Raiders
or
Elite Infantry?

Recent Titles in
Contributions in Military Studies

Raiders
or
Elite Infantry?

The Changing Role of the U.S. Army Rangers from Dieppe to Grenada

DAVID W. HOGAN, JR.

Contributions in Military Studies, Number 128

Greenwood Press
Westport, Connecticut • London

Library of Congress Cataloging-in-Publication Data

Hogan, David W., 1958-
   Raiders or elite infantry? : the changing role of the U.S. Army
Rangers from Dieppe to Grenada / David W. Hogan, Jr.
     p.   cm.—(Contributions in military studies, ISSN 0883-6884
; no. 128)
   Includes bibliographical references and index.
   ISBN 0-313-26803-7 (alk. paper)
   1. United States. Army—Commando troops—History—20th century.
I. Title. II. Series.
UA34.R36H64   1992
356'.167'0973—dc20   92-5422

British Library Cataloguing in Publication Data is available.

Library of Congress Catalog Card Number: 92-5422
ISBN: 0-313-26803-7
ISSN: 0883-6884

First published in 1992

Greenwood Press, 88 Post Road West, Westport, CT 06881
An imprint of Greenwood Publishing Group, Inc.

Printed in the United States of America

The paper used in this book complies with the
Permanent Paper Standard issued by the National
Information Standards Organization (Z39.48-1984).

10 9 8 7 6 5 4 3 2 1

To Page

Contents

Illustrations

Maps

Preface

While a graduate student at Duke University, I first became interested in the subject of elite units, particularly Rangers. Beneath tales of heroic exploits and occasionally embarrassing failures, one finds a fascinating story that says much about the way in which Americans view both their military and their past. Few terms have more legendary connotations attached to them than "Ranger," a word deeply rooted in America's frontier heritage. For a public that is hungry for heroes in an impersonal mass society, Rangers, past and present, have a special appeal, even given American traditions of the citizen soldier and suspicion of elitism. Furthermore, the increasing need for Ranger and other special units in the turbulent international scene of recent years has aroused interest in such formations on the part of both the military and society as a whole. When successful in brushfire conflicts and counterterrorist raids, Ranger-type units have boosted national pride. On the other hand, failures have often caused considerable soul-searching. Given the growing interest in the Rangers in the past few years, a thorough examination of the underlying concept seems more important now than ever before.

Within this space, it is impossible to thank all who helped to make this book possible. I would, however, particularly like to express my appreciation to Mildred Vasan and Lynn Flint of Greenwood Press; Ed Reese, Wil Mahoney, Rich Boylan, and Bill Lewis of the National Archives; Romana Danysh, Hannah Zeidlik, Gerrie Harcarik, Terry Kraus, and Mary Sawyer of the U.S. Army Center of Military History; Richard Sommers, David Keogh, John Slonicker, Louise Arnold, and Randy Hackenburg of the U.S. Army Military History Institute; John Jacob of the George C. Marshall Library; Steve Eldridge, Maj. Jim McKernan USA, and Tom Gaskins of the Access and Release Branch, U.S. Army Adjutant General's Office; Vivian Dodson and Al Garland of the U.S. Army Infantry School; Nancy Cooke and Capt. William F. Gerhards USA of the

Public Affairs Office, 1st Special Operations Command; Maj. Del Dailey USA
of the 75th Ranger Regiment; the Public Affairs Office of the Department of the
Army; Shelby Stanton; John Guillenhammer; Stephen Gregory; and Col. Rod
Paschall USA (Ret.), who originally suggested the idea of a work on the
Rangers. For help with photographs, I would like to thank the National Archives,
the Department of Defense Still Media Records Center, Howell Brewer of the
U.S. Army Center of Military History, Benjamin Schemmer of *Armed Forces
Journal International*, Dr. Homer House, Bettman Newsphotos, and the George
C. Marshall and Dwight D. Eisenhower Libraries. Sherri Dowdy of the Center
of Military History helped with the maps. A special note of appreciation goes to
those who agreed to be interviewed and took the time to go through the
transcripts of those conversations. Dr. Alex Roland, Dr. I. B. Holley, Jr., Col.
Robert Sholly USA, Lt. Col. Gary Bounds USA (Ret.), Maj. Henry Keirsey
USA, Romana Danysh, Dale Andrade, Shelby Stanton, George MacGarrigle, Dr.
Edgar Raines, Lt. Col. Jonathan House USA, and Maj. Charles Kirkpatrick USA
read all or portions of the manuscript and made many helpful suggestions.
Obviously, they are in no way responsible for any interpretations or errors of
fact within the manuscript. It should be mentioned that the views expressed in
this work are those of the author and do not necessarily represent those of the
U.S. Army or the Department of Defense. Research for this study was greatly
aided by grants from the U.S. Army Center of Military History and the U.S.
Army Military History Institute. At this point, I would like to express my
appreciation to my family and to the late Dr. Rowena Reed, who first interested
me in a career in military history. To my wife, Page, this book is affectionately
dedicated. Throughout its composition, she has been a constant source of
encouragement and loving support.

Abbreviations

AFHQ	Allied Force Headquarters		COSSAC	Chief of Staff to the Supreme Allied Commander
CIA	Central Intelligence Agency		DCSOPS	Deputy Chief of Staff for Operations
CIDG	Civilian Irregular Defense Group		DCSPER	Deputy Chief of Staff for Personnel
CMH	U.S. Army Center of Military History, Washington, D.C.		DMZ	Demilitarized Zone
CINC	Commander in Chief		ETO	European Theater of Operations, U.S. Army
CINCEUR	Commander in Chief, Europe		ETOUSA	European Theater of Operations, U.S. Army
CINCFE	Commander in Chief, Far East		EUSAK	Eighth U.S. Army, Korea
COHQ	Combined Operations Headquarters		FECOM	Far East Command
CONARC	Continental Army Command		FORSCOM	Forces Command

FSSF	1st Special Service Force	OCMH	Office of the Chief of Military History
GPO	Government Printing Office	OG	Operational Group
JFKSWC	John F. Kennedy Special Warfare Center, Fort Bragg, N.C.	ORLL	Operational Report, Lessons Learned
		OSS	Office of Strategic Services
JSOC	Joint Special Operations Command	PX	Post Exchange
		SAG	Special Activities Group
LRP	Long-range patrol		
LRRP	Long-range reconnaissance patrol	SAS	Special Air Service (UK)
MACV	Military Assistance Command, Vietnam	SEAL	Sea-Air-Land teams
		SF	Special Forces
MMHB	Modern Military Headquarters Branch	SHAEF	Supreme Headquarters, Allied Expeditionary Force
NA	National Archives and Records Administration, Washington, D.C.	SLAM	Search, Location, Annihilation, and Monitors
NATO	North Atlantic Treaty Organization	SOCCOM	Special Operations Command (Joint)
NCO	Noncommissioned Officer	SOCOM	Special Operations Command (Army)
OACSFOR	Office of the Assistant Chief of Staff for Force Development	SOF	Special Operations Forces
		SOG	Studies and Observation Group
OCAFF	Office of the Chief of Army Field Forces		

SOS	Services of Supply, U.S. Army
SWPA	Southwest Pacific Theater
TRADOC	Training and Doctrine Command
UN	United Nations
USA	U.S. Army
USAFBI	U.S. Army Forces, British Isles
USAFCBI	U.S. Army Forces, China-Burma-India
USAFFE	U.S. Army Forces, Far East
USAFNI	U.S. Army Forces, Northern Ireland
USAMHI	U.S. Army Military History Institute, Carlisle Barracks, Pennsylvania
USARPAC	U.S. Army Pacific
USAWC	U.S. Army War College, Carlisle Barracks, Pennsylvania
VCCO	Vice Chief, Combined Operations (UK)
WNRC	Washington National Records Center, Suitland, Maryland

Introduction

Elite formations, consisting of carefully selected soldiers of above-average abilities, have been part of the military landscape almost since the advent of organized armed forces. Until the nineteenth century, elite units generally had the character of a "palace guard," protecting the person of the commander and providing a shock force for the climactic moment of battle. Alexander had his "Companions," the Roman emperors relied on their Praetorian Guard, rulers of early modern Europe used Swiss mercenaries, and Frederick and Napoleon employed formations of Guards. In contrast, the people's wars of the nineteenth and early twentieth centuries featured conscript armies led by professionals who used the technology of the Industrial Revolution to fight increasingly unheroic and impersonal engagements. Such mass formations proved unsuitable for certain special missions that demanded especially capable units. Aided by nostalgic romanticism and the trend toward specialization, elite units for unique tasks have proliferated in the past half century.[1]

Among the revived elites are the U.S. Army's Rangers, proud holders of an enviable combat record but also survivors of a roller-coaster existence over the past 50 years. Ranger units spearheaded amphibious landings and raided enemy prison camps during World War II, fought toe-to-toe with Chinese infantry in Korea, and earned praise even from Army critics for their performance as patrol specialists and as a ready reaction force in Vietnam and Grenada. Indeed, they have acquired such a reputation for resourcefulness and heroism that the Army has conducted a "Ranger School" for both individual and noncommissioned officers since 1951. However, the Army has also gone through lengthy periods without Ranger units, notably for 5 years after World War II and 15 years after the Korean War. Since 1974, the Rangers have maintained their existence and even expanded from two battalions to a full regiment. Nonetheless, if they feel some insecurity, it is understandable, given their stormy past.

Why have the Rangers had such an erratic history? To answer this question, one must go beyond the legends to examine the evolving concept—the underlying nature and purpose—of the Rangers in the minds of the American military and public. Such an analysis must take into account the overall American approach to warfare and the use of military force in the period since 1942. On the one hand, the interplay of attitudes, convictions, and values of professional officers, as expressed, for example, in strategy, missions, and organizations, must be evaluated. On the other hand, these officers operate within the context of a specific society, with its own ideals, beliefs, and institutions, as well as an increasingly uncertain international environment. This study, therefore, will seek to accomplish three things: first, to trace the development of the Ranger concept over the past 50 years, second, to evaluate that concept and discover its underlying elements, and third, to assess its application.

As a conceptual study, this book takes a different approach from that of other recent studies of the Rangers. While not ignoring campaigns and battles, this study will treat them only in general terms, focusing instead on what they reveal of the role and image of the Rangers in the American military and society. In exploring the Ranger concept, the discussion goes beyond formations that bore the designation "Ranger" to include units that carried out Ranger-type tasks, such as the 1st Special Service Force, Merrill's Marauders, and, later, long-range patrols, and Special Forces. With the passage of time, the Ranger story also becomes increasingly interwoven with that of other "special operations forces" which perform similar, but not identical, missions.

In a work of this type, the definition of terms is crucial. The phrase "special operations," for example, has come to stand for a wide variety of activities. In this study, it signifies military operations that do not fit the traditional World War II–style pattern of opposing lines, mass, and firepower. Among these activities, a distinction can be made between Ranger missions, such as raids and long-range reconnaissance by regular troops from bases within friendly lines, and unconventional warfare, which includes such operations as guerrilla warfare, escape and evasion, subversion, and psychological warfare. Guerrilla warfare, which has frequently been confused with Ranger operations, involves the use of indigenous forces, which are often organized and trained by regular personnel, to conduct operations either without fixed bases or from bases behind enemy lines. When capitalized, the word "Regular" stands for soldiers or units of the Regular Army. When not capitalized, the term indicates troops of a regular military force, in contrast to irregulars or partisans. Another vaguely defined word, "doctrine," signifies in this study an officially approved statement, based on experience, of the proper mission and methods of a military force.[2] This work also distinguishes between "elite" or especially capable formations, and "special" forces, which are units formed for a particular task. The degree to which the Rangers represent an elite or a special force, or both, will be one of the major themes of this work.

NOTES

1. Samuel P. Huntington, "Foreword," in Eliot A. Cohen, *Commandos and Politicians: Elite Military Units in Modern Democracies,* Harvard Studies in International Affairs no. 40 (Cambridge, Mass.: Harvard University Press, 1978), pp. 11–12. See also Roger A. Beaumont, *Military Elites* (Indianapolis: Bobbs–Merrill, 1974).

2. See I. B. Holley, "The Role of Doctrine," *Air Force Journal of Logistics* 10 (Winter 1986): 9.

1

Origins of a Legend

The best of them were commonly employed on Lake George, and
nothing can surpass the adventurous hardihood of their lives. Summer
and winter, day and night, were alike to them. Embarked in whale-
boats or birch canoes, they glided under the silent moon or in the
languid glare of a breathless August day, when islands floated in
dreamy haze and the hot air was thick with odors of pine, or in the
bright October . . . when gay mountains basked in light, maples
dropped leaves of rustling gold, sumachs glowed like rubies under the
dark green of the unchanging spruce and mossed rocks with all their
painted plumage lay double in the watery mirror. Or in the tomblike
silence of the winter forest, with breath frozen on his beard, the
ranger strode on snowshoes over the spotless drifts and like Durer's
knight, a ghastly death stalked ever at his side. There were those
among them for whom this stern life had a fascination that made all
other existence tame.[1]

When Francis Parkman composed that passage in the late nineteenth century, the
Rangers of Col. Robert Rogers had long since disappeared into the mists of
legend. Concerned with the strains of urbanization and immigration, Americans
of the time found escape and romance in the struggle of their ancestors to tame
the wilderness, overcome their French and Indian rivals, and win independence
from the British. Any evaluation of the Ranger concept must take into account
the mythical connotations attached to the term "Ranger" since Rogers and his
hardy frontiersmen traversed the waters of Lake Champlain in the 1750s.

The American Rangers traced their origins to the need of British
colonists for special military units and methods to meet the peculiar conditions
of the New World. Conventional linear tactics, involving solid masses drilled to
maneuver and fire volleys as a unit, had served the Europeans well on the plains
of Flanders, but they proved ineffective against elusive enemies in the forests,

lakes, and mountains of early America. As long as a colonial community bordered on the frontier, the local militia usually possessed enough skills in woodcraft and marksmanship to meet the Indians on their own terms. Once the frontier moved west to the Appalachians, however, the residents of the more established communities met only periodically to drill in European-style warfare and soon lost their prowess in woodland tactics. To guard the frontier from New York to Virginia, the colonists erected blockhouses at regular intervals, but Indian war parties could easily slip between these posts. This fact, as well as the increasing specialization within colonial society, caused colonial governments to hire scouts to patrol the gaps between the outposts on a full-time basis.[2]

Those scouts who guarded the early frontier became known as "rangers." Derived from the Frankish word "hring" which means circle or ring, the term "ranger" may have originated in England, where it applied to keepers of the royal forest. Legend has undoubtedly exaggerated the prowess of the early American rangers. While many possessed the skills of seasoned woodsmen, others probably chose such a lonely duty, far from civilization, because they lacked other options. Drawn from the rustic border peoples and lower classes, they were viewed with ambivalence, if not condescension, by the more refined citizens of the Atlantic seaboard.[3]

By the late 1600s, rangers were serving several functions in addition to guarding the frontier. Parties of rangers escorted surveyors and searched for escaped slaves. When the colonists took the offensive against hostile Indian tribes, ranger units served as scouts and raiders. In 1676, Capt. Benjamin Church's company of friendly Indians and white frontiersmen killed the Wampanoag chieftain, King Philip, ending the Indian resistance to white settlement of Massachusetts. During "King George's War" in the 1740s, a mixed company of whites and Mohawks under Capt. John Gorham raided Indian settlements in Nova Scotia and accompanied Sir William Pepperrill's expedition to Louisbourg. Both Church's and Gorham's units drew much of their identity from the personalities of the commanders, whose charisma was often necessary to hold together their unruly bands.[4]

It was through the personality and deeds of Robert Rogers, however, that the Ranger legend first assumed real form. A product of the rugged frontier of New Hampshire, Rogers lacked formal education, but his courage, presence of mind, woodcraft, and physical strength made him a leader among the yeomen who, in 1755, answered the call for volunteers to fight the French and Indians. Hard experience with Indian tactics, notably Maj. Gen. Edward Braddock's disastrous expedition against Fort Duquesne, had already shown British regulars the need for skilled woodsmen to reconnoiter and serve as flank guards in the wooded terrain. Rogers's success as a scout in the Lake George region during the winter of 1755–1756 prompted Governor William Shirley of Massachusetts to commission him as captain of an independent company of 60 Rangers, who were recruited from Rogers's fellow New Hampshire woodsmen. From a base on an island across the Hudson from Fort Edward, the Rangers penetrated deep into French-held territory, reconnoitering enemy positions, harassing supply convoys, and raiding Indian villages. When British regulars advanced into the Lake Champlain region, the Rangers screened the flanks and vanguard of the columns.

The exploits of Rogers's Rangers aroused mixed emotions on both sides of the Atlantic. On the one hand, they provided a tonic to colonials and Britons who were hungry for good news after a series of defeats. Accounts from America stirred romantic imaginations with tales of Rangers threading through green forests or gliding in canoes over autumn-tinted waters to surprise a French outpost. Even British generals grudgingly conceded the value of the Rangers and expanded Rogers's force. On the other hand, British officers looked down on the fiercely independent woodsmen as an undisciplined rabble who stole provisions and rioted to free comrades who had been imprisoned for disciplinary infractions. Rogers himself often seemed beyond control, frequently departing on unauthorized missions. Seeking a more tractable scouting force, the British formed their own Ranger-type units, notably Col. Thomas Gage's regiment. In the wilds of western Pennsylvania, Col. Henry Bouquet's four battalions of Royal Americans effectively used Ranger tactics. Few, however, could match Rogers's leadership and the skills of his Rangers in forest warfare.[5]

At the same time as the British Army's introduction of Ranger units in North America, other European armies were also experimenting with "light infantry," including riflemen who could maneuver in open order, scout, and screen the flanks of conventional units in rugged terrain. The light muskets or rifles of light troops provided greater accuracy at longer ranges, although they had too slow a rate of fire to suit line battalions. Such units met the most favorable reception from armies that were involved in colonial struggles, notably the Austrians, who found *Grenzer* units of Croatians to be so valuable in operations along the rough Turkish frontier that they later used them in raids against Prussian convoys and depots. An irritated Frederick the Great responded with his *Freikorps*, consisting largely of undisciplined foreigners attracted by the opportunity for plunder. While many European armies disbanded their light units after the close of the Seven Years War in 1763, light infantry reappeared in the revolutionary wars of the late 1700s.[6]

Generations of Americans have grown up with the myth that the American Revolution was won by the colonial riflemen, who used their woodcraft and wits to overcome the effete British regulars. The embattled farmers of Lexington and Concord and the sharpshooting frontiersmen of King's Mountain inspired a host of legends, but most of the battles were fought in the European style by massed formations on open ground, where riflemen, with their lack of bayonets and slow rate of fire, were at a disadvantage. Nevertheless, both sides found Ranger-type units invaluable for maneuvering and skirmishing in the wooded, broken terrain that covered much of the 13 colonies. Although at heart a conventional soldier, Gen. George Washington encouraged the formation of light units, including rifle companies, for missions of reconnaissance and harassment. Of these units, Lt. Col. Thomas Knowlton's Rangers distinguished themselves at the Battle of Harlem Heights, and a crack light brigade under Brig. Gen. Anthony Wayne used a night bayonet assault to capture the British post at Stony Point. In a more traditional role, Maj. Benjamin Whitcomb's Rangers patrolled the frigid northern frontier and mounted rangers campaigned in the swamps of South Carolina.[7]

Of the "Rangers" who served in the American Revolution, the riflemen of Col. Daniel Morgan achieved the greatest fame. Responding to a Congressional call for 10 companies of riflemen in June 1775, Morgan raised a company of expert marksmen, seasoned in Indian warfare, from the Shenandoah region of Virginia. On their way to join the army at Boston, they staged frequent exhibitions of their skills for appreciative audiences. At Boston, they terrorized British outposts with their skill in marksmanship and patrolling, but they also displayed the same lack of discipline that had been the scourge of Rogers's Rangers, discharging their rifles on whim and brawling among themselves. Fortunately, they possessed a chief with the toughness and common touch necessary to keep them under a degree of control. Morgan's riflemen served as scouts and flank guards in the American invasion of Canada, but most, including Morgan, were captured in the unsuccessful assault on Quebec. After his exchange, Morgan, now a colonel, took command of a new 600-man rifle corps, which distinguished itself at Saratoga. When Morgan received a promotion to brigadier general, the few remaining riflemen joined other units.[8]

The exploits of Morgan's riflemen and, later, the western volunteers during the War of 1812 reinforced the new nation's idealization of the American as a natural soldier, a legend increasingly linked in the popular mind with the Ranger concept. Where officers in the tiny standing army remembered Winfield Scott's Regulars at Chippewa, the country as a whole thrilled to the memory of Andrew Jackson's Kentucky and Tennessee riflemen at New Orleans. In the view of most Americans during the years after the War of 1812, Jackson's riflemen overcame the effete British precisely because they were unschooled, spontaneous, and natural. Regulars understandably resented the negative attitudes of the Jacksonian period toward any special military training or a professional military force. One officer noted with irritation the speech of a "Western senator, who branded the regular army as the 'sweepings of cities,' etc. etc., and extolled the frontier men—militia—rangers (our friends, the volunteers) as infinitely superior."[9]

Ranger units that served from the Revolution to the Civil War thus tended to be temporary volunteer forces rather than professionals. The tiny Regular Army retained barely enough troops to garrison frontier outposts, let alone form elite, European-style "palace guards" which, in any case, struck egalitarian Americans as too royalist and as possible seedbeds for reaction.

Nonetheless, Americans did see a need for volunteer Rangers to help guard the frontier and hunt down hostile Indians. Congress authorized 17 volunteer Ranger companies during the War of 1812, and Andrew Jackson used 2 such companies during his campaign against the Seminoles in 1818. As the nation expanded to the prairies, the need for mounted troops to cope with the mobility of the plains tribes caused Congress, in June 1832, to authorize a battalion of "Mounted Rangers," who would enlist for one year and furnish their own arms and horses. To the southwest, the Republic of Texas also called on mounted militia to suppress Indian uprisings. These "Texas Rangers" later served as scouts and guides for U.S. forces during the Mexican War, maintaining in the process the Ranger reputation for self-reliance and lack of discipline. By 1860, the term "Ranger" had become so popular among militia units that over 70 of them used the name.[10]

During the Civil War, over 400 units on both sides used the term "ranger," but it usually referred to the partisans who raided behind the lines in Virginia and the Mississippi Valley. Not surprisingly, the South used guerrilla operations to a much greater degree than did the North. In addition to the fact that most of the fighting took place on Southern territory, as well as the vulnerability of Union lines of communication and the need to compensate for a lack of material resources, the South possessed a romantic outlook on partisan warfare, partly due to a guerrilla tradition dating back to the Revolution. Nevertheless, the Southern war effort was run by conventional soldiers who did not feel comfortable with partisan operations. Although the Confederate Congress authorized the formation of guerrilla units in the Partisan Ranger Act of April 1862, regular officers complained that the rangers attracted too many recruits who were needed by more conventional units. Furthermore, they drew more than their share of shady characters who plundered the people they were supposed to protect. In February 1864, the Confederate Congress repealed the Partisan Ranger Act, but partisan warfare actually intensified as the conflict escalated in bitterness.

The most famous of the partisan rangers was a slight, irascible maverick named John S. Mosby. In January 1863, Mosby, an officer in the 1st Virginia Cavalry, persuaded Maj. Gen. J. E. B. Stuart to permit him and nine other men to conduct raids behind enemy lines. His success earned him a captain's commission and the authority to raise a company of partisan rangers. Assembling a mixture of older men, boys, convalescents, some regulars, and even a few deserters, Mosby destroyed supply trains, captured couriers, and attacked outposts in an attempt to force the Federals to divert troops from the main front. His most famous exploit came in March 1863, when he and 29 men raided the Union outpost at Fairfax Courthouse and snatched a brigadier general from under the noses of a regimental guard. Union troops resorted to extreme measures, including scorched earth tactics, in their efforts to catch Mosby, but the guerrillas were able to blend into a supportive population. Following Appomattox,

Mosby disbanded his regiment of partisans rather than surrender.[11]

After the Civil War, Ranger-type formations almost entirely disappeared from the American landscape. Some units of the Regular Army and militia, notably the Texas Rangers, continued to use the term, and the Army occasionally used special units of frontiersmen and friendly Indians against the hostiles of the Great Plains. With the disappearance of the frontier and the demographic, industrial, and agricultural expansion of the country in the late nineteenth century, however, Rangers seemed increasingly out of place.[12]

The professionalization of the Army of the late 1800s also contributed to the status of the Rangers as an anachronism. Largely isolated from the rest of society and feeling a need to justify their existence, the officer corps had developed a view of war as a science, practiced by educated experts, an outlook that was at odds with the traditional American idealization of the resourceful amateur, with whom the Ranger concept had been so closely tied. These officers looked to the conscript armies and mass warfare of Europe and the Civil War as models and viewed with disdain the individualistic, Ranger formations and raids of the past. To them, the best way to achieve victory lay in the use of overwhelming power to attack and destroy the enemy's armed forces, just as Ulysses S. Grant had done to the Confederate Army of Northern Virginia.[13]

Although some armies created elite units in response to the tactical deadlock of World War I, the U.S. Army did not follow their example. Responding to a disastrous defeat at Caporetto in 1917, the Italians created the *arditi*, an elite corps of black-shirted youths trained in close personal combat, and German storm troopers infiltrated weak points in Allied lines during the 1918 offensive. In contrast, the U.S. Army, hastening to build a mass army capable of combat on the Western Front after American intervention in 1917, devoted little, if any, thought to elite units. With the general trend toward professionalism, Americans in 1917 were more inclined than ever before to leave the conduct of war to the specialists with their predilection for mass warfare. To be sure, even hard-boiled professionals cherished some nostalgia for the rifleman of pre-urbanized America. Despite Gen. John J. Pershing's stress on marksmanship in training and the legend of Sgt. Alvin York, however, the poor initial performance of all too many units suggested that the natural American marksman was part of the past.[14]

World War I reinforced the Army's orientation toward large-unit warfare. While military planners of the 1920s and 1930s returned to the traditional focus on continental defense, the experience of the "Great War" made them more likely to consider the possibility of a major transatlantic effort. The National Defense Act of 1920, in its provisions for mobilization, reflected their continuing assumption that wars were won by the use of mass armies to destroy enemy forces in a quick, climactic campaign. At service schools, future commanders studied the campaigns of the Civil War and World War I for lessons in large-unit operations and examined the problems and possibilities posed by mobilization and such technological innovations as the tank and the plane. For any future wars of such magnitude, the Army would need thousands of staff officers who used similar methods and spoke the same language. To produce large numbers of these officers, instruction at the schools therefore focused on approved or "school" solutions to problems and discouraged free thinking on unorthodox subjects.

Given this outlook, the lack of thought on elite or special units is not surprising. Military thinking of the period lumped raids with amphibious operations, river crossings, overseas expeditions, mountain warfare, and other esoteric "special operations." Some officers did express an interest in German storm troopers, and an occasional article in a professional military journal would advocate special formations for scouting, screening, or night operations. Such views made little headway, however. Even if officers had been more intellectually receptive, the lack of military funds and the generally stagnant atmosphere of the interwar Army tended to discourage any impulse toward experimentation.[15]

While the Army had become increasingly antagonistic to the idea of special units, Americans in general were nourishing a growing fascination with Rangers of the remote past. The exploits of Rogers's Rangers fired the imagination of the young Francis Parkman, whose monumental works on the epic struggle between France and Great Britain for control of North America secured the place of the Rangers in American folklore. As the nation's society and culture became more urbanized, diverse, and complex in the early years of the twentieth century, Americans increasingly looked back with fondness to an earlier, simpler era. In 1937, Kenneth Roberts published *Northwest Passage*, a best-selling novel about a youth who found his identity through service with Rogers's Rangers. Rogers appeared as a tragic hero who, in the end, fell victim to scheming rivals and his own human faults. As the United States edged closer to intervention in World War II, Americans thrilled to the screen version of Roberts's book, starring Spencer Tracy as Rogers.[16]

By the time of Pearl Harbor, the conceptual framework, the underlying thought, needed for effective Ranger operations by special units no longer existed in the U.S. Army. American attitudes toward the Rangers were split between the skepticism of the military professionals and the naive romanticism of the American public. Within the American popular psyche, the legend of the Ranger as the highest exemplification of the American fighting man, overcoming all odds through persistence and resourcefulness, had become firmly established. Nevertheless, military force structure and strategy had become largely, if not exclusively, the province of professionals who viewed warfare as a systematically managed contest of resources and instinctively dismissed special units as costly, superfluous, and undisciplined. As the United States entered the greatest war in its history, an observer would have found few indications that the Army was about to revive Ranger units.

NOTES

1. Francis Parkman, *The Battle for North America*, 2d ed., ed., John W. Tebbel (Norwalk, Conn.: Easton Press, 1987), pp. 583–584.

2. Russell F. Weigley, *History of the United States Army*, 2d ed. (Bloomington: Indiana University Press, 1984), pp. 9–10; John K. Mahon, "Anglo-American Methods of Indian Warfare, 1676–1794," *Mississippi Valley Historical Review* 45 (September 1958): 254–275; Robert W. Black, "The Beginning of the American Ranger," *Gung-Ho*, October 1984, p. 21.

3. Eric Partridge, *Origins: A Short Etymological Dictionary of Modern English* (New York: Macmillan, 1963), p. 549; John R. Elting, Dan Cragg, and Ernest L. Deal, *A Dictionary of Soldier Talk* (New York: Scribner's, 1984), p. 253.

4. Allan R. Millett and Peter Maslowski, *For the Common Defense: A Military History of the United States of America* (New York: Free Press, 1984), p. 16; John R. Elting, "Further Light on the Beginnings of Gorham's Rangers," *Military Collector and Historian* 12 (Fall 1960): 74–77. Governor James Oglethorpe of Georgia used mounted rangers as scouts against the Spanish; see Douglas E. Leach, *Arms for Empire: A Military History of the British Colonies in North America* (New York: Macmillan, 1973), p. 221.

5. The standard source on Rogers is John R. Cuneo, *Robert Rogers of the Rangers* (New York: Oxford University Press, 1959). See also Weigley, *History of the United States Army*, pp. 25–26, and Mahon, "Anglo-American Methods," for more on the British response to Indian warfare. Rogers's subsequent history did not improve the image of the Rangers. With the end of the French and Indian War, the British dissolved the Ranger units, leaving Rogers without permanent rank or pay. Deeply in debt and given to bouts of drunkenness, he briefly led British rangers in the Revolution before he died, penniless, in a cheap London boardinghouse in 1795.

6. Correlli Barnett, *Britain and Her Army, 1509–1970: A Military, Political, and Social Survey* (New York: William Morrow, 1970), pp. 177–178, 227, 242–245; John Childs, *Armies and Warfare in Europe, 1648–1789* (New York: Holmes and Meier, 1982), pp. 116–120; E. M. Lloyd, *A Review of the History of Infantry*, 2d ed. (Westport, Conn.: Greenwood Press, 1976), pp. 175–176.

7. Marcus Cunliffe, *Soldiers and Civilians: The Martial Spirit in America, 1775–1865* (Boston: Little Brown, 1968), pp. 148, 179; Weigley, *History of the United States Army*, pp. 33, 36, 66–67; Albert S. Batchellor, "The Ranger Service in the Upper Valley of the Connecticut and the Most Northerly Regiment of the New Hampshire Militia in the Period of the Revolution," *Magazine of History with Notes and Inquiries* 6 (October 1907): 187–205; "American Rangers from the Colonial Era to the Present," 1 October 1984, in "Rangers—General," Organizational History Branch, U.S. Army Center of Military History, (CMH).

8. The standard biographies of Morgan are Don Higginbotham, *Daniel Morgan: Revolutionary Rifleman* (Chapel Hill: University of North Carolina Press, 1961), and North Callahan, *Daniel Morgan: Ranger of the Revolution* (New York: Holt Rhinehart and Winston, 1961). See also Don Higginbotham, *The War of American Independence: Military Attitudes, Policies, and Practices* (New York: Macmillan, 1971), pp. 102–103.

9. Quoted in Cunliffe, *Soldiers and Civilians*, p. 268; see also pp. 53–54, 179, 204, 415–416. Also see Weigley, *History of the United States Army*, p. 154.

10. Beaumont, *Military Elites*, pp. 7, 49; Weigley, *History of the United States Army*, pp. 159–161; John K. Mahon, *The War of 1812* (Gainesville: University of Florida Press, 1972), pp. 68–69, 288–289; Larry Ivers, "Rangers in Florida—1818," *Infantry* 53 (September–October 1963): 37; Otis E. Young, "United States Mounted Ranger Battalion, 1832–1833," *Mississippi Valley Historical Review* 41 (December 1954): 453–470; Walter P. Webb, *The Texas Rangers*, 2d ed. (Boston: Houghton Mifflin, 1965), pp. 23–33, 67, 72–83, 91–94, 118, 140; Richard C. Drum, *List of Synonyms of Organizations in the Volunteer Service of the United States during the Years 1861, 1862, 1863, 1864, and 1865* (Washington: U.S. Government Printing Office (GPO), 1885), pp. 270–271.

11. The standard work on Mosby is V. C. Jones, *Ranger Mosby* (Chapel Hill: University of North Carolina Press, 1944). See also John S. Mosby, *Mosby's War Reminiscences*, Rev. ed. (New York: Pageant Book Co., 1958), pp. 29–45, 62, 85, 98–99. On the partisans, see "American Rangers from the Colonial Era;" Millett and Maslowski, *Common Defense*, pp. 170–171; and Carl E. Grant, "Partisan Warfare, Model 1861–1865," *Military Review* 38 (November 1958): 43–46.

12. Robert M. Utley, *Frontier Regulars: The United States Army and the Indian, 1866–1891* (New York: Macmillan, 1973), pp. 44–46, 50–53; "American Rangers from the Colonial Era;" Weigley, *History of the United States Army*, pp. 320–322, 336–337. To subdue the Plains Indians, the Army did use individual frontiersmen as scouts, and Maj. George A. Forsyth recruited 50 seasoned plainsmen into a light unit which fought well at the battle of Beecher's Island. During the Philippine Insurrection, Brig. Gen. Frederick Funston used a mixed force of American officers, native scouts, and former guerrillas to capture the rebel leader, Emilio Aguinaldo, in a Ranger-type raid. See Utley, *Frontier Regulars*, pp. 152–153 and John M. Gates, *Schoolbooks and Krags: The United States Army in the Philippines, 1898–1902* (Westport, Conn.: Greenwood Press, 1973), p. 233.

13. Samuel P. Huntington, *The Soldier and the State: The Theory and Politics of Civil Military Relations* (Cambridge, Mass.: Harvard University Press, 1957), pp. 227–269. For the development of American strategic thought, see Russell F. Weigley's *The American Way of War: A History of United States Military Strategy and Policy* (New York: Macmillan, 1973).

14. Weigley, *History of the United States Army*, pp. 375, 391; Beaumont, *Military Elites*, pp. 13, 19–24; Allan R. Millett, "Cantigny," in Charles E. Heller and William A. Stofft, eds., *America's First Battles, 1775–1965* (Lawrence: University Press of Kansas, 1986), p. 165.

15. Maurice Matloff, "The American Approach to War, 1919–1945," in Michael Howard, ed., *The Theory and Practice of War* (London: Cassell, 1965), pp. 215–229; Weigley, *American Way of War*, pp. 207–222; Martin Blumenson, "Kasserine Pass," in Charles E. Heller and William A. Stofft, eds., *America's First Battles, 1775–1965* (Lawrence: University Press of Kansas, 1986), pp. 226–231; Martin Blumenson, *Mark Clark: The Last of the Great World War II Commanders* (New York: Congdon and Weed, 1984), pp. 29, 33–37; Harry P. Ball, *Of Responsible Command: A History of the U.S. Army War College* (Carlisle, Pa.: Alumni Association of the U.S. Army War College, 1983), pp. 152–156, 167, 195–199, 210–214, 244–247; "A Military History of the U.S. Army Command and General Staff College, 1881–1963," unpublished manuscript, pp. 24–30, CMH Library; Gen. Theodore J. Conway USA (Ret.), interview with author, Durham, N.C., 2 May 1984; William N. Hauser, "The Peacetime Army: Retrospect and

Prospect," in Robin Higham and Carol Brandt, eds., *The United States Army in Peacetime: Essays in Honor of the Bicentennial* (Manhattan, Kans.: Military Affairs, 1975), pp. 207–211. Numerous interviews from the Senior Officers Debriefing Program at the U.S. Army Military History Institute (USAMHI), Carlisle Barracks, Pa., testify to the leisurely atmosphere of the interwar Army.

16. Cuneo, *Robert Rogers*, p. 277; Kenneth Roberts, *Northwest Passage*, 4th ed. (New York: Ballantine, 1964), p. 9.

2

American Commandos

April 1942 was a gloomy month for the Allies. Four months after Pearl Harbor, the Axis tide showed no signs of ebbing. With the fall of Bataan in the Philippines, only the tiny island outpost of Corregidor disputed Japanese supremacy in the western Pacific. Japanese armies had occupied Malaya and were driving the British from Burma. Winter and determined resistance by the Red Army had saved Moscow, but Soviet prospects against a renewed German summer offensive appeared doubtful at best. While Field Marshal Erwin Rommel prepared to launch a final offensive against the British Empire's lifeline at Suez, German U-boats were carrying their raids against Allied shipping to the East Coast of the United States. American and British planners had agreed to concentrate first on Europe and the defeat of Germany, but they differed on the timing for the climactic invasion of Northwest Europe. Lack of material resources, bitter memories of the Western Front of 1914–1918, and imperial interests in the Mediterranean inclined the British to favor such an operation only as the coup de grace to an already beaten enemy. In contrast, the Americans, who had been schooled in direct, massive campaigns of annihilation and were concerned about the plight of the Soviets, wanted to launch an invasion as soon as practicable. To present the American case, the Army's chief of staff, Gen. George C. Marshall, and presidential aide Harry Hopkins arrived in London in early April.

Despite a conventional background and a forbidding exterior, the 61-year-old Marshall would demonstrate considerable open-mindedness toward special operations. A graduate of Virginia Military Institute, Marshall had distinguished himself as a staff officer during World War I. He had also served in China and had held several teaching, staff, and line positions before assuming the post of chief of staff in September 1939. Austere and reserved, he could be intimidating to staff officers who were unprepared for the clear, concise briefings

Gen. George C. Marshall
(Courtesy of the George C. Marshall Research Foundation)

that he demanded, but he often showed a willingness to try new ideas. As assistant commandant of the Infantry School during the early 1930s, he encouraged officers to develop alternatives to the "school solution," and, as chief of staff, he pushed for bold exploitation of such new concepts as the use of airborne troops.[1]

While Marshall sought the earliest possible invasion of the Continent, he was gravely concerned about the U.S. Army's lack of combat experience. In the year and a half leading up to Pearl Harbor, the Army had grown from a small volunteer force of about 200,000 men to over 1.6 million Regulars, National Guardsmen, and draftees. Although a comprehensive, realistic training program was finally in place by April 1942, few of the recruits added by the hasty mobilization had completed it, and, in maneuvers, those few still displayed deficiencies in basic soldiering and command skills. Many used mock-up weapons and equipment in training to compensate for shortages. Furthermore, as Marshall knew all too well, even the most realistic training was no substitute for combat experience against troops as battle-tested as the Germans. The Americans would not enjoy the luxury of gradually working units into an active front, as they had in World War I. Instead, if American planners had their way, their troops would receive their baptism of fire in an amphibious assault, one of the most difficult military operations.[2]

How would American soldiers acquire the necessary combat experience? Searching for an answer, Marshall's gaze came to rest on the British commandos, elite raiders who traced their origins to the dark days of 1940 when Britain stood alone. In this atmosphere of gloom, but with grim determination, the British had turned to their long tradition of seaborne raids as a means of striking back against the enemy until the British Army could return in force to the Continent. At the instigation of Lt. Col. Dudley Clarke, and with the strong support of Prime Minister Winston Churchill, the British had formed 440-man battalions, known as Commandos after the parties of Boer farmers who had bedeviled British forces in South Africa at the turn of the century. All the men were volunteers, selected through interviews by troop commanders who looked for youth, daring, resourcefulness, physical fitness, and an ability to swim. Those selected endured a grueling program of specialized infantry training, stressing conditioning, instruction in weapons and demolitions, realism, and self-reliance. The strenuous training, as well as the sense of adventure and camaraderie of a special unit, contributed to an esprit that standard units rarely, if ever, matched.[3]

For all the capabilities of the commandos, the value of their operations became a matter of debate among British officials. After initial forays failed due to poor planning and equipment shortages, an angry Churchill, in July 1940, created an interservice Combined Operations Headquarters (COHQ) to plan and conduct the raids. Under the charismatic Admiral Sir Roger Keyes, COHQ planned raids by over 5,000 troops against Dakar and Pantelleria in the

Mediterranean but the British War Office shied away from such endeavors as too risky and an unnecessary diversion of resources. Such inhibitions did not sit well with the cantankerous Keyes, whose biting criticisms, to the point of calling the other service chiefs "cowards," forced his removal in October 1941. His replacement, the youthful Lord Louis Mountbatten, appeared to be a lightweight but soon showed energy, a sense of purpose, and a receptivity to new ideas. Emphasizing smaller-scale raids, his commandos wiped out the garrison of the Norwegian port of Vaagso, reconnoitered the French coast near Boulogne, and seriously damaged submarine dry docks at St. Nazaire. However, critics argued that these accomplishments were mere pinpricks, hardly worth the diversion of manpower and equipment from other tasks. Even the leader of the Boulogne raid later admitted that 2 scouts could have accomplished as much as his force of 150.[4]

While the true value of the raids remained a controversial topic, the British public hailed the commandos as heroes, an image that soon spread to the United States. On both sides of the ocean, readers devoured available information on the raiders. The British Ministry of Information's booklet on combined operations went through a record printing order of 1.25 million copies, and COHQ's official history was chosen by the Book of the Month Club as its June selection. American newspapers and magazines portrayed the commandos as modern-day Apaches, throwbacks to Tarzan and Daniel Boone, and focused on their tough training, special equipment, and glamorous chief. Some accounts pointed to commando raids as a sign that the period of defense was over and the tide was turning in favor of the Allies.[5]

Marshall might not have shared the public's rosy view of commando achievements, but he did see in the British raiding program a way for American soldiers to gain combat experience as well as meet President Franklin D. Roosevelt's demand for action on the European continent in 1942. Prior to his departure for London, his staff had prepared a plan to establish an active front in Europe during the summer through steadily increasing air operations and raids by small task forces along the German-held coast. Such operations would boost public morale and help the Soviets by diverting German troops from the Eastern Front, but their greatest benefit would be "the increase in the battle efficiency of the participating troops." Soldiers would receive intensive training in amphibious operations, and the theater would gradually feed them into combat under conditions favorable to success, thereby building confidence. They would then "enter upon the final venture with an ability to meet, on equal terms, the battle trained veterans of the German Army."[6]

When Marshall presented his memorandum in London, the British, while taking issue with many of the provisions on the cross-Channel attack, heartily assented to American participation in their raiding program. From the opening session on April 9, Marshall and Mountbatten got along well, particularly after the chief of staff singled out COHQ as the agency he would most like to visit. Fascinated by COHQ's experiment in joint planning, he agreed to Mountbatten's suggestion that officers from all the American armed services be stationed there. After he had expressed his desire for American troops to take part in the raiding program, staff officers from both sides hammered out a proposal for 12 officers and 60 enlisted men to undergo commando training and serve as the nucleus of an American Commando. On his way home following the close of the conference, Marshall visited the Commando Depot in Scotland and was favorably impressed.[7]

Back in his office in Washington, Marshall summoned Col. Lucian K. Truscott, Jr. A native of Texas, the 47-year-old Truscott had received his commission in the cavalry in 1917. During the interwar years, he had served on several stateside posts, where he met and played polo with a fellow cavalryman named George S. Patton, Jr. Small in stature and wiry, with deep-set gray eyes, a ruddy complexion, and a gravelly voice, the dashing, imaginative Truscott would later become a lieutenant general and one of the outstanding American field commanders of World War II. In April 1942, however, one of his main qualifications for the COHQ post seems to have been his polo-playing ability, given Mountbatten's avid interest in the sport.[8]

Arriving in Washington from Fort Bliss, Texas, where he had been supervising maneuvers of the 5th Cavalry, Truscott was ushered into Marshall's office and told that he would head the American mission at COHQ. He and his officers would study the concept of combined operations, especially of the commando type, and provide information on training, methods, and equipment to the U.S. War Department. After describing Mountbatten's organization, Marshall voiced his belief that participation in COHQ's raiding program would help the U.S. Army overcome its lack of combat experience. A few battle-hardened men in every assault unit, said Marshall, "would be able to counter the fears and uncertainties which imagination and rumor always multiply in combat." Truscott and his contingent would arrange for American participation in such a way as to ensure the broadest possible dispersal of combat-hardened troops among American units. Despite the preliminary steps in London to create an American commando unit, Marshall apparently left to Truscott's discretion the final decision on whether to proceed with such a formation.[9]

It did not take long for Truscott to conclude that rotation of individual soldiers through an American commando unit would indeed be the most efficient way to spread combat experience. When he arrived in London on May 16, he found that the American theater headquarters had already launched preparations for such a formation, detailing observers to commando training camps and beginning work on a table of organization. Truscott could either continue preparations for this formation or put line units in succession through the training and raiding programs. He chose the former course. While recognizing the hostility toward elite units in the U.S. Army, he preferred to organize along British lines, since the program would be conducted under COHQ's auspices.

Lt. Gen. Lucian K. Truscott, Jr. (U.S. Army photograph)

Furthermore, given the prospect of only a limited number of raids, rotation of individuals through a special unit seemed the best way for the maximum number of troops to participate. On May 26, theater headquarters forwarded his recommendation for a provisional Commando. Despite opposition in London and Washington, Marshall quickly approved the proposal.[10]

After receiving Marshall's authorization, Truscott directed Lt. Col. Haskell H. Cleaves and Maj. Theodore J. Conway to draw up an organizational table for the new unit. For two weeks, Conway toured commando bases and training depots, gathering data. Upon his return, he and Cleaves prepared a table based on that of the commandos. The unit would consist of a headquarters company, containing 77 staff personnel, and six line companies, each with three officers and 64 men. Most of the weapons, such as the M-1 rifle, were standard among American infantry units, but the table listed some unique items, including special demolition equipment and collapsible rubber dinghies. In line with the stress on a light force able to fit into small landing craft, the heaviest weapons were 60-millimeter and 81-millimeter (mm) mortars, and provisions for support personnel were so minimal that the commanders would later have to file a special request for cooks.[11]

For personnel to man the unit, Truscott turned to the two divisions and supporting troops that had arrived in Northern Ireland. In a directive to the American commander in Northern Ireland, Maj. Gen. Russell P. Hartle, and in conferences with Hartle's subordinates, Truscott laid out his need for volunteers with athletic ability, endurance, and initiative, especially sailors, mountaineers, and individuals with experience in judo, woodcraft, weapons, demolitions, railroads, power plants, and radios. His appeal met with a less than warm response. The 34th Infantry Division, a National Guard outfit from Iowa and Minnesota, and the 1st Armored Division, a mix of Regulars and draftees, had already undergone heavy personnel turnover and several drastic reorganizations, and their commanders viewed a further loss of manpower, however temporary, with little enthusiasm. Maj. Gen. Orlando P. Ward, the ascetic commander of the 1st Armored Division, grumbled that his unit would probably never see its detached personnel again. Nevertheless, he and the others promised their cooperation.[12]

Among the officers attending the conference was Maj. William O. Darby. A native of Fort Smith, Arkansas, Darby had graduated in 1933 from West Point. Joining the field artillery, he had spent the next eight years in a variety of assignments, attending courses and acquiring experience as a troop leader. Unlike most American officers, he possessed some experience in amphibious operations, having participated in joint landing exercises in Puerto Rico in early 1941. After the attack on Pearl Harbor, he had become an aide to Hartle, who at the time was commander of the 34th Division. Chafing at the inactivity, Darby had asked the 34th's chief of staff for a transfer. When Hartle mentioned the importance of a good leader for Truscott's project, the chief of

staff suggested Darby. Finding Truscott to be agreeable, Hartle assigned his aide
to command the new unit on June 8.

Around Darby, a legend would grow that, with time, would rival those
of Rogers and Morgan. Perhaps no combat leader in World War II was so
praised by his superiors and idolized by his men. He showed great concern for
the welfare of his troops, and they responded with deep devotion. Handsome,
outgoing, smart, and enthusiastic, he also won the confidence of Truscott and
other general officers who came into contact with him. In part, his popularity
with superiors can be traced to his conventional outlook, for Darby was hardly
the maverick one so often finds in command of a special unit. Lacking
commitment to a concept of special operations, he perceived his unit more as an
elite fighting force than as a formation with a unique mission, and he does not
seem to have opposed the use of his men as line infantry. To be sure, he
probably recognized that a rigid stand against misuse might well have resulted
in his force's disbandment.[13]

Establishing his headquarters in the town of Carrickfergus, Darby acted
quickly to select officers and men. A circular letter calling for volunteers soon
appeared on the bulletin board of every American unit in Northern Ireland.
Darby and a colonel from Hartle's staff personally interviewed and chose
officers, who, in turn, formed two-man boards to canvass the 2,000 enlisted
volunteers. At each unit headquarters, volunteers assembled, received a thorough
physical examination, and were questioned by the boards on their reasons for
joining and such matters as their sports background and their willingness to use
a knife. Those who passed assembled in a temporary camp at Carrickfergus.[14]

Who were these American commandos? Almost half, 217, of the 489
originally selected came from infantry units. Of the rest, 89 were artillerymen,
80 transferred from armored formations, and the rest came from a variety of
support units. Regulars from the prewar Army accounted for few of the enlisted
men and none of the officers, except for Darby. The enlisted men ranged in age
from 18 to 35, but most were between 18 and 20. They included midwestern
farmers, steelworkers from eastern cities, truck drivers, boxers, coal miners,
cowboys, morticians, railroaders, photographers, and even a lion tamer and a
stock broker. In accordance with the Army's policy of segregation in combat
units, no blacks could join, but the enlistees did include a Sioux Indian. Several
men volunteered out of boredom or even a love for combat, while others joined
because of peer pressure or the desire to fight with an elite force. Even more
than other American soldiers, the volunteers showed individualism and the ability
to improvise, as well as a frequent disregard for authority. Despite Hartle's
attempts to ensure a qualified body of recruits, many commanders seized the
chance to unload malingerers and thugs. Given the limited number of volunteers,
the selection process could weed out some, but not all, of these malcontents.[15]

On June 19, Darby activated the American Commando, which he
designated the "1st Ranger Battalion (Prov.)." Before leaving Washington,

Truscott had discussed the new formation with Maj. Gen. Dwight D. Eisenhower, who headed the War Plans Division of the War Department at the time. Eisenhower had remarked that the term "commando" properly belonged to the British and suggested that Truscott find a distinctively American name for any new unit. When Conway submitted his table of organization, Truscott replaced the word "commando" with "Ranger." He later stated that he had selected the term because of its legendary connotations of courage, initiative, ruggedness, and fighting ability. Thus, although the Rangers would later cite Rogers's maxims in their training literature and claim inspiration from the forays of the New Hampshire frontiersman, any real link to the Rangers of the past seems tenuous at best. The British commandos, and not Rogers's Rangers, provided the model for the Rangers of World War II.[16]

Having established their organization, the Rangers moved to Scotland for three months of intensive commando training. At a railway station near the Commando Depot at Achnacarry Castle they were met by the camp's commander, a cheerful ex-Guardsman named Lt. Col. Charles Vaughan, who introduced them to commando training with a seven-mile speed march to the depot. The trek foreshadowed a month of rigorous training, involving instruction in weapons and fieldcraft, work with small boats, obstacle courses, lifts of huge logs by teams, and more hikes over rugged mountains and through frigid rivers under the watchful eye of commando instructors. From Achnacarry, the Rangers moved to the rocky Scottish coast near Argyle for a month of amphibious training with the Royal Navy and then to the coastal village of Dundee for instruction in assault tactics. To develop responsibility at lower levels, officers frequently permitted sergeants to lead the units and adopted the commando practice of billeting individual Rangers in private homes. By late September, after training so realistic that live grenades would occasionally land in boats crowded with Rangers, the battalion was ready to begin the raiding program that Marshall had envisioned.[17]

For some Rangers, the raiding program had already begun. In early August, Mountbatten had contacted Truscott and arranged for 50 Rangers to take part in a large-scale raid on the French port of Dieppe. Even today, the objectives of the operation remain obscure and shrouded in controversy. As with other raids, Allied planners wanted to test amphibious techniques and gather data on coastal defenses. A large-scale raid might also bring the German air force to battle under favorable conditions. At the same time, higher considerations also appear to have been at work. Allied leaders were under considerable pressure, at home and abroad, to create a second front in France and aid the hard-pressed Russians. A large raid might create such a diversion, as well as provide experience for the thousands of restless but green soldiers, many of them Canadian, who were stationed in Britain. Thus, in mid-May, the British chiefs of staff approved COHQ's proposal for a raid and set late June or early July as the date for its execution.

Almost from the beginning, the project encountered problems. Bad weather forced a cancellation of the raid in July, but, for reasons that remain a matter of debate, it was rescheduled for mid-August. By then, British Home Forces, the agency responsible for planning the raid, had modified COHQ's preliminary design for flank attacks on either side of Dieppe to include a frontal assault on the port by the 2d Canadian Division. Based on poor intelligence, the plan underestimated the strength of the German defenses and, worse yet, did not provide enough prior bombardment due to concern that shelling would alienate civilians and clutter the streets for the tanks. When the task force launched its assault on the morning of August 19, it ran into disaster. The commandos, accompanied by most of the 50 Rangers, captured one battery flanking the port and neutralized another with sniper fire, but the main assault and two other flanking attacks ran into a heavy fire which pinned down the infantry and knocked out tanks and landing craft. At about 11:00 a.m., the attackers withdrew. Of the 5,000 participants in the raid, about 3,400 were casualties, including 1,900 prisoners. The Ranger contingent counted seven killed or missing and seven wounded.

Debate still continues over the ultimate value of the Dieppe raid. Apologists have argued that the lessons learned made possible the Normandy invasion two years later, that the German air force suffered crippling losses, and that the Allies, in any case, had to try something during the long wait before D Day. To be sure, the raid clearly demonstrated the need for flexible plans, more rehearsals, better communications, more fire support, and intelligence from sources other than air photographs. However, it achieved few of its other goals. Agitation for a second front subsided only briefly. Postwar figures showed that the Germans actually lost half as many planes as the British. While the Allies learned several lessons, the raid also showed the Germans some weaknesses in their coastal defenses. In the view of the critics, an entire division and large numbers of aircraft had been sacrificed for dubious political and strategic gains.[18]

In the United States, however, such sober assessments were initially lost in the euphoria surrounding the first action by American troops against the Germans. When the Rangers returned with their British and Canadian comrades, they were engulfed by reporters anxious to interview them. Individual Rangers appeared on NBC's Army Hour and were interviewed by Edward Murrow, Quentin Reynolds, and Charles Collingwood. Despite attempts by COHQ and the U.S. theater headquarters to play down American participation, headlines in New York City trumpeted "U.S. and Britain Invade France," "U.S. Troops Land with Commandos in the Biggest Raid!" and "Tanks and U.S. Troops Smash at the French Coast!" Both the *New York Times* and *Newsweek* published features on "Truscott's Rangers," describing training exercises in which men drilled until their lungs burst and then hiked 36 miles over bleak, trackless mountains, carrying only half-rations. Behind much of the enthusiasm lay a pride that

Americans were operating as partners with the fabled commandos.[19]

The Rangers of Dieppe were only one expression of the interest of many American officers in commando operations during the spring and summer of 1942. Commando raids provided not only a means of striking back during that difficult time, but also a way to develop amphibious techniques that would be essential to the eventual counteroffensive. In Scotland, about 500 Rangers surplus to the 1st Ranger Battalion joined with British commandos to form the 1st and 6th "Commandies." Several divisions training in the United States were forming commando units within their organizations. In Massachusetts, at the Amphibious Training Center, a commando section instructed division staffs in commando operations and trained a unit within each division in conditioning, hand-to-hand fighting, the use of small boats, night raids, demolitions, and other commando subjects. Even the Marine Corps joined the bandwagon, forming Raider battalions despite grumbles among leathernecks that they already were elite light infantry.[20]

One of the elite raiding formations that appeared at this time, the 1st Special Service Force, traced its roots to Marshall's openness to original ideas, particularly those that promised action. During the chief of staff's visit to London in April, Mountbatten had introduced him to Geoffrey Pyke, COHQ's "Director of Programmes." The ungainly, often argumentative Pyke could be a trial to work with, especially given his inattention to personal cleanliness. Nevertheless, he possessed a mind full of innovative ideas, one of which he now described to Marshall. Figuring that over 70 percent of Europe's surface was covered with snow for five months of the year, he wanted to develop a special snow vehicle that would enable the Allies to conduct winter raids against such key points as hydroelectric stations in Norway and oil refineries in Romania. To contain the raiders, the Germans would have to divert thousands of troops from other fronts. Someone had to design and produce the vehicle, and a special force was needed to conduct the raids. Marshall liked the idea and gave it the highest priority when he returned to Washington.

Even with Marshall's backing, the concept still had to overcome several obstacles before it could become a reality. Planners in the War Department thought little of the scheme, particularly after Pyke paid a visit and angered many of them with his condescending attitude. A young coast artilleryman on the department's staff, Lt. Col. Robert T. Frederick, prepared a memorandum urging cancellation of the project as too great a diversion of resources for a task that could be accomplished by other means. Nevertheless, the project enjoyed too much high-level support to be dismissed. Studebaker received a contract to manufacture the vehicle, known as the Weasel, and, when Mountbatten visited Washington in June, he completed arrangements for a Canadian-American force to carry out the raids. Since he had worked on the project longer than anyone else, Frederick received the command. It proved to be an inspired choice, for the vigorous, charismatic Frederick, like Darby, possessed the qualities of a born leader.[21]

In his search for volunteers, Frederick encountered many of the problems that had plagued Darby. His dispatches to American and Canadian officials requested rugged, mentally agile types from 18 to 35 years of age with a willingness to take airborne training and, preferably, with experience as forest rangers, hunters, mountaineers, lumberjacks, or prospectors. Those who volunteered fell far short of these requirements. While the Canadians made an effort to provide some of their best troops, too many American post commanders emptied their stockades and otherwise unloaded their malcontents on the new formation. One telegram to Frederick blandly stated, "All volunteers for your command have departed this date. Direct the officer in charge and armed guards to return to this station as soon as practicable."[22] Within the ranks of the unit, one could find former miners, farmers, teachers, ex-thieves, safecrackers, and murderers. The rough Americans, about 60 percent of the unit, combined with the disciplined Canadians to produce an aggressive but often unruly fighting force that took some pride in its reputation as a unit of thugs.

Assembling the volunteers at Fort William Henry Harrison, a remote mountain outpost near Helena, Montana, Frederick soon weeded out misfits with an intensive training program that sought to have the unit ready for raids into Norway during the winter of 1942–1943. Since many recruits had not yet received basic training, much of the initial training phase from August to October was devoted to instruction in basic subjects such as weapons, demolitions, small-unit tactics, and physical hardening, along with a mere six days for airborne training. The unit then practiced larger-unit tactics until late November, when it began to receive cold-weather training and instruction in rock climbing and operation of the Weasel. The raiders also learned to ski from Norwegian instructors while living out of boxcars along the frigid Continental Divide. As training proceeded, Frederick and his staff developed a unique organization for the force, consisting of a combat echelon of three 417-man "regiments" and a service echelon, containing all the support elements.

All the hard work, however, seemed to be for naught when the raid into Norway was canceled. When Frederick flew to London in September, he found that much of the enthusiasm for the project had subsided. The chief of the British Air Staff would agree to loan the necessary planes only if Frederick could demonstrate that the raid would accomplish more than a bombing run. Furthermore, Norway's government in exile showed more interest in a plan, devised by the British Special Operations Executive, which would sabotage many of the same targets, but on a scale less likely to create hardships for the Norwegian population. Mountbatten and Frederick conferred and decided to let the plan die. Nevertheless, Marshall would not disband the force until all possible alternatives for its employment had been examined. At his direction, the General Staff's Operations Division considered missions in the Caucasus Mountains, New Guinea, and the Aleutians. In Montana, Frederick added heavier, more conventional weaponry to the unit and drilled his men for a broader array of tasks. As winter passed, the force was still searching for a purpose, illustrating by its inaction the danger of creating a special unit for too narrow a mission.[23]

While the concept of commandos as raiders or amphibious specialists interested many American officers, others were fascinated by the notion that commando training would provide the test needed to turn spoiled boys from an affluent society into soldiers. They shared the view of many Americans that the prosperity of the 1920s had encouraged softness and that Roosevelt's New Deal had rewarded self-pity, eroded traditional values of self-reliance, and left in its wake a spineless, dependent generation. Even those who were less likely to brand American society as self-indulgent expressed some worry about the effect of the urbanization of American life on prospective soldiers. Marshall, for one, admitted that "the ordinary military quality is not dominant in the American any more. It is no longer the question of taking the gun off the mantlepiece and fighting the savages." The concerns of such officers were not eased by the poor levels of health among young men examined for Selective Service. Gen. Omar N. Bradley later commented on the appalling physical condition of the 82d Division's draftees, some of whom could not walk a mile without collapsing.[24]

To develop soldiers able and willing to meet a ruthless and experienced enemy on battlefields far from home, training camps around the United States initiated "Ranger" programs. The best known, the Second Army Ranger School at Camp Forrest, Tennessee, was the brainchild of Lt. Gen. Ben Lear, Second Army's commander and a hard-bitten old Regular who perceived the growth, in the twentieth century, of "an ascetism [sic] which has belittled the development of strength." His realistic two-week course, based on Marine combat training, drilled picked men from Second Army in physical conditioning, hand-to-hand combat, sniping, camouflage, demolitions, tank hunting, infiltration, ambushes, patrols, and street fighting. The men would then return to their units and spread the creed of "Rangerism," which, roughly translated, meant being tougher and nastier than the enemy.[25]

As the commando craze continued in the United States during the summer of 1942, Allied leaders were making decisions with far-reaching implications for the program of raids envisioned by Marshall. Ever aware of the impatience of public opinion and under pressure from the Soviets, President Roosevelt was anxious to come to grips with the Germans on some front in 1942. When Allied strategists had conferred in Washington in June, however, the British had made clear their opposition to a cross-Channel attack in 1942, and Churchill had instead pressed for a landing in North Africa. In July, the president sent Hopkins, Marshall, and Admiral Ernest J. King, the chief of naval operations, to London for one last attempt to win over the British. If they still did not yield, the American delegation must agree on an alternative operation to take place before the end of the year. Given these instructions and continued

British recalcitrance, the Americans, on July 24, reluctantly agreed to an invasion of Northwest Africa.

The decision to invade North Africa had an almost immediate effect on plans for the 1st Ranger Battalion. In any competition for resources, the invasion, christened TORCH, had priority over the raiding program, and as planners considered the problems posed by TORCH, they saw the value of the Rangers as an assault force that could seize key points in the defense and clear the way for ensuing waves of troops. Initial plans called for the Rangers to make a predawn landing near Bone and secure a nearby airfield in advance of a British brigade, but the planners rejected a landing so far east along the Mediterranean coast as too risky. Instead, the Rangers would land at Arzew in advance of the 1st Infantry Division and capture two batteries dominating the approaches to the harbor. Although a naval bombardment could also knock out the guns, a surprise attack would cause less damage to port facilities and inflict fewer losses on the defenders and civilian populace, a major consideration in view of the Allies's hope that the French would rally to their side.[26]

In their first mission as a unit, the careful training and preparation of the Rangers paid off in a striking success. In the early-morning darkness of November 8, two companies under Darby's able executive officer, Maj. Herman W. Dammer, slipped through a boom blocking the entrance to the inner harbor of Arzew and stealthily approached Fort de la Pointe. After climbing over a sea wall and cutting through barbed wire, two groups of Rangers assaulted the fort from opposite directions. Within 15 minutes, they had captured the fort and 60 startled French prisoners. Meanwhile, Darby and the other four companies landed further up the coast and climbed a ravine to reach Batterie du Nord, overlooking the harbor. Supported by the fire of Company D's four 81-mm mortars, the Rangers overran the position, capturing over 60 more French soldiers. Except for a delay in communicating the success to the waiting fleet, due to the loss of the battalion's radio in the landing, the operation had been almost flawless.

The euphoria of the Rangers over the success of their first mission was tempered somewhat by the use of Ranger companies as line infantry in the expansion of the beachhead. When a battalion of the 16th Infantry encountered resistance in its drive toward LeMacta on the afternoon of November 8, Maj. Gen. Terry Allen, commander of the 1st Infantry Division, directed Darby to send a company to help. Placed on the front line, the Rangers, backed by two self-propelled guns, outflanked the French position and went into LaMacta unmolested. That same afternoon, Allen ordered another Ranger company to report to the 18th Infantry, which attached the Rangers to one of its battalions for the advance on St. Cloud. Moving by night to cut off the exits from the town, the Rangers hit a motor column at dawn, but heavy mortar and artillery fire pinned them down and reduced them to sniping at the French position. About mid-afternoon, the French surrendered, and the Rangers returned to Arzew.[27]

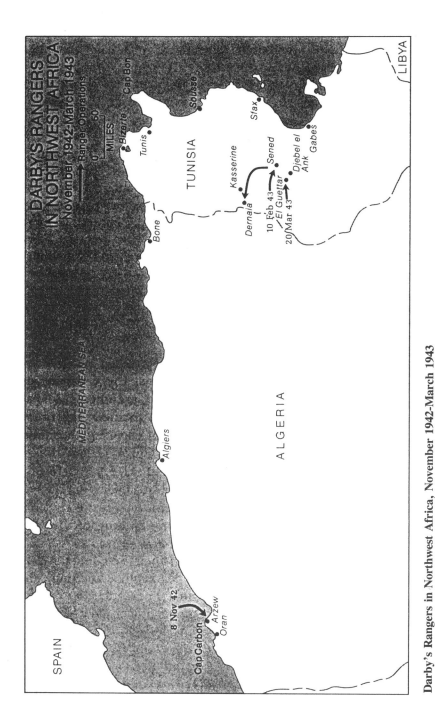

Darby's Rangers in Northwest Africa, November 1942–March 1943

U.S. Army Center of Military History.

Losses at LeMacta and St. Cloud had been light, but the two engagements foreshadowed the future use of the Rangers as line infantry, an unsuitable role given their organization and training. Many of the factors in their misuse in later battles were also present at Arzew. Probably because of the battalion's temporary status, no doctrinal statement, laying out missions and capabilities, existed to guide officers in the employment of the Rangers. Field commanders were left with only a vague, intuitive sense of the purpose of such troops. Only an extraordinarily perceptive officer would have seen the danger of misuse, and General Allen, a pugnacious cavalryman who had risen from the ranks after dropping out of West Point, was hardly the type to worry about distinctions.

In common with many other American officers, Allen perceived the Rangers to be elite infantry rather than raiding specialists. As Capt. Ralph Ingersoll, a journalist who later accompanied the Rangers to El Guettar, wrote in *The Battle Is the Payoff*, "The Rangers are somewhat misunderstood young men. They are thought of as American Commandos. And as the term Commandos is popularly thought of, that would make them specialists in raiding enemy coastal defenses. Actually, they are either more or less than that, depending on the point of view." Ingersoll reviewed Ranger selection procedures and training, concluding, "In the end, the Ranger turned out neither a special new kind of soldier—like a paratrooper—nor a superman as the feature stories would have him but simply a close approximate to the ideal basic unit of any army—the perfectly trained infantryman." Allen himself indicated his state of mind at Arzew when he later called the Rangers "a specially trained unit of high combat value." As far as he was concerned, the Rangers were proven troops that were available. Faced with an uncertain battlefield situation, he would not hesitate to throw them into the breach.[28]

Allen's employment of the Rangers met with some protest from enlisted Rangers, but little, if any, from their leaders. In a report on TORCH, Dammer mentioned that the Rangers were trained and equipped for "combined operational duties" but did not complain about misuse. He later stated that the Rangers were in no position to take the attitude that line duty was not their responsibility. James J. Altieri, in his memoir, *The Spearheaders*, recalled the response of a company commander to grumbling among the ranks, "Remember, [Darby] is only a lieutenant colonel and we're still a young outfit. It'll take some time for senior field commanders to know the exact capabilities of the Rangers and how to use us effectively." Darby himself seems to have had little sense of the Rangers as a special unit, and he never forgot that his battalion, as a temporary outfit, existed at the sufferance of superiors who might disband it if it remained inactive.[29]

Indeed, the battalion remained idle in the Arzew area for three months while higher headquarters debated what to do with them. Until January, the Allies had no plans for more major amphibious landings in the Mediterranean, and nothing existed to guide commanders in the use of the Rangers on an active

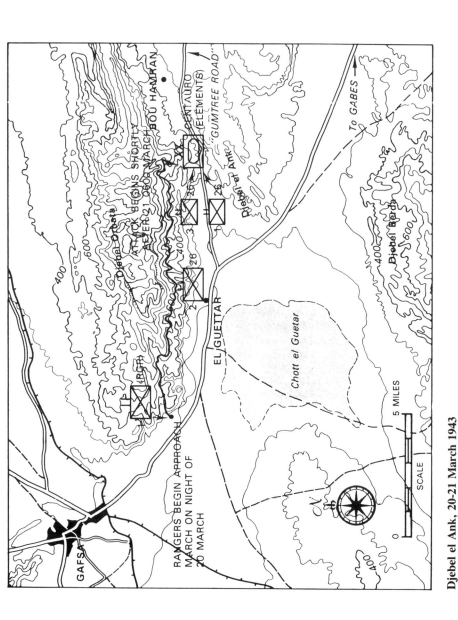

Djebel el Ank, 20-21 March 1943
U.S. Army Combat Studies Institute.

land front. The battalion did receive orders in mid-December for a raid against a radar and radio station on Galite, an island off the North African coast, but that operation was soon canceled. As Eisenhower's Allied forces drove across North Africa to Tunisia in an attempt to cut off the retreat of Rommel's Afrika Korps from the battlefield of El Alamein, the Rangers endured more speed marches and amphibious training and fought a growing sense of boredom. Many of the more disgruntled, convinced that the war was passing them by, transferred to other units.[30]

In early February, the battalion finally received a mission. Eisenhower's headquarters attached the Rangers to Lt. Gen. Lloyd R. Fredendall's II Corps, which held the Allied right in Tunisia. Shifting troops to meet a threat to his left, Fredendall wanted the Rangers to conduct a series of night raids from his right flank, near Gafsa, in order to gather information on enemy deployments, disguise Allied strength and intentions, and weaken enemy morale. Darby laid plans for three raids, beginning with one against the Italian outpost at Sened. On the night of February 10–11, three Ranger companies marched through eight miles of rugged terrain to a chain of hills overlooking the position. After observing the outpost by day, at midnight, the Rangers began their approach, using colored lights to keep formation. At 200 yards, the Italians discovered their advance and opened fire, but most of the shots passed harmlessly overhead. The Rangers waited until they were within 50 yards to launch a bayonet assault. Within about 20 minutes, they had overrun the garrison, killing 50 and capturing 11. Almost perfect in execution, the raid boosted Ranger morale and unnerved the Italians, who dubbed the raiders "Black Death."[31]

The raiding program was soon cut short by developments to the north. Within days of the action at Sened, German tanks attacked through Kasserine Pass, roughly handling the green American units and forcing Fredendall to withdraw his exposed right. In the emergency, II Corps once again pressed the Rangers into service as line troops, After serving as a rear guard in the retreat, the Rangers held a regimental-sized front at Dernaia Pass and patrolled in anticipation of a German attack until their relief on March 1.[32]

When the Rangers rejoined II Corps in mid-March, that force, now under Maj. Gen. George S. Patton, Jr., had launched a limited offensive in an attempt to divert enemy troops from the front of the British Eighth Army. Attached to the 1st Infantry Division, the Rangers spearheaded the Allied advance past El Guettar, only to find the Italians blocking the road at the pass of Djebel El Ank. The terrain to either side of the position appeared impassable, but Ranger patrols found a 12-mile path through the mountains and ravines north of the pass to the Italian rear. During the night of March 20–21, the battalion, accompanied by a mortar company, followed this tortuous route, reaching a plateau overlooking the Italian position. As the sun rose, the Rangers, supported by the fire of the mortars, struck the surprised Italians from flank and rear, while the 26th Infantry made a frontal assault. The enemy fled, leaving the pass and 700 prisoners in American hands. For a week, the Rangers patrolled and repelled counterattacks from a position near Djebel Berda, before returning to Algeria for reorganization.[33]

Even more than the clashes at Arzew and Sened, the performance of the Rangers at the battle of El Guettar, showing their value in support of conventional operations, won over their superiors. Patton offered Darby a promotion to colonel and command of a regiment, but Darby chose to stay with the battalion. While the Rangers rested, the North African campaign was coming to a victorious conclusion. On May 7, Tunis and Bizerte fell to the Allies, and, by May 13, over 275,000 Axis troops had surrendered. With North Africa secure, the Allies could turn to Operation HUSKY, the invasion of Sicily.[34]

The success of the Rangers in North Africa went a long way toward overcoming their status as a provisional unit. Along with other Ranger formations and training programs, the 1st Ranger Battalion represented an improvised response to the crisis of early and mid-1942: the unending string of defeats to Allied arms; the desire for action among the public, the president, and the military; the incomplete mobilization of an unready society; the inexperience of American troops; and the daunting prospect of amphibious landings. While Dieppe provided lessons on amphibious methods and thrilled a public that was hungry for heroes, the raiding program, as far as the Americans were concerned, never had a chance to achieve the goals envisioned by Marshall. High-level political factors and the demands of other operations killed the 1st Special Service Force's plan to raid Norway, and the TORCH landings claimed the services of the 1st Ranger Battalion. By the winter of 1942–1943, both units, lacking any stated purpose beyond the narrow task for which they were formed, were searching for a mission. The success of Darby's men in both special and line missions increased the natural reluctance of field commanders to disband a fine unit, but it was the need for amphibious spearheaders that ultimately led to the expansion of the Rangers in the spring of 1943.

NOTES

    1. Forrest C. Pogue, *George C. Marshall: Education of a General* (New York: Viking Press, 1963), p. 254; Forrest C. Pogue, *George C. Marshall: Ordeal and Hope*, 2d ed. (New York: Viking Press, 1966), p. 12–14, 305–306, 316; Forrest C. Pogue, *George C. Marshall: Organizer of Victory* (New York: Viking Press, 1973), p. 379; Maurice Matloff and Edwin M. Snell, *Strategic Planning for Coalition Warfare, 1941–1942*, U.S. Army in World War II (Washington: Office of the Chief of Military History (OCMH), 1953), pp. 156–159, 178–181; Millett and Maslowski, *Common Defense*, p. 404.

    2. "Documents Relating to Subjects Considered by U.S.-British Representatives in London Conferences, April 6–18, 1942," (hereafter cited as "Documents Relating to London Conferences"), Box 61, Folder 49, George C. Marshall Papers, George C.

Marshall Research Library, Lexington, Va.; Weigley, *History of the United States Army*, pp. 429–431, 435, 569; Blumenson, "Kasserine Pass," pp. 237–240. Contrary to popular belief, the Army had worked on amphibious operations before the war, although it had not yet fully developed a doctrine; see William F. Atwater, "United States Army and Navy Development of Joint Landing Operations, 1898–1942" (Ph.D. dissertation, Duke University, 1986).

3. Peter Young, *Commando* (New York: Ballantine, 1969), pp. 6–12; Simon Christopher Joseph Fraser Lord Lovat, *March Past: A Memoir* (New York: Holmes and Meier, 1978), pp. 150–152, 157; John Durnford–Slater, *Commando* (London: Kimber, 1953), pp. v, 16, 20; Hilary St. George Saunders, *Combined Operations: The Official Story of the Commandos* (New York: Macmillan, 1943), pp. 4–7; U.S. War Department, Military Intelligence Service, *British Commandos*, Special Series no. 1 (Washington, D.C.: U.S. War Department, 1942), pp. 5–13, 27–33; Roger Keyes, *Amphibious Warfare and Combined Operations* (Cambridge: Cambridge University Press, 1943), p. 7; "Documents Relating to London Conferences," Tab U: "Notes of a Meeting between the VCCO [Vice Chief, Combined Operations] and Representatives of the U.S. Army," p. 2, Box 62, Folder 3, Marshall Papers, Marshall Library; Maj. Theodore J. Conway to Truscott, 5 June 1942, Box 10, Folder 3, Lucian K. Truscott, Jr. Papers, George C. Marshall Research Library; Cohen, *Commandos and Politicians*, pp. 37–40. Originally, personnel from all units were eligible to join with the stipulation that they would return to their units after six months of training or one raid. When this stipulation was dropped, the resentment of the commanders caused recruiters to turn to training centers.

4. Young, *Commando*, pp. 12–24, 34–37, 56–111; Lovat, *March Past*, pp. 184–189, 199, 215, 222–223, 269; Saunders, *Combined Operations*, pp. 19–21, 26, 65; Glen S. Barclay, "Butcher and Bolt: Admiral Roger Keyes and British Combined Operations, 1940–1941," *Naval War College Review* 35 (March–April 1982): 18–29; Arthur Swinson, *Mountbatten* (New York: Ballantine, 1971), pp. 38, 41; J. Hughes-Hallet, "The Mounting of Raids," *Military Review* 31 (May 1951): 85–93.

5. "How Combined Operations Are Organised Beforehand by Scale Models," *Illustrated London News*, 22 May 1943, p. 576; R. Maillard Stead, "Witness Describes Sortie," *New York Times*, 5 June 1942, p. 6; "Commando Chief Hails War Spirit," *New York Times*, 6 June 1942, p. 3; Peter Locke, "Hard Hitting Commandos," *New York Times Magazine*, 5 April 1942, sec. 7, p. 6; Bruce Thomas "The Commando," *Harper's*, March 1942, pp. 438–440.

6. "Documents Relating to London Conferences," Tab A: "Memorandum: American Proposal for Operations in Western Europe (Referred to by British as General Marshall's Memorandum)," pp. 1–2, Box 61, Folder 49, Marshall Papers, Marshall Library; Matloff and Snell, *Strategic Planning, 1941–1942*, pp. 184–187.

7. Along with those who would serve with the Commando, another 20 officers and 40 enlisted men would attend the training and return to the United States as instructors; see "Documents Relating to London Conferences," Tab D: "Resume of Meeting on April 9, 1942 of British JCS with American Representatives," p. 3, Box 61, Folder 50, Marshall Papers, Marshall Library; "Documents Relating to London Conferences," Tab U: "Notes of a Meeting between the VCCO and Representatives of the U.S. Army," pp. 1–2, Box 62, Folder 3, Marshall Papers, Marshall Library; "Documents Relating to London Conferences," Tab V: Box 62, Folder 3, Marshall Papers, Marshall Library; William O. Darby and William H. Baumer, *Darby's Rangers: We Led the Way* (San

Rafael, Calif: Presidio Press, 1980), p. 25; Matloff and Snell, *Strategic Planning, 1941-1942*, pp. 187-188; Pogue, *Ordeal and Hope*, pp. 311-312.

8. Lucian K. Truscott, Jr., *Command Missions: A Personal Story* (New York: E. P. Dutton, 1954), p. 20; Edmund F. Ball, *Staff Officer with the Fifth Army* (New York: Exposition Press, 1958), pp. 315-316; "Truscott, Lucian King Jr.," *Generals of the Army*, January 1954, p. 21; Russell F. Weigley, *Eisenhower's Lieutenants: The Campaigns of France and Germany, 1944-1945* (Bloomington: Indiana University Press, 1981), p. 223.

9. Quotes from Truscott, *Command Missions*, pp. 22-23. See also pp. 19-24; Conway interview.

10. Truscott to Brig. Gen. Charles L. Bolte, Chief of Staff, U.S. Army Forces in British Isles (USAFBI), 26 May 1942, Box 10, Folder 3, Truscott Papers, Marshall Library; Maj. Gen. J.C. Haydon, Vice Chief, Combined Operations, to Brig. Gen. L. M. McClelland, 13 May 1942, Box 10, Folder 4, Truscott Papers, Marshall Library; Truscott, *Command Missions*, pp. 25, 37-38; London to Adjutant General, U.S. War Department, No. 1695, 26 May 1942, U.S. War Department, Operations Division, ABC Files, 381 Bolero (3-16-42), Sec. 1, RG 165, Modern Military Headquarters Branch (MMHB), National Archives, Washington, D.C.; Marshall to USFOR, 27 May 1942, Section IA, U.S. Army, Assistant Chief of Staff, G-3, Records Section, Decimal File, March 1950-1951 322 Ranger, RG 319, MMHB, National Archives.

11. Conway to Truscott, 5 June 1942; Truscott to Adjutant General, 8 July 1942, Sgt. Harry Perlmutter Ranger Battalions of World War II Collection, "Ranger Battalions: Historical Background Information on Ranger Battalions and Tables of Organization and Equipment" (hereafter cited as Perlmutter Collection), Call No. MP 63-8, Roll No. 8, John F. Kennedy Special Warfare Center (JFKSWC), Fort Bragg, N.C.; Col. I. B. Summers, Adjutant General USAFBI, to Commanding General, U.S. Army Forces Northern Ireland (USAFNI), 13 June 1942, Theodore J. Conway Papers, USAMHI; Conway interview; Col. Herman W. Dammer USA (Ret.), interview with author, McLean, Va., 23 August 1984.

12. Summers to Hartle, 1 June 1942, Adjutant General's Office, World War II Operations Reports, 1940-1948, Infantry (hereafter cited as WWII Ops. Reports), INBN 1-0, RG 407, Washington National Records Center (WNRC), Suitland, Md.; Truscott to Commanding General, USAFBI, 5 June 1942, Box 10, Folder 3, Truscott Papers, Marshall Library; Truscott, *Command Missions*, p. 39; Martin Blumenson, *Kasserine Pass* (Boston: Houghton Mifflin, 1967), p. 82; Blumenson, "Kasserine Pass," pp. 235, 238-240.

13. Michael J. King, *William Orlando Darby: A Military Biography* (Hamden, Conn.: Archon Books, 1981), pp. 10, 16-27, 32, 177; Robert C. Williams, "Amphibious Scouts and Raiders," *Military Affairs* 13 (Fall 1949): 157. Testimonies of Darby's leadership ability abound; see James J. Altieri, *The Spearheaders* (Indianapolis, Ind.: Bobbs-Merrill, 1960), pp. 31-32; Brig. Gen. Norman D. Cota, Combined Operations, to Commanding General, European Theater of Operations (ETO), 10 August 1943, Perlmutter Collection, Call No. 63-8, Roll 8, JFKSWC; Milton Lehman, "The Rangers Fought Ahead of Everybody," *Saturday Evening Post*, 15 June 1946, p. 28.

14. Darby and Baumer, *Darby's Rangers*, pp. 25-26; "Report on Organization of American Commando Unit," Box 10, Folder 4, Truscott Papers, Marshall Library; Ranger Questionnaire, Theodore J. Conway Papers, USAMHI; Altieri, *Spearheaders*, pp.

15–22; James J. Altieri, "Darby's Rangers: Activation of the First Ranger Battalion," *Gung Ho*, 4 October 1984, pp. 54–55.

15. Darby was later quoted as saying that if he had the job to do again, he would not have created a special formation of volunteers but instead would have selected a unit for a particular job and given the men special training and equipment. In this, his views were not so different from those later expressed by opponents of Ranger units. See Williams, "Amphibious Scouts," p. 157. See also Special Orders no. 20, Headquarters (HQ), USAFNI, 22 June 1942, Conway Papers, USAMHI; Darby and Baumer, *Darby's Rangers*, pp. 25–27, 84; Mack Morriss, "Rangers Come Home and Bring Stories of Their Tough Campaigns in Africa and Europe," *Yank*, 4 August 1944, p. 3; "The Rangers," *Life*, 31 July 1944, pp. 59–63; Altieri, *Spearheaders*, p. 15–19, 66–67; members of the Ranger Battalions Association, interviews with author, Carlisle, Pa., 4 May 1984; Dammer interview; Brig. Gen. John W. Dobson USA (Ret.), interview with author, Hilton Head, S.C., 16 November 1984; Morris J. MacGregor, Jr., *Integration of the Armed Forces, 1940–1965*, Defense Studies Series (Washington: OCMH, 1981), pp. 18–21.

16. General Orders no. 7, HQ, USAFNI, 19 June 1942, WWII Ops. Reports, INBN 1–0, RG 407, WNRC; Truscott, *Command Missions*, p. 40; Conway interview; Maj. Leonard O. Friesz, Assistant Executive Officer, OCMH, to Roy Boatman, 23 May 1952, and Col. D. G. Gilbert, Historical Services Division, OCMH to Mr. George C. Singer, 17 February 1960, in HRC 314.7 Ranger Battalion, Historical Records Branch, CMH.

17. "Instructions and Key to Programme of Work for U.S.A. Rangers, 1st to 31st July 1942," and Darby's Progress Report to Truscott, 17 July 1942, Perlmutter Collection, Call No. MP 63–8, Roll 8, JFKSWC; Darby and Baumer, *Darby's Rangers*, pp. 27–38, 46–49; Altieri, *Spearheaders*, pp. 22–28, 38–44, 80–85; Darby to Commanding General, II Corps, 30 November 1942, WWII Ops. Reports, INBN 1–0, RG 407, WNRC; Young, *Commando*, pp. 115, 122.

18. Charles W. Schreiner, "The Dieppe Raid: Its Origins, Aims, and Results," *Naval War College Review* 25 (May–June 1973): 83–97; Lovat, *March Past*, pp. 238–239, 269–278; John Mellor, *Forgotten Heroes: The Canadians at Dieppe* (Toronto: Methuen, 1975), pp. 12–15, 19–26, 30–35; "Outline Plan and Narrative of Events," along with reports on lessons learned in SHAEF, General Staff, G-3 Division, Administrative Section, Subject File, 1942–1945: Dieppe Raid, Boxes 16–17, RG 331, MMHB, National Archives; Robert P. Arnoldt, "The Dieppe Raid: A Failure That Led to Success," *Armor* 90 (July–August 1981): 12–19; Young, *Commando*, pp. 128–153; Keyes, *Amphibious Warfare*, pp. 96–99; Darby to Adjutant General, 11 January 1943, and Capt. Roy Murray's report on Dieppe, 26 August 1942, WWII Ops. Reports, INBN 1–0, RG 407, WNRC; Darby and Baumer, *Darby's Rangers*, pp. 42–46. For the controversy on the decision to launch the raid, see Brian Loring Villa, "Mountbatten, the British Chiefs of Staff, and Approval of the Dieppe Raid," *Journal of Military History* 54 (April 1990): 201–226.

19. Sgt. Alex Szima File, Ranger Collection, USAMHI; Eisenhower to Marshall, 20 August 1942, in Alfred D. Chandler, Jr. and Stephen E. Ambrose, eds., *The Papers of Dwight David Eisenhower*, 9 vols. (Baltimore, Md.: Johns Hopkins University Press, 1970), I:483–484; Jerome J. Haggerty, "A History of the Ranger Battalions in World War II" (Ph.D. dissertation, Fordham University, 1982), pp. 101–103; Larry Meier, "With the Ranger Commandos on Their Journey To and Return From Dieppe," *New York*

Times, 21 August 1942, p. 3, and other articles in the *New York Times* in the days following the raid; "Truscott's Rangers," *Newsweek*, 31 August 1942, pp. 21–22.

20. Alexander P. Shine, "Stepchildren: The Rangers of World War II," May 1970, p. 27, HRC 314.7 Ranger Battalion, Historical Records Branch, CMH; Marshall Becker, *The Amphibious Training Center*, Army Ground Forces Study no. 22 (Washington, D.C.: Army Ground Forces, 1946), pp. 3, 7, 50–52; Matloff and Snell, *Strategic Planning, 1941-1942*, p. 221; Allan R. Millett, *Semper Fidelis: The History of the United States Marine Corps* (New York: Macmillan, 1980), p. 346; "Princeton 'Commandos' to Stage Raid Tonight," *New York Times*, 21 August 1942, p. 8.

21. Robert D. Burhans, *The First Special Service Force: A War History of the North Americans, 1942-1944* (Washington, D.C.: Infantry Journal Press, 1947), pp. 1–12, 37; Robert H. Adleman and George Walton, *The Devil's Brigade* (Philadelphia: Chilton Books, 1966), pp. 2–3, 10–35; Stanley W. Dziuban, *Military Relations Between the United States and Canada, 1939-1945*, U.S. Army in World War II (Washington, D.C.: OCMH, 1959), pp. 259–260; Albert C. Wedemeyer, *Wedemeyer Reports!* (New York: Holt, 1958), pp. 109–111; USAMHI, "Senior Officers Debriefing Program: Conversations between General Paul DeWitt Adams and Colonel Irving Monclova, Lt. Colonel Marlin Lang," (Carlisle, Pa., 1975), I:56–58.

22. Quoted in Adleman and Walton, *Devil's Brigade*, p. 49.

23. Frederick to Military Personnel Division, SOS, 6 July 1942, and Fort Douglas, Utah to Adjutant General, 13 July 1942, in AG 320.2 (6-15-42)(16) U.S. Army, Adjutant General's Office, Classified Decimal File, 1940-1942, Box 299, RG 407, MMHB, National Archives; Burhans, *Special Service Force*, pp. 14–15, 23–24, 35–37, 44–46, 60; Adleman and Walton, *Devil's Brigade*, pp. 48–50, 64–68, 73, 77, 86–91; Scott R. McMichael, *A Historical Perspective on Light Infantry*, Research Survey no. 6 (Fort Leavenworth, Kans.: Combat Studies Institute, 1987), pp. 169–173, 212; Maj. Gen. Frederick, interview at the Pentagon, WWII Mediterranean, Stanley Mathews Collection, USAMHI; Dziuban, *Military Relations*, pp. 260–262; USAMHI, "Senior Officers Debriefing Program: Adams," I:59–62.

24. Marshall quoted in Pogue, *Organizer of Victory*, p. 83; see also Clay Blair and Omar N. Bradley, *A General's Life* (New York: Simon and Schuster, 1983), pp. 106, 171–172; Blumenson,"Kasserine Pass," p. 237; Richard Polenberg, *War and Society: The United States, 1941-1945* (Philadelphia: Lippincott, 1972), p. 2; Geoffrey Perret, *Days of Sadness, Years of Triumph: The American People, 1939-1945* (New York: Coward, McCann and Geoghegan, 1973), pp. 136, 197–198; Arthur Goodfriend, *Scouting and Patrolling* (Washington, D.C.: Infantry Journal, 1943), pp. vii–viii.

25. Lear quoted in Bell I. Wiley and William P. Govan, *History of the Second Army*, Army Ground Forces Study no. 16 (Washington, D.C.: Army Ground Forces, 1946), p. 139; see also pp. 139–140; enclosure folder to 353/729 1/2 (Second Army) 1943, U.S. Army, Army Ground Forces, Ground Adjutant General Section, Records Division, Project Decimal File: Second Army, 1942-3, 1946-7, Box 1158, RG 337, MMHB, National Archives; Milton Bracker, "Rangers Toughen But Are Still Boys," *New York Times*, 6 March 1943, p. 5, and other articles in the *New York Times* in late 1942 and 1943 on Ranger training.

26. Matloff and Snell, *Strategic Planning, 1941-1942*, pp. 222, 232–239, 243, 273, 282, 287–292, 317, 325, 354; Pogue, *Ordeal and Hope*, pp. 327–330, 403; Tab CCS 103, Enclosure B, HQ, European Theater of Operations, U.S. Army (ETOUSA), Norfolk

Group Outline Plan, Operation TORCH, 21 August 1942, and AFHQ Outline Plan, Operation TORCH, 20 September 1942, in U.S. Army, Army Staff, Plans and Operations Division, ABC Decimal File, 1942-8, 381, (7-25-42) Sec. 1 to 4, RG 319, MMHB, National Archives; King, *Darby*, p. 44.

27. Darby's report of Arzew, 1 January 1943, WWII Ops. Reports, INBN 1-0, RG 407, WNRC; Darby and Baumer, *Darby's Rangers*, pp. 9-23.

28. Ralph M. Ingersoll, *The Battle Is the Payoff*, Fighting Forces Series (Washington, D.C.: Infantry Journal Press, 1943), pp. 122-123; Terry Allen, "Combat Operations of the 1st Infantry Division during World War II," p. 8, Terry Allen Papers, USAMHI; "Allen, Terry de la Mesa, (1888-1969)," Robert McHenry, ed., *Webster's American Military Biographies* (Springfield, Mass.: Merriam, 1978), p. 5. I have found no evidence of a doctrine for the World War II Rangers, nor have any of the Rangers interviewed indicated that such a doctrine existed. See Dammer and Dobson interviews; Col. Robert W. Garrett USA (Ret.), interview with author, Potomac, Md., 8 October 1985; Col. James F. Greene, Jr., USA (Ret.), interview with author, Carlisle, Pa., 8 March 1984.

29. Altieri, *Spearheaders*, p. 137; Dammer to Commanding General, Center Task Force, 10 January 1943, WWII Ops. Reports, INBN 1-0, RG 407, WNRC; Dammer interview.

30. Journal, 1st Ranger Battalion, 1325, Part III, 1942-5 February 1944, WWII Ops. Reports, INBN 1-0.3, RG 407, WNRC; Darby and Baumer, *Darby's Rangers*, pp. 53-55; Altieri, *Spearheaders*, pp. 146-153, 169-171; Michael J. King, *Rangers: Selected Combat Operations in World War II*, Leavenworth Papers no. 11 (Fort Leavenworth, Kans.: Combat Studies Institute, 1985), p. 14.

31. Darby's report of Sened, 5 March 1943, WWII Ops. Reports, INBN 1-0, RG 407, WNRC; Darby and Baumer, *Darby's Rangers*, pp. 56-60; Leilyn M. Young, "Rangers in a Night Operation," *Military Review* 24 (July 1944): 64-69; Fredendall to Eisenhower, 10 March 1943, U.S. Army Ground Forces, General Staff, G-2 Section, Intelligence Reports Numerical File, 1943-1946, RG 337, MMHB, National Archives.

32. Darby's report for the period 14-28 February 1943, 5 March 1943, WWII Ops. Reports, INBN 1-0, RG 407, WNRC; Darby and Baumer, *Darby's Rangers*, pp. 60-63; King, *Darby*, p. 62.

33. Darby's report of El Guettar, 9 April 1943, WWII Ops. Reports, INBN 1-0, RG 407, WNRC; Darby and Baumer, *Darby's Rangers*, pp. 68-77; King, *Rangers*, pp. 13-22; George F. Howe, *Northwest Africa: Seizing the Initiative in the West*, U.S. Army in World War II (Washington, D.C.: OCMH, 1957), pp. 546-548, 557-558, 562-563.

34. Darby and Baumer, *Darby's Rangers*, p. 78; King, *Darby*, p. 68; Howe, *Northwest Africa*, p. 666.

3

The Spearheaders

Although considerable hard fighting lay ahead of the Allies, the tide was definitely shifting in their favor by early 1943. While American and British forces were converging on Tunisia, the German surrender at Stalingrad in February marked a turning point on the Eastern Front. That same month, American forces drove the last Japanese troops from Guadalcanal, bringing to a successful conclusion the initial step in the advance across the Pacific. In the Far East, Japanese attempts to invade India had bogged down in the rugged terrain along the frontier, and the Allies could begin to contemplate a counteroffensive. Despite the improving global situation, in January, American planners left the conference of Allied leaders at Casablanca in an irate mood. Once again, the British had used divisions among their allies to obtain consent for operations in the Mediterranean, in this case an invasion of Sicily following the North African campaign. The disgruntled Americans realized that the decision effectively postponed any cross-Channel attack until 1944 at the earliest.

In theory, the Americans and British remained committed to their raiding program. The lack of combat veterans in the divisions expected to carry out the cross-Channel attack concerned planners almost as much as the shortage of landing craft and aviation. In addition, the Allies continued to see raids as a means of provoking a major air battle under conditions favorable to the attrition of the German Air Force. The final directive of the Casablanca Conference provided for continued planning for small raids, and Marshall apparently indicated to Mountbatten his interest in more Ranger units.[1]

To replace the 1st Ranger Battalion in the raiding program, European Theater of Operations, U.S. Army (ETOUSA), the American theater headquarters in Britain, had already created a new Ranger unit. On September 30, 1942, ETOUSA had directed II Corps, still in Britain at the time, to form a provisional Ranger battalion "as a training unit for a maximum number of officers and enlisted men of combat units to receive training and experience in actual combat, after which they will return to their organizations." Most of the American units in the British Isles soon departed for TORCH, leaving only the 29th Infantry Division, a recently arrived National Guard outfit from Maryland and Virginia, as a source for recruits. In mid-December, the division's chief, Maj. Gen. Leonard T. Gerow, asked Maj. Randolph Milholland, a recent graduate of the British General Headquarters Battle School, to organize the new unit. Using the same recruiting procedures employed by Darby, Milholland selected officers, who, in turn, interviewed and chose enlisted volunteers. A tiny cadre from the 1st Ranger Battalion filled out the headquarters element and two companies which initially composed the unit. After some preliminary training in the divisional area, the Rangers, in February, endured five weeks at Achnacarry and then practiced amphibious landings and raids with the commandos.[2]

By the spring of 1943, however, enthusiasm in London and Washington for the raiding program had begun to subside. In the year since Marshall's first trip to Britain, the program had yielded meager results. From May to September 1942, Combined Operations Headquarters had carried out only one operation, the raid at Dieppe. Five others had been canceled at the last moment, and nine had been abandoned at some stage in planning. In part the inactivity resulted from the vagaries of weather, but it could also be traced to complexities of planning and coordination among the three services, and, in the case of larger-scale raids, competition with other operations for scarce planes, landing craft, and other resources. The problems of the program confirmed the suspicions of officers who had never thought much of raids. Among other things, they argued that such operations merely pointed out to the Germans the weaknesses in their coastal defenses.

Despite the waning interest in raids, commando units found a basis for their continued existence in the need for spearheaders for landing operations. Along with unique problems of command, communications, and supply, an assault across an open beach raked by hostile fire presented a formidable test of even a veteran's courage and initiative. Amphibious planners prized special units that possessed the skills and aggressiveness needed to seize key fortifications or certain critical areas in coastal defenses, thereby easing the way for the main assault. The Marines, as experts in amphibious warfare, would have been the logical choice for such a role, but the Joint Chiefs of Staff had committed almost the entire Corps to the Pacific. Consequently, the Army would have to rely on its own special units to spearhead the landings.[3]

As early as December 2, 1942, ETOUSA had requested that the War Department form another Ranger battalion to serve as a spearhead for the cross Channel invasion. "Experience has proven," ETOUSA's memorandum stated, "that specially trained units of this character are invaluable in landing operations, for the reduction of coast defenses and similar missions." Since the 1st Ranger Battalion would probably not return to Britain and Milholland's Rangers were supposed to return to the 29th Division before the invasion, ETOUSA wanted the War Department to form a 2d Ranger Battalion in the United States and send it to Britain for training without delay.[4]

ETOUSA's request met a cold reception from Army Ground Forces, the War Department agency responsible for organizing and training ground combat units. To fight a war of large armies, Army Ground Forces preferred to mass produce large numbers of standard units that could perform a variety of tasks rather than create special formations for special jobs. In this, it reflected the views of its chief, Lt. Gen. Lesley J. McNair, a gruff but efficient artilleryman who remarked in response to the pressure for commando units, "Hell, we rehearsed trench raids in the last war, only we didn't call them 'Commandos.'" Under his leadership, Army Ground Forces had already abolished commando training at the Amphibious Training Center and would soon discontinue the Second Army Ranger School after a pair of two-week courses. McNair's headquarters preferred programs that would prepare all troops for combat rather than create a few "superkillers" and disapproved of training that diverted large numbers of men from their units for lengthy periods of time.[5]

The response by Army Ground Forces to ETOUSA's request listed many of the arguments that are repeatedly cited in opposition to elite units. McNair's agency contended, with some reason, that a special unit unless employed for a specific mission, would probably remain inactive for lengthy periods and might even seek "unprofitable missions" to justify its existence. The memorandum implied that such a formation, demanding special arrangements, would be an administrative headache and warned that if too many qualified personnel were diverted to a Ranger unit, "it will seriously handicap the selection and training of [line unit] leaders who are so essential in the present training program." With special equipment and training, the memorandum argued, any separate infantry battalion could perform Ranger missions. On the basis of this statement, the War Department turned down ETOUSA's request, but it did authorize the theater to designate a company within a battalion or regiment to perform special tasks.[6]

ETOUSA would not give up that easily. Considerable interest in the Ranger concept existed within the theater, especially within the American mission at COHQ. Following Marshall's original orders to Truscott, those officers had been gathering data on commando training, methods, and equipment, and were preparing a tentative table of organization for a Ranger battalion. They showed especially great enthusiasm for Ranger training, to the point of advocating it for all infantry instructional programs, and even suggested that Darby return to Britain to head a Ranger Training Center. They also sought a Ranger Division, organized along the lines of the commandos' 1st Special Service Brigade. Probably as a step toward that end, ETOUSA, on March 12, renewed its request for a 2d Ranger Battalion and also asked to turn Milholland's two companies into a fully manned and equipped "29th Ranger Battalion" for operations later in the year.

In this conflict between the desires of a theater and the misgivings of the headquarters responsible for the Army's organization, Marshall sided with his field commanders. At his direction, Army Ground Forces activated the 2d Ranger Battalion at Camp Forrest on April 1. Later in the month, he approved the expansion of Milholland's unit to full strength but stipulated that the men should return to their parent organizations when the battalion was no longer needed or was replaced by a similar unit from the United States.[7]

Thus, the 29th Ranger Battalion lingered for a few more months. Expanding to four companies, the unit trained through April and May while detachments accompanied British commandos in three raids on the coast of Norway. The first, an attempt to destroy a bridge over a fjord, ended in failure when a Norwegian guide dropped the magazine for his submachine gun on a concrete quay, alerting the German guards. The second, a three-day reconnaissance of a harbor, was more successful, but the third aborted when commandos and Rangers found their objective, a German command post, abandoned. During the summer, the Rangers practiced amphibious methods and developed a film on assault tactics for use by training programs in the United States. In early September, the Rangers destroyed a German radar station on the Ile d'Ouessant, an island off the coast of Brittany, and left a helmet and cartridge belt on the beach as calling cards. This raid proved to be their final mission. Although ETOUSA apparently wanted more Ranger units, it had to consider the 29th Division's desire for the return of its men, and the War Department, having already decided to form another battalion in the United States, responded coolly to the idea of granting permanent status to the 29th. On October 15, ETOUSA inactivated the 29th Ranger Battalion, the only Ranger unit of World War II to follow Marshall's original concept.[8]

While ETOUSA had been calling for more Ranger units in early 1943, Eisenhower's headquarters in the Mediterranean had obtained authorization to expand its Ranger force for the invasion of Sicily. In April, Allied planners had conferred with Darby on the number of Ranger battalions needed to knock out the coastal defenses of Palermo, the original target of Patton's Western Task Force. Darby's response, 15, was too exorbitant for the planners, who instead requested authority from the War Department to expand Darby's force to 3 battalions. Marshall gave his approval but directed that the units disband once the requirement for their services had passed. His response, while again deferring to the wishes of his field commanders, indicates that he still perceived the Rangers as temporary units for transitory tasks. Once the tasks were performed, in his view, it made little sense to retain the battalions at a time when the Army faced a growing shortage of replacements for combat units.[9]

Remembering his experience with misfits in Northern Ireland, Darby chose to seek out prospective Rangers rather than rely on other units to provide volunteers. He and his officers avoided existing combat units, most of which

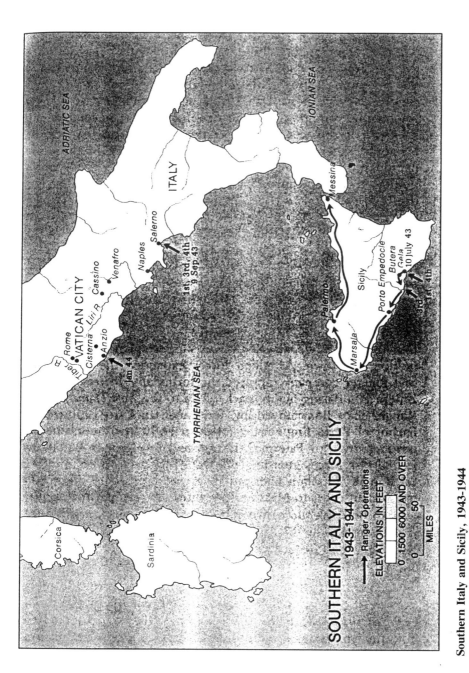

Southern Italy and Sicily, 1943-1944

U.S. Army Center of Military History.

were either at the front or likely to see combat soon, and instead focused on the replacement depots and rear echelon formations in Algeria and French Morocco. They posted bulletins, talked to likely candidates in bars, and made stump speeches, emphasizing the exacting discipline and less glamorous sides of Ranger life and warning that the recruits would receive no special privileges. About 10 percent of the soldiers who were contacted joined. Many were eager to be part of the unit that had carried out the Dieppe raid. Others, especially transient replacements, found the appeal of a "home" in one of the best combat units in the Army irresistible. Those accepted by Darby and his party assembled at a bleak plateau overlooking the port of Nemours, Algeria, where, at a replica of the Commando Depot, they endured six weeks of speed marches, cliff climbing, weapons training, instruction in fieldcraft and night operations, and amphibious exercises.[10]

Darby's excitement over the expansion of the Rangers was tempered somewhat by his inability to obtain a regimental or force headquarters to command the three battalions. He had turned down a promotion and regimental command partly out of loyalty to his Rangers but also because he believed that he would soon fulfill his dream to command an elite Ranger regiment that would serve as a model unit for the rest of the Army. The War Department, however, still viewed the battalions as temporary units and disapproved his request for a regimental or group headquarters. This left Darby in an awkward position. Although he technically commanded only one battalion, he was responsible for the organization and training of all three, as well as overall command when they functioned as a group. For the time being, the Rangers, when operating together, settled for an informal arrangement in which Darby, as senior battalion commander, directed his own 1st Ranger Battalion, the 3d Ranger Battalion under Dammer, and the 4th Ranger Battalion, under Lt. Col. Roy Murray.[11]

In Sicily, at least, the improvised command arrangement worked well enough. Attached to the 1st Infantry Division, the 1st and 4th Ranger Battalions stormed across a mined beach on the early morning of July 10 to capture the port of Gela and adjacent shore batteries. They then held on for two days of enemy counterattacks, using thermite grenades and a 37-mm gun against tanks that penetrated into the streets of the town. Despite such heroics, the Rangers could not have held Gela without naval gunfire, which compensated for their lack of heavy weapons. As the Allies expanded the beachhead, a Ranger company overran the surprised defenders of the fortress town of Butera in a night attack. To the west, the 3d Ranger Battalion met light resistance when it landed at Licata with the 3d Infantry Division. It then moved by foot and truck to capture Porto Empedocle and over 700 prisoners.

As Patton's Seventh Army swept across Sicily, the Rangers operated with task forces on the flanks of the main body. Under Darby's command, a task force that included the 1st and 4th Ranger Battalions guarded the left flank of the 2d Armored Division in the drive to Palermo on the western tip of the island.

After the fall of Palermo, the 1st and 4th went into reserve, while the 3d Ranger Battalion joined the 3d Infantry Division's slow advance against successive German delaying positions along the coastal road to Messina. To speed the march, Patton infiltrated the Rangers through the mountains around one German flank, while other formations staged amphibious end runs around the seaward flank. The fall of Messina on August 17 brought the campaign to a close and set the stage for the invasion of Italy.[12]

By the conclusion of the Sicilian campaign, it was becoming increasingly clear to Darby that the Ranger battalions must become more versatile if they were to maintain their existence. Once the Allies had established themselves on the Continent and no longer needed amphibious spearheaders, field commanders would either disband the Rangers, find other missions suited to their unique capabilities, or, most likely, use them as line troops. Darby had never been tied to the notion of the Rangers as troops for a special task, and, as a former artilleryman, he valued firepower. Impressed with the long-range capabilities of the 4.2-inch mortar, he had arranged for the 83d Chemical Warfare Battalion and its mortars to accompany the Rangers at Gela, but that battle convinced him that his Rangers needed something more. As the Rangers prepared for the invasion of Italy, he formed a cannon company of four French 75-mm guns, mounted on half-tracked vehicles. The addition of this unit and the 83d made the Rangers a heavier, more conventional force.[13]

The heavier weapons proved their value in the landings at Salerno when the Rangers, cut off from the main force, had to hold on for three weeks against German counterattacks. Landing on a narrow, rocky shore to the left of the main beachhead in the early hours of September 9, the Rangers quickly occupied the high ground of the Sorrentino Peninsula, dominating the routes between the invasion beaches and Naples. The Germans contained the main landing, preventing Lt. Gen. Mark W. Clark's Fifth Army from linking up with the Ranger position. Nevertheless, under Darby's overall command, the three Ranger battalions, paratroopers, and commandos fought off repeated German attacks. Lacking enough troops to hold a continuous line, the Rangers relied on a system of mutually supporting strong points, the terrain, naval gunfire, and their cannon company, which shelled the Germans from passes in the heights. On September 29, Clark's force finally relieved the Rangers, who withdrew into reserve.[14]

As Fifth Army's advance north stalled against the twin obstacles of mud and the German Winter Line, Clark pressed the Rangers into duty as line troops. From early November to mid-December, the three battalions, attached to divisions, engaged in bitter mountain fighting at such close quarters that in places, the Rangers lobbed grenades on German soldiers clinging to the rocks below. Despite the addition of heavier weapons, the Rangers were ill-suited to this static warfare, which stressed prepared positions and the use of firepower to blast the Germans out of their positions. By mid-December, the continuous fighting, rain, and snow had taken a toll. In a month, the 1st Ranger Battalion had lost 350 men, including 200 nonbattle casualties, and the other two battalions had also suffered heavily. Lacking a system to ensure a flow of specially trained replacements, each battalion detached an officer and a few enlisted men to remain in the rear and select and train volunteers for Ranger duty, but this improvised arrangement provided only limited time in which to train recruits. Thus, the quality of the battalions declined as veteran casualties were replaced by enthusiastic but inadequately trained personnel.[15]

The issue of replacements was overshadowed by Darby's larger battle for a Ranger force headquarters. Shortly after Gela, where he had again turned down an offer of a regimental command, the Ranger leader, with Patton's backing, had written a letter to Eisenhower, arguing that the performance of the Rangers justified the formation of the battalions into a permanent organization with a force headquarters. Once again, Eisenhower rejected the idea, leaving Darby to ponder the future of his Rangers.[16] Nevertheless, as the battalions slogged through mud and snow against the Winter Line, he and his officers intensified their push for a unified Ranger organization. In a dispatch to Army Ground Forces, Murray called for a force headquarters to handle administration, intelligence, planning, the assignment of missions, and "most important, to decide if the assignment is a proper one for the battalions." While Murray apparently never received a response, he and Darby soon received a partial reward for their efforts. In December, Fifth Army authorized a 6615th Ranger Force (Prov.) under Darby, who was finally promoted to colonel. Within days, the Rangers withdrew from the line to prepare for their next, and final, amphibious landing.[17]

One of the units that replaced the Rangers in line was the 1st Special Service Force, which had taken a circuitous route to reach Italy. Through the winter and spring of 1943, Frederick's "North Americans" had conducted unit and amphibious training in Montana, Virginia, and Vermont, while Allied strategists debated the best way to employ them. Finally, the War Department sent the unit to the Aleutians to spearhead the landings on Kiska. According to the plan of attack, two Force regiments would conduct a night landing from rubber boats and clear obstacles and resistance prior to the landing of the main force five hours later. Given their training in amphibious and winter warfare, the force appeared ideally suited for the task, but the overall plan was marred by severe flaws. Bright moonlight silhouetted the invaders as they approached on the night of August 15, and lack of noise discipline among the landing craft seemed to nullify any remaining chance of surprise. Fortunately, the Japanese had already evacuated the island and the landing was unopposed.

Within days of the operation, the force received orders to return immediately to the United States. Allied leaders, meeting in Quebec, had been informed of the unit's assignment to the Aleutians, and Churchill reportedly expressed his indignation that he had not been consulted. Once again, planners discussed possible missions for the force, including commando operations against

Col. William O. Darby (U.S. Army photograph)

Norway and the Dalmatian Coast of the Balkans. Finally, they sent Frederick's restless troopers to Italy, where Eisenhower planned to use them for special reconnaissance and raids. In practice, however, they were to function in an entirely different role.[18]

Soon after the 1st Special Service Force's arrival in November, it showed its capabilities in convincing fashion. Looming over Fifth Army's front, the twin peaks of Monte La Difensa and Monte La Rementanea presented formidable barriers to the Allied advance into the Liri River valley. A German panzer grenadier division, deeply entrenched along the slopes of the two masses, had already thrown back repeated Allied attempts to gain control of the heights. Attached to the 36th Infantry Division, the force received orders to carry the two peaks. After a personal reconnaissance of the 3,000-foot La Difensa, Frederick decided to avoid the trail leading up the south side and instead launch a surprise attack via a 200-foot cliff on the opposite slope. On the night of December 2–3, 600 riflemen of the 2d Regiment moved silently up the face to a position only yards away from the German defenders on the crest. When noise from displaced stones alerted the enemy, the North Americans assaulted the position and, within two hours, gained control of the crest. Over the next few days, they pushed down a saddle to capture Monte La Rementanea and link up with British units on the other side of the valley. The fall of the twin peaks cracked the Winter Line and opened the way for the Allied advance to Cassino.[19]

Any euphoria that Frederick's men might have felt over their success soon dissipated after the unit reentered the fighting as line infantry in late December. Poor weather and a skillful German defense among rocks and gullies slowed the advance to a crawl and took a heavy toll of the 1st Special Service Force. After a bitter struggle, the 1st Regiment took Monte Sammucro but lost much of its fighting power. The 3d Regiment overwhelmed the defenders of Monte Majo in a surprise night assault but then suffered heavy losses in a three-day defense of the height against German counterattacks. Like the Rangers, the force lacked the heavier weapons needed to blast the Germans out of their positions, and they were paying dearly for that deficiency.[20]

Why did Fifth Army use the Rangers and 1st Special Service Force to perform tasks for which they were so ill-suited? Clark later stated that, lacking troops, he could not afford to hold special formations in reserve until suitable missions presented themselves. To be sure, the shortage of manpower and the exhaustion of the few troops available made it difficult to exclude proven fighters like the Rangers and the North Americans from line duty. The static nature of the campaign, with its grinding offensives through mountains against prepared defenses in depth, also seemed to preclude infiltration and raids. Nevertheless, Sixth Army in the Philippines faced a comparable situation and did not misuse its Ranger battalion. The difference between the two cases seems to lie in the leadership. Although Clark had some appreciation of special operations, having supervised the organization of guerrillas in North Africa, he was at heart a conventional soldier. Hard-driving and ambitious, he would put every available man on the front line to achieve victory. Like Allen and other field commanders, he perceived Rangers and Forcemen to be shock troops rather than specialists.[21]

Clark's favorable opinion of the Rangers as fighters was shared by several others in the Army during World War II. Field commanders appreciated them as troops who could be relied on to achieve their mission, whatever that task might be. Patton, characteristically, called them "the best damned combat soldiers in Africa" but also remarked that they were the "worst garrison troops I ever saw in my whole professional life." Bradley stated that "by the war's end, I honestly believed there was nothing they could not do." On different occasions after the war, Eisenhower spoke of his admiration for the Rangers and even claimed credit for their creation. These positive impressions seem to have been held by many in the lower ranks, particularly when the Rangers performed their share of the line fighting. Three officers of the 47th Armored Infantry Battalion remembered that "our morale went up in a hurry" when the 2d Ranger Battalion reinforced their unit's section of the line.[22]

Not all military personnel held such positive views of the Rangers. The Army maintained the fiction that all units began with equal status, but, in practice, the Rangers and other elites received privileges and publicity that other units did not enjoy. Rangers naturally assumed that they were special and often flaunted their status, especially in rear areas. While many Rangers behaved themselves, others adopted a "bars belong to us" attitude and acquired a reputation for rowdiness, terrorizing military policemen and brawling with other soldiers. Some outfits, notably the 1st Special Service Force, actually took pride in their image as thugs. Such posturing tended to confirm the suspicion of those line troops who were more than ready to view the Rangers as prima donnas and hooligans. One airborne officer, while generally extolling Rangers, compared their appearance, with stubble beards and a variety of uniforms, to that of a bunch of cutthroats. When the 2d Ranger Battalion arrived in an English town for training, they found the residents in a state of fear, having been informed by the previous unit stationed there that the Rangers were convicts pulled from penal institutions to do the Army's dirty work. To be sure, unruly behavior was hardly limited to the Rangers, but they seem to have been more guilty than most. As Patton's comment implies, they represented, in many ways, the best, and worst, of the American soldier.[23]

While the rest of the Army held ambivalent views of the Rangers, these commandos did appeal to the popular yearning for heroes in the middle of an impersonal mass war. Most news features on the Rangers displayed traits common in other stories on American servicemen, portraying Rangers as normal American boys who had risen to the challenge of war without losing more civilized qualities of kindness and love for home and family. A photograph in *Life* magazine showed a tough Ranger captain playing with his children, while the *Saturday Evening Post* carried a photograph of a Ranger having dinner with his family in Brooklyn after his escape from a German prison camp. Reporters were also intrigued by the Rangers' diverse backgrounds. *Life*'s story, for example, gave profiles of individual Rangers, including a miner from West Virginia, a detective from Minnesota, an auto worker from Michigan, and a locomotive fireman from New York.[24]

Having depicted the Rangers as ordinary Americans, the media then built up their image as rugged fighters to almost mythical proportions. Readers thrilled to accounts of dangerous operations behind enemy lines or scrutinized stories under such banner headlines as "Daring Rangers Silence Coastal Guns" and "Night Fighters Take Arzew on D Day, Then Smash Way to Oran." Encouraged by Army press releases that described "steel muscled Rangers . . . writing a new, exciting and heroic chapter in the history of American arms," various features elaborated on the theme of toughness through stories of individuals taking on tanks with their bare hands and continuing to fight even when severely wounded. Other accounts exalted Ranger marksmanship and resourcefulness, and several tied them to legendary raiders of the past, including Rogers, Mosby, and the commandos. Ranger doctrine and organization received less attention, no doubt because of military secrecy and the fascination of the American press and public with more dramatic subjects. This positive image of the Rangers, despite the traditional discomfort of American antimilitarism with the martial spirit implied in the Ranger ethos, reflected the war's relative popularity in the nation.[25]

The acclaim that the Rangers received in the United States spurred recruitment of the 2d Ranger Battalion, which had been formed in the spring of 1943 to meet ETOUSA's need for a special assault unit. Responding to Marshall's directive, McNair called on each command within the continental United States to furnish volunteers of above-average physical ability from formations that had completed unit training. The latter must have been a bitter pill for units which, having reached an advanced stage of training, now faced the prospect of losing some of their best men, and, as with other Ranger units, many commanders unloaded their misfits on the new formation. Recruits were slow to arrive at Camp Forrest, and several of those who did were too old or unfit for Ranger duty and had to be replaced. Fortunately, others supplied able volunteers, including some graduates of the Second Army Ranger School. Many had heard of "Darby's Rangers" and wanted to be part of a similar outfit, while others simply wanted to get overseas.

Following its activation on April 1, the unit went through a series of commanders until Maj. James E. Rudder took command on June 30. A graduate of Texas A&M University in 1932, Rudder had been a teacher and football coach at Brady High School and Tarleton Agricultural College in Texas until, as a reserve officer, he was called to active duty in 1941. He had served as a company commander and as a staff officer with the 83d Infantry Division before his assignment to the Rangers. A master of human relations, the tough but genial

Rudder possessed the rare ability to relate to his men without sacrificing high standards of military proficiency and discipline. He won the gratitude of his men through monthly "gripe" sessions and efforts to improve their food and quarters, but he also earned their respect by refusing to tolerate poor performances on the training field.

Although the battalion apparently modeled its organization on Darby's Rangers, it based much of its training on concepts developed by Army Ground Forces and the Second Army Ranger School. The 2d's initial training program at Camp Forrest, in particular, incorporated many of the features of the school in its stress on toughness and infantry skills. Rangers lifted 14-foot logs, wrestled each other in square pits, ran obstacle courses, scaled the cliffs of the Cumberlands, and endured speed marches through the heat and dust of a Tennessee summer. They also practiced hand-to-hand fighting, conducted night exercises, and trained in weapons, demolitions, and patrolling. In early September, the battalion moved to the Scout and Raiders School at Fort Pierce, Florida. Camped on an insect-infested island, the Rangers practiced small-scale amphibious raids with rubber boats and similar craft. They concluded two weeks of training with a simulated raid against the town of Fort Pierce. From there, they moved to Fort Dix, New Jersey, for instruction in advanced tactics, including larger unit exercises. Having completed their stateside training, the Rangers departed New York City for Great Britain on November 23.[26]

Meanwhile, ETOUSA's need for a stronger assault force had led Army Ground Forces to form yet another Ranger battalion. On June 23, ETOUSA asked for the unit, citing the additional requirements of the cross-Channel invasion. This time, ETOUSA's request does not seem to have stirred much debate at Army headquarters, but McNair did direct Second Army to furnish the volunteers, probably in the hope that, by giving the responsibility to a single headquarters, he could ensure a more qualified pool of recruits. Perhaps because of this precaution, the new unit obtained adequate personnel more quickly than did the 2d. Over 500 prospective Rangers had arrived at Camp Forrest by the activation of the new 5th Ranger Battalion on September 1. The 5th followed the same training regimen as the 2d, undergoing physical conditioning and infantry training at Camp Forrest, amphibious instruction at Fort Pierce, and tactical exercises at Fort Dix before leaving for the British Isles on January 8, 1944.[27]

As Allied forces assembled in late 1943 for the climactic assault on Hitler's Fortress Europe, Allied planners on the other side of the globe were preparing for another long-delayed offensive. By occupying Burma in 1942, the Japanese had not only threatened the British position in India, they had also cut the Burma Road, China's main lifeline to the outside world in its war with Japan. Allied plans to retake Burma repeatedly foundered on the formidable obstacles of terrain and climate, the theater's low priority for manpower and supplies, and the differing goals of the powers. Chiang Kai-shek's Chinese government hoped that its Allied partners would subdue the Japanese while it preserved its forces to deal with bitter internal enemies. The British, who were skeptical of the Chinese ability and will to fight, were determined to hold India and, with time, regain the portions of their empire that had been lost to the Japanese. While, by late 1943, American leaders had tempered earlier romantic notions of Chinese military potential, they still wanted to reopen a line of supply to China as a means of diverting Japanese troops from the Pacific and establishing bases in China for the bomber offensive against the enemy's homeland. Frustrated with delays, they were ready to seize on almost any idea that promised action in the theater.[28]

At the Quebec Conference in August 1943, American leaders became enthralled with the *Chindits*, a British raiding force that drew its name from the stone guardians of Burmese temples and its inspiration from one of the war's most original thinkers. Moody, suspicious, a bit fanatical, and intolerant of staff foibles, Maj. Gen. Orde C. Wingate could be hard to work with, but he possessed a brilliant mind, persuasiveness, and a charisma that inspired an almost religious fervor among his men. Arriving in Burma in the midst of the defeat of 1942, he conceived the idea of "long-range penetration groups," columns of light infantry which, supplied by air drop, would penetrate deep into the Japanese rear and conduct hit-and-run raids against the vulnerable roads and railroads supplying the enemy's front. With the support of Field Marshal Sir Archibald Wavell, the British commander in India, he converted British, Gurkha, and Burmese infantry units into a "77th Brigade" of 3,000 men. In their first raid during the spring of 1943, the *Chindits* wrought enough havoc to tie down an estimated six to eight enemy battalions, but relentless Japanese pressure, long marches, and infrequent supply drops left only 600 fit for another campaign. More orthodox British officers were inclined to dismiss the affair as a costly fiasco. Nevertheless, the raid boosted morale and caught the attention of the Allied media, which lionized the "ghost army" and hailed Wingate as another Lawrence of Arabia.[29]

The concept also looked appealing to Marshall and other Allied strategists searching for a way to overcome the terrain, lack of resources, disputes, and bureaucratic inertia that had delayed the offensive in Burma. Churchill, who was receptive to any idea that appealed to his romantic notion of war, saw in Wingate "a man of genius and audacity," and he impulsively brought the latter along to the conference of Allied leaders at Quebec. There, the arguments of the founder of the *Chindits* for an expanded long-range penetration force found a receptive audience among the assembled chiefs, notably Marshall, who perceived in Wingate a rare talent. The chiefs agreed to enlarge the *Chindits* to six brigades and add a special American air group for supply, transport, and evacuation. Marshall, on his part, promised to form a special unit of jungle tested troops to serve under Wingate.[30]

When the new unit assembled under the code name GALAHAD, it proved to be a far cry from the elite formation that Marshall had envisioned.

Recruiters in the South and Southwest Pacific, the Caribbean, and the continental United States found few jungle veterans with any inclination to volunteer for an unspecified "hazardous" mission, and many of those who did suffered from malaria. Lacking qualified recruits, commanders once again seized the opportunity to get rid of personnel who, for various reasons, did not fit with their units. When the troops from the Caribbean and the United States gathered at San Francisco, one officer remarked, "We've got the misfits of half the divisions in the country." Although the War Department issued no official word, rumors, spread perhaps by overly zealous recruiters, circulated to the effect that the unit would be withdrawn from action after an operation of about three months duration. These rumors would have dire consequences later.[31]

Almost from the start, the collection of undisciplined individualists, adventurers, and professional soldiers who made up GALAHAD seem to have shared a sense that they were a "bastard organization." While some of Army Ground Forces's actions regarding GALAHAD indicate a concern for secrecy, they also reflect the lack of enthusiasm for yet another special formation, especially one that, by some estimates, was expected to suffer 85 percent losses. As a new unit, GALAHAD needed a sense of identity, as embodied in a mission and a recognizable leader. However, few of the recruits who assembled in San Francisco, including senior officers, had any idea of the unit's purpose. The designation of "5307th Composite Unit (Prov.)" might have been chosen for security reasons, but it met with almost universal derision among the rank and file. Finally, the men of GALAHAD did not have a leader around whom they could rally. As the senior officer, Col. Charles N. Hunter, a dour, colorless professional and former instructor at the Infantry School, took them across the Pacific, but many months would pass before higher authority selected a commander for GALAHAD. Such conditions were hardly conducive to the spirit of an elite unit.[32]

After adding contingents from the South and Southwest Pacific on the voyage to India, GALAHAD arrived in Bombay in late October and began training under Wingate's overall supervision. The command situation remained ambiguous, as the American theater headquarters appointed Col. Francis G. Brink to conduct training while Hunter continued to handle administrative matters. At Deolali, outside Bombay, Brink put the troops through two weeks of conditioning and close-order drill. The unit then moved to Deogarh, in central India, where it received more intensive training in small-unit tactics, stream crossings, weapons, demolitions, evacuation of wounded troops, and the novel technique of supply by airdrop. In December, GALAHAD joined the *Chindits* for a week of maneuvers. As the campaign season approached, the troops were showing great proficiency in small-unit operations and rifle marksmanship, but Hunter felt that they needed work in larger-unit tactics and supply procedures. They also were presenting disciplinary problems, for example, discharging their guns into the air on a whim and even commandeering trains to Bombay.[33]

If GALAHAD's personnel struck observers as unruly, its organization, which was modeled after that of the *Chindits*, seemed radically unconventional. Each of the three "battalions" included two combat teams of about 470 men each. Designed to operate as self-contained units, each contained scout, demolition, medical, and mortar elements in addition to one or two rifle companies. At least initially, GALAHAD eschewed heavy weapons, relying on 81-mm and 60-mm mortars to support its rifles and machine guns. Its most distinctive feature was its ability to supply itself by air. A separate rear echelon at Dinjan kept prepackaged supplies ready for delivery. When the tactical situation permitted, the combat teams found a clearing, and C-47 transport planes dropped food, ammunition, and other supplies by parachute or free fall. Pack mules and horses carried supplies and other equipment through the narrow jungle trails. For the most part, GALAHAD subsisted on K-rations. While these light parcels required little preparation, experience would show that they did not provide sufficient bulk or nutrition over long periods of time.[34]

As GALAHAD trained and organized, Wingate was laying plans for an even more ambitious employment of his *Chindits* in support of the 1944 offensive. The availability of No. 1 Air Commando and conversations with the unit's commander, Col. Philip Cochran, led him to envision the infiltration of his raiders by glider to defensible landing zones, which they would turn into fortified bases for attacks on Japanese communications. Supply, evacuation, and close support by Cochran's planes would compensate for the isolation of these bases and their lack of heavy artillery. To carry out this design, Wingate expanded his force to five brigades in addition to GALAHAD, converting an entire division over the anguished protests of orthodox theater staff officers.[35]

When GALAHAD went into combat, however, it would not be with Wingate. In his plans for the unit, the *Chindit* leader ran afoul of Lt. Gen. Joseph W. "Vinegar Joe" Stilwell, the commander of American forces in the theater and one of the war's most controversial personalities. A favorite of Marshall since their days at the Infantry School, Stilwell had been considered for a command in Europe, but the War Department had instead sent him to China, where, in addition to his duties as American theater chief, he served as Chiang's chief of staff with responsibility for building the Chinese Army. While intelligent, fluent in Chinese, and a believer in the fighting ability of the Chinese soldier, his cynicism toward Chiang's regime, contempt for the British, and general irascibility ill fitted him for a post with such strong diplomatic overtones. At heart a combat soldier, he had been eager for a chance to return to Burma and redeem his reputation ever since the well-publicized retreat of his Chinese troops from that country in the spring of 1942.

On the eve of the long-awaited offensive, Stilwell used his influence with Marshall and the new Allied theater chief, Lord Mountbatten, to obtain control of GALAHAD. Hoping to use the unit as a model for his new Chinese formations, he was in no mood, in any case, to permit the only American combat force in the theater to operate under British command. In response to Stilwell's persistent pleas, Marshall referred the matter to Mountbatten, who reassigned the unit over Wingate's furious protests. As a permanent commander for GALA- HAD, Stilwell chose an old friend on his staff, Brig. Gen. Frank D. Merrill. A former cavalryman and student of Japanese with little infantry experience, Merrill won respect with his outgoing nature, self-denial, and courage, but his poor health should have disqualified him from such an active command. As an intimate of Stilwell's, he would be also be an unlikely candidate to stand up to his chief on the issue of the unit's employment. Although correspondents were already dubbing the unit "Merrill's Marauders," Stilwell, not Merrill, and certainly not Wingate, would determine its mission.[36]

Formed in response to Marshall's prodding, official impatience, and local lack of resources, GALAHAD's origins resembled those of Ranger units created in 1942, not 1943. As the tide turned in favor of the Allies and American forces grew in strength and experience, most of the factors that had inspired the formation of the original Rangers had ceased to exist. However, it would be hard to disband units whose feats had thrilled millions. Furthermore, the need for amphibious spearheaders in Normandy, the Mediterranean, and even far-off Kiska provided justification for continuation, and even expansion, of the Ranger force. Field generals who were worried about the obstacles of an amphibious assault and impressed by the exploits of Darby's Rangers wanted their own special troops for the capture of key points on or adjoining the beachhead. Their desires prevailed over rear echelon officers who were concerned about the most efficient use of manpower, the administrative challenge of a special unit, and other, very genuine considerations involved in the management of a mass war. Thus, as amphibious specialists, the Rangers survived, and even thrived, but as temporary units with a fleeting role and an uncertain future. Their experience in Italy only emphasized that the question of their use once Allied armies were established on the Continent remained to be solved.

NOTES

1. Maurice Matloff, *Strategic Planning for Coalition Warfare, 1943–1944*, U.S. Army in World War II (Washington, D.C.: OCMH, 1959), pp. 21–26; Maurice Matloff, "Grand Strategy and the Washington High Command," in Maurice Matloff, ed., *American Military History*, 2d ed., Army Historical Series (Washington, D.C.: OCMH, 1973), pp. 447–448; Wedemeyer, *Wedemeyer Reports!*, p. 176; CCS 167, 22 January 1943, "Continental Operations in 1943," and CCS 170, 22 January 1943, "Report to the President and the Prime Minister," in Casablanca Conference, January 1943: Papers and Minutes of Meetings, pp. 90–91, 106, CMH Library; Commanding General, ETO, to Adjutant General, 12 March 1943, AG 320.2 Ranger Battalions for ETO (12 March 1943), AG Classified File, RG 407, MMHB, National Archives.

2. Lt. Col. C. E. Lundquist, ETOUSA, to Commanding General, II Corps, 30 September 1942; Capt. Cleaves A. Jones, Liaison Section, to Brig. Gen. Norman D. Cota, 18 March 1943; and Jones to Col. Claude E. Stadtman, February 1943, in Perlmutter Collection, Call No. MP 63–8, Roll 8, JFKSWC; Joseph H. Ewing, *29 Let's Go! A History of the 29th Infantry Division in World War II* (Washington, D.C.: Infantry Journal Press, 1948), pp. 18–19; Haggerty, "Ranger Battalions," p. 129. Haggerty obtained much of his information on the 29th Ranger Battalion from a letter from Milholland, dated 14 August 1979.

3. Col. J. A. Dabney, Chief of Staff, Center Task Force, to Commander in Chief, Allied Force Headquarters (AFHQ), 29 December 1942, AFHQ-Mediterranean, G-3 Section, Organization Division, Campaign Lessons, January 1943–August 1943, Microfilm Roll R–83–Spec., RG 331, WNRC; Truscott, *Command Missions*, pp. 55–56; Hughes-Hallett, "The Mounting of Raids," pp. 86–93; Samuel A. Stouffer, *The American Soldier*, vol. 2, *Combat and Its Aftermath* (Princeton, N.J.: Princeton University Press, 1949), pp. 67–68; Millett and Maslowski, *Common Defense*, p. 372.

4. Maj. Richard P. Fisk, Assistant Adjutant General, ETO, to Adjutant General, 2 December 1942, Perlmutter Collection, Call No. 63–8, Roll 8, JFKSWC.

5. McNair quoted in U.S. Army, Army Ground Forces, *A Short History of the Army Ground Forces*, Army Ground Forces Study no. 2 (Washington, D.C.: Army Ground Forces, 1946), p. 32; see also pp. 31–32; Weigley, *Eisenhower's Lieutenants*, p. 10; Weigley, *History of the United States Army*, pp. 465–466, 470; Becker, *Amphibious Training Center*, pp. 17, 58; Wiley and Govan, *Second Army*, p. 142. Army Ground Forces permitted continuance of some Ranger training on a part-time basis and also allowed the integration of some elements of Ranger training into regular programs.

6. Maj. James D. Tanner, Assistant Ground Adjutant General, Army Ground Forces to Assistant Chief of Staff, Operations Division, War Department, 4 January 1943; and Assistant Chief of Staff, Operations Division, to Adjutant General, 10 January 1943, in AG 320.2 (12–2–42), AG Classified File, RG 407, MMHB, National Archives.

7. Commanding General, ETO, to Adjutant General, 12 March 1943; and Col. C. B. Ferenbaugh, Chief, European Section, Theater Group, OPD, to Adjutant General, 21 April 1943, in AG 320.2, Ranger Battalions for ETO (12 March 1943), AG Classified File, RG 407, MMHB, National Archives; 1st Lt. H. W. Madducks, Adjutant, 11th Detachment, Special Troops, Second Army, to Adjutant General, 1 April 1943, AG 320.2 (3–11–43) (Activation of 2d Ranger Battalion), AG Classified File, RG 407, MMHB, National Archives; Cota to Commanding General, ETOUSA, 10 August 1943; "The U.S. Rangers," Folder 279 Rangers (U.S.), U.S. Army, ETO, Historical Division, Administrative File, 1942–Jan. 1946, Box 55, RG 332, WNRC.

8. Ewing, *29 Let's Go!*, pp. 19, 25–26; Haggerty, "Ranger Battalions," pp. 131–135; Lt. Col. L. W. Merriam, G-3, Combined Operations, to Cota, 25 September 1943, Perlmutter Collection, Call No. 63–8, Roll 8, JFKSWC; Cota to Commanding General, ETOUSA, 10 August 1943; "U.S. Rangers."

9. Darby and Baumer, *Darby's Rangers*, p. 82; Algiers to War Department, 18 April 1943, U.S. War Department, Operations Division, War Department Message File: Incoming Top Secret, April 1–30, 1943, RG 165, MMHB, National Archives; Marshall to Eisenhower, 19 April 1943, WWII Ops. Reports, INBN 1–0, RG 407, WNRC.

10. Darby to Eisenhower, 14 April 1943; and Announcement by HQ, Atlantic Base Section, 17 May 1943, WWII Ops. Reports, INBN 1-0, RG 407, WNRC; Darby and Baumer, *Darby's Rangers*, pp. 83–85; Altieri, *Spearheaders*, pp. 244–247; Stouffer, *Combat and Its Aftermath*, pp. 272–276; John F. Hummer, *An Infantryman's Journal* (Manassas, Va.: Ranger Associates, 1981), pp. 12–18; Lt. Col. J. R. Dryden, Adjutant General, Army Ground Forces, to Marshall, 8 November 1943, Folder 4-1.67/43, U.S. Army, Adjutant General's Office, World War II Operations Reports, 1940–1948: Special File, Box 24410, RG 407, WNRC.

11. Lt. Col. James M. Churchill, Assistant G-1, Fifth Army, to Darby, 29 April 1943, WWII Ops. Reports, INBN 1-0, RG 407, WNRC; King, *Darby*, pp. 75–76.

12. Darby's report of action at Gela, Sicily, 5 August 1943, U.S. War Department, Operations Division, OPD 381 ETO, Section V, Case 108, RG 165, MMHB, National Archives; Dammer to Adjutant General, 31 July 1943, WWII Ops. Reports, INBN 3-0.3, RG 407, WNRC; Darby and Baumer, *Darby's Rangers*, pp. 85–99, 103–109; King, *Rangers*, pp. 23–28; Dryden to Marshall, 8 November 1943; Albert N. Garland and Howard M. Smyth, *Sicily and the Surrender of Italy*, U.S. Army in World War II (Washington, D.C.: OCMH, 1965), pp. 125, 131–139, 169–170, 220, 252–253.

13. King, *Darby*, pp. 82, 106, 185.

14. At Salerno, Darby had about 8,500 men, an amazing number for a lieutenant colonel and an indication of the regard that commanders had for him. See Darby's Field Order no. 1, 2 September 1943, INBN 1-0.3; as well as Darby's report of Salerno, 15 November 1943, INBN 1-0; and Dammer's report, 25 November 1943, INBN 3-0.3, in WWII Ops. Reports, RG 407, WNRC; Darby and Baumer, *Darby's Rangers*, pp. 113–122; Alexander M. Worth, Jr., "Supporting Weapons and High Ground: The Rangers at Salerno," *Infantry Journal* 56 (May 1945): 33–34; Martin Blumenson, *Salerno to Cassino*, The U.S. Army in World War II (Washington, D.C.: OCMH, 1969), pp. 73–74, 91, 97, 163–165.

15. Darby's report for 8 November–13 December 1943, 29 March 1944, WWII Ops. Reports, INBN 1-0, RG 407, WNRC; Darby and Baumer, *Darby's Rangers*, pp. 127–139; Haggerty, "Ranger Battalions," pp. 169–173; Blumenson, *Salerno to Cassino*, pp. 222, 231, 273–277. Murray suggested to Army Ground Forces the establishment at Camp Forrest of a Ranger Training Center which would turn out 100 graduates a month, but no response was made to his suggestion. See Murray to Commander in Chief, Ground Forces, War Department, 28 November 1943, WWII Ops. Reports, INBN 4-0.1, RG 407, WNRC. Although Darby hoped to create a special center for replacements, he had only taken a few steps in that direction by the end of 1943. See Dammer interview; Dobson interview; King, *Darby*, pp. 103, 121, 129–137, 145; Administrative Annex, Operation SHINGLE, HQ Ranger Force, 13 January 1944, WWII Ops. Reports, INBN 1-0.3, RG 407, WNRC; Hummer, *Infantryman's Journal*, pp. 29, 38–43.

16. Darby to CINC, AFHQ, 10 August 1943; Patton to Eisenhower, 12 August 1943; and Eisenhower to Patton, 3 September 1943, in WWII Ops. Reports, INBN 1-0, RG 407, WNRC; Dryden to Marshall, 8 November 1943. On the dispatch notifying Fifth Army of the decision, a staff officer had written, "Back where you were, Bill, a red-haired stepchild."

17. Murray to Commander in Chief, Ground Forces, 28 November 1943; A.W.G. to Clark, 14 October 1943, WWII Ops. Reports, INBN 1-0, RG 407, WNRC; King, *Darby*, p. 145; Darby and Baumer, *Darby's Rangers*, p. 139. Ironically, lineage records

show that the Rangers had, on paper, already received permanent status, at least for the war's duration. The 1st Ranger Battalion was constituted in the Army of the United States in May 1942, and the 3d and 4th in July 1943. Either word had not reached the theater, the officers there were unversed in lineage terminology, or, most likely, the War Department still intended to disband the units once the need for them had passed. See John K. Mahon and Romana Danysh, *Infantry*, part 1, *Regular Army* (Washington, D.C.: OCMH, 1972), pp. 888–889.

18. Burhans, *Special Service Force*, pp. 48–57, 67–68, 76–86; Adleman and Walton, *Devil's Brigade*, pp. 91, 95, 103–112; CCS TRIDENT Minutes, 6th Meeting, The White House, 11:30 a.m., 25 May 1943, TRIDENT Conference, May 1943: Papers and Minutes of Meetings, pp. 310–311, CMH Library; Williams, "Amphibious Scouts," p. 156; McMichael, *Light Infantry*, pp. 175–176; "Senior Officers Debriefing Program: Adams," II:3; CCS 316, "Combined Chiefs of Staff, The 'Plough' Force," 18 August 1943, in QUADRANT Conference August 1943: Papers and Minutes of Meetings, pp. 202–203, CMH Library.

19. Adleman and Walton, *Devil's Brigade*, pp. 119–132, 142–145; "Narrative Report, First Special Service Force, 17 November 1943–1 February 1944," World War II Operations Reports, 1940–1948: Special Service Force, SSFE 1-0.3, Box 23274, RG 407, WNRC; Blumenson, *Salerno to Cassino*, pp. 265–266; Burhans, *Special Service Force*, pp. 87–90, 97–125.

20. Adleman and Walton, *Devil's Brigade*, pp. 148, 159–161; "Narrative Report, 17 November 1943–1 February 1944"; McMichael, *Light Infantry*, pp. 186–192.

21. King, *Darby*, p. 137; Mark W. Clark, *Calculated Risk* (New York: Harper, 1950), p. 231; McMichael, *Light Infantry*, p. 186; Carleton S. Coon, *A North Africa Story: The Anthropologist as OSS Agent* (Ipswich, Mass: Gambit Press, 1980), pp. 124–125; Blumenson, *Mark Clark*, p. 2.

22. Patton quoted in Lehman, "Rangers Fought Ahead," p. 45; Bradley quoted in Omar N. Bradley, *A Soldier's Story* (New York: Holt, 1951), p. 139; Eisenhower to Lehman, 13 July 1946, in Chandler and Ambrose, *Eisenhower*, VII:1194–1195; "CBS Reports: D Day plus 20 Years: Eisenhower Returns to Normandy," Louis F. Lisko Papers, USAMHI; officers quoted in Charles B. MacDonald, *The Siegfried Line Campaign*, U.S. Army in World War II (Washington, D.C.: OCMH, 1963), pp. 461–462.

23. Samuel A. Stouffer, *The American Soldier*, vol. 1, *Adjustment during Army Life* (Princeton, N.J.: Princeton University Press, 1949), pp. 304, 329; Hummer, *Infantryman's Journal*, p. 44; Edwin M. Sorvisto, *2nd Ranger Battalion: Roughing It with Charlie* (Williamstown, N.J.: Antietam National Museum, n.d.), pp. 10–11; Alfred E. Baer, Jr., *D for Dog: The Story of a Ranger Company* (Memphis, Tenn., 1946), pp. 5–8; Adleman and Walton, *Devil's Brigade*, p. 94; Dammer interview; Lt. Gen. William P. Yarborough USA (Ret.), interview by Col. John R. Meese and Lt. Col. H. P. Houser III, 28 March 1975, sess. 1, side 2, pp. 54–55, William P. Yarborough Papers, USAMHI; Morris Prince, "Co. A, 2nd Ranger Battalion: Overseas and Then—Over the Top," I:42, WWII Ops. Reports, INBN 2-0, RG 407, WNRC. Although Darby frowned on individuals who flaunted their status as Rangers, he did nothing to discourage that impression on a visit he made with some of his men to a supply depot. When the personnel on duty told him that the items available in quantity were for officers only, he snapped, "All of my men are officers," and told his men to help themselves; see King,

Darby, p. 95.

24. John M. Blum, *V Was for Victory: Politics and American Culture during World War II* (New York: Harcourt, Brace and Jovanovich, 1976), pp. 53–59; Polenberg, *War and Society*, p. 134; "The Rangers," *Life*, 31 July 1944, pp. 59–63; Cecil Carnes, "The 101 Days of Private Perlmutter," *Saturday Evening Post*, 21 April 1945, pp. 14–16.

25. Altieri, *Spearheaders*, pp. 154–155; U.S. War Department, "Rangers Writing New Chapter in History of American Army," War Department Release, 12 February 1944, HRC Geog L. Italy 370.2-Anzio, Historical Records Branch, CMH; Lehman, "Rangers Fought Ahead," pp. 28–29, 49–52; Thomas M. Johnson, "The Army's Fightingest Outfit Comes Home," *Reader's Digest*, December 1944, pp. 51–54; "Another One Man Army," *New York Times*, 11 June 1944, p. 36; "Enemy in Dread of Black Devils," *New York Times*, 22 August 1944, p. 5; Polenberg, *War and Society*, pp. 38, 132; Blum, *V Was for Victory*, pp. 7–8.

26. Ronald L. Lane, *Rudder's Rangers* (Manassas, Va.: Ranger Associates, 1979), pp. 16–37, 179–180; Baer, *D for Dog*, pp. 2–14; Sorvisto, *2nd Ranger Battalion*, pp. 6–11; Wiley and Govan, *Second Army*, pp. 154–155; McNair to Commanding Generals, Second and Third Armies et al., 11 March 1943, and 22 March 1943; and Lear to Commanding Generals, Second and Third Armies et al., 26 April 1943, in U.S. War Department, Operations Division, OPD 320.2 Plans Section: Organization, RG 165, MMHB, National Archives; McNair to Marshall, 10 August 1943, U.S. War Department, Operations Division, OPD 353 Amphibious Force, Section V, Case 167, RG 165, MMHB, National Archives; Ranger Battalions Association interviews by author; James J. Altieri, "Lead the Way Rangers," *Gung Ho*, October 1984, p. 25.

27. Commanding General, ETO, to Adjutant General, 23 June 1943, AG 320.2 Ranger Battalions for ETO (12 March 1943), AG Classified File, RG 407, MMHB, National Archives; McNair to Commanding Generals, Second and Third Armies et al., 24 July 1943, and 4 August 1943, 5th Ranger Infantry Battalion File, "Ranger Battalions of World War II," Organizational History Branch, CMH; Wiley and Govan, *Second Army*, p. 155; Henry S. Glassman, *"Lead the Way, Rangers!" A History of the Fifth Ranger Battalion* (Markt Grafing, Germany: Buchdruckerei Hausser, 1945), pp. 2, 10–12.

28. Ronald H. Spector, *Eagle against the Sun: The American War with Japan* (New York: Free Press, 1985), pp. 324–327, 330–338; Shelford Bidwell, *The Chindit War: Stilwell, Wingate, and the Campaign in Burma, 1944* (New York: Macmillan, 1979), pp. 21–22, 27, 30–31, 66, 282–283.

29. Christopher Sykes, *Orde Wingate: A Biography* (Cleveland, Ohio: World, 1959), pp. 360, 370–375, 388–442, 538; Bidwell, *Chindit War*, pp. 18, 25–26, 37–42, 51, 62; McMichael, *Light Infantry*, pp. 1, 13–22, 27; U.S. War Department, Military Intelligence Division, *Merrill's Marauders, February–May, 1944*, American Forces in Action (Washington, D.C.: U.S. GPO, 1945), pp. 5–7.

30. Pogue, *Organizer of Victory*, pp. 256–257; Sykes, *Orde Wingate*, pp. 445–456; CCS 329/2, CCS, "Implementation of Assumed Basic Undertakings and Specific Operations for the Conduct of the War, 1943–4," 26 August 1943; CCS, 107th Meeting, "Minutes of Meeting Held in Room 2008, Chateau Frontenac, on Tuesday, 14 August 1943, at 1630"; and CCS, 110th Meeting, "Minutes of Meeting Held in Room 2208, Chateau Frontenac, on Tuesday, 17 August 1943, at 1430," in QUADRANT, pp. 336, 427–428, 449–450; Bidwell, *Chindit War*, p. 68.

31. Officer quoted in Charlton Ogburn, *The Marauders*, 2d ed. (New York: Harper and Bros., 1959), p. 34; see also pp. 9, 29–30, 34–43, 271; USAMHI, "Senior Officers Debriefing Program: Conversations between General Paul L. Freeman (Ret.) and Colonel James N. Ellis, USAWC," (Carlisle, Pa., 1973), side 1, interview 1, p. 57; Charles N. Hunter, "Report of Overseas Observations," 75th Ranger Regiment File, Organizational History Branch, CMH; Col. George E. McGee, Jr., "Comments Relating to an Article, 'Common Man, Uncommon Leadership: Colonel Charles N. Hunter with GALAHAD in Burma,' Summer 1986 edition of *Parameters*," p. 4, Scott R. McMichael Papers, USAMHI; John J. McCloy, Acting Secretary of War, to Senator Robert R. Reynolds, 25 August 1944, Folder 333.1, U.S. Army Operations Division, Decimal File, 1942–1944, Box 35, RG 165, MMHB, National Archives.

32. Charles N. Hunter, *GALAHAD* (San Antonio, Tex.: Naylor, 1963), pp. 1–2; Ogburn, *Marauders*, pp. 183, 282; Bidwell, *Chindit War*, pp. 81–84; McMichael, *Light Infantry*, pp. 14–15, 35; Scott R. McMichael, "Common Man, Uncommon Leadership: Colonel Charles N. Hunter with GALAHAD in Burma," *Parameters: Journal of the U.S. Army War College* 16 (Summer 1986): 46; Riley Sunderland's comments on McMichael article, p. 5, McMichael Papers, USAMHI; Hunter, "Report."

33. Ogburn, *Marauders*, pp. 44–56, 63, 72; U.S. War Department, *Merrill's Marauders*, pp. 11–16; Hunter, *GALAHAD*, pp. 3–4, 12–13; McMichael, "Uncommon Man," pp. 47–48; Mountbatten to Marshall, 16 January 1944, Box 77, Folder 10, Marshall Papers, Marshall Library.

34. Hunter, *GALAHAD*, pp. 16, 24–25; Ogburn, *Marauders*, pp. 23–32, 45, 60–61, 65–67, 136; U.S. War Department, *Merrill's Marauders*, pp. 11–14, 29–30; Hunter, "Report"; Memorandum, Rear Echelon HQ, USAFCBI, 28 March 1944; and Col. Frank Milani, Adjutant General, Rear Echelon, USAFCBI, to OPD Asiatic Section, 28 March 1944, in Folder 92 TF 1–0.2 (2627) Report—GALAHAD Force, North Burma Operations Feb.–Mar 44, U.S. Army, Adjutant General, World War II Operations Reports, 1940–1948: Asiatic Theater, Box 90, RG 407, WNRC.

35. P. W. Mead, "The *Chindit* Operations of 1944," *Journal of the Royal United Service Institution* 100 (May 1955): 253; Bidwell, *Chindit War*, pp. 52–53, 64–65, 69, 75; Sykes, *Orde Wingate*, pp. 459, 483–486.

36. Bidwell, *Chindit War*, pp. 22–23, 29–36, 73, 84–85; Ogburn, *Marauders*, pp. 16, 59–70; "Merrill, Frank Dow, (1903-1955)," in Robert McHenry, ed., *Webster's American Military Biographies* (Springfield, Mass.: Merriam, 1978) p. 281.

4

Line Infantry

As 1944 began, the Allies were preparing for the decisive offensives that would take them to the gates of Germany and Japan. On the Russian Front, the Red Army was methodically expelling the Germans from the western Ukraine. In Western Europe, as Allied armies bogged down in the Italian mountains against stubborn German resistance, attention was shifting to the English Channel, where the British and Americans would soon open their long-awaited Second Front. American naval forces and Marines had launched their drive across the Central Pacific, while, in the Southwest Pacific, Gen. Douglas MacArthur's Americans and Australians were advancing along the northern coast of New Guinea with an eye toward MacArthur's eventual objective, the Philippines. Finally, a long-delayed Allied offensive was about to begin in Burma. Around the globe, Allied fortunes surged as their mass armies, navies, and air forces, backed by their superior resources, came into play. What role would Ranger units have in this clash of large formations?

In Italy, Darby's men played a familiar role as the Allies tried to outflank the Winter Line with an amphibious landing by VI Corps at Anzio. Attached to that corps, the Ranger Force received orders to land between two divisions in the assault and clear the town of Anzio. Darby anticipated fierce resistance and was concerned about the need, due to a lack of landing craft, to land his battalions in successive waves. In the end, his fears proved groundless. The landing on the morning of January 22, 1944, met no opposition. Rather than exploit his advantage, the VI Corps chief, Maj. Gen. John P. Lucas, chose to consolidate the beachhead, permitting the Germans to rush in reserves and contain the Allies within a small perimeter. For a week, the Rangers fought on line with VI Corps, beating off repeated counterattacks.[1]

On the night of January 28–29, the Rangers pulled out of the line and joined Truscott's 3d Infantry Division, where they received a new, risky mission.

Irritated by Lucas's caution, Clark had pushed for a bold attack to break out of the beachhead, and Lucas, in response, ordered an all-out assault. The Rangers were attached to the 3d Division, which would capture the key crossroads town of Cisterna. Drawing on intelligence reports indicating that the Germans were on the defensive and would retreat if pressed, Truscott's staff drew up a plan for the 1st and 3d Ranger Battalions to infiltrate four miles to Cisterna on the night of January 29–30. One hour after their departure, the 4th Ranger Battalion and the 3d Division would attack and use the confusion created by the 1st and 3d to break through the German lines. While Darby did not participate in the actual planning and decried the lack of reconnaissance of the target area, he apparently approved the basic concept. He was later quoted as stating: "The plan was not an unusual one for my Rangers. In fact, it was down our alley and one that would have delighted the heart of Major Rogers in pre-Revolutionary days."[2]

The mission ended in disaster. During the previous night, the Germans had secretly moved a panzer grenadier division into the area for an attack that would crush the beachhead. When the Rangers began their infiltration early on the morning of January 30, the Germans quickly detected them and, by dawn, had surrounded them with infantry and tanks in the flat, open fields just south of Cisterna. The 4th Ranger Battalion and supporting tanks desperately tried to break through to the beleaguered battalions but were stopped by a fierce German defense, aided by muddy ground and mines that channeled the American advance. About noon, the remnants of the encircled Rangers surrendered. Only eight men escaped to American lines. The 4th, on its part, lost half its men in a vain effort to reach the 1st and 3d.[3]

The loss of the two battalions created an uproar. When Clark and Lucas visited Truscott's headquarters on the day following the debacle, the Fifth Army commander implied that Truscott had misused the Rangers. Truscott replied, with some heat, that the mission had, in fact, been a suitable one, and that he and Darby probably understood the capabilities of the Rangers better than any other American officer. Clark said no more, but, worried about publicity, he ordered an inquiry, an impossible task with so many witnesses in German hands. His concern over public reaction was well-founded. German propagandists were soon circulating photographs of the U.S. Army's elite being paraded through the streets of Rome, and, back home, newspapers compared Cisterna to Thermopylae, the Alamo, and Custer's Last Stand, describing "guys from American farms, towns, and cities" fighting heroically to the end against tanks. American leaders were discovering that commando missions, although glorious when successful, could bring considerable negative publicity when they failed.[4]

What, in fact, had gone wrong at Cisterna? Lucas later blamed the catastrophe on the failure of the Rangers to conceal their infiltration. To be sure, declining Ranger skills due to the influx of inadequately trained replacements may well have contributed to their early detection by the Germans, but other factors seem more directly responsible for the fiasco. By its nature, the

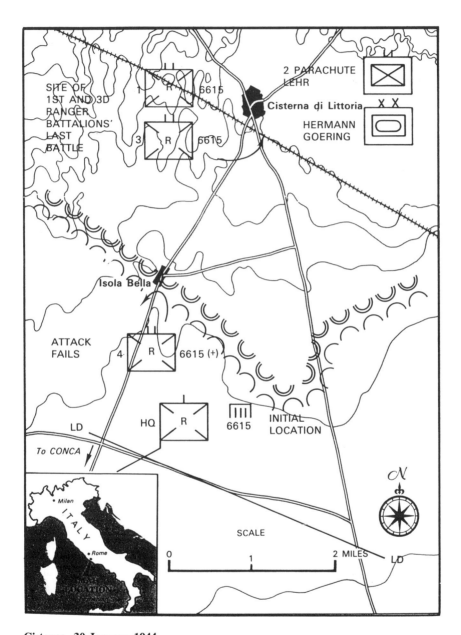

Cisterna, 30 January 1944

U.S. Army Combat Studies Institute.

operation was a risky venture, exposing the infiltrators to an enemy of uncertain strength and intentions before the main force could reach them. Unfortunately for the Rangers, American assumptions of German weakness were invalidated by the arrival of enemy reinforcements on the night before the attack. Under pressure for action and concerned that overt activity in the target area might alert the Germans, divisional headquarters decided against a prior reconnaissance, which might have revealed the buildup. Darby sensed the need for a reconnaissance, but his supreme faith in his men apparently overrode his better instincts. Confident in the Rangers and relying on faulty intelligence, he and Truscott gambled for a breakout and lost.[5]

The destruction of the three Ranger battalions brought to a head the issue of their future. For a change, it was the field commanders—Clark and Lt. Gen. Jacob L. Devers, the new American theater chief—who advocated disbandment of the Rangers, partly due to an awareness of the time it would take to reconstruct the battalions and partly because of concern that the Rangers would deplete the already dwindling pool of infantry replacements. Unable to foresee any special mission that would justify such a diversion of resources, they preferred disbandment and the use of the ex-Rangers as fillers for the 1st Special Service Force. Marshall, however, hesitated to disband the battalions until he could be sure that no other requirement for them existed. When Clark and Devers reaffirmed that they could see no further need for Ranger units in their theater, Marshall directed them to use the less experienced Rangers as fillers for the 1st Special Service Force, while those who had served since the formation of the 1st Ranger Battalion would return to the United States. In late March, 150 veteran Rangers left Naples for home, arriving at Camp Butner, North Carolina, in May.[6]

Although the vast majority of those arriving at Camp Butner volunteered for additional service with Ranger units, the War Department soon concluded that reconstitution of the three battalions would not only be unnecessary but would also aggravate the growing problem of insufficient combat manpower. McNair figured it would take six months to rebuild the battalions and also pointed out that much of the manpower would have to come either from units set to go overseas or from available fillers at a time of serious shortages of infantry replacements. He would have agreed with Brig. Gen. W. W. Irvine of the General Staff's Training Division, who argued that Ranger units possessed "an inequitable proportion of skills, intelligence, and the will to perform, all of which must be attained at the expense of other units."[7] While the European and Pacific sections of the Operations Division believed that their theaters might desire more Ranger units, the deputy chief of the Theater Group pointed out that none of these theaters had registered a need for such formations and that they would more likely want versatile, standard units, capable of sustained action. Faced with these arguments, Marshall approved the disbandment of the three battalions.[8]

Thus, Darby's Rangers moved on to other duties. Most of the veterans served as instructors and administrators in training camps within the United States. As for Darby, he led an infantry regiment at Anzio before returning in April to the United States and a desk in the Operations Division. The former leader of the Rangers soon tired of routine tours of training posts and, while on a visit overseas in March 1945, managed to obtain a position as assistant division commander of the 10th Mountain Division in Italy. On April 30, a week before the end of the war in Europe, he was killed by a shell fragment while on an inspection tour. Reporting his death, Truscott, who by then was commander of Fifth Army, sadly remarked, "Never have I known a more gallant, heroic officer."[9]

Those Rangers who had not returned to the United States joined the 1st Special Service Force, which had arrived at the Anzio beachhead in early February 1944 and taken station on the right flank of the perimeter. This mission of static defense, which was unsuitable for light infantry, was made even more imposing by the force's position in open farmlands, which were cut by occasional irrigation canals and exposed to artillery fire from overlooking heights. Nevertheless, Frederick's men held firm with the aid of two field artillery battalions and a few tank destroyers. Taking cover from artillery fire during the day, they emerged at night to seize control of no-man's-land with aggressive patrolling and raids, earning a reputation in VI Corps as patrolling experts and in the United States as the "Black Devils of Anzio." More important, they deceived the Germans into believing that they had a full division. Actually, after a month of duty opposite the Winter Line, the force had only 1,300 combat troops to defend 13 kilometers of perimeter, and casualties soon cut that total. Under these conditions, the ex-Rangers were a welcome addition.[10]

Despite the need for such highly capable replacements, the former Rangers experienced a difficult, and even rancorous, assimilation into the force. A few were impressed by the capabilities of the North Americans in airborne and mountain warfare and expressed pride in their new unit. Many, however, retained their identity with Darby's Rangers, feeling that they had already belonged to an elite fighting force, and took offense at any implication that they were new recruits. Frederick did not ease this resentment when he forbade the wearing of the Ranger patch. For their part, many soldiers in the force expressed antagonism toward cocky Rangers who boasted of their exploits. In the end, time and shared experiences tended to bring the two groups together, but some ex-Rangers never felt that they were totally accepted by their comrades.[11]

In late May, two months after the addition of the Rangers, the 1st Special Service Force joined the breakout from the Anzio beachhead. Frederick had devoted much of the two months to training his men in mobile operations in conjunction with tanks, and the results justified his efforts. Advancing on the right flank of the 3d Infantry Division, the force helped spearhead the breakout from the beachhead on May 23 and then drove inland to link up with Allied troops which had cracked the main German line across the Italian peninsula. As the Allies turned toward Rome, the North Americans were joined by an armored task force which, along with an artillery battalion and the former Ranger cannon company, provided them with more mobility and firepower. This task force drove toward Rome, using tank-infantry teams to overcome German resistance on the high ground above the right flank of the main drive. On the morning of June 4, the first elements of the combined force entered Rome and secured the bridges over the Tiber River. Frederick's weary troopers then withdrew to Lake Albano for rest and reorganization.

One more special mission remained for the 1st Special Service Force before it closed its career as line infantry. Assigned to Seventh Army for the invasion of southern France, the unit received orders to seize German batteries on the Hyeres Islands, three rocky land masses on the left flank of the invasion beaches. It would be their first mission without Frederick, who had left to take command of the 1st Airborne Task Force. Under the command of Col. Edwin A. Walker, the North Americans used rubber boats to land on the shores of Ile de Port Cros and Ile du Levant during the night of August 14–15. Within 48 hours, the surprised defenders on both islands had surrendered, and Walker's men prepared to join Frederick's airborne task force on the mainland. Guarding the right flank of Seventh Army's advance, the Forcemen's lightly contested drive along the Riviera, the "champagne campaign," seemed more like an extended route march than a battle. In early September, they reached the mountains on the Italian border and assumed a static defensive position.[12]

For the next three months, Walker's bored troopers held this quiet sector at the extreme right of the front, while Allied leaders once again debated their fate. Ironically, the initial impetus for inactivation came from Frederick, perhaps due to recognition that no special tasks lay on the horizon and that his old unit was wasting away in a mission that was more suitable for line infantry. Given its binational nature, the Force's fate could only be determined at the highest levels of decision making. The War Department and the Canadian Ministry of National Defense, which had long since tired of the burden of providing Canadian fillers for the formation, favored disbandment, but Devers, now the chief of 6th Army Group in southern France, wanted to form the American contingent into a separate infantry regiment for use in the mountains of southern Germany. His idea appealed to Marshall, who wanted to preserve the unit's expertise in some form. On December 5, 1944, the 1st Special Service Force was dissolved. The Canadians returned to their own army, and the Americans transferred to the new 474th Infantry. Since Devers had just received nine new regiments, Eisenhower's headquarters reassigned the 474th to Bradley's 12th Army Group, where it performed rear area security for the rest of the war.[13]

For all the laurels won by the 1st Special Service Force, one can seriously question whether its employment justified its formation. Their initial purpose notwithstanding, the North Americans never conducted any deep raids or parachute assaults. In all, they performed perhaps three missions which might be considered special: the landings at Kiska and at the Hyeres Islands, and the capture of Monte La Difensa. They, as well as the Rangers, could have contributed to the advance up the Italian peninsula through amphibious raids against the exposed, enemy-held coastline or by special missions against key points on the model of the attack on Monte La Difensa, but the Allies had not developed an imaginative, consistent strategy for their employment. Instead, the North Americans and Rangers either endured a restless inactivity or carried out tasks that any line unit could have performed, even if not with the same élan. In the case of the latter, they suffered heavy casualties, partly because of a lack of heavy weapons to support a conventional attack or prolonged defense, partly out of occasional overaggressiveness, and partly due to the attritional nature of line combat. Losses while performing such missions hardly compensated for the administrative burden, especially to the Canadians, or the waste of superior infantrymen needed as leaders in other formations.[14]

On the other side of the globe, another unit of raiders was, for all practical purposes, destroyed through service as line infantry. In late January and early February 1944, GALAHAD moved from its training sites to Ningbyen in northern Burma, its jump-off point for the 1944 offensive. Under the original plan, Stilwell's Chinese troops would drive up the Hukawng Valley toward the north Burmese city of Myitkyina, while two British corps advanced from India and another Chinese force attacked from China into eastern Burma. The *Chindits* would aid these advances with raids on Japanese communications. The capture of Myitkyina, a key transportation center with a nearby airfield, would not only move the Allies much closer to a linkup with the old Burma Road but would also eliminate a base for Japanese fighters harassing Allied transport planes on the aerial supply route to China. As the date for the offensive approached, the British, under pressure from a renewed Japanese offensive toward India, postponed their drive, and the Chinese reneged on their offer of an advance into eastern Burma. Nevertheless, Stilwell proceeded, hoping to gain as much ground as possible before the monsoon in June closed operations.

GALAHAD's role in the coming campaign would depend on Stilwell, who had his own views on the new unit's employment. The sardonic theater chief, who was proud of his image as a regular doughboy, was hardly the type to favor special units, particularly if they demanded privileges in such areas as promotions and decorations. Like so many other American officers, he tended to think in mass terms. He and Merrill envisioned GALAHAD's role as similar to that of the old strategic cavalry, which would turn the enemy's flank and strike his communications, but in closer coordination with the main body than Wingate had proposed. They also hoped that GALAHAD would serve as a model for the recalcitrant Chinese. On Stilwell's behalf, it must be said that considerable debate continued in Allied circles over the role of a long-range penetration

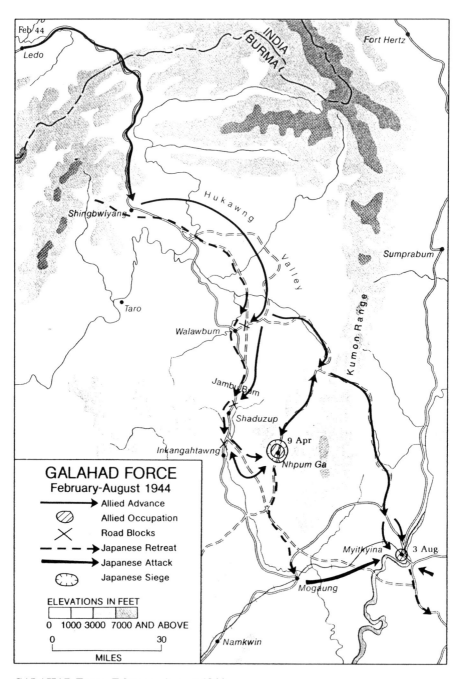

GALAHAD Force, February-August 1944

U.S. Army Center of Military History.

force. He also had some grounds to distrust the Chinese will to fight, for Chiang, wishing to preserve his forces for the future clash with the Communists, had secretly directed his generals not to risk their men unduly. Unaware of, but suspecting, these orders, Stilwell ordered GALAHAD to envelope the Japanese right and cut the enemy's supply line, but he also told Merrill to avoid heavy losses to his only American combat unit.[15]

On February 24, the Marauders began their movement around the flank of the Japanese 18th Division. Screened by their reconnaissance platoons, and receiving supply drops in the few jungle clearings, the three battalions followed obscure trails to a pair of positions near Walawbum, astride the expected Japanese line of retreat. On the main front, Stilwell's two Chinese divisions, in accordance with Chiang's orders, advanced at a snail's pace, permitting the 18th Division to concentrate against GALAHAD. A Chinese relief force, including a tank group, had not yet reached the roadblocks, leaving the Marauders with only rifles, a few machine guns, and mortars to resist the aroused Japanese. The Americans held on grimly, losing about 200 men but inflicting 800 casualties. Concerned to avoid excessive losses, Merrill withdrew his weary men from their positions on March 7. By then, the enemy had bypassed the roadblocks and fallen back to a line along the rugged Jambu Bum mountain range.

Anxious to capture the Jambu Bum before the onset of the monsoon season, Stilwell directed another, deeper envelopment of the Japanese right. Accompanied by the Chinese 113th Regiment, GALAHAD's 1st Battalion hacked its way through dense foliage to establish a roadblock south of Shaduzup. The other two battalions took a wider path to cut the Japanese line of retreat further south, but the 2d Battalion had no sooner reached the road than Stilwell's staff ordered both units to head off a Japanese drive against the left flank of the Allied advance. This change from a flanking mission, holding blocking positions for only brief periods of time, to a static defensive role represented "a radical change" in GALAHAD's concept of employment. For 11 days, the 2d Battalion held an isolated ridgeline at Nhpum Ga against repeated attacks. Merrill, leading a relief force, had to be evacuated due to a heart attack. Under Hunter's command, and with help from artillery airdropped to them, the 1st and 3d Battalions finally broke through to the beleaguered 2d on April 9, and the Japanese withdrew south.[16]

With the Jambu Bum in Allied hands, the 1,400 surviving Marauders anticipated a lengthy rest, but Stilwell had other ideas. Under pressure from the Joint Chiefs of Staff to take Myitkyina, he ordered GALAHAD to strike for the airfield near the city. The American commander recognized GALAHAD's poor condition after two months of hard campaigning but believed he had no option if the Allies were to capture Myitkyina before the monsoon. He promised to evacuate the Marauders without delay "if everything worked out as expected."[17]

Guided and screened by the "Kachin Rangers," native guerrillas organized and trained by the American Office of Strategic Services (OSS), the

Marauders and two Chinese regiments hiked 65 miles east over the 6,000-foot
Kumon Range to Myitkyina. Lt. Charlton Ogburn later wrote:

> We set off with that what-the-hell-did-you-expect-anyway spirit that
> served the 5307th in place of morale, and I dare say served it better.
> Mere morale would never have carried us through the country we
> now had to cross. . . . The saw-toothed ridges would have been
> difficult enough to traverse when dry. Greased with mud, the trail
> that went over them was all but impossible.[18]

Mules fell off ledges to their deaths in the crevices below. Marauders left their
packs by the side of the trail; straggling was rampant. Despite all obstacles, the
Marauders and their allies surprised the defenders of the airbase on May 17,
seized the strip, and probed toward Myitkyina itself. A delighted Stilwell quickly
arranged for Chinese reinforcements to fly into the airfield and crowed in his
diary, "WILL THIS BURN UP THE LIMEYS!"[19]

The exultation over the capture of the airfield soon dissolved as the task
force faltered in its attempts to take the city. Disorder reigned at the airstrip, due
to the lack of an on-site commander, the absence of a clear plan, and a shortage
of information on enemy strength. Although in command of the task force,
Merrill made only a brief visit to the airfield on May 19. Shortly afterward, he
was evacuated with his second heart attack, leaving the task force leaderless for
three days until Stilwell finally appointed a new commander. Lacking overall
direction and underestimating the strength of the Japanese defense, Chinese
troops made uncoordinated, piecemeal attacks and were repulsed with heavy loss.
Meanwhile, the confused, improvised process of resupply and reinforcement was
further upset by the decision of the theater's air chief to ship antiaircraft units to
the airfield ahead of additional troops, food, and ammunition. As the Allies
fumbled, the Japanese recovered from their shock and rushed in reinforcements.
By June, these troops and the onset of the monsoon had forced the Allies to
settle for a siege, a task for which GALAHAD was ill-suited.[20]

Stilwell should have relieved GALAHAD at this point, but political
considerations intervened. Both the British and the Chinese may well have
viewed with disapproval the relief of the only American combat force when their
own troops were heavily engaged. GALAHAD's earlier retreats from threatened
roadblocks had not impressed the Chinese, who believed the Americans were too
quick to leave them with the defense of dangerous positions. As for the British,
the decisive battle of Imphal, which would end the Japanese threat to India, was
just passing its climax. When Stilwell appealed for a division on May 27, the
British responded that they could not spare one until late June. They had already
given Stilwell control of the *Chindits*, who had become exhausted after more than
two months of raids behind Japanese lines. Nevertheless, hoping to cut
Myitkyina's communications to the south, Stilwell ordered them to attack the
railroad center of Mogaung, despite protests from *Chindit* commanders against

employment in set-piece battles. While pressing the *Chindits* past the point of endurance, Stilwell could hardly evacuate his own Americans.[21]

GALAHAD, therefore, stayed on the line, with predictable results. By late May, the organization, with its component units scattered throughout the Allied perimeter, had lost much of its coherence, and the few remaining men were so exhausted that some fell asleep in the middle of engagements. Daily, the Marauders were evacuating 75 to 100 men with malaria, dysentery, or typhus. In their plans for GALAHAD, the Joint Chiefs had not arranged for replacements, although they had just sent personnel for a new GALAHAD-type force to India. Desperate for manpower, Stilwell's headquarters threw these inadequately trained "New GALAHADs" and some engineers into the line, where they suffered heavy casualties. Overzealous staff officers, trying to hold down the rate of evacuation, pressed sick or wounded troops who could still walk into service. Such episodes, along with broken promises of relief, confirmed GALAHAD's self-image as the maltreated stepchild of higher headquarters. Hunter, who was nominally in command of GALAHAD, bitterly protested the treatment of his unit and was relieved on August 3—ironically the same day as the long-awaited fall of Myitkyina.[22]

When word of GALAHAD's plight reached the United States, a political firestorm erupted. The Marauders had received a great deal of favorable publicity through their image as elite jungle fighters and their status as the only American combat unit in Burma. When reports of their dire situation filtered back to the United States in August, they were met with shock and disbelief. Under such headlines as "Sick Merrill Marauders Sent to Front through Error" and "The Bitter Tea of Uncle Joe," the media blamed the collapse in morale on ill-advised promises and the impressment of convalescents for combat duty, and the chairman of the Senate Military Affairs Committee called for an official explanation. Remembering too well the furor that ensued when Patton slapped a soldier who was suffering from battle fatigue, the War Department investigated and concluded that unauthorized statements might well have led the men to believe in an early relief. It assured the chairman that morale had recovered and that sick and wounded soldiers, as well as those with a year of overseas service, were being returned to the United States as quickly as possible.[23]

The uproar soon died down, but the episode left a bitter taste, even in victory. Indeed, the Myitkyina campaign was a major triumph, enabling an expansion of the airlift to Chiang's forces and putting the Allies on the road and rail network of Burma, close to China. Without GALAHAD's capability for infiltration, that triumph would have been impossible to achieve, at least before the summer monsoon. Stilwell's gamble, unlike Truscott's, succeeded. Nevertheless, while the results may well have justified GALAHAD's sacrifices, Stilwell and his staff could have done much that might have prevented the unit's collapse in morale. Political complications, the lack of troops, and an incompletely developed concept of employment might have made the use of the

Marauders as line infantry inevitable. However, higher levels could have shown more appreciation for their ordeal. In a letter to Stilwell and a bitter memoir, Hunter, who was an orthodox officer, did not complain about the misuse of GALAHAD, but he did accuse Stilwell and his staff of ignoring recommendations for decorations and promotions and of otherwise treating the unit as an unwanted stepchild. The angry reaction at home proved, had any doubt existed, the sensitivity of Americans to mistreatment of their soldiers, even in victory.[24]

A brief epilogue concludes GALAHAD's story. In August 1944, the survivors reorganized into the 475th Infantry and then combined with the 124th Cavalry and supporting units to form a new long-range penetration group, the Mars Task Force. When the campaign resumed, the new unit made a killing hike south and east through mountains to outflank Japanese positions along the Burma Road near Lashio. By January 17, 1945, advance patrols of Kachins and "Marsmen" were clashing with Japanese outposts along the Burma Road. Wishing to avoid the heavy casualties that had decimated GALAHAD, Brig. Gen. John P. Willey, the commander of the task force, avoided the main road. Instead, he placed his troops on adjacent high ground, from which they could interdict the highway with patrols and artillery. Their lines of supply cut, the Japanese evacuated Lashio on March 7, enabling the Allies to link a road from their base at Ledo to the Burma Road and reopen the route to China. Transferred to China for training duties, the Mars Task Force disbanded in July 1945.[25]

While the Marauders were hiking through the jungles of Burma to Myitkyina, the 2d and 5th Ranger Battalions were training on the beaches and cliffs of Britain for D Day, the Normandy invasion. When they arrived during the winter of 1943–1944, Allied planners were contemplating the use of Rangers and commandos in a preparatory raiding program to obtain information, mislead the Germans on the eventual target of the assault, and provide the men with combat experience. After considering raids against Norway, COHQ, in consultation with Colonel Rudder of the 2d Ranger Battalion, laid plans for descents on the French coast by two Ranger companies, one to snatch a prisoner from the shore near Calais and one to reconnoiter the Isle of Herm in the Channel Islands. Rough seas, often a nemesis of COHQ planners, forced the cancellation of the two forays, and Gen. Sir Bernard L. Montgomery, who was in charge of ground forces for the D Day assault, decided against further raids, which would aggravate the shortage of landing craft and might alert the Germans without providing new information. In February, Eisenhower's Allied headquarters canceled the raiding program.[26]

The Rangers did not have much time to mull over their aborted program, for they had just received a formidable task for D Day. In January, Rudder and Maj. Max Schneider, the jaunty, good-natured commander of the 5th Ranger Battalion, journeyed to General Bradley's First Army headquarters in London, where staff officers laid out their mission. Four miles west of the American point of attack at Omaha Beach, the Germans had emplaced a battery of six 155-mm guns on Pointe du Hoc, a line of steep, rocky cliffs dominating the approaches to the beaches. Although planners had provided for naval and air bombardment of the point, a direct assault was the only certain way of neutralizing the fortification. To reach the position by sea, attackers would first have to land on a narrow shoreline and then scale an 83- to 100-foot cliff. One intelligence officer remarked, "It can't be done. Three old women with brooms could keep the Rangers from climbing that cliff." Although initially stunned by what was, to all appearances, a suicide mission, Rudder and Schneider stepped up training, emphasizing cliff climbing and amphibious assaults. To coordinate the two battalions, First Army authorized the formation of a "Provisional Ranger Group" under Rudder, as senior battalion commander.[27]

In retrospect, planners overrated the threat of the guns on Pointe du Hoc, but that in no way detracts from what the Rangers accomplished on June 6, 1944. Early that morning, the first assault wave, consisting of three companies of the 2d Ranger Battalion under Rudder's personal leadership, pounded through heavy Channel seas toward the Normandy coast. After correcting a course error, he and his men landed at 7:10 a.m., 35 minutes behind schedule. Covered by naval gunfire, they scrambled up ropes and ladders to reach the top of the cliff. Incredulous German defenders kept up a withering fire, cut the ropes, and tossed grenades down the slope, but within 10 minutes, the first Rangers had reached the top and secured a precarious foothold. As more soldiers reached the summit, they expanded the perimeter and swept the area. One patrol finally found and destroyed the guns, which the Germans had moved to a more concealed location from which they could still fire on the invasion beaches. The cost had been heavy. Of the 230 Rangers who made the assault, only 70 remained by late afternoon. Lacking men and supplies, these few grimly prepared to hold out against counterattack.[28]

When the 5th Ranger Battalion and the remainder of the 2d did not hear from Rudder's party within 30 minutes of the scheduled landing at the point, they joined the 29th Infantry Division's assault on Omaha Beach. There, heavy fire raked the shoreline, pinning the Rangers and troops of the 29th behind a seawall. At this point, according to legend, Brig. Gen. Norman D. Cota, the division's assistant commander, roared, "We have to get the hell off this beach. Rangers, lead the way!" Whether under Cota's inspiration or not, small parties of Rangers and infantry scrambled over the seawall and, under cover of the rising smoke, carried the heights. After linking up with a Ranger company that had seized nearby Pointe de la Percée, Schneider's force finally relieved Rudder's battered contingent on June 8.[29]

Having accomplished the mission that had justified their creation, the Rangers had to wait for higher levels to decide their future. Before D Day, planners at Eisenhower's headquarters had vaguely envisioned the use of commandos for "amphibious operations," and, as First Army's advance bogged down in the Norman hedgerows during June and July, 1st (later 12th) Army

**Rangers scaling the cliffs of Pointe du Hoc on the day after D Day
(U.S. Navy photograph)**

Group was considering the use of Rangers, commandos, and paratroopers to seize a badly needed port in Quiberon Bay on the coast of Brittany. Perhaps with such operations in mind, Rudder, in the days after the invasion, wanted to take the two badly depleted Ranger battalions back to Britain for reconstitution, but Bradley refused, stating that he could not spare anybody from the growing battle. However, First Army headquarters, which was beset with the myriad strategic and logistical problems of the buildup of corps and divisions in Normandy, could devote little time to consider the proper employment of, or even the need for, the two battalions. Thus, the Rangers, when not resting and training replacements, performed a series of odd jobs, mopping up bypassed German detachments, guarding prisoners, and serving as a reserve against attack from the German-held Channel Islands.[30]

When Allied armies broke out of their Normandy beachhead and drove across France into Germany in the late summer and fall of 1944, the two Ranger battalions played only a minor role. Attached to various divisions, they creditably carried out missions within the capability of most line units. In August, they joined VIII Corps for the drive into Brittany, screening flanks, filling gaps, and assaulting strongpoints. The Lochrist Battery, one of the forts and pillboxes guarding Brest, fell to a four-man Ranger patrol that infiltrated the position and forced its commander to surrender. After a two-month respite following the fall of Brest on September 18, the two battalions joined the offensive against the Siegfried Line, a system of fortifications guarding the German border. Assuming a defensive position in the dense, gloomy woods of the Huertgen Forest, the graveyard of many an American unit, the 2d suffered heavily from artillery and frostbite.

Rudder, who had reverted to command of the 2d following D Day, complained to higher headquarters about the misuse of his Rangers and received orders to move his battalion to Bergstein for an assault on nearby Castle Hill. This wooded hill mass dominated the region, including Bergstein, where troops and tanks of the 5th Armored Division clung to a tenuous position. In its attack on the hill, the Rangers used tactics similar to those of line units, but executed perhaps with more skill, and certainly with more élan. After a Ranger patrol reconnoitered the height in the predawn darkness of December 7, one company took position to provide fire support, while two others charged up the slope. Catching the Germans by surprise, the Rangers seized control of the crest but were hit almost immediately by enemy shell fire and two counterattacks. By late afternoon, only 25 Rangers remained on top of the hill. Reinforced by a platoon and supported by artillery fire, they held until a battalion relieved them on the evening of December 8. In the end, the battle for Bergstein cost the battalion over half its strength, most of which was expended in defense of the hill.[31]

To the south, the 5th Ranger Battalion performed the only deep infiltration mission assigned to the two battalions after D Day. Under a new chief, Lt. Col. Richard P. Sullivan, the 5th had worked with mechanized task forces in the drive by Patton's Third Army into the Saar-Moselle region in late November and had covered a division-sized sector in the front during the Battle of the Bulge. In late February 1945, Lt. Gen. Walton H. Walker of XX Corps directed the Rangers to penetrate the German front and cut enemy communications in support of the corps's expansion of a bridgehead over the Saar River. On the night of February 23–24, the Rangers, using the woods and hills of the area as concealment, quietly moved through German lines. By the morning of February 25, they had reached a position on high ground dominating the Irsch–Zerf Road, the enemy's main route of retreat. Aided by a battery of field artillery firing from American lines, the Rangers withstood repeated attacks by the retreating Germans. Although the advance of the 10th Armored Division bypassed the Ranger positions on February 26, it was not until March 5 that the 180 remaining Rangers could withdraw to a rest area. Their stand contributed directly to the collapse of German defenses in the area and XX Corps's advance to the Rhine.[32]

After these two Ranger missions, the remainder of the war in Europe proved anticlimactic for the two battalions. The 2d had barely begun to train replacements following its ordeal at Bergstein when the German Ardennes offensive compelled First Army to throw the unit into the line at Simmerath in an effort to shore up the northern flank of the growing "Bulge." Following the repulse of this last German offensive, the 2d, in February, patrolled in preparation for Allied crossings of the Roer River. Once the Allies had breached the German defenses along the Roer and the Rhine, the two Ranger battalions, operating alone and in conjunction with mechanized cavalry, joined the rapid advance across Germany, patrolling rear areas and mopping up the last pockets of resistance prior to the surrender on May 8.[33]

In the eleven months since the Rangers had spearheaded the landings at Normandy, they had endured lengthy inactive periods, punctuated occasionally by operations that were more suited to standard formations than small, light Ranger units. Higher headquarters, recognizing the problem, often attached tanks, tank destroyers, and self-propelled guns to the Rangers and arranged for access to fire support from corps and division artillery, but such support, while helpful, could not take the place of heavy weapons organic to the organization. Even in the case of the attack on the key point of Castle Hill and the infiltration at Zerf, two Ranger missions, the Rangers, lost heavily when forced to hold a position for days without relief. Given the lack of an established system for Ranger fillers and the difficulty in finding qualified recruits in the dwindling ETOUSA replacement pool, the Rangers could ill afford such casualties. It could be of little consolation that Allied commanders also pressed paratroopers and British commandos into line duty, with predictably heavy losses.[34]

Given this serious attrition of qualified manpower, why did field commanders employ these elite units in wasteful line roles? At first glance, the nature of the war in Europe seemed to preclude effective Ranger operations. With

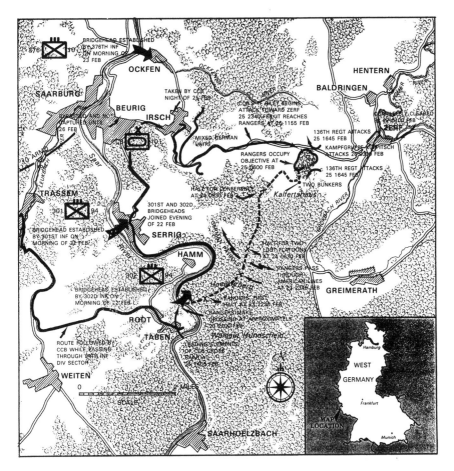

Within the map:

376 19

BRIDGEHEAD ESTABLISHED
BY 376TH INF
ON MORNING OF
23 FEB

OCKFEN

HENTERN

BALDRINGEN

SAARBURG

BEURIG

IRSCH

TAKEN BY CCB
NIGHT OF 25 FEB

BYPASSED AND NOT
CAPTURED UNTIL
26 FEB

301

CCB OF RILEY BEGINS
ATTACK TOWARD ZERF
25 2340 FEB. IT REACHES
RANGERS AT 26 1155 FEB

MIXED GERMAN
UNITS

RANGERS OCCUPY
OBJECTIVE AT
25 0600 FEB

HALT FOR CONFERENCE
AT 24 0930 FEB

BRIEFLY CLEARED
25 1700 FEB

ZERF

136TH REGT ATTACKS
25 1645 FEB

KAMPFGRUPPE KLEPITSCH
ATTACKS 26 0330 FEB

136TH REGT ATTACKS
25 1645 FEB

TWO BUNKERS

Kaltertshaus

TRASSEM

301 94

301ST AND 302D
BRIDGEHEADS
JOINED EVENING
OF 22 FEB

BRIDGEHEAD ESTABLISHED
BY 301ST INF ON
MORNING OF 22 FEB

SERRIG

HAMM

302 94

BRIDGEHEAD ESTABLISHED
BY 302D INF ON
MORNING OF 22 FEB

Hoecker Berg

HALT FOR TWO
29TH PLATOONS
AT 24 0630 FEB

RANGERS PASS
THROUGH
AMERICAN LINES
AT 24 2345 FEB

GREIMERATH

RANGERS FIRST
HALT AT 25 2230 FEB

RODT

TABEN

ROUTE FOLLOWED BY
CCB WHILE PASSING
THROUGH 94TH INF
DIV SECTOR

RANGERS MAKE
CROSSING AT APPROXIMATELY
25 0300 FEB

LEADING ELEMENTS
OF CCB CROSS
SAAR AT
25 1705 FEB

Wald bei Hunoldscheid

WEITEN

0   2 MILES

SCALE

SAARHOELZBACH

WEST
GERMANY

Hamburg

Frankfurt

Munich

MAP
LOCATION

Zerf, 23 February–5 March 1945

U.S. Army Combat Studies Institute.

Allied forces established on the Continent, the war became a clash of mass armies in generally open terrain, employing artillery and aerial firepower against fortifications, and exploiting breakthroughs with fast-moving tanks and mechanized columns. Nonetheless, opportunities for Ranger operations did exist for the alert general who perceived the potential of such activities. In his comments on the Zerf operation, Sullivan pointed out that German overextension and lack of reserves offered numerous openings for infiltration, as long as the infiltrators did not allow their movements to become predictable. Wedded to the cavalry, the Rangers possessed the mobility to seize key road junctions, river crossings, and prisoner of war camps in advance of the main forces. Indeed, III Corps considered the use of a picked band of Rangers to seize the bridge at Remagen but decided the likelihood of taking it intact was too slim to justify the effort.[35]

Thus, while the nature of the campaigns in France and Germany explains to a degree the wasteful use of the Rangers, other factors were even more responsible. While the Rangers dodged the threat of disbandment after D Day, they never did establish a clear purpose. Part of the problem lay in the absence of some kind of doctrine defining the proper use of the Rangers. The American mission at COHQ had been collecting data that might have been helpful in the formulation of a doctrine, but, given the lack of documentation and Army Ground Forces's prior attitude, one can only assume that the Army's chief doctrinal agency was not interested in such a statement. Ranger battalion commanders occasionally protested misuse, as they saw it, and suggested suitable tasks, with some success in the case of Castle Hill. However, Sullivan, Rudder, and Maj. George S. Williams, who replaced Rudder in December, lacked the stature at higher levels that a Darby would have enjoyed. The provisional group headquarters, as a center for planning Ranger missions, might have had that leverage, but, after a brief existence under Col. Eugene Slappey, that organization dissolved in August. From then on, the battalions never again worked as a team.[36]

Underlying all other factors in the wasteful use, or lack of use, of the Rangers was the orientation of the U.S. Army and its commanders toward big-unit warfare. Once the Army had established itself on the Continent, it was fighting the kind of conflict for which it had prepared during those long interwar years: an enormous contest of mass units, machines, and complex logistics, conducted by efficient managers rather than charismatic leaders. At the Command and General Staff College, the Army Industrial College, and the Army War College, future commanders had learned to apply massive force along broad fronts to destroy the enemy's means of resistance rather than employ raids and other special operations by small elite units to wear down his will to fight. Under the circumstances, it is not surprising that officers who modeled themselves after Ulysses S. Grant, William T. Sherman, and John J. Pershing tended to perceive infiltration and other Ranger operations as unnecessarily risky sideshows. Like other field commanders, Bradley, Patton, and Lt. Gen. Courtney H. Hodges of First Army proved reluctant to disband such excellent fighting units. However, busy with the management of mass armies, they had little time or inclination to define a unique role for the Rangers. Under pressure from the lack of combat troops, the restlessness of the high-spirited Rangers, and their own inclinations against special treatment, they used the battalions as line infantry, at a great cost in specially trained manpower.[37]

One should not, of course, criticize too much the Army's orientation toward big-unit warfare in World War II. In the end, it was campaigns by mass armies, navies, and air forces, and not amphibious raids, which brought the Axis powers to their knees. Furthermore, as Cisterna and Myitkyina demonstrated, Ranger operations could not only result in the destruction of fine units but also create a backlash in public opinion. Nevertheless, the Army undoubtedly could have made more efficient use of its Rangers. Lacking a doctrine or stated purpose for Ranger units, commanders should have either disbanded them, using the manpower to replenish badly depleted replacement pools, or employed them within their capabilities. In the case of Darby's Rangers, where a fragment of the unit remained, and the 1st Special Service Force, where the recommendation of the former commander and international considerations governed, they did inactivate the unit. For the most part, however, they either allowed Ranger units to waste away or assigned unsuitable missions to them. Thus, in Italy, Burma, and Western Europe, the Rangers paid the price for the lack of a clear concept of employment.

NOTES

1. Ranger Force report for 22 January–5 February 1944, WWII Ops. Reports, INBN 1-0.3, RG 407, WNRC; 3d Ranger Battalion's report for 20–30 January 1944, WWII Ops. Reports, INBN 3-0.3, RG 407, WNRC; Darby and Baumer, *Darby's Rangers*, pp. 143–154; Dobson interview.

2. Darby quoted in Darby and Baumer, *Darby's Rangers*, p. 157. See also Clark, *Calculated Risk*, p. 296; Darby's report for 28–31 January 1944; and G-2, 3d Infantry Division, "G-2 Estimate of the Situation," 29 January 1944, in WWII Ops. Reports, INBN 1-0.3, RG 407, WNRC; Darby and Baumer, *Darby's Rangers*, pp. 155–169; Truscott, *Command Missions*, pp. 312–313; Fred Sheehan, *Anzio: Epic of Bravery* (Norman: University of Oklahoma Press, 1964), pp. 72–73. Many observers later claimed that Darby was against the operation from the beginning; see Dobson interview and Lehman, "Rangers Fought Ahead," p. 50.

3. "The German Operation at Anzio," pp. 13–20, John W. O'Daniel Papers, USAMHI; Darby's report for 28–31 January 1944; Darby and Baumer, *Darby's Rangers*, pp. 160–169; Dobson interview; James J. Altieri, *Darby's Rangers* (Durham, N.C.: Seeman Printery, 1945), pp. 75–84; King, *Rangers*, pp. 32–40; Sheehan, *Anzio*, pp. 73, 78–82.

4. Truscott, *Command Missions*, p. 314; Lucas Diary, III:351–352, John P. Lucas Papers, USAMHI; Ivan H. Peterman, "Peterman Discloses Story of Lost Rangers at Anzio Beachhead," *Philadelphia Inquirer*, 15 April 1944, p. 1; John Lardner, "The Beachhead Alamo of the Rangers," in Lisko Papers, USAMHI; Milton Lehman, "The Rangers Died Fighting at Dawn," *Stars and Stripes*, 11 March 1944, in WWII Ops. Reports, INBN 1-0.3, RG 407, WNRC; Sheehan, *Anzio*, p. 83; Blumenson, *Mark Clark*, p. 178.

5. Lucas Diary, III:352; King, *Rangers*, p. 31; King, *Darby*, pp. 152–154; Dobson interview.

6. Correspondence between Devers and the War Department in U.S. War Department, Operations Division, OPD 320.2 Africa, Case 616, RG 165, MMHB, National Archives; correspondence in AG 320.2 Disposition of Ranger Battalions (28 April 1944), AG Classified File, RG 407, MMHB, National Archives.

7. Brig. Gen. W. W. Irvine, G-3 Division, to OPD, 30 May 1944, U.S. War Department, Operations Division, OPD 320.2 Africa, Case 616, RG 165, MMHB, National Archives.

8. Commanding Officer, Camp Butner, to Commanding General, XIII Corps, 10 May 1944, AG 320.2 Disposition of Ranger Battalions (28 April 1944) AG Classified File, RG 407, MMHB, National Archives; correspondence in OPD 320.2 Africa, Case 616, RG 165, MMHB, National Archives. Interestingly, the 4th Ranger Battalion disbanded on October 24, two months after the others. The most likely explanation is that Marshall still believed that a need for one Ranger battalion might exist in another theater; see Chapter 5, p. 85.

9. Truscott quoted in Altieri, *Darby's Rangers*, p. 11. See also King, *Darby*, pp. 160–175.

10. Reports of 1st Special Service Force for February to May 1944 in WWII Ops. Reports, SSFE 1-0.3, Box 23274, RG 407, WNRC; Burhans, *Special Service Force*, pp. 166–210; Adleman and Walton, *Devil's Brigade*, pp. 165–199; McMichael, *Light Infantry*, 192–198.

11. Adleman and Walton, *Devil's Brigade*, p. 197; Hummer, *Infantryman's Journal*, pp. 51–57, 63.

12. 1st Special Service Force reports for May to September 1944, WWII Ops. Reports, SSFE 1-0.3, Box 23274, RG 407, WNRC; Burhans, *Special Service Force*, pp. 211–246, 257–293; Adleman and Walton, *Devil's Brigade*, pp. 200–239; McMichael, *Light Infantry*, pp. 198–204.

13. Eisenhower to Maj. Gen. Walter B. Smith, 17 October 1944, and footnote, in Chandler and Ambrose, *Eisenhower*, IV:2232; Dziuban, *Military Relations*, pp. 265–267; McMichael, *Light Infantry*, pp. 204, 211–212; Burhans, *Special Service Force*, pp. 299, 316–320. Ironically, the 474th Infantry finally reached the force's original destination, when it went to Norway to repatriate German prisoners at war's end.

14. McMichael, *Light Infantry*, pp. 198, 211–212; Adleman and Walton, *Devil's Brigade*, p. 244; Dziuban, *Military Relations*, p. 267.

15. U.S. War Department, *Merrill's Marauders*, p. 16; Charles F. Romanus and Riley Sunderland, *Stilwell's Command Problems*, U.S. Army in World War II (Washington, D.C.: OCMH, 1956), pp. 36, 131, 146, 149; Bidwell, *Chindit War*, pp. 45, 67–73; Sunderland memorandum, pp. 6–7, 12, in McMichael Papers, USAMHI; John Randolph, *Marsmen in Burma* (Houston, Tex.: Gulf Publishing, 1946), p. 26; Hunter,

GALAHAD, p. 53; Sykes, *Orde Wingate*, pp. 457, 489; Ogburn, *Marauders*, p. 60; USAMHI, "Senior Officers Debriefing Program: Conversations between Lt. Gen. William R. Peers and Lt. Col. Jim Breen, Lt. Col. Charlie Moore" (Carlisle, Pa., 1977), I:5-7.

16. Quotation in Romanus and Sunderland, *Stilwell's Command Problems*, p. 182; see also pp. 149-154, 175-191, 212; Hunter, *GALAHAD*, pp. 19-46, 52-80; Ogburn, *Marauders*, pp. 91-134, 188-228.

17. Stilwell quoted in Romanus and Sunderland, *Stilwell's Command Problems*, p. 225; see also pp. 201, 223-225.

18. Ogburn, *Marauders*, pp. 229-230.

19. Ogburn, *Marauders*, pp. 229-230; Romanus and Sunderland, *Stilwell's Command Problems*, pp. 225-227; Hunter, *GALAHAD*, pp. 103-113; Theodore H. White, ed., *The Stilwell Papers* (New York: Wm. Sloane, 1948), p. 296. For more on the Kachin Rangers, see William R. Peers and Dean Brelis, *Behind the Burma Road: The Story of America's Most Successful Guerrilla Force* (Boston: Little Brown, 1963), and Richard Dunlop, *Behind Japanese Lines: With the OSS in Burma* (Chicago: Rand McNally, 1979).

20. Romanus and Sunderland, *Stilwell's Command Problems*, pp. 229-236; Hunter, *GALAHAD*, pp. 99, 116-128, 146; Sunderland memorandum, pp. 8-9, McMichael Papers, USAMHI.

21. Romanus and Sunderland, *Stilwell's Command Problems*, pp. 188-189; Hunter, *GALAHAD*, pp. 168-169; Bidwell, *Chindit War*, pp. 242, 252-254; Sunderland memo, pp. 10-11, McMichael Papers, USAMHI.

22. McGee comments, p. 7, in McMichael Papers, USAMHI; Hunter, *GALAHAD*, pp. 84, 130-137, 147-149, 164, 179, 195-196, 205, 212; Romanus and Sunderland, *Stilwell's Command Problems*, p. 237; James H. Stone, "The Marauders and the Microbes," *Infantry Journal* 64 (March 1949): 8; Ogburn, *Marauders*, pp. 250-261.

23. See Tillman Durdin, "U.S. Unit in Burma a Dashing Outfit," *New York Times*, 8 March 1944, p. 3, and other articles in *New York Times* during March and May 1944; "Merrill's Marauders Break in Morale," *New York Times*, 6 August 1944, p. 1; Clay Gowran, "Sick Merrill Marauders Sent to Front through Error," *Washington Times-Herald*, 6 August 1944, p. 1; Hunter, *GALAHAD*, p. 214; Acting Secretary of War John J. McCloy to Senator Robert R. Reynolds, 25 August 1944, U.S. Army, Operations Division, Decimal File, 1942-1944, Folder 333.1, Box 35, RG 165, MMHB, National Archives.

24. Sunderland memorandum, p. 12, McMichael Papers, USAMHI; Hunter, *GALAHAD*, pp. 146, 172; Ogburn, *Marauders*, pp. 256-257.

25. Charles S. Romanus and Riley Sunderland, *Time Runs Out in CBI*, U.S. Army in World War II (Washington, D.C.: OCMH, 1958), pp. 126, 134, 183-214; Randolph, *Marsmen*, pp. xi, 28, 100-160, 218-219.

26. Chief of Staff to Supreme Allied Commander (COSSAC) to ETOUSA, 14 December 1943, U.S. Army Headquarters, 12th Army Group, Special Staff, Adjutant General's Section, Administrative Branch, Top Secret Decimal File 1943-5, 322 Rangers to T Force, Box 32, RG 331, MMHB, National Archives; "Raids & Recon Policy and Ops," in SHAEF, General Staff, G-3 Division, Operations "A" Section, Numeric File, 1943-5, Box 120, Folder 17225, RG 331, MMHB, National Archives; "The Narrative History of the Second Ranger Infantry Battalion, 1944" (hereafter cited as "Narrative of 2d Ranger Battalion,"), pp. 1-6, WWII Ops. Reports, INBN 2-0.3, Box 21072, RG 407,

WNRC.

27. Officer quoted in Lane, *Rudder's Rangers*, p. 68; see also pp. 67–68; "Normandy Landings, 2nd and 5th Ranger Battalions, June 6–8, 1944," Perlmutter Collection, Roll No. 7, JFKSWC; Staff Study by 21st Army Group, 27 December 1943, HQ, 12th Army Group, Top Secret Decimal File, 1943–5, 322 Rangers to T-Force, Box 32, RG 331, MMHB, National Archives.

28. "Narrative of 2d Ranger Battalion," pp. 6–8; 2d Ranger Battalion report for June 1944, 22 July 1944, in WWII Ops. Reports, INBN 2-0.3, Box 21072, RG 407, WNRC; "Normandy Landings"; Lane, *Rudder's Rangers*, p. 68; Prince, "Co. A," I:33–36; Glassman, *"Lead the Way Rangers!"*, p. 13; Sorvisto, *2nd Ranger Battalion*, pp. 16–20; Baer, *D for Dog*, pp. 26–28, 35–37. The patrol that located the guns found them sighted on Utah Beach with ammunition nearby, but they found no sign of crews or a guard, nor any indication that the guns had been fired.

29. Cota quoted in Haggerty, "Ranger Battalions," p. 218; see also Glassman, *"Lead the Way Rangers!"*, pp. 20–25; Prince, "Co. A," II:5–15; 2d Ranger Battalion report for June 1944, 22 July 1944; 5th Ranger Battalion report for 6–10 June 1944, 22 July 1944, WWII Ops. Reports, INBN 5-0.3, Box 21076, RG 407, WNRC. Cota's statement later became the Ranger motto.

30. "Strategic Reserves for Overlord," in "Pre-D-Day Planning Papers (Operations)," SHAEF, General Staff, G-3 Division, Administrative Section, Subject File, 1942–5, Box 53, RG 331, MMHB, National Archives; Chester B. Hansen Diary entries for 16 and 20 June 1944, Chester B. Hansen Papers, USAMHI; 2d Ranger Battalion report for June 1944, 22 July 1944; Prince, "Co. A," II:21–33; Glassman, *"Lead the Way Rangers!"*, p. 28; Sorvisto, *2nd Ranger Battalion*, p. 38; 5th Ranger Battalion unit journal for June 1944, WWII Ops. Reports, INBN 5-0.7, Box 21078, RG 407, WNRC; Martin Blumenson, *Breakout and Pursuit*, U.S. Army in World War II (Washington, D.C.: OCMH, 1961), p. 186.

31. 2d Ranger Battalion after-action reports for August to December 1944, in WWII Ops. Reports, INBN 2-0.3, Box 21072, RG 407, WNRC; 5th Ranger Battalion after-action reports for August through December 1944, WWII Ops. Reports, INBN 5-0.3, Box 21076, RG 407, WNRC; Prince, "Co. A," II:39–49, 59–66; Glassman, *"Lead the Way Rangers!"*, pp. 31–38, 42–43; Sorvisto, *2nd Ranger Battalion*, pp. 42–56; Baer, *D for Dog*, pp. 48–87; Haggerty, "Ranger Battalions," p. 227; "Narrative History of the 2nd Ranger Battalion: The Huertgen Forest Campaign, 3 Nov.–5 Dec. 1944," p. 1, WWII Ops. Reports, INBN 2-0.3, Box 21072, RG 407, WNRC; "Huertgen Forest Action (Nov. 23–Dec. 10, 1944) 2nd Ranger Battalion: Interview With Major George S. Williams, Commanding Officer, Captain Edgar L. Arnold, Executive Officer, Bn. CP, Mayschoss, Germany, March 21, 1945," Perlmutter Collection, Roll 7, JFKSWC; MacDonald, *Siegfried Line*, pp. 455, 461–463, 493; ETO unit assignment cards, Organizational History Branch, CMH; John A. English, *On Infantry*, 2d ed. (New York: Praeger, 1984), p. 134.

32. 5th Ranger Battalion after action reports for November 1944 through February 1945, WWII Ops. Reports, INBN 5-0.3, Boxes 21076–21077, RG 407, WNRC; "Operation behind German Lines Vicinity Zerf (Feb. 25–March 4, 1945) 5th Ranger Battalion—Written Report Prepared by Major Hugo W. Heffelfinger, Executive Officer, March 9, 1945 at Remich, Luxembourg," and "Operations inside German Lines in the Vicinity of Zerf (Feb. 23–March 4, 1945) Lieutenant Colonel Richard P. Sullivan, March

9, 1945, Remich Luxembourg," in Perlmutter Collection, Roll 7, JFKSWC; Glassman, *"Lead the Way Rangers!"*, pp. 47–70; Greene interview; "5th Ranger Infantry Battalion," in Ranger Files, Organizational History Branch, CMH; King, *Rangers*, pp. 43–54.

33. 2d Ranger Battalion after action reports for December 1944 through May 1945, WWII Ops. Reports, INBN 2-0.3, Boxes 21072–21073, RG 407, WNRC; 5th Ranger Battalion after-action reports for December 1944 through May 1945, WWII Ops. Reports, INBN 5-0.3, Boxes 21076–21078, RG 407, WNRC; Glassman, *"Lead the Way Rangers!"*, pp. 71–73; Baer, *D for Dog*, pp. 87–88, 101; Greene interview; Prince, "Co. A," III:39–69.

34. 2d Ranger Battalion after action reports for October to December 1944, WWII Ops. Reports, INBN 2-0.3, Box 21072, RG 407, WNRC; Prince, "Co. A," II:65; Glassman, *"Lead the Way Rangers!"*, pp. 34, 48–49; Greene interview; McMichael, *Light Infantry*, p. 211; Weigley, *Eisenhower's Lieutenants*, pp. 370–373; Lovat, *March Past*, pp. 326–327. By the third month of OVERLORD, No. 4 Commando had lost 100 percent of its paper strength.

35. Weigley, *American Way of War*, pp. 316, 327, 347, 359; "Operation Inside German Lines;" Charles B. MacDonald, *The Last Offensive*, U.S. Army in World War II (Washington, D.C.: OCMH, 1973), p. 211.

36. "Narrative History of the 2nd Ranger Battalion: Reorganization," WWII Ops. Reports, INBN 2-0.3, Box 21072, RG 407, WNRC; Hansen Diary entry for 20 June 1944; Greene interview. See Chapter 2, page 34, on doctrine.

37. See the discussion in the previous chapter and Weigley, *American Way of War*, pp. 212–222. Martin Van Creveld discussed the American army's mass approach to warfare in *Fighting Power: German and U.S. Army Performance, 1939-1945* (Westport, Conn.: Greenwood Press, 1982). See also Weigley, *Eisenhower's Lieutenants*, pp. 80–85; Robert H. Ferrell, ed., *The Eisenhower Diaries* (New York: Norton, 1981), p. 6; Blair and Bradley, *A General's Life*, pp. 53–54; Martin Blumenson, *The Patton Papers*, 2 vols. (Boston: Houghton Mifflin, 1974), II:848; Bradley, *Soldier's Story*, p. 226.

5

The Anomaly of the 6th Ranger Battalion

While Rangers in Europe and Burma saw their ranks depleted and their unique talents wasted through service as line infantry, a different concept of Ranger operations was emerging in the Pacific. The Allies had planned to remain on the defensive there until the defeat of Germany enabled them to concentrate their forces against Japan, but after the decisive victory at Midway, American forces had seized the initiative and never lost it. By November 1943, American soldiers and Marines had occupied much of the Solomon Islands chain in the South Pacific, and naval and air strikes were beginning to isolate the key Japanese naval base of Rabaul. In the Southwest Pacific theater (SWPA), General MacArthur's American and Australian forces had used amphibious end runs to gain control of much of the northern coast of New Guinea. To the north lay the Philippines, whose redemption had been a near obsessive goal for MacArthur since his departure from Corregidor two years earlier. Anticipating a need for long-range reconnaissance and other special operations during the approach to, and invasion of, those islands, he and Lt. Gen. Walter Krueger, commander of Sixth Army, were considering the creation of special units to carry out those missions.[1]

In their attitudes toward special operations, the two men were a different breed from commanders in Europe and Burma. On the surface, it would be hard to imagine two more dissimilar personalities than the brilliant, charismatic, articulate MacArthur and the austere, cautious, thoroughly professional Krueger, but they found common ground in many areas. They were older than counterparts in other theaters, having started their careers in a pre–World War I Army that showed many of the traits of the old frontier constabulary. Each had served extensively in the Philippines and knew of the peculiar conditions of operations in that archipelago. Each possessed the flexibility to adjust to strategic and tactical demands. Finally, each knew the value of moral and spiritual factors in war and understood the disproportionately great effect of a small unit of determined, well-trained men.[2]

One area in which a small, elite unit could make a major contribution lay in the field of reconnaissance. By late 1943, Krueger was concerned about the lack of reliable ground intelligence available to his command. As his Sixth Army drove toward the Philippines, it would need advance data on beaches designated for amphibious landings. Furthermore, to operate effectively, his troops needed reliable information on Japanese troop movements and dispositions. Such intelligence was hard to obtain in the dense jungles of the Southwest Pacific. Aerial photographs could not penetrate the dense jungle canopy, and standard infantry formations lacked the skills for long-range patrols to collect the needed data. The situation clearly called for a special unit.

At Krueger's direction, in November 1943, Sixth Army formed the Alamo Scouts to reconnoiter behind enemy lines and perform other covert operations. From the ranks of Sixth Army, volunteers who had been selected for courage, stamina, adaptability, and intelligence assembled at Fergusson Island off the southeast tip of New Guinea. The group included husky college football heroes, restless adventurers, and, in anticipation of future activities, a number of Filipino-Americans. For nearly four weeks, they endured long marches, swimming tests, and instruction in marksmanship, communications, navigation, rubber boats, and hand-to-hand combat. They then participated in two weeks of field exercises, including landings from PT boats under live fire. Survivors of this regimen, through secret ballots, named the fellow trainees with whom they would most like to serve. On this basis, Sixth Army formed teams, each with one officer and six or seven enlisted men, while those not selected returned to their original units.

Beginning in February 1944, 10 Scout teams carried out about 60 covert missions without the loss of a single man. Operating under Sixth Army's intelligence section, they reconnoitered beaches, established radio and coast-watcher stations, observed Japanese movements and garrisons, called in air strikes against enemy formations, and organized and trained guerrillas. Infiltrating by submarine, PT boat, seaplane, or parachute, they generally stayed in the field for three to five days, although they often remained in action for longer periods when cooperating with guerrillas. They avoided combat except when essential to their mission, as when two Scout teams rescued 32 natives from a Japanese prison camp in New Guinea. Careful selection and rugged training contributed to the success of the Scouts, but they also benefited greatly from the presence of an active guerrilla movement in the Philippines.[3]

For all their success, the Scouts did not have the organization to handle larger-scale special missions, and the American high command decided that a Ranger battalion was needed. Available evidence reveals little on the individual or the reasoning behind the creation of the 6th Ranger Battalion, but it seems clear that the prospect of a number of amphibious landings, and MacArthur's fondness for amphibious diversions to disguise the main effort, inclined him and Krueger to favor a battalion-sized elite infantry unit that could operate independently against key points. The plight of captives who might still be lingering in Japanese prison camps in the Philippines never strayed far from the mind of MacArthur, who felt a special sense of obligation to the veterans of Bataan and Corregidor. At the same time, the SWPA chief, with his insatiable appetite for publicity, could not have been blind to the attention that successful special operations attract. For such tasks, MacArthur and Krueger did not want to detail a standard unit and thereby weaken its parent formation. They preferred to organize a special unit along the lines of the European theater's Rangers, of which they were vaguely aware, and the Pacific's Marine Raiders.[4]

By late 1943, much of the initial glow surrounding the Raiders had faded through repeated misuse, but, in almost two years, they had certainly made their mark. The Raiders traced their origins to prewar experiments with raids and diversions by Marine rubber boat companies, but the real impetus for their formation in early 1942 came from a handful of commando enthusiasts, one of whom, Capt. James Roosevelt, urged his father to prod the Corps into action. From the rubber boat companies, the Marines formed the two Raider battalions for raids, landings on especially difficult beaches, and vaguely defined "guerrilla operations." Their initial mission, a raid on Makin Atoll in the Gilbert Islands, ended in near chaos but won much acclaim, as did a raid behind Japanese lines on Guadalcanal. Even on Guadalcanal, higher levels were already employing the Raiders as line infantry, and Raider units later lost heavily in line operations on New Georgia and Bougainville, where their élan could not make up for their lack of heavy weapons in attacks against fixed positions. These problems strengthened the case of opponents within the Corps, who argued that the Marines already represented an elite light infantry force, that too few special missions existed to justify special units, and that Raider battalions were drawing potential leaders from new Marine divisions. In late 1943, the commandant of the Corps decided that the need for Raider units had passed, and, in February 1944, the four existing battalions combined to form a standard regiment.[5]

Ironically, at about the same time as the demise of the Marine Raiders, MacArthur directed the creation of the 6th Ranger Battalion. The SWPA chief could see, even if the commandant of Marines could not, the prospect of a number of Raider-type missions. Furthermore, the Marines were not only converting the Raiders into more conventional units, but also concentrating their forces for the developing offensive in the Central Pacific. If MacArthur wanted an elite light infantry unit for SWPA, he would have to rely on resources within his theater. Thus, on December 27, he directed Krueger to convert the 98th Field Artillery Battalion into a provisional Ranger battalion for "employment on amphibious raids and diversionary attacks of limited duration."[6]

Krueger's choice to command the 6th Ranger Battalion, Lt. Col. Henry A. Mucci, would soon demonstrate the kind of tough, resourceful leadership needed in special operations. A graduate of West Point in 1932, the 33-year-old Mucci had served as provost marshal of Honolulu and as a battalion leader in the 24th Infantry Division before taking command of the Rangers. At first glance, the new chief did not cut a very impressive figure. Short and stocky, he looked almost professorial with his receding hairline, trim mustache, and pipe. His piercing eyes were the greatest indication of his personal magnetism. In the months to come, he would show both considerable dynamism and a natural ability to motivate men.[7]

Rather than select personnel from a pool of volunteers as Darby and other Ranger leaders had done, Mucci faced the task of converting an inactive artillery unit into an elite Ranger infantry battalion. Fortunately, the 98th, a pack artillery battalion that had been marking time since its arrival in New Guinea in January 1943, enjoyed some unique qualifications for Ranger duty. Recruiters for the unit had selected men who were six feet tall or over for the anticipated rugged service with the mule-borne howitzers, and most of these soldiers came from farms and mountain areas where they had grown accustomed to hard outdoor labor. Nevertheless, Sixth Army was still concerned about the maintenance of elite standards in a converted unit, and it preserved the volunteer principle by offering each artilleryman the option of the replacement depot if he did not want to perform Ranger duty. Married men were urged to give the new mission some thought. Bored and glad to be rid of the mules, most battalion members stayed, and volunteers from the depots filled the spaces of those who did leave. In April 1944, a team from Sixth Army headquarters inspected the unit and pronounced itself satisfied with the quality of the personnel.[8]

Given the background of most of the men, Mucci's rigorous training program, not surprisingly, stressed infantry skills. In a sparse training camp among the hills near Port Moresby, he whipped his new charges into shape with a series of 5-mile runs before breakfast, 20-mile hikes, and races up the aptly named, 500-foot high "Misery Knoll." Games, swimming, group exercises, and an obstacle course completed the conditioning regimen, in which Mucci and the other officers participated alongside their men. The Rangers also received instruction in weapons, communications, patrols, scouting, and night operations. In June, they moved to Finschhafen in northern New Guinea for unit and amphibious training, which stressed night landings and the use of rubber boats. Already, word of this battalion was beginning to reach the press, which portrayed the Rangers as the biggest and roughest collection of soldiers in Sixth Army. Unfortunately, they were also encountering some friction with other soldiers, who resented the battalion's favored status.[9]

When Ranger leaders were not arbitrating clashes with other units, they were looking for a suitable organization for the new battalion. MacArthur's orders had suggested the Marine Raider battalion as a model, and the Rangers did temporarily adopt the Raider organization. In Finschhafen, however, they received a new, War Department–approved table, which was based on the experiences of Rangers in Europe. In many ways, the new table was not well suited for operations in the Pacific. The 6th needed to substitute items for much of the equipment listed, such as lighter Browning Automatic Rifles for machine guns. Experience showed that the stipulated jungle pack was too large, and the battalion had to obtain more cooks than the table provided. Nevertheless, the Rangers reorganized according to the table, one of the very few contacts between Rangers in Europe and in the Pacific.[10]

Although little contact existed between the Rangers in Europe and the Pacific, to the point that individual Rangers in the Pacific claimed not to have heard of those in Europe until late in the war, the status of the Rangers in Europe affected that of the 6th Ranger Battalion. Several months passed before the activation of the 6th as a permanent unit, partly due to Sixth Army's desire to train the unit thoroughly prior to its commitment to combat, but also because the Army's official troop basis at the start of 1944 only provided for the five Ranger battalions in Europe. Not until the decimation of the 1st, 3d, and 4th Ranger Battalions at Cisterna, and their later disbandment, did enough spaces become available in the troop basis for SWPA to activate the 6th Ranger Battalion on September 26.

By then, the Rangers had experienced a change in mission. In late September, SWPA and Sixth Army were no longer thinking of amphibious diversions by Rangers, but rather were contemplating the seizure of points that were critical to the success of an amphibious assault, the same role that Rangers had played in Europe. Krueger had originally planned that the veteran 112th Cavalry and 158th Regimental Combat Team, the Bushmasters, would do the job, but, when Sixth Army learned that these units would be unavailable, it gave the mission to the Rangers. Three days before the invasion, the battalion would seize three islands flanking the entrances to Leyte Gulf. One company would land on Homonhon Island, occupy Colasi Point, and clear any installations there. Another would occupy Suluan Island, demolish the radio, radar station, and other facilities in the lighthouse area, and seize any documents. The rest of the battalion would land on Dinagat Island, secure a perimeter, and destroy installations at Desolation Point and the town of Loretto. Beacons placed on Dinagat and Homonhon would guide the invasion fleet through the channel between them into Leyte Gulf. The mission, which required a small, independent force to secure points vital to the success of the main operation, was ideal for the Rangers.[11]

In its first combat mission, the 6th Ranger Battalion generally encountered little opposition, but it did get a chance to demonstrate its capabilities on Suluan. There, Capt. Arthur D. "Bull" Simons of Company B found the Japanese in the lighthouse, surrounded by imposing cliffs on three sides and a steep trail on the fourth. In a daring night attack, part of the company cut off a security detachment at the foot of the trail, while the other Rangers climbed the cliffs, struck the surprised garrison from the rear, and annihilated them. The attack showed the battalion's ability to surmount difficult terrain and its expertise in night fighting, the latter being an uncommon quality in American units. From Suluan, Company B moved to Leyte, where the rest of the battalion had assembled after carrying out its mission on Dinagat and Homonhon. For the next two months, the Rangers patrolled rear areas and served as a guard for the army headquarters and supply depot. Such tasks mostly served to occupy them pending another special mission, but rear area personnel certainly appreciated their presence in early December, when Japanese paratroopers launched an abortive attack on airfields in Sixth Army's rear.[12]

After the unopposed American landing in Luzon in early January, the 6th Ranger Battalion received its most famous mission. Krueger and his staff had known of the Japanese prison enclosure near the central Luzon city of Cabanatuan since shortly after the landing, when Capt. Robert Lapham's Filipino guerrillas had notified Sixth Army of the camp's existence. The information stirred deep emotions among American officers, who had long been concerned about the fate of the survivors of the defense of the Philippines in early 1942. Reports of mistreatment of prisoners only heightened the anxiety and determination to rescue them if possible. By January 26, the American advance had reached Guimba, only 24 miles from the camp. After receiving a report from Lapham on the situation there, Col. Horton White, Sixth Army's intelligence chief, conferred with Krueger, who authorized a rescue. Fortunately for Sixth Army, it had special units ready for such contingencies. On January 27, Mucci and three Scout team leaders received orders to rescue the prisoners.

In the early afternoon of January 28, a reinforced company of 107 Rangers infiltrated Japanese lines and began the march to the compound with the Scouts moving in advance to reconnoiter the position. Guided by guerrillas, the Rangers hiked through forests and grasslands, narrowly avoiding a Japanese tank on the National Highway by following a ravine that ran under the road. At Balincarin on January 29, Lt. Thomas Rounsaville and Lt. William Nellist of the Scouts notified Mucci of heavy traffic around the compound, causing the Ranger chief to postpone the raid for a day. While the Rangers rested at the hamlet of Platero, a 40-minute march from the camp, two Scouts disguised as natives watched the enclosure from a hut across the road.

After receiving reports from the Scouts, Mucci issued orders for the attack. In the early evening of January 30, the Rangers began their approach march, crawling across the last mile of open rice fields to take up a position on two sides of the camp. While one platoon, on signal, eliminated the guards in the rear and on one side of the stockade, another broke through the main gate to rake the garrison's quarters with automatic fire, and a third broke into the prisoner's section and liberated the astonished captives, most of whom had to be carried to freedom. Within half an hour, the Rangers had destroyed the installation, killing about 200 Japanese guards and rescuing over 500 prisoners at the cost of two dead and seven seriously wounded. Covered by the guerrillas,

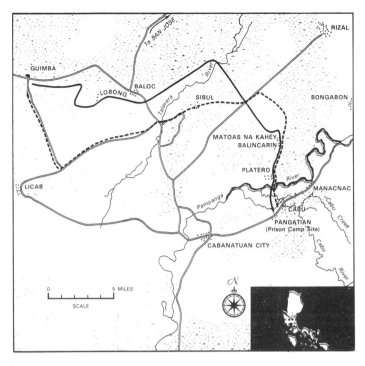

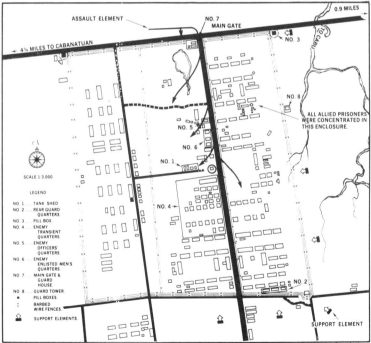

Cabanatuan Operation

U.S. Army Combat Studies Institute.

who stopped an enemy relief effort northeast of the camp, the column of Rangers and liberated prisoners finally reached friendly lines by the following morning.[13]

The returning Rangers were met by a wave of public emotion, for the raid represented, to many, a symbol that America had kept faith with its sons who were captured at Bataan and Corregidor. Reporters were waiting when the Rangers, Scouts, and former captives returned, and they lost little time in flashing news of the raid to the world. Editorials hailed the rescue, and newspaper articles described the deep emotions of men who were finally free after almost three years of captivity. Mucci contributed an article to the *Saturday Evening Post*, and *Life* magazine ran a feature story that portrayed the Rangers as "pistol packing farm boys, hand picked for just such a job as this." Within a few months of the raid, the War Department brought 10 of the Rangers home for a morale-boosting tour of war plants. In a war that was seemingly short of glamour and heroes, the romance of the raid touched a nerve among the public. However, while the rescue boosted morale on the home front, the publicity created resentment among more conventional units in Sixth Army. Members of the 6th Infantry Division, on the line near Guimba, grumbled that they would have overrun the camp within a few days in any case, and the 37th Infantry Division turned down a plan for a Ranger company to spearhead its attack on Manila, claiming that the Rangers already had enough publicity.[14]

Such comments were unjustified. Indeed, the raid at Cabanatuan represents perhaps the best conceived and executed Ranger mission of World War II. Not knowing for sure if the Japanese would remove or even kill the prisoners, Krueger and his advisors felt that they had to act before the American advance reached the camp. Having made that decision, they, as well as Mucci and his men, acted with great efficiency. The raiders benefited from good intelligence, largely the work of the guerrillas and prior reconnaissance by the Scouts. They also enjoyed a clear chain of command from Krueger down to Mucci. In the field, the Ranger commander possessed sole authority and responsibility, without interference from higher levels. His plan for the attack on the enclosure was simple but flexible, and his Rangers performed it with great skill. To be sure, the operation was greatly aided by the fluidity and confusion of the Japanese front, and, above all, by help from the guerrillas and a friendly native population. Still, future American rescue operations could have learned much from the raid, and it is amazing that the Army made so little effort to incorporate its lessons into doctrine.[15]

From Cabanatuan until the close of the campaign in Luzon, the Rangers performed a variety of military odd jobs in support of Sixth Army's drive across central Luzon and slow advance into the mountains of the north. Under Lt. Col. Robert W. Garrett, who replaced the newly promoted Mucci in February, the Rangers used groups of platoon, company, and task force size to conduct long-range reconnaissance and a few raids, mop up bypassed pockets of resistance,

Rangers of the 6th Ranger Battalion after their return from the raid on Cabanatuan (The Bettmann Archive)

and serve as headquarters guards. In February, for example, a company patrolled the dense bamboo thickets of the Cabaruan Hills for Japanese troops who were bypassed in the drive on Manila. During the spring, two companies reconnoitered in collaboration with Col. Russell W. Volckmann's guerrillas in North Luzon, while two other companies intercepted individual Japanese trying to flee through American lines to the north. Meanwhile, 10 picked Ranger noncommissioned officers drilled two companies of Filipino guerrillas. The final major combat mission came in June, when Company B and Col. Donald D. Blackburn's guerrillas infiltrated enemy lines to seize the northern port of Aparri and a nearby airfield, clearing the way for the 11th Airborne Division.[16]

Although disease and the rotation home of veterans who had served their time overseas took a heavy toll of the unit, the Rangers suffered few combat losses, largely because of Sixth Army's resolve not to misuse them as line infantry. In part, the nature of operations in the Philippines, with its rugged terrain, stress on small groups and decentralized control, and opportunities for small, elite units to make a major contribution, helps explain the disparity between Sixth Army's concept of employment and that prevailing in Europe, but the basic attitudes of the commanders constituted an even greater factor. From the beginning, Krueger and Mucci had an understanding that the Rangers would not serve on the line, and Sixth Army kept that promise. The overseer for this policy was Col. Clyde D. Eddleman, a slight young infantryman who had served in the Philippines before the war and now was Krueger's operations officer. Lacking a Ranger doctrine, his idea of Ranger tasks was so broad that it defied definition. Nonetheless, he had an intuitive sense for the capabilities and limitations of Ranger units. Keeping in close contact with Ranger commanders, he made sure that the battalion did not receive unsuitable missions or assignments to separate divisions, brigades, or regiments which might misuse them.[17]

In the Pacific, therefore, local conditions produced a different concept of employment for the Rangers. To be sure, the Pacific version was not much more clearly defined than its European counterpart, and it, too, changed with time. Instead of its original mission of amphibious raids and diversions, the 6th Ranger Battalion carried out a variety of tasks, including some, such as rear area patrols and headquarters security, that a line unit could have handled. The major difference between the concept in the Pacific and elsewhere lay in the fact that, from the beginning, higher command levels understood that the Rangers would not serve as line infantry. As in Europe, temptations undoubtedly existed to use them in such a role, particularly given Sixth Army's lack of numerical superiority over the Japanese on its front. The special treatment of the Rangers also created some resentment among members of other units, who felt that the Rangers were getting too much coddling and publicity. Nevertheless, because of the careful policy of Krueger and Eddleman, Sixth Army made productive use of the Rangers without wasting the battalion's strength on missions beyond its capabilities.

NOTES

1. Forrest B. Johnson, *Hour of Redemption: The Ranger Raid at Cabanatuan* (New York: Manor Books, 1978), pp. 119–120, 128, 132; MacArthur to Commanding General, U.S. Army Forces, Far East (USAFFE), 27 December 1943, [paraphrased copy], and MacArthur to Commanding General, Sixth Army, 28 December 1943, U.S. Army, HQ, Sixth Army, G-3 Section, Decimal File, 1943–6, Box 36, RG 338, WNRC.

2. Krueger was famous in Sixth Army for his concern for the well-being of his men. Stories abound of his rigorous inspections of mess halls and even the feet of infantrymen on the front line. Gen. Clyde D. Eddleman USA (Ret.), interview with author, Arlington, Va., 13 September 1988; William M. Leary, "Walter Krueger: MacArthur's Fighting General," in William M. Leary, ed., *We Shall Return! MacArthur's Commanders and the Defeat of Japan* (Lexington: University Press of Kentucky, 1988), pp. 62–65. For more on MacArthur and Krueger, see Stanley L. Falk, "Douglas MacArthur and the War against Japan," in William M. Leary, ed., *We Shall Return! MacArthur's Commanders and the Defeat of Japan* (Lexington: University Press of Kentucky, 1988), pp. 1–2; Leary, "Krueger," pp. 60–71, 86; D. Clayton James, *The Years of MacArthur* (Boston: Houghton Mifflin, 1975), I:557–559, 571–575, II:90–91, 153–154; USAMHI, "Senior Officers Debriefing Program: Conversations between Gen. George H. Decker USA (Ret.) and Lt. Col. Dan H. Ralls USAWC" (Carlisle, Pa., 1976), II:19–21, 31.

3. See G-2 sections in Sixth Army's reports on the Luzon operation, Box 1477, and the Leyte campaign, Box 1478, in Philippine Archives, Liberation, RG 407, MMHB, National Archives; Johnson, *Hour of Redemption*, pp. 119–120, 182; Leary, "Krueger," p. 69; U.S. War Department, Military Intelligence Service, "The Alamo Scouts—Sixth Army," in U.S. Army, Intelligence, Decimal File, 1941–8, Box 874, RG 319, WNRC; George C. Shelton, "The Alamo Scouts," *Armor* 91 (September–October 1982): 29–30; Williams, "Amphibious Scouts," pp. 151, 155.

4. Johnson, *Hour of Redemption*, p. 127; Eddleman interview; MacArthur to Commanding General, USAFFE, 27 December 1943; MacArthur to Commanding General, Sixth Army, 28 December 1943; Falk, "MacArthur," pp. 1–2; James, *Years of MacArthur*, II:153–154.

5. Shaun M. Darragh, "The Raider Experience," *Infantry* 69 (March–April 1979): 35–41; Jeter A. Isely and Philip A. Crowl, *The U.S. Marines and Amphibious War: Its Theory and Practice in the Pacific* (Princeton, N.J.: Princeton University Press, 1951), pp. 65, 154, 168, 172; James D. Ladd, *Commandos and Rangers of World War II* (New York: St. Martin's Press, 1978), pp. 95–105; Millett, *Semper Fidelis*, pp. 346, 372, 380; Robert D. Heinl, *Soldiers of the Sea: The United States Marine Corps, 1775–1962* (Annapolis, Md.: U.S. Naval Institute Press, 1962), pp. 357–358, 372; U.S. Marine Corps Historical Branch, *U.S. Marine Corps in World War II: Pearl Harbor to Guadalcanal* (Washington, D.C.: GPO, 1961), pp. 261–262, 285–286, 298, 305–306, 350; U.S. Marine Corps Historical Branch, *U.S. Marine Corps in World War II: Isolation of Rabaul* (Washington, D.C.: GPO, 1963), pp. 55, 134–138, 145, 239, 519.

6. MacArthur to Commanding General, Sixth Army, 28 December 1943. See also MacArthur to Commanding General, USAFFE, 27 December 1943; James, *Years of MacArthur*, II:345.

7. Johnson, *Hour of Redemption*, pp. 128, 132; Eddleman interview; Garrett interview; Lt. Col. Benjamin O. Turnage, Assistant G-3, Sixth Army, to G-3, Sixth Army, 13 April 1944, U.S. Army, HQ, Sixth Army, G-3 Section, Decimal File, 1943–6, Box 36, RG 338, WNRC.

8. Turnage to G-3, 13 April 1944, Brig. Gen. Edwin D. Patrick, Chief of Staff, Sixth Army, to G-3, 11 April 1944, C.F.A., Assistant G-3, to G-3, 12 April 1944, and Mucci to Krueger, 9 March 1944, in U.S. Army, HQ, Sixth Army, G-3 Section, Decimal File, 1943–6, Box 36, RG 338, WNRC; Edwin W. Hundertmark, "The Sixth Ranger Infantry Battalion," *Herald's Trumpet*, September–October 1984, p. 1; USAMHI, "Senior Officers Debriefing Program: Conversations between Lieutenant General Jonathan O. Seaman USA (Ret.) and Col. Clyde H. Patterson Jr., AWC [Army War College]" (Carlisle, Pa., 1976), II:11; Johnson, *Hour of Redemption*, pp. 114–115, 129–136; Garrett interview; Eddleman interview.

9. On one occasion, the Rangers protested to the local corps headquarters that the 33d Infantry Division was destroying its assault course by moving tanks across it. The corps commander directed the division to repair the course. See Garrett interview; see also Johnson, *Hour of Redemption*, pp. 133–135, 145–146; King, *Rangers*, p. 55; 6th Ranger Battalion file in Sixth Army, G-3 Section, Decimal File, 1943–6, Box 36, RG 338, WNRC; Hundertmark, "Sixth Ranger Infantry Battalion," pp. 3–4.

10. 6th Ranger Battalion file in Sixth Army; Garrett interview; U.S. War Department, "Table of Organization and Equipment 7–85: Ranger Infantry Battalion," 29 February 1944; and U.S. War Department, "Table of Organization 7–87: Ranger Company, Ranger Infantry Battalion," 29 February 1944, in Organizational History Branch, USAMHI; "History of the 6th Ranger Battalion in KING II Operation," WWII Ops. Reports, INBN 6–0.3, RG 407, WNRC; "Historical Data, 6th Ranger Infantry Battalion," Ranger File, Organizational History Branch, CMH; Johnson, *Hour of Redemption*, p. 131; Eddleman interview.

11. "History of the 6th Ranger Battalion in KING II Operation"; Garrett interview; Walter Krueger, *From Down Under to Nippon: The Story of the Sixth Army in World War II* (Washington, D.C.: Combat Forces Press, 1953), p. 150; "Historical Data, 6th Ranger Infantry Battalion."

12. "History of the 6th Ranger Battalion in KING II Operation" and operational reports of the 6th Ranger Battalion in WWII Ops. Reports, INBN 6–0.3, RG 407, WNRC; Simons to G-3, Sixth Army, 19 March 1945, WWII Ops. Reports, INBN 6–0.4, RG 407, WNRC; Haggerty, "Ranger Battalions," p. 256; Garrett interview; Eddleman interview.

13. "Narrative, 6th Ranger Battalion, January–July 1945," pp. 4–8, WWII Ops. Reports, INBN 6–0.3, RG 407, WNRC; Henry A. Mucci, "Rescue at Cabanatuan," *Infantry Journal* 56 (April 1945): 15–19; Henry A. Mucci, "We Swore We'd Die or Do It," *Saturday Evening Post*, 7 April 1945, pp. 18–19; Johnson, *Hour of Redemption*, pp. 179–306; King, *Rangers*, pp. 56–71.

14. Johnson, *Hour of Redemption*, pp. 327, 347; Carl Mydans, "The Rescue at Cabanatuan," *Life*, 26 February 1945, p. 34, in Lisko Papers, USAMHI; Mucci, "Rescue," pp. 15–19; Mucci, "We Swore We'd Die," pp. 18–19; "Rangers Pierce Foe's Lines, Rescue 513, Many of Bataan," *New York Times*, 2 February 1945, p. 1; "Escape from Hell," *New York Times*, 2 February 1945, p. 18; "Luzon Rangers Here," *New York Times*, 13 March 1945, p. 12; George E. Jones "Luzon Prison Camp Rescue Made in

Region Thick with Japanese," *New York Times*, 3 February 1945, p. 1; "Narrative, 6th Ranger Battalion, January–July 1945," pp. 9–10; USAMHI, "Senior Officers Debriefing Program: Conversations between General Bruce Palmer Jr. and Lieutenant Colonel James E. Shelton, Lieutenant Colonel Edward P. Smith" (Carlisle, Pa., 1976), p. 347.

15. See King, *Rangers*, pp. 56–71 for a thoughtful analysis. Postwar doctrinal documents show no sign that the Army took into account the lessons of the raid. A similar rescue mission by American paratroopers and Filipino guerrillas at Los Banos received only slightly more attention.

16. 6th Ranger Battalion operational reports in WWII Ops. Reports, INBN 6-0.3, RG 407, WNRC; "Narrative, 6th Ranger Battalion, January–July 1945," pp. 13–14; King, *Rangers*, p. 71; Eddleman interview; Garrett interview; USAMHI, "Senior Officers Debriefing Program: Palmer," p. 348; Hundertmark, "Sixth Ranger Infantry Battalion," p. 4.

17. When the battalion first came into existence, Krueger and his chief of staff at the time, Brig. Gen. Edwin D. Patrick, reportedly promised Mucci that they would not use the Rangers as line infantry. Existing documents do not reveal what the men discussed, and Mucci, the only surviving participant, declined to be interviewed for this book. USAMHI, "Senior Officers Debriefing Program: Palmer," p. 346; USAMHI, "Senior Officers Oral History Program: General Walter T. Kerwin USA Retired. Interviewed by Colonel D. A. Doehle USA," Project 80-2, 2 vols. (Carlisle, Pa., 1980), I:197; Eddleman interview; Garrett interview; Leary, "Krueger," p. 71; "Eddleman, Clyde David, Maj. Gen.," *Generals of the Army*, February 1953, p. 24.

6

The Rangers in Eclipse

When World War II came to a close in September 1945 with the Japanese surrender aboard the battleship *Missouri* in Tokyo Bay, the United States stood alone as the world's most powerful nation. While other nations had contributed mightily to the defeat of the Axis powers, the United States possessed not only powerful armed forces and a heartland untouched by war but also a monopoly on the most devastating weapon in human history. Internationalists argued that the nation must accept a more active role in the world. Nevertheless, most Americans, while exultant in victory and proud of their country's new status, looked forward to a period of calm and prosperity, free from global respon- sibilities, and demanded rapid demobilization of the armies and navies. The Army's staff had worked out a plan for the orderly discharge of troops, based on a point system that rewarded length and arduousness of service, but under pressure from Congress, the public, and the soldiers themselves, it soon released all men with over two years of service. By June 1947, the Army had shrunk from a wartime peak of over 8 million troops to about 980,000.[1]

To return to peacetime levels, the Army inactivated hundreds of units, including the Rangers. In Europe, the 2d and 5th Ranger Battalions were serving as police for the military government and marking time with drill and athletics when, in June 1945, theater headquarters decided to inactivate them. At Sullivan's request, the War Department returned the two units to the United States before inactivating them in late October. The Army had planned to use some of the veterans of the 2d and 5th as fillers for the 6th Ranger Battalion in the invasion of Japan, but the Japanese surrendered before they could reach the Pacific. Instead of spearheading Sixth Army's assault, the 6th Ranger Battalion disembarked peacefully at Japan's Wakayama Beach on September 25. While serving as guards and ceremonial troops at the old capital of Kyoto during the fall, the battalion was losing large numbers of its veterans to demobilization, and many of the bored, young replacements who remained were creating disciplinary problems. Concerned about the unit's reputation, Garrett requested inactivation, and MacArthur agreed. The 6th Ranger Battalion was officially inactivated in the Philippines on December 30.

In retrospect, the lack of prolonged consideration regarding the inactivation of the Rangers is striking but not surprising. Demobilization required the Army to inactivate most of its units, and the Ranger battalions, for a number of reasons, figured to be prime candidates. In both Europe and Japan, they were struggling to maintain their strength levels and standards as veterans accumulated enough points to return home and were replaced by whatever fillers Ranger officers could muster from a shrinking replacement pool. Furthermore, occupation authorities could see no special need for Rangers in a military government. Given these circumstances, and the fact that military planners had never envisioned a role for the Rangers beyond a few temporary wartime tasks, even Ranger leaders were urging the inactivation of their units.[2]

Thus, the Rangers of World War II faded into history, leaving a distinguished but limited legacy and mixed assessments of their value. Some enthusiasts have contended that Ranger missions provided a laboratory for new methods, a claim that has only partial validity at best. While commando operations influenced the program at the Army's Amphibious Training Center and the Dieppe raid provided critical lessons for the cross-Channel invasion, the Army, over time, deferred to the Navy and Marines in the development of amphibious doctrine. In North Africa, Italy, and the Pacific, field commanders praised Ranger expertise in night operations, and both Army Ground Forces and the Infantry School requested information on a system of colored lights that was developed by Darby to coordinate movements at night. A War Department observer in Europe found that 8 of the 10 divisions he visited had become so disgusted with the performance of their combat patrols that they had organized ad hoc "Ranger" units to carry out those tasks. Still, while such instances show the widespread respect for Ranger skills in patrols and night operations, Ranger methods did not have any lasting influence on Army doctrine for such activities, nor did the Army's inadequate doctrinal process devote much attention to the Ranger concept in general.[3]

Part of the reason for the Rangers' lack of influence on doctrine lay in their blurred image within the postwar Army. An occasional postwar study accurately described them as raiding or amphibious specialists. However, as the controversy over the proposed Ranger Group would show, the Ranger concept, for several officers, embraced almost any mission behind enemy lines, including assistance to guerrillas as well as commando raids. Others simply viewed Rangers as shock troops, capable of the toughest infantry missions. Ranger heroics at Salerno, Monte La Difensa, Normandy, Cabanatuan, and numerous other locales impressed these officers with their capabilities, if not with the merits of raids or patrols as part of an overall strategy. In the end, this view of

Rangers as elite infantry ensured that their most enduring legacy from World War II would lie in the realm of training. The mass indoctrination of soldiers in Ranger conditioning and methods held an appeal for orthodox soldiers who respected the quality of fighter produced by Ranger training and also felt that this training lay within the abilities of the average recruit.[4]

Ranger training held an especially great attraction given the continuing concern in the Army over the quality of its infantry. While victory confirmed the superiority of the American fighting man in the eyes of many professional soldiers, two postwar analyses raised some disturbing questions. One study prepared by veterans of the Army's Information and Education Division found that the Army had used the infantry as a dumping ground for soldiers who had passed the necessary physical standards but did not satisfy any other test. Despite efforts to improve the infantry's image through higher pay, publicity, and decorations, its status had remained low. Those concerned about the result on the battlefield found confirmation for their fears in S. L. A. Marshall's *Men Against Fire*. Drawing on after-action interviews with combat personnel in Europe and the Pacific, Marshall found that, due to fear, religious inhibitions, or other factors, less than 25 percent of those who were engaged actually fired their weapons. His conclusion that the same soldiers bore the burden in each battle could only strengthen the arguments of antielitists against the concentration of this valuable nucleus in a few special units.[5]

For all the anxiety over the quality of its infantry, the Army was more absorbed with other developments in the last years of the decade. By 1947, postwar optimism had given way to concern over Communist expansion in Eastern Europe, the Near East, and Asia. In March, President Harry S Truman pledged American aid to free peoples resisting subjugation by armed minorities and outside pressures. This policy of "containment," which soon became the cornerstone of American foreign policy, was supported by the Marshall Plan, which provided economic aid to a devastated Western Europe, and the North Atlantic Treaty Organization (NATO), a military alliance. To deter attack, in the absence of sizable conventional forces, NATO relied on American possession of the atomic bomb, a weapon whose immense implications policymakers were just beginning to grasp. Nevertheless, most Americans confidently assumed that any act of aggression would result in an all-out war in which their atomic monopoly would ensure victory.

Given the emphasis on air-atomic warfare, the Army faced a struggle to maintain some semblance of a fighting force. Determined to balance the national budget, Truman calculated the military's share by subtracting all other expenditures from revenues, and Secretary of Defense Louis Johnson favored the Air Force in his allocation of this remainder. To cut costs, the Army staff reduced manpower levels, eliminated many of the support units necessary for sustained combat, and deferred modernization of old equipment. By 1950, the 591,000-man Army represented little more than a police force. Of its 10 understrength divisions, only the 82d Airborne Division was even remotely ready for battle. In doctrine, as well as equipment, the Army looked back to World War II, focusing on a European conflict of mass armies, firepower, and mobility. One finds little evidence of thought on the problems posed by limited wars, insurgencies, or rapid deployment to global flash points.

Under these circumstances, the Army's lack of Ranger units in the postwar period hardly seems surprising. From time to time, an enthusiast would propose the formation of units of amphibious scouts or raiders, but such advocacy was rare. Many more officers disparaged Rangers as arrogant, reckless mavericks who performed tasks that any line unit with special training could handle, a view that the misuse of commandos in the Greek Civil War seemed to confirm. Although the inactivation, rather than outright disbandment, of the World War II battalions indicates that the Army's leaders perceived some future role for Rangers, limits on funds and manpower discouraged any inclination to form Ranger units. Military leaders believed that they could not afford to waste scarce troop spaces and resources on such formations, particularly in the absence of a strategic rationale. Devers, who, as chief of Army Ground Forces, was responsible for Army organization and doctrine during the postwar period, could hardly be expected to push for Ranger units. During World War II, he had shown little hesitation in disbanding similar formations when they no longer appeared to serve a clear purpose. He and other postwar military leaders were too concerned with universal military training, service unification, and the role of a mass army in an atomic war to devote much thought to seemingly esoteric Ranger operations.[6]

On those rare occasions when the Army considered Ranger operations, it lumped them with the activities of the Office of Strategic Services (OSS) in World War II. The OSS was the brainchild of William J. Donovan, a hero of World War I, corporate lawyer, and friend of President Roosevelt. After watching both sides employ special operations to good effect, he persuaded the president, in July 1941, to form an agency for the collection and analysis of data and "supplemental activities." The new organization's role soon expanded far beyond intelligence gathering to include propaganda, sabotage, aid to partisans, and commando raids, often by military personnel. For commando raids and aid to guerrillas, the OSS relied on "Operational Groups" (OGs), elite 15-man teams vaguely similar to Ranger units but with additional skills, including parachute qualification and fluency in a foreign language. While many of their missions resembled those of the Rangers, Donovan distinguished between them, stating that Rangers operated against the enemy's front, while OGs "fitted into the pattern of OSS activities behind enemy lines."[7]

Donovan's distinction between Rangers and OGs was lost on the Army, which viewed with suspicion an agency working outside the conventional services but claiming a charter to perform quasi-military operations. Reflecting the common confusion of Ranger and partisan concepts, Maj. Gen. George V.

Strong, the Army's intelligence chief, argued that guerrilla warfare, if conducted at all, should consist of raids by regular task forces. The Joint Chiefs of Staff attempted to settle the issue by granting responsibility for guerrilla warfare to the OSS as long as its teams served only as nuclei for partisans, but this solution hardly satisfied everyone. The OSS still had to justify itself to the theater chiefs, and MacArthur, for one, never allowed the OSS to operate in his command. Nonetheless, Donovan's personal influence with the president ensured the agency's survival until the end of the war and Roosevelt's death. In October 1945, President Truman, largely at the behest of the services, directed the disbandment of the OSS.[8]

Having eliminated its main rival in the field of special operations, the Army did little more with the subject until its civilian leadership nudged it into action. In August 1946, Secretary of War Robert P. Patterson suggested that Army Ground Forces consider the formation of an airborne reconnaissance formation similar to those developed by the OSS. Patterson noted the value of the OSS's airborne reconnaissance agents and, implicitly, the OGs, and he directed Army Ground Forces to produce a study on the employment, organization, and training of a similar unit.

Although skeptical, the Army could not ignore the wishes of its civilian leader. The study that Army Ground Forces produced in December recommended an experimental airborne reconnaissance unit of 6 officers and 35 enlisted men. At the prompting of the Army Staff's intelligence section, which viewed the idea with great enthusiasm, Lt. Gen. Charles P. Hall, the Army's director of organization and training, approved the study in April and ordered Army Ground Forces to develop a table of organization, tactics, techniques, and training for airborne reconnaissance units. For an organization, Hall suggested a flexible cellular arrangement, which a commander could alter depending on the mission. Once Army Ground Forces had prepared such a table, the War Department would activate the formation. Thus, by April 1947, it appeared that the new unit would soon become a reality.[9]

This initial impetus soon dissipated in endless discussions as the Army struggled to grasp the concept behind the proposed formation. Patterson retired as secretary in July 1947, and his successor, Kenneth C. Royall, was not as inclined to push the subject. Not until the summer of 1948 did Army Field Forces, the successor to Army Ground Forces, produce a study on a "Ranger Group" of 115 officers and 135 men. Assigned at the theater level but operating under an army and army group, the group would carry out a hodgepodge of missions ranging from psychological warfare and espionage to reconnaissance, raids, and aid to resistance movements. In short, the Army tried to combine in one unit all the missions performed by the Rangers and OSS without considering the different types of individuals and training needed for activities as dissimilar as the dissemination of propaganda and commando raids. As pointed out by Lt. Col. W. R. "Ray" Peers, the former chief of OSS Detachment 101 in Burma, such a unit would face problems when it tried to deal with the vast scope and political nature of special missions at the theater level.[10]

Largely at Peers's suggestion, organizational planners focused on the development of a more conventional unit which would perform deep reconnaissance for an army headquarters, but the concept still made little headway. In an attempt to speed the process, in August 1948, Army Intelligence urged the formation of two "Ranger Groups," to be organized along the lines of the Alamo Scouts. Maj. Gen. Harold R. Bull, Hall's successor as director of organization and training, agreed to form a group once troop spaces became available after June 1949, but he pointed out that Army Field Forces still had not produced a table of organization for the new unit. There the matter rested for the next two years, lacking any sense of urgency. When war broke out once again in June 1950, Army Field Forces was still examining the concept of a Ranger Group.[11]

The endless discussions over the Ranger Group reflected the Army's lack of any sense of a need for Ranger units or even a clear idea of the term "Ranger," throughout the postwar years. Rather than inspire discussion on the possibilities of such activities, Ranger operations in World War II generated little interest in an Army that was simultaneously complacent in its orientation toward mass warfare but uncertain of its role in the Atomic Age. As yet, the Army was devoting little thought to the idea of limited war, let alone assessing the contribution that Rangers might make in such a contingency. Instead, military planners focused on the prospect of an all-out war, especially in a European context. In such a conflict, Ranger operations, in the view of the planners, were sideshows, with only a marginal impact on the outcome. When, under pressure from its civilian leader, the Army considered special operations, it soon showed its inadequate grasp of the subject, attempting to combine within one "Ranger" formation a wide range of conventional, unconventional, overt, covert, tactical, and strategic missions. The idea of a Ranger Group undoubtedly would have died in committee, had the Korean War not intervened.

NOTES

1. Weigley, *History of the United States Army*, pp. 486, 599–600; B.C. Mossman, "Peace Becomes Cold War, 1945–1950," in Maurice Matloff, ed., *American Military History*, 2d ed., Army Historical Series (Washington: OCMH, 1973), p. 530; Frederick F. Siegel, *Troubled Journey: From Pearl Harbor to Ronald Reagan* (New York: Hill and Wang, 1984), pp. 26–27, 35; William E. Leuchtenburg, *A Troubled Feast: American Society since 1945*, rev. ed. (Boston: Little Brown, 1979), p. 23.

2. 2d Ranger Battalion's report for May 1945, WWII Ops. Reports, INBN 2-0.3, Box 21073, RG 407, WNRC; "Narrative, 6th Ranger Battalion, January–July 1945"; HQ, 6th Ranger Battalion to Commanding General, Sixth Army, 21 December 1945, WWII Ops. Reports, INBN 6-0.3, RG 407, WNRC; Garrett interview; Greene interview; William G. Weaver, "Demobilizing the Ground Army 1 September 1945–10 March

1948," Studies in the History of Army Ground Forces during the Demobilization Period, no. 2, unpublished manuscript (Washington, D.C.: Historical Section, Army Field Forces, 1948), pp. 9–10; Sullivan to Commanding General, ETO, 24 June 1945; Lt. Col. Richard P. Fisk, Assistant Adjutant General, ETO, to Adjutant General, 15 July 1945; and Adjutant General to Commanding General, U.S. Forces, European Theater (Rear), 7 August 1945, in U.S. Army, Operations Division, Decimal File, 1942–1945, 370.5 PTO, RG 165, MMHB, National Archives; lineage statements for 2d, 5th, and 6th Ranger Battalions, Organizational History Branch, CMH.

3. Altieri, *Spearheaders*, pp. 172–173; Williams, "Amphibious Scouts," pp. 155–157; Amphibious Training Command to Col. John W. O'Daniel, 19 June 1942, John W. O'Daniel Papers, USAMHI; USAMHI, "Senior Officers Debriefing Program: Conversations between General Theodore J. Conway and Colonel Robert F. Ensslin" (Carlisle, Pa., 1977), p. 19; Albert N. Garland, "Amphibious Doctrine Training," Studies in the History of Army Ground Forces during the Demobilization Period, no. 6, unpublished manuscript (Washington, D.C.: OCMH, 1949), pp. 24–25, 37, 91; Brig. Gen. George H. Weems, Assistant Commandant, Infantry School, to Darby, 27 May 1944, and Darby to Weems [draft], in WWII Ops. Reports, INBN 1-0.3, RG 407, WNRC; HQ, Army Ground Forces, 18 May 1944, Subject: Notes on Interview with Col. William Darby; and report of Col. Gilbert E. Parker, Infantry Observer, 2 October 1945, in HRC 314.7 Ranger Battalion, Historical Records Branch, CMH; Fredendall to Eisenhower, 10 March 1943, Report no. 47; extracts from report on the Italian campaign, December 1943–March 1944 by Maj. A. G. Crist, Army Ground Forces Observer, Report no. 87; Pacific Warfare Board, "Battle Experiences against the Japanese: What the Rangers Think," Report no. 241; and Night Operations in Pacific Ocean Areas, 1 April 1945, Report no. 284, in Army Ground Forces, Intelligence Reports, Numerical File, 1943–6, RG 337, MMHB, National Archives. For more on the Army's doctrinal process, see Stephen L. Bowman, "The Evolution of United States Army Doctrine for Counterinsurgency Warfare from World War II to the Commitment of Combat Units in Vietnam" (Ph.D. dissertation, Duke University, 1985), pp. 48–65.

4. Williams, "Amphibious Scouts," pp. 155–157; Dobson interview.

5. Stouffer, *Combat and Its Aftermath*, I:309–310; S. L. A. Marshall, *Men against Fire: The Problem of Battle Command in Future War* (Washington, D.C.: Combat Forces Press, 1947), pp. 54–60, 78–80. For an example of postwar thought in the Army on the quality of American infantrymen, see USAMHI, "Senior Officers Debriefing Program: Conversations between General Ralph E. Haines, Jr. and Capt. William J. Hudson" (Carlisle, Pa., 1976), I:21. Recent research has raised serious questions about Marshall's evidence, but that does not change the enormous influence of the book when it first appeared; see Roger J. Spiller, "S. L. A. Marshall and the Ratio of Fire," *RUSI Journal* (Winter 1988): 63–71; Fredric Smoler, "The Secret of the Soldiers Who Didn't Wish to Shoot," *American Heritage* 40 (March 1989): 37–45.

6. Mossman, "Peace Becomes Cold War," pp. 530–540; Millett and Maslowski, *Common Defense*, pp. 472, 477–478; Robert A. Doughty, *The Evolution of U.S. Army Tactical Doctrine, 1946–1976*, Leavenworth Papers no. 1 (Fort Leavenworth, Kans.: Combat Studies Institute, 1979), pp. 2–7; T. R. Fehrenbach, *This Kind of War: A Study in Unpreparedness* (New York: Macmillan, 1963), pp. 87, 91; Blair and Bradley, *General's Life*, p. 474; Weigley, *History of the United States Army*, pp. 489, 497, 501–503, 506; USAMHI, "Senior Officers Debriefing Program: Conversations between

Gen. Barksdale Hamlett and Col. Jack Ridgway and LTC Paul Walter" (Carlisle, Pa., 1976), IV:22; USAMHI, "Senior Officers Debriefing Program: Palmer," p. 124; USAMHI, "Senior Officers Oral History Project: Kerwin," pp. 197–198; Williams, "Amphibious Scouts," pp. 156–157; Aaron Bank, *From OSS to Green Berets* (Novato, Calif.: Presidio Press, 1986), p. 140; Charles M. Simpson III, *Inside the Green Berets* (Novato, Calif.: Presidio Press, 1983), p. 14; Garrett interview; Larry E. Cable, *Conflict of Myths: The Development of American Counterinsurgency Doctrine and the Vietnam War* (New York: New York University Press, 1986), pp. 18–19.

7. Donovan quoted in Alfred H. Paddock, Jr., *U.S. Army Special Warfare: Its Origins: Psychological and Unconventional Warfare, 1941–1952* (Washington, D.C.: National Defense University Press, 1982), p. 28; see also pp. 24–28; Kermit Roosevelt, *War Report of the OSS*, 2 vols. (New York: Walker, 1976), I:5–8, 16, 26, 225; Stewart Alsop and Thomas Braden, *The OSS and American Espionage*, 2d ed. (New York: Harcourt, Brace and World, 1964), p. 9; "OSS Missions and Functions," JCS 155/11/D, 27 October 1943, U.S. Army, Intelligence, Decimal File, 1941–1948, 370.5, 1–31–42, to 373.2, Box 874, RG 319, WNRC; Anthony Cave Brown, *The Last Hero: Wild Bill Donovan* (New York: Times Books, 1982), p. 473.

8. Paddock, *Special Warfare*, pp. 26–27, 30–33; "Special Operations Branch," Appendix A, JCS 155/4/D, U.S. Army Intelligence, Decimal File, 1941–1948, Box 874, RG 319, WNRC.

9. Maj. Gen. S. J. Chamberlin, Director of Intelligence, to Adjutant General, 19 August 1946; Col. L. R. Forney, Chief, Security Group, to Chief, Combat Intelligence and Training Group, 18 June 1946; Lt. Gen. C. P. Hall, Director of Organization and Training, to Commanding General, Army Ground Forces, 9 April 1947; Director of Intelligence to Director, Organization and Training, 6 March 1947; and Col. C. V. Allan, Chief, Training Group, to Commanding General, Army Ground Forces, 27 January 1947, in U.S. Army Intelligence, Decimal File, 1941–1948, Box 874, RG 319, WNRC.

10. Farris, Intelligence Section, Army Field Forces, to Lt. Col. Roland M. Gleszer, Intelligence Division, General Staff [undated], and Peers to Maj. Ernest Samusson, Jr., Intelligence Division, Army Field Forces, 9 July 1948, in U.S. Army, Intelligence, Decimal File, 1941–1948, Box 874, RG 319, WNRC; Paddock, *Special Warfare*, pp. 70–71; Bank, *From OSS to Green Berets*, pp. 143–144, 147.

11. "The Airborne Reconnaissance Unit??" 9 August 1948; Director of Intelligence, General Staff, to Organization and Training, General Staff, 9 August 1948; and Bull to Director of Intelligence, 13 September 1948, in U.S. Army, Intelligence, Decimal File, 1941–1948, Box 874, RG 319, WNRC; Conference Notes on Marauder Company, 7 September 1950, U.S. Army, Assistant Chief of Staff, G-3, Operations, Records Section, Decimal File, March 1950–1951, 322 Ranger, Box 380, RG 319, MMHB, National Archives. During conferences on formation of the Ranger companies, conferees discussed the table of distribution of a proposed unit whose description matched that of the Ranger Group. Similar indications that the idea was still floating around Army Field Forces can be found in Waller B. Booth, "The Pattern That Got Lost," *Army* 31 (April 1981): 62–67.

7

Raiders for Korea

Those who lived through both events recalled an eerie resemblance between June 25, 1950, and another Sunday morning almost nine years earlier. Even more than Pearl Harbor, the North Korean invasion caught Americans by surprise. The Pentagon had not prepared any war plans to deal with a Communist attack on South Korea, an understandable omission given Secretary of State Dean Acheson's public exclusion of Korea from the American defensive perimeter. Nonetheless, the invasion seemed to represent such a clear Soviet challenge that American leaders felt compelled to help the hard-pressed South Koreans. Aided by a fortuitous Soviet boycott of the United Nations Security Council in protest of the exclusion of Communist China, the United States secured UN approval of a series of resolutions authorizing the use of force to repel the attack. At first, member nations hoped that air and naval power would be sufficient, but it soon became clear that troops would be necessary to halt the North Korean onslaught. On June 30, President Truman approved the deployment to Korea of two divisions from Eighth Army in Japan.[1]

Like the rest of the American military, Eighth Army was physically and psychologically unprepared for war. For most of the previous five years, it had concentrated on administration, police work, and other occupation duties, to the detriment of combat readiness. American soldiers, largely youngsters lured by the GI Bill and other benefits, inhabited a comfortable world of regular workdays, dinner parties, formal dances, and athletics. Many had brought their families to Japan, while others lived with Japanese women outside the bases. After transferring most of its occupation functions to the Japanese in late 1949, Eighth Army finally made training a priority, but understrength units, equipment shortages, lack of sizable training areas, and the absence of any sense of urgency hindered the effort. When the call came to deploy to Korea, American soldiers lacked not only certain basic skills but also the physical and mental toughness for

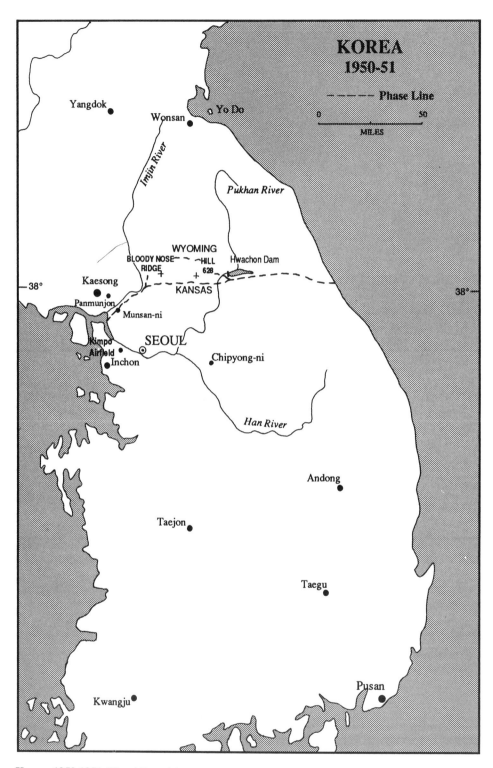

Korea, 1950-1951 (Sherri Dowdy)

combat. They went to war confident that the North Koreans would flee at the first sight of American troops.[2]

Far from running, the North Koreans jolted the Americans out of their complacency with their unorthodox tactics and brutal atrocities. They drove Eighth Army's initial arrivals down the peninsula with a combination of double envelopments of American positions and raids against communications. Fifteen-man parties, disguised as refugees and transporting their disassembled weapons by cart and porter, infiltrated to positions behind or adjacent to American lines. Assembling their rifles, machine guns, and mortars, they established roadblocks, ambushed convoys, raided command posts and artillery positions, and blew up bridges. The terror that they created in the American rear was heightened by a ruthless disregard for what Americans considered to be the rules of civilized warfare. They shot prisoners, mutilated the dead, used flags of truce as a ruse, and even drove helpless refugees before them as a shield for their assaults.

Such tactics shocked and angered the Americans, but they could not deny their effectiveness. For an army that had molded its doctrine and equipment for mechanized, mass warfare on the plains of Western Europe, such activities represented an especially formidable challenge. The rugged terrain of the Korean peninsula restricted tanks and trucks to the valleys, and poorly conditioned American infantry showed little inclination to forsake their transportation and venture into the mountains. Flanks and lines of supply, on which Eighth Army's mechanized formations were so dependent, were exposed to hit-and-run attacks from the Communist-controlled high ground. American officers who, before the war, had viewed raids with distaste and dismissed the threat that they posed now wanted to turn these tactics against the North Koreans. Since the draftees who manned most American formations did not possess the skills to carry out such tasks, special units would clearly be necessary.[3]

During the crisis of late summer, as United Nations forces withdrew toward the port of Pusan on the southern tip of the peninsula, MacArthur's Far East Command (FECOM) in Tokyo was flooded with suggestions for ad hoc raiding units. As in World War II, MacArthur was receptive to the notion of special formations, and a number were formed. To carry out amphibious raids against enemy communications north of the 38th Parallel, FECOM combined a Royal Marine Commando, a 12-man party from the Royal Navy, a raider company of former staff personnel, and South Koreans to form a "Special Activities Group." In practice, SAG, as a unit, performed few of the missions for which it was designed. After an abortive attempt to seize Kimpo Airfield in support of the Inchon landing, SAG hunted guerrillas and served on the line until its disbandment in April 1951. Throughout its brief history, SAG struggled with equipment shortages, an inadequate staff, and lack of awareness of its mission, problems reflecting the rushed, improvised circumstances of its formation.[4]

In the rush to form special units during the late summer of 1950, it was inevitable that a bright staff officer would suggest a unit along the lines of the

Rangers of World War II. When Lt. Col. John H. McGee of Eighth Army's staff proposed the formation of a Ranger company, however, considerable confusion arose over the vague meaning of the term "Ranger." McGee apparently wanted a unit that could reconnoiter a salient on the right flank of the developing UN defensive perimeter above Pusan, and the dispatch that Eighth Army's staff forwarded to FECOM called for a formation similar to the Alamo Scouts of World War II. FECOM, nonetheless, adopted a table for a Ranger company as the basis for the unit's organization. Under orders not to recruit scarce riflemen, Lt. Ralph Puckett, a brash, young airborne officer who had volunteered for service in Korea, combed the clerks, cooks, typists, and mechanics of FECOM for volunteers. Two of his classmates from West Point became platoon leaders. After its organization in Japan in late August, the 8213th Army Unit, or Eighth Army Ranger Company as it became known, deployed to Korea, where it was attached to the 25th Infantry Division.[5]

By late August, UN forces had managed to establish a stable defensive line along a 140-mile front in the southeast corner of the Korean peninsula. For the first time, Lt. Gen. Walton H. Walker's Eighth Army could form a continuous battle line with a reserve and no exposed flanks, and it responded by repulsing repeated North Korean attacks. With each week, the UN position grew stronger as reinforcements arrived from the United States and the other United Nations. As the situation improved, MacArthur pondered an amphibious landing at the port of Inchon, deep in the rear of the North Korean Army, to cut the enemy's communications and force his retreat from the Pusan area. Believing the proposal to be too risky, the Joint Chiefs of Staff delegated two of their number, Gen. J. Lawton Collins of the Army and Adm. Forrest P. Sherman of the Navy, to go to the Far East, examine the situation, and hear MacArthur's case.

After meeting MacArthur in Tokyo on August 21, Collins flew to Korea the next morning to visit Eighth Army and confer with its leadership. Following a briefing at army headquarters, Collins and Walker toured the front lines and talked with local commanders, who convinced the chief of staff that Eighth Army could hold its position. From the standpoint of the Ranger concept, the trip was important for another reason. The problem of enemy infiltration frequently surfaced in the briefing and discussions with field commanders and staff operations officers at the corps and army levels. Available evidence does not reveal who originally proposed the idea of Ranger units as a counter to North Korean tactics, but the concept had certainly been prevalent in FECOM for some time. It must have held an especially great attraction in late August, given the overextended state of the enemy's supply lines. Whatever the impetus, Collins came back to the United States with a determination that the U.S. Army should revive Ranger formations as soon as possible.[6]

While Collins might have been converted to the notion of Ranger units, his subsequent actions demonstrated that he did not really understand the concept underlying their use. Like other American officers of the time, he had developed

Gen. J. Lawton Collins (U.S. Army photograph)

his concepts of warfare during the 1920s and 1930s, when Army schools wei a
preparing students for another mass conflict in Europe. During World War II,
he had won acclaim as the aggressive corps commander who had spearheaded
First Army's advance across Europe, and his performance in various roles since
then had confirmed his reputation and rise to the post of chief of staff. A disciple
of Marshall, he admired his former chief's openness to new ideas, but he was
not a deep thinker. He saw in North Korean infiltration tactics a major challenge
to the Army's tactical doctrine and, thus, was receptive to proposals to develop
the Army's capability in that area. However, his response to the problem showed
haste and little grasp of its complexities. Although he was not anti-Ranger, his
lack of experience with Ranger operations was obvious.[7]

Once he had returned to the United States, Collins, on August 29,
directed the formation of "marauder companies" on an experimental basis. "One
of the major lessons to be learned from the Korean fighting," he stated, "appears

to be the fact that the North Koreans have made very successful use of small groups, trained, armed, and equipped for the specific purpose of infiltrating into our lines and attacking command posts and artillery positions. During the latter stages of the war with Germany, the Germans developed similar units. The results obtained from such units warrant specific action to develop such units in the American Army." Collins wanted each division to have a lightly armed and equipped marauder company supplied with jeeps to infiltrate through enemy lines and attack command posts, artillery, tank parks, and key communications installations. Volunteers would receive extra pay and instruction at a special training section to be established at the Infantry Center.[8]

Sadly, the directive showed a lack of deep consideration of the issues involved in the rush to get a unit into the field. The name "marauder" obviously referred to the Marauders of World War II, but these companies would be very different from Merrill's combat teams. They bore even less resemblance to the *Brandenburgers*, an elite German SS unit which, disguised in American uniforms, had created havoc in the Allied rear during the Battle of the Bulge. In his haste, Collins had obviously confused several different concepts of raiders, a common phenomenon in the Army of the period.[9] The mission statement in the directive was clear enough, but the organizational provision, assigning the companies to divisions, again showed a lack of thought and boded ill for the employment of the companies. In short, the dispatch reflected the quick, ad hoc nature of the response to the infiltration crisis, as well as the American belief that courage, ingenuity, and skillful improvisation would make up for any deficiencies in the basic concept.

Responding to Collins's directive, representatives of Army Field Forces, the Army Staff, and the Central Intelligence Agency met at the Pentagon on September 6. The concept of a Ranger Group, which was still circulating in the offices of Army Field Forces, was shelved, apparently because the conferees thought that the proposed companies could handle the group's mission of reconnaissance. Focusing on these companies, which they designated as "Ranger," they made arrangements for a special training section, which would organize and train one company for deployment to the Far East as soon as possible. Three other companies would follow. All four would require their recruits to be parachutists, not due to mission requirements but because their elite status would be enhanced by the extra pay and prestige that airborne qualification conferred in the Army of the 1950s. To save time in parachute training, the first group of volunteers would come from the 82d Airborne Division. Details on doctrine and arrangements for intelligence, communications, and interservice coordination would be worked out later.[10]

While Army Field Forces hastened to carry out the directive, Collins personally selected Col. John G. Van Houten to head the prospective Ranger Training Section. A graduate of the University of Georgia, the Infantry Center, and the Command and General Staff College, Van Houten had compiled a distinguished record during World War II as commander of an infantry regiment in the 75th Infantry Division and as chief of staff of the 9th Infantry Division in the European theater. After the war, he had served as a staff officer with Second Army, attended the National War College, and taught at the Command and General Staff College. A veteran of considerable combat, he was regarded as one of the most promising young colonels in the Army, but he lacked experience with Rangers or even an airborne qualification. Given the unruly reputation of the Rangers in World War II, Collins may well have wanted an outsider with Van Houten's reputation as a disciplinarian to bring the Rangers to heel. Despite the new commander's conventional attitude toward special operations when he arrived at the Infantry Center, he proved receptive to new ideas and became a forceful advocate of the Ranger concept.[11]

Arriving at Fort Benning on September 21, Van Houten established the Ranger Training Section with headquarters in the Harmony Church area, home of the present-day Ranger Department and about eight miles from the main post. Most of the 50 instructors and administrative personnel who were initially available came from the Infantry Center, but additional help soon arrived as Army personnel officers screened records for those who had served with the Rangers, Merrill's Marauders, 1st Special Service Force, and OSS in World War II. Van Houten's deputy and the man directly responsible for training, Col. Edwin Walker, had commanded the 1st Special Service Force in World War II. Like many who were involved in special operations, he possessed little regard for the fine points of garrison protocol, an attitude that occasionally brought him into conflict with Van Houten. Among the staff, Maj. William Bond, formerly of Darby's Rangers, had provided guidance to the Infantry Center when the directive to form the section had first arrived at Fort Benning. The corps of instructors also included Maj. James Y. Adams, Capt. "Bull" Simons of the 6th Ranger Battalion, colorful Capt. Wilbur "Coal Bin Willie" Wilson, and intense, young Maj. John K. Singlaub, who had parachuted into France for the OSS.[12]

By the beginning of October, the first recruits had begun to arrive. Selection teams from Army Field Forces had solicited enlisted men from airborne units, particularly the 82d and 11th Airborne Divisions, and officer volunteers from jump-qualified personnel throughout the country. To avoid the perennial problem of misfits, Army Field Forces asked the various headquarters in the continental United States to conduct preliminary screening. The selection teams interviewed the prescreened volunteers, looking for rugged 19-year-olds with initiative, high aptitude-test scores, and a knack for hand-to-hand combat. Those who were rejected by the teams returned to their old units. Among the airborne formations, recruiters found numerous cocky, young paratroopers who were eager to escape the routine of garrison duty and see some action, but, despite prescreening, not all the volunteers necessarily represented elite troops. One commander even sent an officer to the Rangers for receiving a parking ticket.[13]

In contrast to the situation in World War II, blacks could volunteer for the Rangers, and many did. Although President Truman, in 1948, had directed equal treatment and opportunity in the armed forces, considerable resistance to integration remained among many officers who were concerned that blacks could not compete with whites, feared the effect on morale and efficiency, and believed that the Army should not be used as an instrument of social change. Thus, the Army moved slowly to integrate below the battalion level, and, in June 1950, most blacks still served in segregated units. When the Army issued its call for Rangers, black paratroopers in one of those units, the 3d Battalion of the 505th Airborne Infantry, responded with enthusiasm. Of the 491 enlisted recruits who went through training at Fort Benning in mid-October, 27 percent were black. In accordance with Army policy, they formed a separate unit, the 2d Ranger Infantry Company (Abn.), which impressed observers with its performance in training.[14]

Training reflected the range of concepts embodied in the term "Ranger" at the time. The product of intense debate among the instructors, with their different backgrounds, it included such traditional Ranger subjects as weapons, demolitions, fieldcraft, communications, amphibious assaults, close combat, air support, and supply methods, including aerial resupply. At the same time, it covered escape and evasion, cooperation with natives, and the language and characteristics of the target area, which were topics closer to the OSS concept. To cover this array of material, the center allotted 48 hours per week for 6 weeks, and, even then, it did not include everything that the instructors would have desired. As in past Ranger courses, conditioning and realism received considerable emphasis. Soldiers who failed to finish the 50-mile speed marches could board a white-flagged jeep, return to quarters, and leave the center before the other recruits returned. Over 50 percent of the training took place at night, and the promiscuous use of live ammunition, including artillery rounds, concerned more safety-conscious officers at the post. The course culminated in "Hell Week," in which trainees performed a low-level jump, organized into small parties, and blew up targets over a 49-square-mile area.[15]

While the first four companies were training, Army Field Forces and the Army Staff, in mid-October, produced a paper organization for a light raiding unit with the firepower to hit hard and fast at the objective. The organization, which provided for a company headquarters of 6 personnel and three platoons of 1 officer and 32 men each, was larger than the Ranger companies of World War II but only half the size of a standard infantry company. In firepower, it eclipsed the latter with its high proportion of submachine guns, automatic rifles, bazookas, grenade launchers, light mortars, and machine guns. To carry these weapons and other equipment, which was estimated by some to require five trucks, the table only provided two jeeps and one truck, a far cry from Collins's original concept. The lack of motor transport was certainly justifiable, given the need to move by foot in the mountains of

Korea, but it did mean that the Rangers would have to carry a lot of equipment on their backs, with predictable losses in unit efficiency. Nor did the table provide for much of a support element. The small headquarters, which lacked even cooks or clerks, reflected the view of the planners that the company should rely for support on its parent division.[16]

For the moment, the tiny support element did not concern the staff of the Ranger training center as much as the need to define a mission and doctrine for the companies. The veterans on the staff knew, from bitter experience, of the danger of misuse, and they sought to prevent it through the preparation of a tentative doctrine. Largely authored by Major Bond, it provided a reasonably clear statement of the Ranger mission as attacks against command posts, artillery, motor pools, airfields, communications centers, and other targets in the enemy's rear area. On the other hand, the inclusion of aggressive action against vaguely defined "critical objectives" left considerable room for interpretation as to whether a given objective was worth the use of a Ranger company. The statement clearly listed intelligence collection as a secondary task for the Rangers and, while anticipating cooperation with guerrillas, foreclosed a role for Rangers as trainers of partisans. Above all, it warned that the Ranger companies, with their small size, lack of heavy weapons, and small support echelon, were not suited for sustained combat. It also suggested that a liaison officer be detailed from the division staff to keep track of the Rangers' employment.

Bond's proposed doctrine was not adopted by the Army. The Army Staff and Army Field Forces regarded the Ranger companies as experimental and hesitated to issue an official statement on their use until they had shown their value in the field. While General Mark Clark, now the chief of Army Field Forces, and Maj. Gen. Charles L. Bolte, the Army's assistant chief of staff for operations and training, were not anti-Ranger, neither could see the need for a doctrine to prevent misuse. Bolte had been chief of staff of the European theater at the time of the creation of the 1st Ranger Battalion, but the experience had not left much of an impression on this conventional soldier, who, like many others, tended to lump guerrilla activities with Ranger operations. He and his staff focused more on the deployment of the Ranger companies to the Far East as soon as possible, assuming that, once they arrived, the commanders on the spot would know how to use them. However, the lack of a guiding doctrine would have dire consequences for Ranger employment.[17]

Discussions of Ranger doctrine, of course, could have held little interest for an American public that, after the reverses of the conflict's early months, was more than ready to welcome back the heroes of World War II. Within days of the Army's October 10 announcement of the return of the Rangers, Americans were reading in their newspapers of these new commandos, who were described variously as "the masters of stealth," "the Army's happy hatchetmen," and "rougher than a stucco bathtub." One *Washington Post* story described the tough training of the Rangers and compared these "rugged specimens" to Jackson's "foot cavalry" of the Civil War. However, behind these accounts, one can perceive a certain ambivalence toward these men. The idolization of an individual or a small, elite group, common in a crisis, as well as a barely suppressed glee that the Army was finally unleashing its roughest fighters, is apparent. At the same time, one can sense that, in an affluent, postwar America that would not even declare war, such men, with their eagerness to fight, seemed a curiosity, out of place except in the current crisis.[18]

Ironically, by the time the Army announced the revival of the Rangers, the public mood was shifting from dismay to euphoria as the news from the front improved. On September 15, MacArthur had launched his counterstroke, landing the 1st Marine Division at Inchon. Their communications cut, the North Koreans fled northward in disorder. By early October, UN forces were crossing the 38th Parallel and driving north toward the Yalu River, the border between Korea and China, in an effort to unify Korea by force. The end of the war appeared within reach. In this air of general optimism, the Army actually became anxious that the war would end before it had a chance to test the Ranger concept. On October 19, Bolte pressed Collins to send three Ranger companies to Korea as soon as possible, stating that "even though major hostilities may be terminated in the near future, it is felt that these units will have potential value in an antiguerrilla role." Collins and other policymakers, however, suspected that the Korean conflict might be a mere diversion, preliminary to a Soviet attack on Western Europe. The chief of staff directed that only one of the first three companies would go to Korea, while the other two would deploy to Europe.[19]

Within a few weeks, the Army's leaders had to change their plans. After several warnings that Western diplomats chose to ignore, the Communist Chinese, in late November, launched a massive offensive against the exposed flanks of UN forces approaching the Yalu. Among the units hit by the Chinese assault was the Eighth Army Ranger Company, which threw back four enemy assaults before its hilltop position was overrun. Only 20 Rangers survived to join the general retreat down the Korean peninsula to a position below the 38th Parallel. Following the anticipation of an early victory, the debacle along the Yalu represented a great military and psychological setback. Although MacArthur called for air raids against Chinese bases in Manchuria, other nations in the UN coalition argued against any further expansion of the war, and Truman, fearing Soviet intervention and the outbreak of World War III, agreed. The United Nations returned to its original goal, the preservation of a free South Korea.[20]

Faced with "an entirely new war," the Army ordered three Ranger companies to the Far East, kept a fourth at Fort Benning as a demonstration unit, and took steps to achieve Collins's goal of one Ranger company per active division. With the lengthening of the Ranger course to 8 weeks, the addition of cold weather training, and the increasing need of recruits for airborne instruction prior to Ranger training, the total length of time necessary to prepare a company for action in Korea was approaching 16 weeks by early 1951. At that time, the number of companies that would take this elongated program remained unclear, in part because of uncertainty over the number of active divisions that the Army would eventually organize, but also because of proposals to further expand the force. Brig. Gen. Ridgely Gaither, a veteran paratrooper on Bolte's staff, foreshadowed a future role for the Rangers with his suggestion that the Army form more companies as ready reaction forces for its commands in Iceland, the Caribbean, and Alaska, and some enthusiasts even pushed for a Ranger company for each regiment. In March 1951, however, Army Field Forces recommended postponing consideration of these proposals until the Army could evaluate the performance of the companies in Korea.

One reason for Army Field Forces's opposition to further expansion lay in the growing challenge of finding recruits who were able and willing to serve as Rangers. For the remaining companies, Army Field Forces had planned to draw volunteers from the parent divisions, except in the case of overseas divisions, which would provide a cadre and let recruiters fill out their companies with volunteers from the rest of the Army. Through this policy, Army Field Forces hoped to avoid further draws from the manpower of the airborne divisions, which, as the Army's main strategic reserve, were supposed to avoid such disruptions and maintain a constant state of readiness. By early February 1951, however, recruiters were having so many problems meeting their manpower quotas that the Army reluctantly turned once again to the paratroopers. It was becoming clear that the Army's supply of Ranger-qualified manpower was not limitless.[21]

The shortage of Ranger-qualified manpower was not the only ill omen as the companies prepared for combat. The general haste surrounding the revival of the Rangers reflected the fact that, after five years of neglect of special operations and elite infantry units, the Army was in crisis and was attempting a quick fix with little grasp of the concept underlying such units. Communist infiltrators in Korea had demonstrated some major gaps in American doctrine and capabilities, embarrassed the Army in the process, and stunned both the military and the American public with their viciousness. In this atmosphere, the Army and the public were ready to remove restraints and form special units that were capable of similar tactics. However, for all the enthusiasm to deploy Rangers overseas as soon as possible, the Army possessed only a vague idea of their mission as operators behind enemy lines, even lumping Ranger raids with guerrilla operations as appropriate tasks. While a small body of Ranger instructors with experience in special operations attempted to define the unit and its missions, their efforts were not well received by the Army hierarchy, which assumed that the divisions in Korea would know how to employ them. Experience would soon show, at great cost, the fallacy of this assumption.

NOTES

1. Robert J. Donovan, *Tumultuous Years: The Presidency of Harry S Truman, 1949-1953* (New York: Norton, 1982), pp. 182-183, 194; Weigley, *History of the United States Army*, p. 506; J. Lawton Collins, *War in Peacetime: The History and Lessons of Korea* (Boston: Houghton Mifflin, 1969), pp. 1-2.

2. Weigley, *History of the United States Army*, pp. 503-507; Roy K. Flint, "Task Force Smith and the 24th Division: Delay and Withdrawal, 5-19 July 1950," in Charles E. Heller and William A. Stofft, eds., *America's First Battles, 1775-1965* (Lawrence: University Press of Kansas, 1986), pp. 269-284, 297-299; Fehrenbach, *This Kind of War*, pp. 91, 98-100.

3. "Report on Visit of LTC Everett (Rep. of G-3, D/A) to FECOM and USARPAC, 19-30 Aug. 1950," Tab E: HQ, Eighth U.S. Army Korea, "Combat Information Bulletin No. 1," Section I, U.S. Army, Operations, General Decimal File, 1950-1951, 333 Middle East to 333 Pacific, RG 319, MMHB, National Archives; Fehrenbach, *This Kind of War*, pp. 127, 144, 158-160, 199-201; Doughty, *Evolution*, pp. 7-10; Joseph C. Goulden, *Korea: The Untold Story of the War* (New York: Times Books, 1982), pp. 170-171; Matthew B. Ridgway, *The Korean War* (Garden City, N.Y.: Doubleday, 1967), pp. 17, 28; Flint, "Task Force Smith," p. 299; Weigley, *History of the United States Army*, p. 519; Maxwell D. Taylor, *Swords and Plowshares* (New York: Norton, 1972), pp. 158-159; Maj. Gen. John K. Singlaub USA (Ret.), interview with author, Alexandria, Va., 1 February 1989.

4. By February, the commandos had left the organization and were conducting raids along the Korean coast in conjunction with the Navy. See D. B. Drysdale, "41 Commando," *Marine Corps Gazette* 37 (August 1953): 28-32; Bolte to Chief, Army Field Forces, 26 September 1950, Ranger File, U.S. Army, Assistant Chief of Staff, G-3, Operations, Records Section, Decimal File, March, 1950-1951, 322 Ranger (hereafter cited as G-3 Ranger Records, Korean War), Box 380, RG 319, MMHB, National Archives; documents in 091.#5 Korea 16 July 1950-31 August 1950 and 091.#6 Korea 1 Sept 50 thru 14 Sept 50, U.S. Army, FECOM, G-3 Records, Box 748, RG 338, WNRC; SAG records in U.S. Army, Adjutant General's Office, Command Reports, 1949-1954, Non-Organic Units, Japan Logistic Command, AYUT [Army Unit] 8227, 1950-1951, RG 407, WNRC.

5. Robert W. Black, *Rangers in Korea* (New York: Ballantine, 1989), p. 13; Neil Sheehan, *A Bright, Shining Lie: John Paul Vann and America in Vietnam* (New York: Random House, 1988), pp. 452-454; Capt. F. W. Thiele, Assistant Adjutant General, Eighth Army, to CINCFE [Commander in Chief, Far East], 17 August 1950, U.S. Army, Eighth Army, G-3 Records, Box P559, RG 338, WNRC; "8213th Army Unit (Eighth Army Ranger Company)," Organizational History Branch, CMH; U.S. War Dept., "Table of Organization and Equipment No. 7-87: Ranger Company, Ranger Infantry Battalion," 7 August 1945, USAMHI.

6. B.C. Mossman, "The Korean War, 1950-1953," in Maurice Matloff, ed., *American Military History*, 2d ed., Army Historical Series (Washington, D.C.: OCMH, 1973), pp. 552-553; Fehrenbach, *This Kind of War*, pp. 158-161; Collins, *War in Peacetime*, pp. 108-110; "Report of LTC Everett"; Collins to MacArthur, 18 August 1950, U.S. Army, FECOM, Chief of Staff Records, "Office of Chief of Staff, HQ Far East Cmd + UN Cmd," Box 3, RG 338, WNRC; Singlaub interview.

7. J. Lawton Collins, *Lightning Joe: An Autobiography* (Baton Rouge: Louisiana State University Press, 1979), pp. 22, 49–56, 90–91; Bradley, *Soldier's Story*, p. 228; Blair and Bradley, *General's Life*, p. 472; "General Collins Answers Some Military Questions," Geog. V Korea 350.05 Officer's Call III No. 1, Historical Records Branch, CMH; Eddleman interview.

8. Collins to Bolte, 29 August 1950, Section IA, G-3 Ranger Records, Korean War, Box 380, RG 319, MMHB, National Archives.

9. See the discussion in the previous chapter and later in this chapter on the Army's confusion of raider concepts.

10. Conference Notes on Marauder Company, 7 September 1950; and Bolte to Chief, Army Field Forces, 7 September 1950, in G-3 Ranger Records, Korean War, Box 380, RG 319, MMHB, National Archives; U.S. Army, Office of the Chief of Army Field Forces (OCAFF), "Annual History, 1 January–31 December 1950," unpublished manuscript (Washington, D.C.: OCMH, 1950), Call No. 6–2 AA 1950, vol. 2, sec. 5, ch. 13, pt. 3, pp. 2–3, Historical Records Branch, CMH. For more on the airborne mystique, see Roger A. Beaumont, "Airborne: Life Cycle of a Military Subculture," *Military Review* 51 (June 1971): 52–61.

11. "Van Houten, John Gibson," *Generals of the Army*, May 1953, pp. 27–28; Singlaub interview.

12. Brig. Gen. William S. Lawton, Chief of Staff, Army Field Forces, to Bolte, 10 October 1950, Section I; Bolte to Commanding General, Third Army, 22 September 1950, Section IA; Bolte to Collins, 16 October 1950, Section IA; Memorandum for Record, 22 September 1950, Ranger File; and Memorandum for Record, 5 October 1950, Ranger File, in G-3 Ranger Records, Korean War, Box 380, RG 319, MMHB, National Archives; OCAFF, "Annual History, 1950," vol. 2, sec. 5, ch. 13, pt. 3, pp. 4–5; Robert W. Black, "The Rangers of the Korean War," *Gung Ho*, October 1984, pp. 61–62; Black, *Rangers in Korea*, p. 20; USAMHI, "Senior Officers Debriefing Program: Palmer," pp. 496–497; Singlaub interview.

13. Bolte to Collins, 16 October 1950; and OCAFF to Collins, 21 September 1950, in G-3 Ranger Records, Korean War, Box 380, RG 319, MMHB, National Archives; Black, *Rangers in Korea*, p. 21; Col. Robert W. Black USA (Ret.), interview with author, Carlisle, Pa., 22 March 1984.

14. In a dispatch to Washington, Van Houten reported, "The colored company has the same limitations to a lesser degree as any other such unit, but is by far the best of its type that I have seen;" Van Houten to Bolte, 13 November 1950, Section I, G-3 Ranger Records, Korean War, Box 380, RG 319, MMHB, National Archives. See also Bolte to Collins, 16 October 1950; OCAFF to Collins, 21 September 1950; MacGregor, *Armed Forces*, pp. 312, 318, 321, 350–351, 430, 610; Black, "Rangers of the Korean War," p. 62; Singlaub interview.

15. Memorandum for Record, 24 October 1950, Section I; and Bolte to Collins, 16 October 1950, in G-3 Ranger Records, Korean War, Box 380, RG 319, MMHB, National Archives; Black, *Rangers in Korea*, p. 25; Black, "Rangers of the Korean War," p. 62; "The New Ranger Company," *Military Review* 31 (May 1951): 31; USAMHI, "Senior Officers Debriefing Program: Palmer," pp. 496–497; Black interview.

16. Bolte to Collins, 16 October 1950; Brig. Gen. D. A. D. Ogden, Organization and Training Division, G-3, to Bolte, 3 October 1950; and Memorandum for Record, 13 October 1950, Section I, in G-3 Ranger Records, Korean War, Box 380, RG 319,

MMHB, National Archives; U.S. Army, Department of the Army, "Table of Organization and Equipment No. 7–87: Ranger Infantry Company (Airborne) (Tentative)," 17 October 1950, USAMHI; U.S. Army, Department of the Army, "Table of Organization and Equipment No. 7–17N: Infantry Rifle Company," 9 December 1947, Organizational History Branch, CMH; interview with 1st Lt. Alfred J. Giacherine, Executive Officer, 8th Ranger Company, 5 June 1951, in Martin Blumenson, "Action on Hill 628, 8th Ranger Company (Airborne)," unpublished manuscript (Washington, D.C.: OCMH, n.d.), Call No. 8–5.1A BA99, pp. 10–11; U.S. Army, Eighth U.S. Army Korea, "Special Problems in the Korean Conflict," unpublished manuscript (Washington, D.C.: OCMH, 1955), Call No. 8–5.1A AN, p. 82; Black interview.

17. U.S. Army, Infantry School, Ranger Training Center, "Ranger Company (Tentative)" (Fort Benning, Ga.: Ranger Training Center, 1950), pp. 1–8, USAMHI; Singlaub interview; Bolte to Collins, 16 October 1950; "Bolte, Charles Lawrence, Lt. Gen. (06908)," *Generals of the Army*, February 1953, pp. 5–7.

18. Donovan, *Tumultuous Years*, pp. 253–254, 295; Black, *Rangers in Korea*, p. 27; "Army Ranger Companies," *Army, Navy, Air Force Journal* 88 (14 October 1950): 168; "The Champs Have A New Competitor" *Combat Forces Journal* 1 (December 1950): 7; John G. Norris, "Units of Commandos Organized by Army," *Washington Post*, 11 October 1950, p. 2; Austin Stevens, "December Draft to Call Up 40,000," *New York Times*, 11 October 1950, p. 1.

19. Bolte quoted in Bolte to Collins, 19 October 1950, Section I, G-3 Ranger Records, Korean War, Box 380, RG 319, MMHB, National Archives; see also Donovan, *Tumultuous Years*, pp. 241, 257; Mossman, "The Korean War, 1950–1953," pp. 555–557; Collins, *War in Peacetime*, p. 78; Col. M. F. Haas, Assistant Secretary of the General Staff, to Bolte, 23 October 1950, Section I, G-3 Ranger Records, Korean War, Box 380, RG 319, MMHB, National Archives.

20. Mossman, "The Korean War, 1950–1953," pp. 557–560; Millett and Maslowski, *Common Defense*, p. 488; Maj. Gen. R. E. Duff, Acting Assistant Chief of Staff, to Collins, 6 November 1950, Section I; Duff to CINCEUR, 11 November 1950, Section I; and "Ranger Units Sent to FECOM," Ranger File, in G-3 Ranger Records, Korean War, Box 380, RG 319, MMHB, National Archives; Sheehan, *Bright Shining Lie*, pp. 457–466.

21. Bolte to Collins, 16 October 1950; Bolte to OCAFF, 24 November 1950, Section IA; OCAFF to Bolte, 11 December 1950, Section IA; Adjutant General to CAFF et. al., 16 December 1950, Ranger File; Gaither, Chief, Operations Division, G-3, to Ogden, 31 January 1951, Section II; Memorandum for Record, 1 February 1951, Section IA; and Memorandum for Record, 26 March 1951, Section IA, in G-3 Ranger Records, Korean War, Box 380, RG 319, MMHB, National Archives; Commanding General, Infantry Center, to Adjutant General, 10 January 1951; Memorandum for Record, 19 January 1951, Case no. 13, 353 File, Box 562; and Lt. Col. Neil M. Matzger, Assistant Adjutant General, Army Field Forces, to Van Houten, 21 May 1951, 322 Ranger File, Box 503, in U.S. Army, Army Field Forces, HQ, Adjutant General's Section, Communications and Records Division, Decimal File, 1951–1952, RG 337, MMHB, National Archives; Gaither to Chief, Plans Division, G-3, 3 January 1951, U.S. Army, Operations, General Decimal File, 1950–1951, From 322 to 325, RG 319, MMHB, National Archives; "Gaither, Ridgely, Maj. Gen. (015970)," *Generals of the Army*, June 1953, pp. 14–15.

8

A Turning Point

When the first Ranger companies arrived in Korea in late December 1950 and early January 1951, they found an atmosphere of defeat and despair. Under pressure from the Chinese, Eighth Army was withdrawing below the 38th Parallel. On January 4, Seoul, the capital of South Korea, fell to the Communist forces, and UN leaders frankly discussed evacuation of their forces from the peninsula. Morale fell to a new low among American troops, who lacked food, winter clothing, and an understanding of the reason for their presence in Korea. Poor morale found expression in inadequate patrolling and refusals to leave vehicles in the valleys and battle the enemy on the high ground. When General Walker, the commander of Eighth Army, was killed in a jeep accident on Christmas Eve, it only added to the gloom enveloping UN forces.

Walker's successor, Lt. Gen. Matthew B. Ridgway, proved to be the inspirational leader that Eighth Army needed. His refusal to consider further withdrawals, his visits to the front lines, and his efforts to improve the supply situation, remove poor combat leaders, and explain to the troops the purpose behind their sacrifices invigorated the dispirited UN forces. Under his influence, American troops patrolled with more vigor, employed defenses in depth against infiltration, and used American firepower and local counterattacks to inflict crippling losses on the enemy. These changes had their effect. In mid-January, Eighth Army began a series of limited offensives to regain the initiative and inflict maximum casualties on the Communists. For the next five months, despite repeated Chinese counterattacks, the Rangers and other UN troops slowly pushed toward the 38th Parallel.[1]

Press reports soon filtered back to the United States of Rangers wreaking havoc among enemy forces in the best tradition of Rogers. While the Rangers did not enjoy as high a profile as they did in World War II, they still received considerable publicity. Both the *New York Times* and the *Washington*

Post ran stories on a 26-man Ranger raid that reportedly caused two enemy regiments to flee in disorder, and the *Army Times* described in graphic detail the 3d Ranger Infantry Company's assault on Bloody Nose Ridge. Some of the stories, including one of a Ranger catching a grenade in midair and flinging it back at the startled thrower, and another of a severely wounded sergeant continuing to fire at the Chinese with his automatic rifle, echoed tales of Ranger and infantry combat in World War II. Through such accounts, the American public was developing an image of hard-bitten fighters and "destruction specialists," who lived off the land behind enemy lines for weeks at a time before descending on an isolated command post or another exposed installation.[2]

Actually, the seven Ranger companies attached to divisions in Korea carried out few raids. In this respect, the 1st Ranger Infantry Company was more fortunate than most. Of all the American divisions, the 2d Infantry Division probably had the best appreciation of the Ranger mission, and it occasionally used the 1st Ranger Infantry Company to attack key installations behind enemy lines. It was the company's raid on the headquarters of the 12th North Korean Division that inspired the reports in the *New York Times* and *Washington Post*. The other six companies carried out only a handful of such missions. In some cases, higher headquarters planned a raid and then canceled it. The 4th Ranger Infantry Company, for one, was supposed to drop behind enemy lines in conjunction with Eighth Army's January offensive and capture a party of enemy generals, but Ridgway canceled the operation, apparently out of fear that it would leave the Rangers vulnerable for too long a period.[3]

In the end, the only combat jump, if it can be called that, for the Rangers of the Korean War took place at Munsan-ni. In March, Ridgway launched Operation RIPPER, another limited offensive ostensibly designed to eliminate a salient on the left of the UN line but actually intended to destroy as many Communist units and as much equipment as possible. While I Corps drove northwest from Seoul, the 187th Airborne Regimental Combat Team, with the 2d and 4th Ranger Infantry Companies attached, was supposed to drop behind enemy lines at Munsan-ni and cut the escape route of the North Korean I Corps along the Seoul–Kaesong Road. The airborne assault on March 23 proceeded without mishap and drew publicity, but the enemy had already withdrawn north. Ridgway then tried to use the paratroopers and Rangers to seize high ground behind enemy troops facing the 3d Infantry Division, but once again, the Communists escaped before the trap could close.[4]

In addition to the jump at Munsan-ni, the 4th Ranger Infantry Company performed the only Ranger amphibious mission of the war, the abortive raid on Hwachon Dam. As IX Corps pushed toward the dam, located just north of the 38th Parallel, in early April, Maj. Gen. William M. Hoge directed the 1st Cavalry Division to seize it before the Chinese could release a torrent of water down the Pukhan River and effectively split his corps. When the cavalrymen could not take the dam by head-on assault, Capt. Dorsey B. Anderson of the 4th

Ranger Infantry Company suggested to the division operations officer that his company cross the lake formed by the dam, seize the installation, and blast shut the gates. The order for the operation left him little time to plan and bring needed equipment over rugged terrain to the launch site, and bad weather hindered aerial reconnaissance of the target area. When the company did cross on the night of April 10–11, a shortage of boats hampered the move. On the far shore, the Rangers ran into stiff opposition, which stopped them short of the dam. After holding throughout the day, with help from artillery firing at the limit of its range, the company and a battalion that had joined them withdrew across the lake. An ideal Ranger mission on paper, the raid fell victim to fumbled arrangements and bad luck.[5]

Raids like the one against Hwachon Dam were rare. By shifting their Ranger companies from regiment to regiment, divisions created a situation in which everybody had a task for the Rangers but nobody held responsibility for them. Lacking official guidance, division and regimental commanders used the Rangers for whatever missions occurred to them. Most frequently, the Rangers patrolled and laid ambushes in the disputed area between the lines or a short distance into the enemy rear, an important task in the static warfare that was beginning to settle on the Korean peninsula by the spring of 1951. Night patrols demanded especially capable infantrymen, and the Rangers, with their extensive night training, were natural candidates for the job. Such missions could be quite hazardous, as the 8th Ranger Infantry Company discovered when it ran into a Chinese field army at Hill 628 and was nearly obliterated. Most Ranger patrols, however, carried out tasks that a well-trained line unit should have handled. When not patrolling between the lines, the Rangers hunted guerrillas, screened flanks, guarded command posts, and instructed South Korean troops in Ranger tactics. While most of these odd jobs lay easily within the capability of standard formations, they at least did not cost the Rangers heavy casualties.[6]

The same could not be said of the frequent tendency of field commanders to thrust Ranger companies into the front line. All too often, they used the Rangers either to hold a section of front, counterattack against an enemy penetration, or spearhead an assault against an objective of relatively minor importance. The heavy casualties from these missions were a waste of specially trained personnel. At Chip Yong-ni on February 14, a platoon of the 1st Ranger Infantry Company led a hastily organized attack to regain a hill and restore the defensive perimeter of the 23d Infantry Regiment. Only a handful of Rangers managed to reach the crest, and they were quickly driven off by the Chinese. Two months later, at Bloody Nose Ridge, a platoon of the 3d Ranger Infantry Company lost 24 of its 32 men in an assault on an entrenched position. Not every Ranger attack suffered as high a proportion of losses, but similar episodes occurred often enough to concern thoughtful observers, including Van Houten.[7]

For all their élan, the Rangers, as in World War II, simply did not possess the organization for sustained line duty. Although their tentative doctrine emphasized stealth and short, hard action at the objective, the Rangers often used orthodox tactics, which stressed mass and firepower, in attacks on fortified positions. In such actions, and in a static defensive role, their lack of manpower, compared to a standard company, left them with little ability to absorb losses. Furthermore, while they possessed considerable firepower in small arms, they lacked the heavier weapons that were necessary for line operations. Higher commanders could alleviate this deficiency somewhat through assignment to the Rangers of forward observers from artillery batteries in the rear, but even this step could not substitute for heavy weapons which belonged to the company. Lacking firepower to clear the way, the Rangers had to sacrifice manpower to achieve objectives. In contrast to the improvised system of World War II, the Rangers could at least turn to a system of filler companies at Fort Benning to replace these losses. These units ran into problems in finding enough replacements and shipping them to the Far East in time to serve, but they did manage to keep most Ranger companies near full strength until inactivation.[8]

The inadequacies of the Rangers as line troops combined with a dependence on other units for outside support and the cockiness of Ranger personnel to aggravate an antielitism that many soldiers had held from the prewar period. The reliance on other units for support led at least one regimental commander to call his Ranger company a "parasite," remarking, "They [the Rangers] could barely cook their own meals. They couldn't maintain their vehicles. They couldn't even deliver their mail if there was any, or distribute their rations or go to the rear for additional ammunition." Such dependence seemed especially difficult to accept given the Ranger image as undisciplined prima donnas who dismissed nonairborne troops as legs, made "midnight requisitions" of vehicles from the motor pools of other units, and refused to take orders from anyone below a regimental commander. While aware of heavy Ranger losses in line actions, many orthodox officers believed that they resulted from a Ranger penchant to take unnecessary risks. If higher commanders could not see the waste of misuse, one could not expect subordinates to distinguish the difference.[9]

Van Houten could do little in response to the complaints of misuse that reached him from Ranger company commanders in Korea during the winter and spring of 1951. Since November, he, Adams, and Singlaub had traveled to the Far East to distribute doctrinal literature and explain the missions, capabilities, and limitations of the Ranger companies to staffs at the army, corps, and division levels. Although he had a conventional background, the chief of Ranger Training Command had grown enormously in his grasp of Ranger operations, and he had kept his staff busy with the production of a flood of studies for Army headquarters on the Ranger concept. As early as December, he acknowledged, in one such study, that "the term 'ranger' has been rather loosely used in our military terminology," and argued that the Army should view Rangers as special units for raids into the enemy rear, rather than as elite shock troops. For the first time in

Maj. Gen. John G. Van Houten (U.S. Army photograph)

December, and again in March, he proposed that the Army form Ranger battalions, which would have a large enough headquarters to handle their own planning and administration. His ideas made no headway with an Army Staff that was either unable or unwilling to see any need for a new directive on Ranger organization and use.[10]

Why did field commanders in Korea consistently misuse the Rangers? Part of the answer to this question lies in the change in the nature of the Korean conflict from a war of movement to a war of position. In line with the UN's return to its original objective, the preservation of South Korea, Ridgway sought to regain a defensible position along the 38th Parallel while inflicting enough punishment on the Chinese to make them more amenable to a settlement. By June, Eighth Army had substantially achieved its first goal when it reached the KANSAS-WYOMING line, a network of valleys and high ridges dominating the terrain just north of the 38th Parallel. For the next two years, the opposing sides would conduct a war of trenches, barbed wire, patrols, artillery bombardments, and local attacks in those mountains while peace talks took place in nearby Panmunjom. The stable, densely manned defenses that faced UN forces, as well as the presence of an alert enemy who was most active at night, hampered attempts to infiltrate by foot, and few other alternatives seemed to exist given the infant state of the helicopter and the difficulties involved in the exfiltration of parachutists.[11]

Nevertheless, the argument that the nature of the war precluded effective Ranger operations suffers from two flaws. In the first place, the war did not settle into a stalemate until the summer of 1951, six months after the arrival of the first Ranger companies from the United States. Second, British commandos were conducting productive, Ranger-type raids against targets along the enemy-held Korean coastline. After suffering heavy casualties while serving as line infantry near the Yalu, a reconstituted 41 Royal Marine Commando resumed raiding operations against the east coast of North Korea in April 1951. From a base on Yo Do Island, patrols of 2 to 70 men reconnoitered beaches, snatched prisoners, blew up railroads, and ambushed convoys, in the process tying down an estimated 5,000 Communist troops. Oddly enough, Far East Command does not appear to have considered the use of Rangers in this campaign against the enemy's coastal communications, probably because American theater commanders limited their idea of Ranger operations to local forays under divisional control, without considering deep raids under theater supervision.[12]

Another factor that is often mentioned in official explanations of misuse, racial differences, appears at first glance to be a convenient alibi, but it reveals much about the state of mind among American commanders in Korea. Those commanders complained that Rangers, as Caucasians, could not safely operate in the rear of an Oriental army, especially since the language barrier would preclude cooperation with friendly guerrillas. Such arguments do not withstand serious examination. After all, the 6th Ranger Battalion operated efficiently in the Japanese rear during World War II, and Special Forces would carry out successful raids into enemy-controlled areas during the Vietnam War. In part, the racial explanation demonstrates, once again, the confusion of Ranger, guerrilla, and *Brandenburger* concepts that plagued the Rangers. It also shows the innate hesitancy of commanders to authorize a risky mission behind enemy lines when the enemy has a poor reputation for treatment of prisoners.[13]

Granting the concern about risky operations into the enemy rear, the organizational arrangement that attached Ranger companies to divisions contributed more to the misuse of the Rangers. Ranger operations required considerable planning time and, frequently, coordination with the Air Force, Navy, or CIA. Engrossed in fighting their divisions, divisional commanders and their staffs seldom possessed the time or inclination to consider or plan raids behind enemy lines. Nor could the brave and enthusiastic, but inexperienced, captains and lieutenants of Ranger companies fill the void. They lacked the headquarters organizations to plan properly and the seniority to have much influence on the generals and colonels commanding the divisions. Depending on the views of the staff officer speaking, Ranger companies were either too small or too large for their assigned task. Many thought a company was too small to send on a risky mission into the enemy rear; in the case of parachute drops, they cited the airborne rule, which required a regimental combat team for jumps behind enemy lines. Others complained that a company was too large to infiltrate the dense Chinese front, ignoring the fact that Ranger squads and platoons were trained for such tasks.[14]

Complaints of the size of Ranger units, racial factors, and other excuses point to the simple, underlying fact that the U.S. Army still did not know what it was doing with regard to Ranger operations. For too many officers, "Ranger" represented a fuzzy combination of activities, including guerrilla warfare and patrols. During his trip to the Far East in December 1950, Van Houten noted that press reports had led many in the theater to anticipate that the Rangers would conduct clandestine operations in civilian garb. He and other observers from the Ranger Training Command did their best to inform staff officers of the true nature and purpose of the Rangers, but the Army's rotation policy soon replaced many of these staffers with newcomers who were unfamiliar with the concept. A discussion in February of the plans of corps and division chiefs for the Rangers is revealing. Maj. Gen. Bryant E. Moore of the IX Corps wanted to use the Rangers for antiguerrilla operations, and Maj. Gen. William B. Kean of the 25th Infantry Division stated he would employ his company in "day and night combat-type missions and/or in conjunction with armor or tank-infantry team missions." Only Maj. Gen. Clark Ruffner of the 2d Infantry Division planned to use the Rangers for quick strikes into the enemy rear.

Despite their initial desire to retaliate against North Korean infiltration tactics, raids on rear area facilities did not fit into the concept of warfare held by most American generals. Army, corps, and division commanders had formed their attitudes in a Depression-era Army which looked back to World War I, and World War II had confirmed their bent for mass warfare. Most of them, including Hoge, Kean, Maj. Gen. Claude Ferenbaugh of the 7th Infantry Division, Maj. Gen. Charles Palmer of the 1st Cavalry Division, and Lt. Gen. James Van Fleet, who succeeded Ridgway in command of Eighth Army in April, had participated in the big-unit war in Europe, and many, including Kean, Ferenbaugh, Palmer, and Maj. Gen. Blacksher Bryan of the 24th Infantry Division, had served as staff officers, with little experience in leading troops in battle. When they complained that night raids would throw off prearranged artillery fires, that they lacked intelligence on possible targets for such missions, or that they needed every man in the front lines, they were reflecting an orientation toward firepower and mass as well as an inability to see the benefit of raids, which the trend toward positional warfare in mid-1951 could only reinforce.[15]

While field commanders did not think much of raids as a strategy and complained of the logistical burden presented by Ranger companies, they joined other observers in expressing their admiration for Rangers as fighters. All the Ranger companies served with distinction, with the 1st Ranger Infantry Company receiving the Distinguished Unit Citation. Stories of Ranger aggressiveness abounded in Eighth Army. When news of the Chinese intervention reached a troopship on its way to Korea, according to one account, the Rangers celebrated the prolongation of the war. An officer who visited the 4th Ranger Infantry Company in Korea noted the Mohawk haircuts, switchblade knives, and eagerness for combat, and concluded, "I fear the Commies are going to be searching frantically for some solution to stop this new American menace."[16] Once in action, the Rangers impressed divisional chiefs with their élan. Ferenbaugh noted the high praise of subordinate commanders in his 7th Infantry Division for the performance and esprit of the 2d Ranger Infantry Company, and Ruffner of the 2d Infantry Division remarked on the 1st Ranger Infantry Company, "Their devotion to duty and desire to 'get the job done' is a splendid example of our American soldier's aggressive spirit and will to win."[17]

In part, the enthusiasm over the aggressiveness of the Rangers reflected a concern over the performance of American troops and a grudging but growing respect for the Chinese. Lacking the technical sophistication and logistical apparatus of its UN opposition, the People's Liberation Army relied on the self-reliance and toughness of its infantrymen, who could march great distances in harsh weather, over rugged terrain, with a handful of rice as their only ration. Contrary to legend, the Chinese seldom used frontal "human wave" attacks. Instead, they skillfully probed for weak points, infiltrating and launching surprise assaults from several directions. By comparison, the American soldier seemed soft and uninspired to many observers. Although much improved over its early days in Korea, Eighth Army still showed deficiencies in such areas as conditioning, night operations, and patrolling. To improve the morale of soldiers fighting in a distant land for war aims that often seemed murky at best, the Army adopted a controversial nine-month rotation policy and attempted to transfer some semblance of the affluent American standard of living to the front line. Post exchanges (PX) in rear areas offered soft drinks and radios, and quartermasters supplied turkeys to the troops for Thanksgiving, leading some old timers to grumble about a "creampuff Army" that coddled its men. The shock of the collaboration of American prisoners of war with the enemy only intensified anxiety over the ability of a soft, humanitarian West to compete with the ruthless Communists.[18]

In this atmosphere of concern over the quality of American infantry, the old idea of spreading Ranger-trained soldiers among line units experienced a revival. Once again, orthodox officers complained that Ranger units concentrated the best fighters in a few special formations. Echoing S. L. A. Marshall, one general remarked: "In each squad, you may have only one man who really wants to fight. Under the Ranger program, you have that one man volunteering to be a Ranger, which leaves that squad bare of inspiration to fight." By early March, the notion of attaching personnel from Ranger units to rifle companies had gained enough ground that Army Field Forces asked Van Houten to submit a study of the idea. Van Houten predictably discouraged the concept, warning that it would destroy the integrity of Ranger companies, and that a Ranger, as an outsider in his new unit, would have little influence. He suggested instead the attachment of selected infantrymen to Ranger companies for instruction and then return to their units so they could teach what they had learned.[19]

At this point, General Mark Clark, chief of Army Field Forces, entered the picture. The former commander of Fifth Army in Italy during World War II still regarded infantry as the key element in battle and prided himself on being a foot soldier. Deeply concerned about low evaluations of the Army's infantry, he stressed ruggedness and realism, including the use of live ammunition, in training. He shared the view that Ranger units took too many good troops from the infantry at large and that a few airborne battalions under the control of a field army could handle the occasional mission that required a special formation. Nevertheless, he retained from his experience with Darby's men a high regard for Rangers as fighters. In March, he wrote Ridgway: "As long as we have the Ranger school going, we should use it to give extra training to platoon leaders and gradually infiltrate men of that kind into the infantry companies. We must build up the infantry companies to the caliber of Rangers." During a visit to Fort Benning in mid-March, Clark directed Van Houten to prepare and submit ideas on the use of the Ranger Training Command as a means to raise the standards of the entire infantry.[20]

Van Houten seized on this prospective expansion of the role of the Ranger Training Command to offer a number of alternatives. Cleverly defining the problem in terms of a future Soviet-American war, rather than the Korean conflict, he stated, "It is patent that the United States and her Allies cannot successfully oppose Russia and her satellites by *mass*; obviously, we must turn to *quality* and that quality will be expressed in combat by our infantry." The challenge, he continued, would be to accomplish on a broader scale the same levels of performance that Ranger units had been able to achieve through their special status as well as their rugged training. As possible means to achieve this goal, he proposed Ranger training for volunteers who would return to their units, Ranger instruction for replacements before assignment, a Ranger course for infantry battalions, or an indoctrination course for infantry officers from division chiefs on down. In late April, Clark approved the first option, with the addition of airborne training, and directed Ranger Training Command to work out the details of implementation.[21]

Although Van Houten had deflected an attempt to effectively dissolve the Ranger companies, while at the same time expanding the role of his Ranger Training Command, the battle over the future of the Ranger companies had only just begun. Already, in March, an observer team from Army Field Forces had recommended that the Army send no more Ranger companies to Korea. The Rangers, the team's report stated, were performing missions that properly belonged to the intelligence and reconnaissance platoons of divisions. When, in April, Eighth Army polled its field commanders, it found that nearly all favored some kind of change in the attachment of Ranger companies to divisions. Hoge, Palmer, and Maj. Gen. Frank W. Milburn of I Corps opposed any Ranger units, arguing that such formations drained standard units of needed leaders. Bryan and Brig. Gen. J. S. Bradley of the 25th Infantry Division advocated Ranger battalions at the corps level, and Ferenbaugh suggested that each division have a Ranger battalion. Only Brig. Gen. G. C. Stewart of the 2d Infantry Division backed the existing arrangement. After considering these views, Eighth Army recommended to FECOM the formation of a Ranger battalion assigned to a field army for raids and as a reserve against infiltration.[22]

Eighth Army's proposal largely coincided with the views of Van Houten, although the head of Ranger Training Command would have preferred to attach the battalion to a theater headquarters. In his arguments for such an arrangement, he contended that Ranger battalions would have the personnel to handle their own planning and administration, and would receive more appropriate missions and coordinate more effectively with other services at the theater level. Responding to doubts about the value of Ranger missions, he argued, "Past experience has shown that relatively small military units operating behind enemy lines can achieve results out of proportion to the numbers employed and the costs involved," and he dismissed complaints of the lack of opportunity for Ranger operations, stating that commanders and their staffs "should learn to recognize the many situations in which rangers can be profitably used." To guide these commanders, his staff, in July, issued a training circular, while simultaneously preparing a table of organization and training men for the prospective battalion headquarters.[23]

A patrol of the 3d Ranger Infantry Company in Korea (U.S. Army photograph)

Any experiment with Ranger battalions in Korea, however, would need the approval of Ridgway, who had assumed overall command in the Far East after President Truman's dismissal of MacArthur. Ridgway's views on the Rangers present an enigma. As the commander of the 82d Airborne Division in World War II, he could hardly be viewed as antielite. He knew well the problems of misuse experienced by elites. However, while an independent thinker, he could not be regarded as unconventional. Although he had observed guerrilla warfare in Nicaragua during the 1920s, his experiences in Europe during World War II had a greater influence on his outlook. In Korea, he permitted some sea-based raids by guerrillas and commandos, but he mostly relied on firepower for his strategy of attrition. In one sense, his airborne background might have worked against the Rangers, who had engaged in a spirited rivalry with the paratroopers during World War II. The two groups competed for the same type of soldier, and Ridgway probably believed that paratroopers could handle any Ranger mission. Thus, he may well have agreed that Rangers were a wasteful duplication of resources.[24]

After considering Eighth Army's suggestion of a Ranger battalion under its control, Ridgway recommended to Washington the inactivation of the Ranger companies in the Far East. His separate dispatches of May 19 and June 2 summarized arguments that opponents of the Rangers had been using for months. The peculiar conditions of the Korean War, he argued, made it impractical to assign proper missions to the Rangers. Deep penetration missions involved too much of a risk for Ranger companies due to their small size, their Caucasian appearance, and the lamentable Communist record for treatment of prisoners. He doubted that even a Ranger battalion could fully exploit its capabilities in the Korean environment. Since these formations no longer had a purpose and tended to concentrate the best troops in a few units, he recommended that the Army inactivate them and send no more Ranger units to the Far East. Rather than reform the system to ensure the correct and productive use of the Rangers, Ridgway was proposing the abandonment of the entire concept.[25]

Army headquarters was not disposed to overrule the desires of its field commander. Maj. Gen. Maxwell D. Taylor, the former commander of the 101st Airborne Division in World War II and Bolte's successor as assistant chief of staff for operations and training, sympathized with the views of his fellow paratrooper. When he received Ridgway's dispatch, he directed Army Field Forces to prepare a study on the need for Ranger units in the Army and the feasibility of Ranger training for personnel in infantry, armored, and airborne divisions. He also urged Collins to approve FECOM's recommendations, pointing out the obvious waste in using Rangers for line infantry tasks and arguing that, given the absence of suitable Ranger missions, it made more sense to spread individual Rangers among other units. The chief of staff agreed in principle but delayed an announcement, pending preparation of a statement of the reasons for the action. The Rangers had received so much favorable publicity that the inactivation of the companies without explanation would be sure to provoke an outcry.[26]

In the end, the Army announced the inactivation without a formal press release. On July 10, Army headquarters ordered inactivation of Ranger companies in Korea, transfer of their jump-qualified personnel to the 187th Airborne Regimental Combat Team, and reassignment of their other personnel to their parent divisions. Eighth Army carried out those orders on August 1. Inquisitive Rangers and reporters received the limp explanation that racial differences made it impossible to conduct Ranger operations in Korea and that, in the 187th, ex-Rangers would be joining an elite unit in which they would maintain their special status and pay. Understandably, few Rangers thought that this statement gave the entire reason for their inactivation, and even fewer believed the assurances that the decision would not affect the other Ranger companies and the Ranger Training Command.[27]

Suspicions of the Army's plans for the Rangers were well founded. The Army Staff was authorizing studies and surveying overseas commanders about the Ranger concept, and the results could not have been encouraging to Ranger enthusiasts. Gen. Thomas T. Handy, Commander in Chief, Europe, could foresee no need in his theater for Ranger companies attached to divisions, although he left open the possibility that Ranger battalions might become necessary for some eventualities. Even more damaging was the study produced by Army Field Forces at Taylor's request. Focusing on a global conflict with the Soviet Union as the contingency for which the Army must prepare, the study pointed out that the United States must make efficient use of its relatively limited manpower to neutralize the vast population base of the Soviets. However, the study did not accept operations by Ranger units as a possible counter to this imbalance. On the contrary, it dismissed Ranger formations as an inefficient use of manpower that drained potential leaders of line units for missions that, in the case of shallow raids, well-trained line troops could perform, or, in the case of deeper operations, were better left to partisans trained and supervised by the Americans.[28]

Advocates of Ranger units would not give in without a fight. Eddleman, who was now a brigadier general and head of the Plans Division of the Army Staff, cited the value of the 6th Ranger Battalion to Sixth Army in his argument that every field army should have a Ranger battalion. Responding to complaints that the Rangers took potential leaders from line units, Eddleman pointed out that Ranger formations attracted the kind of soldier who, in the absence of such formations, would probably join the paratroopers or the Marines. Other officers on the Army Staff, while agreeing with Army Field Forces on the value of partisans, contended that a Ranger battalion at the army level would still serve a vital function. They answered proposals to substitute airborne formations, such as the 187th Airborne Regimental Combat Team, for Rangers by stating that such units were accustomed to operations on a larger scale than Ranger tasks generally demanded. Meanwhile, from Fort Benning, Van Houten put in a final plea for a Ranger battalion at the corps level or higher.

Overall sentiment at Army headquarters, however, was turning against the concept of Ranger units and in favor of the views expressed in the study by Army Field Forces. In June, one officer remarked that "working level thinking" on the Army Staff viewed Ranger units as unnecessary but did perceive a role for Ranger-type training in the Army. Both the personnel and operations divisions of the Army Staff favored the incorporation of Ranger training into individual and unit training programs, with the implied goal of making line formations capable of shallow raids and reconnaissance. For deeper raids, the Army Staff increasingly preferred the concept of partisan warfare. If Ranger units continued to exist, in this view, it would be as OSS-type trainers of native irregulars for missions into the enemy rear. Taylor himself was becoming convinced that the Rangers, in their current form, were limited by training and language to shallow patrols and raids and that deeper operations would demand a new concept, probably involving guerrillas.[29]

To the Army, partisan warfare offered a way in which to hit targets in the enemy rear with less risk to Americans than in the case of a raid by a Ranger company. The tendency to lump commando and guerrilla concepts under the vague title of "Ranger," as shown by the prewar discussion of the Ranger Group, had lasted into the war, to the detriment of both.[30] Despite this confusion, the Army had achieved some positive results from its support of partisans in Korea. After the Chinese intervention, Eighth Army had assisted guerrillas in North Korea in order to divert enemy forces and bring into play the UN's naval superiority. A joint staff in Eighth Army's operations section supervised the program, which achieved its greatest success in its support of partisan operations from islands off Korea's western coast. Eleven-man teams trained and equipped guerrillas, who, in turn, collected intelligence and raided enemy communications on the mainland. The effort as a whole suffered from equipment shortages, a faulty command structure, and the lack of an overall plan, but it achieved enough to show the potential of such activities.[31]

Even these accomplishments and lessons might have been forgotten but for a few determined advocates within a small section of the Army Staff. From the Office of the Chief for Psychological Warfare, Lt. Col. Russell Volckmann and Col. Wendell Fertig, who had led guerrillas in the Philippines, and Col. Aaron Bank, who had served with the OSS, flooded their superiors with proposals for unconventional warfare. Through both genuine confusion and shrewd salesmanship at a time when Rangers were popular, they mixed commando and OSS concepts in their initial proposals for special units for partisan warfare, such as their idea of "Ranger" companies of East European émigrés to support guerrillas in their homelands. When the Army was considering alternatives to Ranger units in the summer of 1951, they altered their pitch to distinguish between Rangers and their new concept, pointing out that the problems of race and language faced by Ranger units on deep raids would largely be removed by the use of native forces under American leaders. The inactivation of Ranger companies in Korea, opening previously unavailable spaces in the Army's troop basis, greatly encouraged them. When Bank briefed the Army Staff in July on the ability of a few Americans to form a guerrilla army, he so impressed Taylor that the latter decided to recommend the inactivation of all Ranger companies and the formation of the special cells advocated by Bank.[32]

Before Taylor could act on his decision, he was replaced as assistant chief of staff for operations and training by Maj. Gen. Reuben E. Jenkins, on August 1. Any hopes that the change would save the Ranger companies, however, were soon dispelled, for the new chief was even more opposed to Ranger units than Taylor. A veteran of the Meuse-Argonne campaign in World War I, he had risen from the ranks to serve as Devers's chief of staff in France in World War II. After the war, he accompanied his mentor to Army Ground Forces to supervise the operations and training division. Fundamentally antielitist, he believed that the Army, by setting high standards for the Rangers, had lured its best soldiers from other units to create formations of prima donnas who performed duties of no more difficulty or danger than those of the average infantryman. In sum, he told an associate: "We so oversold ourselves on the special commando units that we expected small Ranger units of supermen could accomplish the impossible. Experience has shown that we were wrong."[33]

Jenkins's initial observations in his new job confirmed his earlier impressions and led him, on August 27, to suggest to Collins the inactivation of the remaining Ranger companies. He bluntly stated that the Army had failed to develop an ability to infiltrate enemy lines in a way acceptable to field commanders. To develop this capability, he continued, the Army must consider the problem in two parts: the capacity to operate deep in the enemy's rear and the ability to penetrate his front lines for harassment and intelligence collection. The Army had formed Ranger companies to meet the latter requirement. These units, Jenkins stated, had not fulfilled expectations. Moreover, they had drained standard divisions of highly qualified infantrymen. Nonetheless, Jenkins praised the Ranger Training Command's program, which, he believed, the Army could use to make all infantry units capable of infiltration tactics. Jenkins thus proposed that the Army drop Ranger companies and instead develop the capability for Ranger tasks in all of its airborne, infantry, and armored units. The Army would accomplish this through a new Ranger program for selected soldiers at the Infantry School and the incorporation of Ranger training into the regular course of instruction for captains, lieutenants, and noncommissioned officers.[34]

Faced with a seeming conflict between Jenkins's desire to spread Ranger methods of infiltration and raids throughout the combat arms and its own notion of Ranger training as a proving ground for small-unit leaders, Army Field Forces chose to fuse the two concepts in its final proposal to Collins. It thus adopted the general, though as yet unproven, belief that a good raider, schooled in Ranger skills, would also make a fine infantryman. Under Army Field Force's plan, about 150 volunteers from the company, platoon, and squad leaders in each infantry division would receive six to eight weeks of practical field training "in scouting and patrolling and small unit Ranger-type operations," but not including airborne training. Noncommissioned officers would make up 75 percent of the 150 trainees in each class. To develop an appreciation for Ranger tactics among senior officers, a separate Ranger Orientation Course would provide five days of instruction for generals, colonels, and majors on Ranger-type operations and the abilities and use of Ranger personnel.[35]

On September 27, Collins formally approved the change from the concept of infiltration by special units to the development of the capability for such tactics in all the Army's infantry, armored, and airborne divisions. He directed the inactivation of the remaining Ranger companies, whose personnel would have the choice of an airborne unit or their parent division for their next assignment. The Ranger Training Command would be dissolved in favor of a new Ranger Department, which would instruct selected students in small-unit leadership and Ranger tactics. Other courses of instruction for commissioned and noncommissioned officers would incorporate elements of Ranger training. The differing objectives of this new Ranger concept were reflected in the announcements of the decision. Public press releases took the angle that Ranger training would enable each soldier to reach his maximum potential, in the tradition of Morgan's Riflemen and the scouts of the Indian Wars. On the other hand, dispatches to field commanders told them to use the new Ranger program to develop in all of their infantry units the capacity to perform Ranger-type missions, which were defined as "those overt operations in enemy territory, the duration of which does not normally exceed 48 hours."[36]

Although the announcement of the decision created some controversy, reaction, on the whole, was relatively subdued. Rumors of the impending inactivation had been circulating in the Army and the public for some time, especially after the dissolution of the Ranger companies in Korea. When the word finally came, press reaction seems to have been rather mild. Reporters quoted officers who pointed out the organizational and conceptual problems presented by Ranger units and argued the need for these "eager beavers" in the Army's other formations. Hanson Baldwin, the respected military columnist of the *New York Times*, had earlier set the tone for much of the coverage with his admission that experience seemed to vindicate the views of the antielitists in the Army. In this atmosphere, the Army moved ahead to establish its new Ranger concept. The various commands in the United States and overseas inactivated their remaining Ranger companies during the fall and winter, and, on October 10, the new Ranger Department of the Infantry School officially came into being, with Col. Henry G. Learnard as its first director.[37]

The events of 1951 were a watershed in the history of the Ranger concept. At the beginning of the year, an Army that was alarmed over its ability to meet the test in Korea had been ready to experiment with improvised special units of raiders. In the end, field commanders used their Ranger companies for line missions, only to discover their inadequacies for such a role. The many reasons given for this misuse—the nature of the war, racial factors, lack of intelligence on targets, and so on—were only expressions of the Army's basic lack of understanding of special operations in the early 1950s. The Army clearly had to do something about its unworkable concept of Ranger units, but, instead of revising the concept, it decided to do away with the units altogether. The character of the war by mid-1951 reinforced the view, already popular in the Army, that a limited war was merely mass warfare on a smaller scale and that if the Army prepared for a big-unit conflict, it could handle all lesser contingencies. Military planners knew well the force imbalance that would face them in the event of a war with the Soviets, but instead of investigating special operations as a means to redress this imbalance, they focused on the quality of their mass units. Hence, they inactivated Ranger formations but expanded the Ranger course to train small-unit leaders and thus make all line units capable of shallow raids and reconnaissance. For 17 years, the American military would do without Ranger units. Like the war in which they fought, the Ranger companies represented an experience that the Army wished to forget.

NOTES

1. Fehrenbach, *This Kind of War*, pp. 381, 386; Matthew B. Ridgway, *Soldier: The Memoirs of Matthew B. Ridgway* (New York: Harper, 1956), pp. 205–208; Ridgway, *Korean War*, pp. 86–91, 108; Doughty, *Evolution*, pp. 9–10; Weigley, *History of the United States Army*, p. 521.

2. "Rangers Fight Toe to Toe on Bloody Nose Ridge," *Army Times*, 2 June 1951, p. 3; Glenn Stackhouse, "2000 of Foe Put to Flight by 26 Rangers: Commando Type Unit Smashes HQ 9 Miles Behind Lines," *Washington Post*, 12 February 1951, p. 1; "Rangers 'Reborn' Filter Red Lines," *New York Times*, 11 March 1951, p. 4; Black, "Rangers of the Korean War," p. 64.

3. Information on the use of the Ranger companies in this and the following paragraphs was drawn from the command reports of the 2d, 3d, 7th, 24th, and 25th Infantry Divisions, the 1st Cavalry Division, and their constituent regiments in RG 407, WNRC, as well as Command Reports, 1949–1954, Non-Organic Units, Japan Logistic Command, AYUT–8213, 1951, Box 5004, RG 407, WNRC. See also U.S. Army, "Special Problems in the Korean Conflict," pp. 82–83; Brig. Gen. G. C. Stewart, 2d Infantry Division, to Ridgway, 5 April 1951, Folder AG 322 General, 1 March–April 30, U.S. Army, Eighth U.S. Army, Assistant Chief of Staff, G-3, Decimal File, Box P570, RG 338, WNRC; "Command Report, Section III: Staff Section Reports: Book I: Office of the CG, HQ 8th U.S. Army Korea (EUSAK), January 1951," U.S. Army, Eighth U.S. Army, Command Reports, Box P732, RG 338, WNRC.

4. Ridgway, *Korean War*, pp. 115–116; "The Good Friday Parachute Operation Which Neutralised Communist Defenses near Seoul," *Illustrated London News*, 7 April 1951, p. 531; Brig. Gen. F. S. Bowen Jr., 187th Airborne Regimental Combat Team, to Commanding General, Eighth Army, 1 April 1951, Folder AG 322 General, 1 March–April 30, U.S. Army, Eighth U.S. Army, Assistant Chief of Staff, G-3, Decimal File, Box P570, RG 338, WNRC; Black, *Rangers in Korea*, pp. 91–93.

5. Martin Blumenson, "The Rangers at Hwachon Dam," *Army* 17 (December 1967): 36–40; U.S. Army, Eighth U.S. Army, 3d Historical Detachment, "Hwachon Dam," unpublished manuscript (Washington, D.C.: OCMH, April 1951); Ridgway, *Korean War*, p. 117.

6. U.S. Army, "Special Problems in the Korean Conflict," pp. 82–84; Report of AFF [Army Field Forces] Observations, FECOM, March 1951, by OCAFF Observer Team no. 4 under Brig. Gen. Robert P. Williams, Item no. 622, U.S. Army, Army Field Forces, Combat Arms Advisory Group, Inspection Reports, 1953, RG 337, MMHB, National Archives; Black, "Rangers of the Korean War," pp. 63–64; Black interview; "Future Employment of Ranger Companies in Korea," 1 May 1951, Folder AG 322 General 1 March–April 30, U.S. Army, Eighth U.S. Army, Assistant Chief of Staff, G-3, Decimal File, Box P570, RG 338, WNRC; David Abshire, "Reflections on the Use and Misuse of Patrols in Korea," *Combat Forces Journal* 4 (July 1954): 20–22; William C. Kimball, "We Need Intelligence and Raider Platoons," *Infantry School Quarterly* 42 (January 1953): 43–50; Taylor, *Swords and Plowshares*, p. 141; 4th Ranger Company File in U.S. Army, Unit Histories, Post WWII, Box 568445, RG 338, WNRC; Blumenson, "Action on Hill 628"; U.S. Army, Eighth U.S. Army, 3d Historical Detachment, "Task Force Byorum," unpublished manuscript (Washington, D.C.: OCMH, n.d.); USAMHI, "Senior Officers Oral History Program: Volney F. Warner, Gen. USA (Ret.)," Project 83-3, interview by Dean M. Owen, Col. USA, (Carlisle, Pa., 1983), p. 161. See also command reports of divisions and regiments, and of the Eighth Army Ranger Company at WNRC.

7. Edward C. Williamson, "Chip Yong-ni: Defense of the South Sector of 23d Regimental Combat Team Perimeter by Company G, 13–15 February 1951," unpublished manuscript (Washington, D.C.: OCMH, n.d.); Black, *Rangers in Korea*, pp. 71–78, 106–110; Black, "Rangers of the Korean War," p. 64.

8. U.S. Army, "Special Problems in the Korean Conflict," pp. 85–86; Bowen to Commanding General, Eighth Army, 1 April 1951; Van Houten to G-3, 4 June 1951, 322 Ranger File, U.S. Army, Army Field Forces, Adjutant General's Section, Communications and Records Division, Decimal File 1951–1952, Box 503, RG 337, MMHB, National Archives; Ogden to Duff, 30 January 1951, and Gaither to Ogden, 31 January 1951, Section II, Distribution Branch, Manpower Control Division, Assistant Chief of Staff, G-1, 12 March 1951, Ranger File, in G-3 Ranger Records, Korean War, Box 380, RG 319, MMHB, National Archives; U.S. Army, "Ranger Company (Tentative)," p. 8; Black, "Rangers of the Korean War," pp. 64–65; Black interview. See Black, *Rangers in Korea*, for descriptions of Ranger actions.

9. Freeman quoted in USAMHI, "Senior Officers Debriefing Program: Freeman," sess. 2, side 1, tape 1, p. 2; U.S. Army, "Special Problems in the Korean Conflict," p. 86; "Unit History, 6th Ranger Infantry Company (Airborne)," p. 5, U.S. Army, Adjutant General's Office, Command Reports, 1949–1954: Non-Organic Units, Box 5235, INCO-6, RG 407, WNRC; Black, "Rangers of the Korean War," pp. 63–64; Black

interview; 2d Lt. R. B. Satterlee, Assistant Adjutant General, EUSAK, to Ruffner, 6 April 1951, Folder 353, U.S. Army, Eighth U.S. Army, Records of the Assistant Chief of Staff, G-1, Box P487, RG 338, WNRC; interview with Capt. John H. Ramsburg, 2 July 1952, Korean War interviews by the Office of the Chief of Military History, USAMHI; Gen. Harold K. Johnson USA (Ret.), interview by Lt. Col. James B. Agnew, Valley Forge, Pa., 21 May 1974, interview no. 15, p. 5, in Harold K. Johnson Papers, USAMHI.

10. Van Houten quoted in Van Houten to Kraus, 2 January 1951, Ranger File, G-3 Ranger Records, Korean War, Box 380, RG 319, MMHB, National Archives; see also Singlaub to Van Houten, 28 November 1950, Section I; Van Houten to Harding, 6 March 1951, Ranger File; Van Houten to Bolte, 28 December 1950, Section II; Van Houten to Collins, 26 March 1951, Section II; Collins to Van Houten, 10 April 1951, Section II; and Memorandum for Record, 16 April 1951, Section II, in G-3 Ranger Records, Korean War, Box 380, RG 319, MMHB, National Archives; Singlaub interview.

11. W. S. Coleman, "Infiltration," *Infantry School Quarterly* 44 (July 1954): 17–20; Ridgway, *Korean War*, p. 183; Bevin Alexander, *Korea: The First War We Lost* (New York: Hippocrene, 1986), pp. 391, 425; Millett and Maslowski, *Common Defense*, pp. 488, 498, 502; Weigley, *History of the United States Army*, p. 524; Doughty, *Evolution*, pp. 10–12; Taylor, *Swords and Plowshares*, p. 141.

12. Drysdale, "41 Commando," p. 32; D. B. Drysdale, "Special Forces," *Marine Corps Gazette* 38 (June 1954): 50; Memorandum for Assistant Chief of Staff, G-3, FECOM, 5 July 1951, Korea no. 6 July 1951, U.S. Army, Far East Command, G-3 Records, Box 752, RG 338, WNRC; David Rees, *Korea: The Limited War* (New York: St. Martin's, 1964), p. 193.

13. Collins to Bolte, 29 August 1950; Ridgway to Taylor, 19 May 1951, Section III, G-3 Ranger Records, Korean War, Box 380, RG 319, MMHB, National Archives; U.S. Army, "Special Problems in the Korean Conflict," p. 83; Report of AFF Observations, FECOM, March 1951.

14. Thomas C. Wyatt, "Butcher and Bolt," *Army* 10 (May 1960): 44; Ridgway to Taylor, 19 May 1951; U.S. Army, "Special Problems in the Korean Conflict," pp. 83–84; Blumenson, "Action on Hill 628," p. 11; Black interview; J. W. Herrington, "Planning an Airborne Assault," *Military Review* 31 (February 1952): 40.

15. Kean quoted in Ogden to Adjutant General, 21 February 1951, Section IA, in G-3 Ranger Records, Korean War, Box 380, RG 319, MMHB, National Archives. For background on the field commanders in Korea, see articles in *Generals of the Army* for the period, as well as USAMHI, "Senior Officers Debriefing Program: Conversations between Lt. Gen. Edward M. Almond and Capt. Thomas G. Fergusson" (Carlisle, Pa., 1975), and USAMHI, "Senior Officers Debriefing Program: Conversations between General William M. Hoge and Lt. Col. George R. Robertson" (Carlisle, Pa., 1974). See also Bolte to Collins, 16 October 1950; and Van Houten to Col. Frank Dorn, Office, Chief of Communication, 28 December 1950, Ranger File, in G-3 Ranger Records, Korean War, Box 380, RG 319, MMHB, National Archives; U.S. Army, "Special Problems in the Korean Conflict," pp. 83–85; USAMHI, "Senior Officers Debriefing Program: Palmer," pp. 123–124; Singlaub interview; Maj. L. R. Skelton, Adjutant, 9th Infantry Regiment, to Assistant Chief of Staff, G-3, 8 February 1951, 302 Inf.(9) Command Report—9th Inf. Regt., 2d Inf. Div., Jan. 1951, U.S. Army, Adjutant General's Office, Command Reports, 1949–1954, Second Infantry Division, RG 407,

WNRC. For more on the U.S. Army's orientation toward strategies of annihilation, see Weigley, *American Way of War*.

16. Quoted in Van Houten to Collins, 29 January 1951, Section II, G-3 Ranger Records, Korean War, Box 380, RG 319, MMHB, National Archives. See also Black, "Rangers of the Korean War," p. 63; 1st Ranger Battalion lineage statement, Organizational History Branch, CMH.

17. Ogden to Adjutant General, 21 February 1951; Van Houten to Collins, 29 January 1951, Section II, G-3 Ranger Records, Korean War, Box 380, RG 319, MMHB, National Archives.

18. Fehrenbach, *This Kind of War*, pp. 256, 289–290, 300–301, 335; U.S. Army, U.S. Military Academy, *Operations in Korea* (West Point, N.Y.: Department of Military Art and Engineering, 1956), pp. 51–52; Taylor, *Swords and Plowshares*, pp. 158–160; Doughty, *Evolution*, pp. 8–9; McMichael, *Light Infantry*, pp. 51–60; S. L. A. Marshall, "Analysis of Infantry Operations and Weapons Usage in Korea during the Winter 1950–1951" (Baltimore, Md.: Operations Research Office, Johns Hopkins University, August 1951), pp. 1–2; Kimball, "We Need Intelligence," pp. 43–50; "The Younger Generation," *Time*, 5 November 1951, pp. 46–52, reprinted in Keith L. Nelson, ed., *The Impact of War on American Life: The Twentieth Century Experience* (New York: Holt, Rhinehart and Winston, 1971), pp. 229–232; Weigley, *History of the United States Army*, pp. 510–511, 520; Hanson W. Baldwin, "Need of Training Revealed in Korea," *New York Times*, 3 November 1950, p. 4; Ridgway to corps and division commanders, 2 January 1951, Correspondence File, General Ridgway, U.S. Army, Eighth U.S. Army, Chief of Staff Records, Box P596, RG 338, WNRC. For opposing viewpoints on the prisoner of war controversy, see Eugene Kinkaid, *In Every War but One* (New York: Norton, 1959) and Albert D. Biderman, *March to Calumny: The Story of American POWs in the Korean War* (New York: Macmillan, 1963).

19. General quoted in "The Rangers Lose," *Time*, 3 September 1951, p. 25; U.S. Army, "Special Problems in the Korean Conflict," p. 85; Memorandum for Record, 5 June 1951, 322 Ranger File, U.S. Army, Army Field Forces, Communications and Records Division, Decimal File, 1951–1952, Box 503, RG 337, MMHB, National Archives; Taylor to Collins, 16 April 1951; Taylor to Adjutant General, 16 April 1951; and Ranger Training Command, "Attachment of Small Groups of Ranger Personnel to Infantry Rifle Companies," 5 March 1951, in Section II, G-3 Ranger Records, Korean War, Box 380, RG 319, MMHB, National Archives.

20. Clark quoted in Clark to Ridgway, 19 March 1951, Matthew B. Ridgway Papers, USAMHI; see also Blumenson, *Mark Clark*, p. 262; "Action Taken on Report of General Clark's Visit to Fort Benning, Georgia," 15–16 March 1951, Item no. 264, U.S. Army, Army Field Forces, Combat Arms Advisory Group, Inspection Reports, 1951, RG 337, MMHB, National Archives.

21. Van Houten quoted in Van Houten to Clark, 9 April 1951, Ranger File, G-3 Ranger Records, Korean War, Box 380, RG 319, MMHB, National Archives. Italics are in original. See also Ranger Training Command, "Staff Study: Project High Standard," 16 August 1951, Infantry School Library, Fort Benning, Ga.

22. Report of AFF Observations, FECOM, March 1951; Memorandum for Record, 27 April 1951, U.S. Army, Far East Command, G-3, Daily Journals, Boxes 840–843, RG 338, WNRC; documents in Folder AG 322 General 1 March–April 30, U.S. Army, Eighth U.S. Army, Assistant Chief of Staff, G-3, Decimal File, Box P570, RG 338,

WNRC.

23. Van Houten quoted in Van Houten to Harding, 6 March 1951, Ranger File, G-3 Ranger Records, Korean War, Box 380, RG 319, MMHB, National Archives; and Van Houten to Distribution List, 13 July 1951, Infantry School Library, Fort Benning, Ga.; see also Van Houten to Maj. John F. Davis, 19 June 1951, Ranger File; Van Houten to Adjutant General, 5 July 1951, Ranger File; and Ranger Training Command, "Ranger Company (Tentative)," 28 March 1951, in G-3 Ranger Records, Korean War, Box 380, RG 319, MMHB, National Archives; Lt. Col. Neil M. Matzger, Assistant Adjutant General, Army Field Forces, to Commanding General, Infantry Center, 14 April 1951, 322 Ranger File, Army Field Forces, Communications and Records Division, Decimal File, 1951–1952, Box 503, RG 337, MMHB, National Archives. To preserve Ranger units, Van Houten was even willing to include such OSS-type missions as the training of partisans within the Ranger concept.

24. For Ridgway's background, see Ridgway, *Soldier*, pp. 11, 37–38, 92–93, 106.

25. In his decision, Ridgway undoubtedly took into account the need of the 187th Airborne Regimental Combat Team for replacements. Ridgway to Taylor, 19 May 1951; Ridgway to Department of the Army, 2 June 1951, Section III, G-3 Ranger Records, Korean War, Box 380, RG 319, MMHB, National Archives.

26. Taylor to Adjutant General, 5 June 1951; Taylor to Collins, 6 June 1951; and Col. M. F. Haas, Secretary, General Staff, to Taylor, 14 June 1951, in Section III, G-3 Ranger Records, Korean War, Box 380, RG 319, MMHB, National Archives.

27. Black, *Rangers in Korea*, pp. 195–196; Taylor to Collins, 25 June 1951, and Memorandum for Record, 3 July 1951, in Section III, G-3 Ranger Records, Korean War, Box 380, RG 319, MMHB, National Archives; Van Fleet to Commanding Generals, I, IX, X Corps, 14 July 1951, AG 322 General 1 March–April 30, U.S. Army, EUSAK, Assistant Chief of Staff, G-3, Decimal File, Box P570, RG 338, WNRC; U.S. Army, "Special Problems in the Korean Conflict," p. 86; U.S. Army, 1st Special Operations Command, "Annual Historical Review, FY 1983–1986," Appendix, p. P–41, Public Relations Office, 1st Special Operations Command, Fort Bragg, N.C.

28. Taylor to Commander in Chief, Europe (CINCEUR), 13 June 1951; CINCEUR to Taylor, 5 July 1951; and Col. R. C. Cooper, Chief, Army War Plans Branch, to Chief, Plans Division, 2 August 1951, Tab C: "Study: Future Need for Ranger Units and Training," Section III, G-3 Ranger Records, Korean War, Box 380, RG 319, MMHB, National Archives.

29. Eddleman to Taylor, 30 June 1951, Section III; Memorandum for Lt. Col. John F. Davis, Organization and Training Division, G-3, 11 July 1951, Ranger File; Van Houten to Maj. Gen. R. E. Duff, Office of Assistant Chief of Staff, G-3, 19 July 1951, Section III; "G-1 Comments of AFF Study re Future Need for Ranger Units and Training," Ranger File; Draft Summary Sheet to the Chief of Staff by Lt. Col. Davis, Ranger File; and Col. Curtis J. Herrick, Chief, Deployments Branch, Operations Division, to Davis, 19 July 1951, Ranger File, in G-3 Ranger Records, Korean War, Box 380, RG 319, MMHB, National Archives; Cooper to Chief, Organization Branch, Organization and Training Division, 23 July 1951, U.S. Army, Operations, General Decimal File, 1950–1951, from 322 to 325, RG 319, MMHB, National Archives; Memorandum for Record, 5 June 1951, 322 Ranger File, U.S. Army, Army Field Forces, Communications and Records Division, Decimal File, 1951–1952, Box 503, RG 337, MMHB, National Archives.

30. Collins illustrated the well-meaning but muddled confusion of Ranger and guerrilla concepts with his remark in April 1951, "The Infantry School should consider using the rangers, as well as other troops and indigenous personnel to initiate subversive activities. I personally established the Rangers with the thought that they might serve as the nucleus for expansion in this direction;" quoted in Lt. Col. Russell W. Volckmann, Acting Chief, Special Operations Division, to Brig. Gen. Robert W. McClure, 337 Conferences TS, U.S. Army, Chief of Special Warfare, TS Decimal Files, 1953-1954, Box 12, RG 319, MMHB, National Archives.

31. Rod Paschall, "Special Operations in Korea," *Conflict* 7, no. 2 (1987): 155-178; Shaun M. Darragh, "Hwanghae Do: The War of the Donkeys," *Army* 34 (November 1984): 66-75.

32. Paddock, *Special Warfare*, pp. 118-129; McClure to Assistant Chief of Staff, G-3, 2 April 1951, and Ogden to McClure, 24 May 1951, in Section II, G-3 Ranger Records, Korean War, Box 380, RG 319, MMHB, National Archives; Bank, *From OSS to Green Berets*, pp. 139-145, 150-160.

33. Jenkins quoted in Col. John G. Hull, Chief, Organization Branch, to Ogden, 18 July 1951, Section III, G-3 Ranger Records, Korean War, Box 380, RG 319, MMHB, National Archives; see also "Jenkins, Reuben E., Lt. Gen. (011658)," *Generals of the Army*, February 1953, pp. 35-36.

34. Jenkins to Collins, 27 August 1951, Ranger File, G-3 Ranger Records, Korean War, Box 380, RG 319, MMHB, National Archives.

35. Lt. Col. L. E. Barber, Assistant Adjutant General, Army Field Forces, to Adjutant General, 3 October 1951, Section III, G-3 Ranger Records, Korean War, Box 380, RG 319, MMHB, National Archives.

36. Quotation from Adjutant General to CINCFE, CINCEUR, Commanding Generals of U.S. Army Alaska, Caribbean, Pacific, Austria, Trieste, Continental Armies, Military District of Washington, Chief of Army Field Forces, 3 October 1951, in HRC 314.7 Ranger Battalion, Historical Records Branch, CMH; see also Brig. Gen. G. J. Higgins, Organization and Training Division, G-3, to Adjutant General, 4 October 1951, Section III, and Memorandum for the Record, 2 October 1951, Ranger File, in G-3 Ranger Records, Korean War, Box 380, RG 319, MMHB, National Archives; Memorandum for Record, 6 October 1951, and Department of the Army to CINCEUR and Commanding Generals of Second, Third, and Fifth Armies, 28 September 1951, in 352 File, Case No. 65, U.S. Army, Army Field Forces, Communications and Records Division, Decimal File, 1951-1952, Box 549, RG 337, MMHB, National Archives; Department of Defense (DOD), Office of Public Information, "Rangers to Join All Army Combat Units: Department Set Up for Training," 28 September 1951, HRC 314.7 Ranger Battalion, Historical Records Branch, CMH.

37. "The Rangers Lose," p. 25; Hanson W. Baldwin, "Rangers Broken Up as Misfits in Korea," *New York Times*, 26 August 1951, p. 1; "Rangers' Training Planned for GI's," *New York Times*, 30 September 1951, p. 6; "Pentagon Studies Fate of Rangers in Army Duty," *Army Times*, 1 September 1951, and "Rangers Lose Jump Pay as Training is Revised," *Army Times*, 6 October 1951, in "Rangers—General", Organizational History Branch, CMH; "Directors Ranger Training Command and Ranger Department," and Col. Owen Elliot, Assistant Adjutant General, Army Field Forces, to the Adjutant General, 22 October 1951, Pamphlet File—Unconventional Warfare, USAMHI.

9

Rangers Lead the Way

The Korean War would last another two years following the inactivation of the Ranger companies, but the atmosphere of confrontation that would characterize the 1950s and 1960s was already determined. For the next two decades, the United States would be obsessed with the global struggle against Communism. Shaken out of their postwar idyll by the Truman Doctrine and the Korean War, Americans were further alarmed by Senator Joseph R. McCarthy's allegations of the presence of Communist spies and sympathizers in government and society. The hysteria of McCarthyism soon subsided, but the American people and government maintained an unswerving opposition to Communism, which they saw as the embodiment of evil arrayed against the forces of good. The Army, for its part, prepared grimly for the anticipated clash with the Soviet Red Army. To counter the Russian masses, the Army sought to enhance the quality of its infantry through special training for small-unit leaders at the new Ranger Department of the Infantry School.[1]

The Ranger course consisted of three phases. After their arrival at the World War II–era barracks, pine trees, and dusty red clay of the Harmony Church area of Fort Benning, students endured brutal physical training, drill, and a refresher course on fundamentals. They also received instruction in leadership, map reading, stream crossing, demolitions, and survival, including a soon-to-be-famous familiarization with poisonous snakes. At the end of three weeks, the program tested the trainees for fitness. Those without the Expert Infantryman's Badge could take qualifying tests at that time. The opening phase, therefore, sought to ensure that the students possessed the conditioning and basic professional knowledge necessary for the rest of the course.

The next two phases provided little formal instruction, emphasizing instead practical fieldwork in rugged terrain. The patrol, with individual trainees rotating through command positions, served as the basic vehicle of instruction.

Amidst snakes and scorpions in the swamps at Eglin Air Force Base near Pensacola, Florida, students learned amphibious and survival techniques and worked with small boats in surf and the inland rivers. On one problem, the trainees landed by night from a ship in the Gulf of Mexico, infiltrated "enemy" defenses, and moved 12 miles through swamps to carry out a mission. After 11 days at Eglin, the students moved to the forested ridges, cliffs, and narrow valleys of the Chattahoochee National Forest near Dahlonega, Georgia. For another 11 days, they learned basic mountaineering methods, navigating precipitous heights and constructing rope bridges to cross gorges, canyons, and streams. Through "confidence tests," notably a steep cable slide from which trainees, on command, dropped into a pool of water, this phase sought to build an individual's faith in his ability to surmount obstacles. The mountain phase concluded with a 72-hour problem involving the simulated destruction of the Blue Ridge Dam on the Ocoee River.[2]

From the highest levels down to the battalions, the Army's leaders were pleased with the initial results from the training but expressed concern about the lack of qualified volunteers, especially noncommissioned officers. Observing the performance of Ranger graduates in Second Army, Lt. Gen. Edward H. Brooks remarked, "We'd have a better combat Army if all squad and platoon leaders in combat units were graduates of this course," and one regimental commander stated, "I now feel that I have nine men who will accept responsibility almost the same as an officer."[3] However, the Army was not meeting its goal of one Ranger-trained officer per company and one Ranger-trained NCO per platoon. With time, fewer soldiers were volunteering, and those who did frequently could not meet the requirements for entry. In the case of NCOs, the lack of incentives and the fact that many of the best sergeants were serving in Korea contributed to the shortage of qualified volunteers. To fill classes, Army Field Forces eased the requirements on the precourse physical fitness test, opened classes to corporals as well as sergeants, and took steps to ensure the promotion of Ranger graduates. Clark even considered the enrollment in the course of some NCOs and junior officers who had distinguished themselves in Korea, but Ridgway and Van Fleet discouraged the idea, comparing it to sending a man to primary school after he had completed a college course.[4]

The continuing inability of the course to attract enough students, as well as its cost in an era of increasingly lean budgets, caused the Army's leaders to consider its dissolution in 1953. Few of the classes were meeting their quotas, and about 75 percent of those who did attend were officers, a reversal of the ratio that Clark had desired at the course's inception. Third Army, the regional headquarters supervising the Infantry School, recommended the elimination of the program, contending that it was too costly and duplicated other offerings at the school. In response, supporters of the course stressed its intangible value and its role as a confidence builder, arguing that "you cannot put a price tag on Ranger graduates." Lt. Gen. John E. Dahlquist, Clark's successor as chief of

A student begins his descent on the "death slide" at the Ranger School, Fort Benning, Ga. (U.S. Army photograph)

Army Field Forces, pointed out that 90 percent of the course's graduates had rated it the best training they had received in the Army, and he further argued that the course's components were too interrelated to incorporate its best features elsewhere. For all its admitted value, if it could not increase enrollment, the program had an uncertain future at best.[5]

After much debate, the course survived, but only by surrendering to a degree its volunteer character. In the Army Staff, the Rangers found an old friend, General Eddleman, who had succeeded Jenkins as chief of the operations division. Eddleman recommended to Ridgway, who was now chief of staff, the continuation of the Ranger program, citing the praise of graduates and pointing out its value in the spread of Ranger techniques throughout the Army. To fill the classes, his division proposed that the Army require every new Regular second lieutenant in the infantry, artillery, armor, Corps of Engineers, and Signal Corps to complete either the Ranger or the airborne course. The airborne option reflected the status of paratroopers in the Army of the 1950s, and it certainly must have made the idea more attractive to Ridgway. However, in the aftermath of the Korean War, Ridgway was also determined to improve the quality of combat training, as well as the competence, character, and public image of the Army's officer corps. On May 10, 1954, he approved the plan. For the moment, the course's enrollment problems were solved, but purists had reason to be concerned about the ongoing quality of the program, especially given the Army Staff's directive to Army Field Forces to minimize its dropout rate and costs.[6]

Costs represented a critical consideration in the Army of the mid- and late 1950s. To contain Communism around the globe without exhausting American resources and patience over the "long haul," the Eisenhower administration elected to cut back expenditures on conventional forces and rely on the threat of air-delivered nuclear weapons to deter aggression. The "New Look," as this policy was called, involved a smaller role for the Army, which was reduced to little more than a tripwire for Western Europe. Between 1953 and 1958, the Army shrank from 1.5 million men in 20 combat divisions to 900,000 men in 15, mostly understrength combat divisions. Both Ridgway and his successor, Maxwell Taylor, resigned in protest of the service's disproportionate share of the budget cuts, and morale in the ground forces sank to a low level. From the Army's point of view, the lone bright spot of the New Look lay in its implicit exclusion of intervention in limited, local conflicts, freeing the Army to focus on its preferred operational environment, a major war with the Soviets in Europe. Army strategists planned to rely on tactical nuclear weapons to offset the Soviet edge in manpower, and they developed a doctrine for the nuclear battlefield involving mobile, fluid operations by highly trained small units which would concentrate quickly to carry out a mission and then disperse before they could be subjected to a nuclear strike.[7]

Observers could view the relevance of Ranger training in this environment in two different ways. On the one hand, the anticipated decentralization of operations in a tactical nuclear conflict in Europe would place a premium on small-unit leaders with initiative, self-confidence, imagination, and daring— precisely the qualities that Ranger training was supposed to develop. One observer went so far to state that "Ranger infantry is the New Look in ground combat forces." On the other hand, the Army of the 1950s was emphasizing technology and management at least as much, if not more than, leadership and the human element in warfare. In his landmark examination of the professional soldier in 1960, the sociologist Morris Janowitz perceived a civilianized officer corps that approached problems in a systematic fashion and reached decisions through group consensus. This managerial model was a far cry from the ideal of the heroic leader embodied in the Ranger ethos, but the Army, in its officer training, was consciously seeking to develop both types.[8]

By the close of the 1950s, therefore, Ranger training had established itself as a program of great prestige in the Army. Even those opposed to Ranger units in Korea, such as Maj. Gen. Paul L. Freeman of the Infantry School, praised the program as a means of producing highly skilled soldiers who could fight under any conditions. Observers noted that the convincing simulation of combat conditions left out only the actual fear of death. In January 1957, Continental Army Command, which had replaced Army Field Forces as the Army agency in charge of training, directed that the Ranger course continue indefinitely, and, the following year, an Army board on officer education, chaired by Lt. Gen. Edward T. Williams, preserved the program from another attempt to incorporate its main features in other courses. As the program grew in permanence and status, it also grew in enrollment. In June 1955, military policemen joined the list of Regular officers required to take Ranger or airborne training, and in 1956, the Army opened the course to officers above the rank of captain. By then, 70 percent of second lieutenants in the Regular Army were taking both Ranger and airborne training.[9]

Enthusiasm for the Ranger course and the type of soldier that it produced had reached such a level in the mid-1950s that several of the Army's combat units experimented with similar training. After a platoon of the 3d Infantry Division attended the course as a unit in the spring of 1955, division commanders noted its high degree of aggressiveness and pride and laid plans to incorporate Ranger-type training into the division's regular program. At Fort Carson, Colorado, the 8th Infantry Division, after a series of tests, added such Ranger subjects as survival, patrol tips, and fieldcraft to its unit training. Meanwhile, the 1st Infantry Division at Fort Riley, Kansas, was proposing that its rifle platoons undergo five weeks of Ranger-type training, including physical conditioning, map reading, demolitions, mines, booby traps, and Ranger-type field problems. Of all the Ranger-type programs, the most famous was the 101st Airborne Division's Recondo School, which used the "patrol of opportunity," a combination of reconnaissance and combat patrol, to drill the division's NCOs in small-unit tactics in the mountains around Fort Campbell, Kentucky. Such programs fit with the theme of Ranger training as a means to improve the quality of the infantry, and, in August 1957, the Ranger Department produced a manual to help units develop these courses.[10]

By the end of the decade, therefore, more soldiers were taking Ranger-type training than ever before, but this expansion did not please everybody. Some critics warned that the broadening of the Ranger course to include almost all Regular combat officers would cause many promising youths to avoid the infantry, armor, and other combat arms, while purists grumbled that the Ranger-airborne requirement had diluted the course's Spartan regimen. No longer truly voluntary, the Ranger program had become a rite of passage, an essential step for a young officer. Instructors were under considerable pressure to relax standards and not ruin the careers of a number of fine young men at the start. One instructor at the Mountain Training Camp even protested that the school was awarding Ranger "tabs," or badges, to trainees who had not finished the course. Whether the program had indeed lowered its standards is difficult to determine, but it would have been hard to convince sweating "mullets" in sawdust pits, thrashing each other with pugil sticks until their urine ran red, that the course was not as tough as it had been.[11]

Unnoticed in the debate over standards, the purpose of the Ranger course had undergone a subtle change since its inception. At first, the course had sought both to produce resourceful small-unit leaders and, through those leaders, to spread methods for infiltration, raids, and other Ranger missions among infantry units. For that reason, it had initially focused on corporals and sergeants, the true teachers of combat troops. By the late 1950s, however, the course had become, for all practical purposes, an endurance test to accustom young officers to operations in a combat environment. To be sure, the curriculum still included raids and long-range patrols, and course literature still paid lip service to the goal of placing in every infantry unit a cadre that was capable of Ranger operations. However, the course handbook in 1959 stated its purpose to be the development of a superb infantry soldier with exceptional endurance and survival skills, and the nature of the program reflected that purpose. The fate of the Ranger Orientation Course illustrated the narrowing focus of the program. Designed to educate senior officers in Ranger missions, it held its last class in 1955.[12]

In part, the declining emphasis on Ranger missions can be traced to growing uncertainty over just what constituted a Ranger mission. Never clear, the meaning of the term "Ranger" had grown more obscure than ever. During World War II, the Army dictionary had defined "Ranger" as a "soldier specially trained to make surprise attacks on enemy territory" and had equated the Rangers with the British commandos.[13] Since World War II, however, the Rangers had carried out numerous other missions, to the point that the Ranger manual of 1957 defined Ranger-type operations as "overt operations conducted in enemy-held territory," including raids, patrols, and "any special mission requiring highly skilled personnel."[14] Such a statement left unclear the line between Ranger missions and normal scouting and patrolling. To the degree that the Army had a concept of Ranger missions, it did not perceive the methods required for such tasks as different from those of line infantrymen but rather saw the Ranger as a soldier with highly developed infantry skills, exceptional endurance and courage, and an ability to work in different environments. The Ranger manual of 1957, with its brief section on actual Ranger operations and lengthy discussion of a Ranger course for line infantry, reflected this perception.[15]

Publicity of the Ranger course in both the Army and the general population encouraged the rugged image of the Rangers. To stimulate enrollment, the Army gave the program plenty of exposure. Articles in newspapers and magazines, both popular and professional, stressed the toughness and realism of the course. A favorite subject was the lecture on poisonous snakes, delivered, according to Hanson W. Baldwin, by "a brawny corporal instructor with tattoo marks all over his arms—and a polite captain who hates snakes." Much of the publicity traced the ancestry of the Ranger program to the legends of early American history, often stretching or falsifying facts in the process. Past Rangers were portrayed as expert riders, crack shots, skilled woodsmen, and "man-for-man . . . without equal." Morgan, Francis Marion, and Mosby all received attention, but the lion's share went to Robert Rogers, whose Standing Orders seemed to appear in almost every piece of literature produced by the Ranger program. Given the emphasis on Rogers, one can imagine the concern of the Ranger Department when it discovered that he had actually fought for the British during the Revolution.[16]

In the development of the Ranger legend, movies played a critical role. By the late 1950s, television and films were largely replacing newspapers and magazines as transmitters of ideas and role models, and, in that media, war exploits were a popular theme. Producers catered to the desire of viewers for romance, adventure, and vicarious excitement through the experiences of others. Like other war movies of the 1950s, *Darby's Rangers* cast a nostalgic glow on overseas service during World War II. It portrayed the Rangers as normal American boys who left in their wake broken hearts from Scotland to Italy, did not take kindly to harsh disciplinarians from West Point, and did their job without enjoying the experience. James Garner portrayed Darby as a surrogate father who listened to his men's fears and then led them to glory. *The Devil's Brigade* took a more sober approach but still stressed the popular theme of rugged individualists molded into a fighting team by a stern father figure.[17]

The romantic picture of the Rangers in films fit with a general idealization of the American as a natural fighter in the popular culture of the 1950s and early 1960s. Quickly forgetting the experience in Korea, which they blamed on the politicians anyway, Americans viewed their military forces as invincible and their soldiers as inherently courageous and self-reliant. They reveled in the legendary exploits of the Kentucky and Tennessee riflemen,

Sergeant York, Audie Murphy, and, above all, Davy Crockett. After 40 million viewers saw the Walt Disney production on the Tennessee frontiersman in 1955, stores sold $100 million worth of coonskin caps and other paraphernalia, and "The Ballad of Davy Crockett" soared to the top of the pop music charts. Numerous articles pointed out that the real Davy Crockett, a lazy and often drunk drifter, was a far cry from the folksy, honest, freshly bathed "king of the wild frontier" portrayed by Fess Parker, but that hardly dampened public enthusiasm. Six years later, Vice President Lyndon B. Johnson told West Point graduates, many of whom would later serve in Vietnam, that "a nation which produced Davy Crockett and Daniel Boone and Jim Bowie is afraid of no forest and no swamp and no game of fighting, however toughly it is played." Moreover, Johnson expressed confidence that they would return and "nail the coonskins to the wall."[18]

As the sentimentalism surrounding the American soldier demonstrated, Americans in the 1950s were in no mood to challenge traditional institutions, including the military. Basking in a prosperity that provided swimming pools, television sets, and two cars in every garage and confident of their ability to solve any problem, they firmly believed they lived in the greatest country in the world. In contrast to the situation in later years, a remarkable degree of consensus existed on the nation's historic mission, particularly as a force for good against the evil of Communism. Even political intellectuals sang the virtues of American culture. American institutions seemed sacrosanct from criticism, and none more so than the military. Movies glorified the military experience, business leaders added retired military heroes to corporate boards, and children read "Sergeant Rock" comics and played with "GI Joe" dolls. In the aftermath of World War II, and with the ongoing Cold War, the military had reached an unprecedented level of status in a traditionally antimilitary society.

Nevertheless, beneath this confidence in American institutions, one could detect a sense of unease as the decade came to an end. The Soviet launch of the Sputnik satellite in October 1957 not only seemed to reveal an alarming Soviet lead in aerospace technology, it also raised the specter of a surprise attack by Soviet intercontinental ballistic missiles against the United States. In the face of this threat to the American homeland, the Eisenhower administration's heavy reliance on nuclear weapons to deter aggression abroad no longer seemed credible. Politicians, retired military officers, and intellectuals called for increased defense spending, especially on conventional arms, and criticized the administration for permitting Soviet technology to catch up with that of the United States. Underlying much of this criticism was a fear that the United States was losing its edge in the global conflict with Communism, that American society had become too complacent, materialistic, and intolerant of new ideas to compete with the Soviets. American leaders called for a new moral toughness and a renewed sense of national purpose to meet the Soviet challenge.[19]

In January 1961, a new administration took office with the goal of restoring American resolve and leadership in the world. In his personality and public statements, John F. Kennedy projected an image of youth, energy, courage, idealism, and confidence in the American ability to solve any problem. He called on Americans to toughen themselves mentally and physically in an article for *Sports Illustrated*, and, in his inaugural address, he committed American power to respond to aggression anywhere in the world with the statement, "We shall pay any price, bear any burden, meet any hardship, support any friend, oppose any foe to assure the survival and success of liberty." To carry out its strategy of responding to each level of aggression with an appropriate level of force, the administration expanded U.S. military forces across the board, but with a particular focus on guerrilla warfare and counterinsurgency. Sensitive to the threat of "wars of national liberation," Kennedy directed the Department of Defense to emphasize organization and training of counterguerrilla forces, pushed the development of appropriate equipment, and even hinted that future promotions in the services would depend on experience in special warfare.[20]

The Army reacted to the administration's enthusiasm with a mixture of skepticism about this latest government fancy and serene confidence that, if it could handle nuclear and conventional warfare, it could manage any other contingency. Generals warned of the need for a balance among several missions, and they clearly did not regard special warfare as a mission requiring unique arrangements. Indeed, *Newsweek* quoted Gen. George H. Decker, the chief of staff, as stating, "Any good soldier can handle guerrillas." After the doldrums of the Eisenhower years, however, the Army welcomed the greater role promised by special warfare, and it beefed up its capabilities in the field. Divisions cleared time in training schedules for counterguerrilla operations, and Army schools added to their curriculums a variety of crash courses on the subject. Ambitious officers hastened to read the mushrooming number of works on guerrilla warfare. Although many claimed expertise, few grasped the intricacies of a subject that was far too complex to yield to cursory examination.[21]

As the Army groped toward a counterinsurgency doctrine, the critical role of small-unit leaders in counterguerrilla operations raised the prestige of the Ranger course in the Army to new heights. For an age concerned about American toughness and moral fiber, the course enjoyed an inherent appeal in any case. Nonetheless, its stress on patrolling, night operations, raids, and endurance seemed particularly relevant to developing the kind of rugged, resourceful, and daring junior officers needed for operations against elusive guerrillas. As the Army became more deeply involved in Vietnam, it increased the number of officers who were required to take Ranger training. By 1964, the Army was directing all Regular officers to take either Ranger or airborne training, and in 1966, it adopted the recommendation of an Army education board chaired by Gen. Ralph E. Haines, Jr., that all Regular officers attend the Ranger course. Gen. Harold K. Johnson, chief of staff from 1964 to 1968, expressed the views of many in the Army when he called the Ranger course "the greatest confidence builder that we have."[22]

Even as the course continued to stress the development of leadership qualities, it gave more attention to patrol techniques to prepare young officers for Vietnam. The Ranger Department had already switched the order of the program's final two phases. It now lengthened the entire course by 200 hours and, with the help of the theatrical Maj. Charlie A. Beckwith and other Vietnam veterans, reoriented the content of the final swamp phase to stress counter-guerrilla methods. Students arriving at Eglin were greeted with explosions, "dead" soldiers, and trucks ablaze from "guerrilla attack." They then endured 17 days of patrols in the swamps, squeezing through narrow tunnels, arriving famished at a landing zone to find that the supply helicopter was carrying batteries, and crossing frigid rivers while Beckwith, lying on his back in the freezing water with a cigar in his mouth, questioned their toughness. Once again, the course had a dual purpose as an instructor of skills and as an endurance test to develop maturity. One could wonder about the program's ability to produce expert patrollers within a few weeks, particularly when students became so exhausted that they had been known to do such things as putting imaginary quarters into a tree to "call for help." Nevertheless, the Army firmly believed that it was providing an "insurance policy" for second lieutenants who would soon be leading patrols in the jungles of Vietnam.[23]

After reaching its peak in popularity during the Vietnam War, the Ranger course declined in favor during the early 1970s. The course seemed an anachronism in the antimilitary atmosphere of the period, with the popular emphasis on individual expression and disdain for martial values. Within the Army itself, several leaders criticized the course's mandatory nature. Facing large budget reductions, many Army leaders noted the program's high cost per graduate and questioned whether it properly prepared young officers for any war outside Southeast Asia. Gen. John K. Woolnough, chief of Continental Army Command, feared that the course was growing too large to retain its elite character and argued that the Army should not stamp a promising officer as a failure just because he could not complete the Ranger program. When Gen. William C. Westmoreland, the chief of staff, asked Woolnough to review the Ranger course in January 1970, the latter suggested that the Army rescind mandatory Ranger training. After a delay to investigate the possibility of incorporating Ranger subjects into the programs of other Army schools, the chief of staff abolished all requirements to attend the Ranger School in mid-1971.[24]

The doldrums of the early 1970s were followed by a revival at the Ranger School in the last years of the decade. As the United States returned to a more activist foreign policy, the Army faced a greater prospect of operations in areas other than Europe. Responding to President Jimmy Carter's "Carter

Doctrine," which committed the United States to protect the oil fields of the Middle East, the Ranger course added a desert phase in April 1983. Between the mountain and swamp phases, students parachuted or were inserted into the desert wastes near Fort Bliss, Texas, where they received seven days of instruction in survival and tactics in a desert environment. Other than the addition of the desert phase, the Ranger course changed little in its basic structure and goals after the 1960s. While paying lip service to methods of Ranger operations, the Ranger Department continued to view its objective as the development of individual qualities of leadership.[25]

The Ranger course's focus on leadership in the 1950s and 1960s combined with other factors in the American military and society to lend an almost mystical connotation to the term "Ranger." Locked in a perceived spiritual struggle with Communism, Americans retained a sense of historic mission but viewed with unease any signs of lack of toughness or moral fiber in their affluent society and looked back with some nostalgia to the legendary heroes of their past. The Army, if anything, held these views to an even greater degree than the general public. For all their confidence in their way of war, with its reliance on technology and firepower, military leaders sensed the ongoing importance of the moral factor and looked to Ranger training to build character in their small-unit leaders. Instruction in Ranger skills of scouting and raids, which was so central to the course's original purpose, became secondary to this main objective. In the process, Ranger training created a cult of toughness, establishing a test of manhood felt to be essential to a young man's military career. It also contributed to a Ranger concept that went beyond functional definitions of the Ranger as raider or expert patroller to evoke an image of the ultimate American fighting man: brave, tough, resourceful, and able to fight anywhere, anytime. Thus, Ranger training, which was initially an alternative to Ranger units, survived even after the Army revived Ranger formations.

NOTES

1. J. Ronald Oakley, *God's Country: America in the Fifties* (New York: Dembner Books, 1986), pp. 7, 48–49, 184–186; Charles C. Alexander, *Holding the Line: The Eisenhower Era, 1952–1961* (Bloomington: Indiana University Press, 1975), pp. xiii, 62–64; Sheehan, *Bright Shining Lie*, p. 480.

2. Joseph Windsor, "Rugged and Ready," *Infantry School Quarterly* 42 (January 1953): 94–103; Jim Mintner and Paul Price, "Rangers Ready!" *Army Information Digest* 8 (January 1953): 13–20; Hanson W. Baldwin, "Our New Shock Troops—The Rangers," *New York Times Magazine*, 27 April 1952, sec. 6, p. 8; Rick Atkinson, *The Long Gray Line* (Boston: Houghton Mifflin, 1989), pp. 153, 161.

3. Brooks to Clark, 1 May 1952, 322 Ranger File, U.S. Army, Army Field Forces, Communications and Records Division, Decimal File, 1951–1952, Box 503, RG 337, MMHB, National Archives; regimental commander quoted in Windsor, "Rugged and

Ready," p. 103; see also items no. 241 and 262 in U.S. Army, Army Field Forces, Combat Arms Advisory Group, Inspection Reports, 1952, RG 337, MMHB, National Archives.

4. Eddleman, Assistant Chief of Staff, G-3, to Ridgway, 30 January 1954, U.S. Army, Chief of Staff, Decimal File, 1953–1954, 322 Rangers, RG 319, MMHB, National Archives; Clark to Ridgway, 18 March 1952; Van Fleet to Ridgway, 3 April 1952; and Ridgway to Clark, 7 April 1952, in Ridgway Papers, USAMHI; correspondence in 322 Ranger File, U.S. Army, Army Field Forces, Communications and Records Division, Decimal File, 1951–1952, Box 503, RG 337, MMHB, National Archives; Gen. John R. Hodge, Chief, Army Field Forces, to Lt. Gen. A. R. Bolling, Commanding General, Third Army, 11 May 1953, U.S. Army, Chief of Staff, Decimal File, 1953–1954, 322 Rangers, RG 319, MMHB, National Archives; Corley to G-3, Army Field Forces, 1 March 1952, and Lt. Col. W. H. Melhorn, Assistant Adjutant General, Army Field Forces, to Commandant, Infantry School, 15 March 1952, Item no. 237, U.S. Army, Army Field Forces, Combat Arms Advisory Group, Inspection Reports, 1952, RG 337, MMHB, National Archives.

5. Quote from Maj. H. R. Coates, G-3 section, OCAFF, to Assistant Chief of Staff, G-3, 12 February 1953, Item no. 204, U.S. Army, Army Field Forces, Combat Arms Advisory Group, Inspection Reports, 1953, RG 337, MMHB, National Archives; see also Item no. 194, U.S. Army, Army Field Forces, Combat Arms Advisory Group, Inspection Reports, 1953, RG 337, MMHB, National Archives; Memorandum for Record and Dahlquist to Eddleman, 24 December 1953, U.S. Army, Assistant Chief of Staff, G-3, General Decimal File, 353, 1954, RG 319, MMHB, National Archives.

6. Eddleman to Ridgway, 30 January 1954; Eddleman to Ridgway, 23 February 1954, U.S. Army, Chief of Staff, Decimal File, 1953–1954, 322 Rangers, RG 319, MMHB, National Archives; correspondence in G-3, 353, Section XIII, Case 266, U.S. Army, Assistant Chief of Staff, G-3, General Decimal File, 353, 1954, RG 319, MMHB, National Archives; Chief of Army Field Forces to Assistant Chief of Staff, G-3, 9 June 1954; and Maj. Gen. James M. Gavin, Assistant Chief of Staff, G-3, to Chief of Army Field Forces, 10 July 1954, in G-3, 353, Section XVI, Case 308, U.S. Army, Assistant Chief of Staff, G-3, General Decimal File, 353, 1954, RG 319, MMHB, National Archives; Ridgway, *Soldier*, pp. 295–301; USAMHI, "Senior Officers Debriefing Program: Conversations between General Matthew B. Ridgway USA (Ret.) and Colonel John M. Blair USA," vol. 2, tape 4, sess. 4, part 2, p. 55; "Help the Army," 18 February 1954, and Mrs. William J. Falsey to Ridgway, 1 September 1953, in D File of Correspondence, Ridgway Papers, USAMHI; "Army Going Back to Tough Training," *New York Times*, 15 August 1954, p. 45.

7. Walter G. Hermes, "The Army and the New Look," in Maurice Matloff, ed., *American Military History*, 2d ed., Army Historical Series (Washington, D.C.: OCMH, 1973), pp. 573–574, 581–587; Alexander, *Holding the Line*, pp. xvi, 8, 66–69; Richard A. Aliano, *American Defense Policy from Eisenhower to Kennedy* (Athens: Ohio University Press, 1975), pp. 38–39; Doughty, *Evolution*, pp. 12–19; Millett and Maslowski, *Common Defense*, pp. 510, 529; Walter Millis, *Arms and Men: A Study in American Military History* (New York: G. P. Putnam's Sons, 1956), pp. 339, 356; Weigley, *History of the United States Army*, pp. 526, 537.

8. Quote from Richard J. Buck, "Rangers Are the New Look," *Combat Forces Journal* 5 (August 1954): 44; see also Armistead D. Mead, "Ranger Type Training for Infantry Units," *Infantry School Quarterly* 46 (April 1956): 33; Ridgway, *Soldier*, p. 298; Hermes, "The Army and the New Look," p. 586; Walter G. Hermes, "Global Pressures and the Flexible Response, " in Maurice Matloff, ed., *American Military History*, 2d ed., Army Historical Series (Washington, D.C.: OCMH, 1973), pp. 610–611; Morris Janowitz, *The Professional Soldier* (Glencoe, Ill.: Free Press, 1960), pp. 8–10, 35–36.

9. "Report of the Department of the Army: Officer Education and Training Review Board" [Williams Board], 1 July 1958, in Historical Records Branch, CMH; Freeman interview, side 1, tape 2, interview 2, 17 April 1974, p. 5; U.S. Army Infantry School, *Ranger* (Fort Benning, Ga.: Infantry School, 1959), p. 8; Corley, Director, Ranger Department to Col. S. W. Foote, OCMH, 30 January 1959, HRC 314.7 Ranger Battalion, Historical Records Branch, CMH; "Field Graders May Volunteer for Ranger Training," *Infantry School Quarterly* 46 (April 1956): 102–103; "Researcher Turns Ranger to Probe Military Skills," *Army Times*, 25 April 1959, p. 19.

10. "Recondo" combined the terms "reconnaissance," "doughboy," and "commando;" see William C. Westmoreland, *A Soldier Reports* (Garden City, N.Y.: Doubleday, 1976), p. 31; "It's a 130-Hour Week at Recondo School; Medal of Honor Commandant," *Army, Navy, Air Force Journal* 96 (16 May 1959): 13; Lewis L. Millett, "Recondo: Patrol of Opportunity," *Army* 10 (February 1960): 54–57. See also Mead, "Ranger Type Training," pp. 34–36; U.S. Army, Department of the Army, *Ranger Training*, FM 21–50 (Washington, D.C.: Department of the Army, 20 August 1957).

11. Donald Lewis, "History of the Ranger Department," *Gung Ho*, October 1984, p. 45; Anthony B. Herbert and James T. Wooten, *Soldier* (New York: Holt, Rhinehart and Winston, 1973), p. 76; Captain Tactic, "U.S. Grant Wasn't a Trooper," *Combat Forces Journal* 5 (May 1955): 49–50; Atkinson, *Long Gray Line*, pp. 155, 175.

12. U.S. Army Infantry School, *Ranger*, pp. 1, 11–16; "Danger Is Routine: Army Ranger's Job Highly Specialized," *Army Times*, 4 August 1956, p. 21; John T. Corley, "Army Ranger Students in 8 Week Course Get Plenty of Rugged Work, Little Sleep," *Army Navy Journal* 96 (20 September 1958): 2; Corley to Foote, 30 January 1959; Herbert and Wooten, *Soldier*, pp. 72–73; Lewis, "Ranger Department," p. 45.

13. U.S. War Department, *Dictionary of United States Army Terms*, Technical Manual 20–205 (Washington, D.C.: War Department, 18 January 1944), p. 223.

14. U.S. Army, *Ranger Training*, p. 5.

15. Herbert and Wooten, *Soldier*, p. 72, Buck, "Rangers," p. 44; USAMHI, "Senior Officers Debriefing Program: Palmer," p. 89; U.S. Army Infantry School, Ranger Department, "Epic of the Rangers," *Infantry School Quarterly* 46 (January 1956): 15.

16. Quote from Baldwin, "Our New Shock Troops," p. 8; see also U.S. Army, *Ranger Training*, pp. 213–226; U.S. Army Infantry School, *Ranger*, pp. 2–10; U.S. Army, Department of the Army, *Ranger Training and Ranger Operations*, FM 21–50 (Washington, D.C.: Department of the Army, January 1962), pp. 321–333; Buck, "Rangers," p. 44; "Danger is Routine," p. 21; U.S. Army, "Epic of the Rangers," p. 15; Corley, "Army Ranger Students," p. 2; "The Rangers Have a Long History," *Army Times*, 11 March 1964, p. E6; A. Porter and S. Sweet, "Rangers Four," *Infantry* 56 (January–February 1966): 60–61; Department of Defense, Office of Public Information Press Release, 23 July 1956, and Corley to OCMH, 24 November 1958, in HRC 314.7 Ranger Battalion, Historical Records Branch, CMH; Richard J. Stillman, ed., *The U.S.*

Infantry: Queen of Battle (New York: Franklin Watts, 1965), p. 17. The Army's Office
of the Chief of Military History returned one Ranger "fact sheet" with the comment,
"This is strictly 'Hollywood stuff' with the usual amount of errors and inaccuracies";
Hazel B. Abbott, Chief of Information, Department of the Army, to OCMH, 2 September
1954, HRC 314.7 Ranger Battalion, Historical Records Branch, CMH.

17. Lawrence H. Suid, *Guts and Glory: Great American War Movies* (Reading, Mass:
Addison-Wesley, 1978), pp. xv–xvii, 2–3, 7–9, 238; Lawrence H. Suid, "The Film
Industry and the Vietnam War" (Ph.D. dissertation: Case Western Reserve University,
1980), p. 103; Bernard F. Dick, *The Star-Spangled Screen: The American World War II
Film* (Lexington: University Press of Kentucky, 1985), pp. vii–viii, 154; Charles C.
Moskos, *The American Enlisted Man: The Rank and File in Today's Military* (New York:
Russell Sage, 1970), p. 3; *Darby's Rangers*, Warner Brothers, 1958, and *The Devil's
Brigade*, David Wolper, 1968, available at the Library of Congress.

18. Johnson quoted in Westmoreland, *Soldier Reports*, p. 33; see also Oakley, *God's
Country*, p. 262; Geoffrey Hodgson, *America in Our Time* (Garden City, N.Y.:
Doubleday, 1976), pp. 493–494; Suid, *Guts and Glory*, p. xv; Stillman, *U.S. Infantry*,
pp. 3–4, 48, 63, 178, 243.

19. Hodgson, *America*, pp. 12, 67–76, 493–494; Oakley, *God's Country*, pp. 95,
314–319, 342–349, 408, 413; Alexander, *Holding the Line*, pp. 101, 133–134, 214–216,
226–230, 268–269; Morris Dickstein, *Gates of Eden: American Culture in the Sixties*
(New York: Basic Books, 1977), pp. 26–28, 40, 50–51; Siegel, *Troubled Journey*, pp.
119–121; Leuchtenburg, *Troubled Feast*, p. 69; Suid, *Guts and Glory*, p. xv; Donald R.
Mrozek, "The Army and Popular Culture," in Robin Higham and Carol Brandt, eds., *The
United States Army in Peacetime* (Manhattan, Kans.: Military Affairs, 1975), p. 144;
Huntington, *Soldier and the State*, pp. 361–362; Millett and Maslowski, *Common
Defense*, pp. 509, 529–530.

20. Kennedy quoted in Siegel, *Troubled Journey*, p. 131; see also pp. 122–132;
Stephen L. Bowman, "The United States Army and Counterinsurgency Warfare: The
Making of Doctrine, 1946–1964" (M.A. thesis, Duke University, 1981), pp. 50–52;
Simpson, *Green Berets*, p. x; Lloyd Norman and John B. Spore, "Big Push in Guerrilla
Warfare," *Army* 12 (March 1962): 28, 32–33; Millett and Maslowski, *Common Defense*,
p. 530; Taylor, *Swords and Plowshares*, p. 200; Weigley, *History of the United States
Army*, p. 528.

21. Decker quoted in Bowman, "Counterinsurgency Warfare," p. 106; see also
Bowman, "Counterinsurgency Warfare," pp. 121–124; Simpson, *Green Berets*, pp.
65–67; Norman and Spore, "Big Push," pp. 34–35; Cable, *Conflict of Myths*, pp. 4–5,
116–117, 136, 141; Bruce Palmer and Roy K. Flint, "Counterinsurgency Training," *Army*
12 (June 1962): 38; Doughty, *Evolution*, pp. 25–26; interview with General William E.
Depuy by Lieutenant Colonels Bill Mullen and Les Brownlee, 26 March 1979, tape 2,
interview 2, pp. 1–2, Historical Records Branch, CMH; Yarborough interview, sess. 2,
pp. 2–4, 7, 17–19; Garrett interview; USAMHI, "Senior Officers Debriefing Program:
Seaman," IV:34; USAMHI, "Senior Officers Debriefing Program: Palmer," p. 381.

22. Johnson quoted in Col. I. A. Edwards, Chief, Ranger Department, to former
Rangers, 27 March 1967, Harry Perlmutter File, Ranger Collection, USAMHI; see also
Palmer and Flint, "Counterinsurgency Training," p. 38; Cable, *Conflict of Myths*, pp.
127, 141; "Don't Forget Nothin': 1759 Ranger Tips Keep GI's Alert," *Washington Star*,
19 December 1965, p. 3; James K. McCrorey, "Ranger Armor," *Armor* 76 (Janu-

ary–February 1967): 24–31; Army Regulation 621–109, 5 August 1964, in Army Regulations 615–370 to 624–300, CMH Library; Army Regulation 350–5, 26 October 1966, in Pentagon Library, Washington, D.C.; U.S. Army, Department of the Army, "Report of the Department of the Army Board to Review Army Officer Schools," [Haines Board], 4 vols. (Washington, D.C.: Department of the Army, February 1966), I:30–31, 76, III:414, 430, 637, in Historical Records Branch, CMH.

23. Lewis, "Ranger Department," p. 45; Shelby L. Stanton, "Rangers at War," manuscript submitted for publication, pp. 1–17; "Vietnam Training Comes to Benning," *Journal of the Armed Forces* 103 (16 October 1965): 15; J. D. O'Brien, "A Ranger's Life," *Canadian Forces Sentinel* 3 (September 1967): 6–9; Charlie A. Beckwith and Donald Knox, *Delta Force* (New York: Harcourt, Brace, Jovanovich, 1983), pp. 85–86; Robert C. Fox, "The New Ranger," *Infantry* 57 (November–December 1967): 47–50; Ronald L. Paramore, "Ranger," *Infantry* 61 (May–June 1971): 18–20; U.S. Army, Department of the Army, *The Army School Catalogue*, DA Pam 20–21 (Washington, D.C.: Department of the Army, August 1962), p. 199; Atkinson, *Long Gray Line*, pp. 162–172.

24. Lewis, "Ranger Department," p. 45; Stanton, "Rangers at War," pp. 16–18; Warren D. Garlock and Michael L. Lanning, "Ranger Training: A Part of the Army's Future?" *Infantry* 62 (November–December 1972): 30; Army Regulation 351–1, 19 August 1971, in Pentagon Library; USAMHI, "Senior Officers Debriefing Program: Conversations between Gen. James K. Woolnough USA (Ret.) and Col. W. D. Macmillan and Lt. Col. W. M. Stevenson," Tab C (Carlisle, Pa., 1971), pp. 29–30; Edward Shils, "American Society and the War in Indochina," in Anthony Lake, *The Legacy of Vietnam: The War, American Society, and the Future of American Foreign Policy* (New York: Council on Foreign Relations, 1976), p. 44.

25. William D. Phillips, "Ranger Desert Phase," *Infantry* 74 (March–April 1984): 10–12; Steve Crawford, "Desert Command Added to Ranger School 'Classload,'" *Army* 34 (November 1984): 26–28; Marc Williams, "Rank Doesn't Cut It: An Officer's Perspective on Ranger School," *Gung Ho*, October 1984, pp. 6–8; and other articles in *Gung Ho*, October 1984; Dan Rifenburgh, "Ranger Making," *Soldiers* 29 (June 1974): 14–16; Garlock and Lanning, "Ranger Training," p. 30; Ernest W. Cooler, "The Ranger Course," *Infantry* 70 (September–October 1980): 31–32; Bill Branley, "Don't Forget Nothing," *Soldiers* 36 (February 1981): 6–13; U.S. Army Infantry School, Ranger Department, "The Ranger Course Pamphlet" (Fort Benning, Ga.: Ranger Department, 1980), pp. 6–12, in U.S. Army Infantry School Library, Fort Benning, Ga.

10

"Lerps" and Green Berets

For almost two decades after the inactivation of the Ranger companies in Korea, the Army did without Ranger units. More than ever before, the Army of the 1950s and 1960s was run by men whose basic outlook had been shaped by big-unit warfare. Entering the service on the eve of World War II, a generation of American officers had risen rapidly to high rank in a conflict that accustomed them to total victory through the application of overwhelming resources. In this environment, the high-level officer, such as an Eddleman, who appreciated elite units was a rarity. Gen. Harold K. Johnson spoke for many when he argued that elites took needless risks to justify their existence, stole the best men from other units, and generally made soldiers in other units feel like second-class citizens. He and his colleagues believed that any properly trained line formation, with a little extra instruction in some cases, could handle short-range infiltration, raids, and patrols. Missions farther into the enemy rear, they felt, should be left to native partisans advised by the new Special Forces. For those sporadic tasks demanding an American combat unit, they would draw on the Army's pool of Ranger-qualified personnel as a cadre, but they saw no consistent need for a regular force to perform deep-penetration raids.[1]

While the U.S. Army was scaling back its elite forces, other nations were finding such units to be invaluable in the brushfire wars of the Third World. In the colonial conflicts and guerrilla wars of the 1950s, elites, with their high morale and readiness to use unconventional methods, usually achieved better results than unenthusiastic conscripts and orthodox professional soldiers. After disbanding most of their elite forces at the end of World War II, the British found a revived Special Air Service to be a valuable asset to the counterinsurgency effort in Malaya. SAS teams infiltrated into the jungle, where they patrolled for guerrillas and won native support through civic action. Overcoming some initial problems of personnel selection, the SAS became one of the world's most professional elite forces, winning distinction in Borneo and Arabia. Nor were they alone in demonstrating the value of elites. The Israelis used airborne forces to raid Arab guerrilla bases and seize key points in conjunction with conventional offensives, and French "paras" spearheaded counterinsurgencies in Indochina and Algeria before involvement in French politics led to their downfall.[2]

As early as the mid-1950s, such American officers as William C. Kimball, John W. Medusky, and Bickford E. Sawyer were urging the U.S. Army to follow the foreign example and form special units. Noting the problems that many American units had encountered in the conduct of deep patrols in Korea, they advocated the formation of special units that could infiltrate 2,000 to 6,000 yards into the enemy's rear, reconnoiter his positions, and call in artillery or air strikes. They responded to misgivings about the risks involved by pointing out the growing capabilities of the helicopter as a vehicle for infiltration and evacuation.[3]

Such arguments met a surprisingly receptive audience. Even by the mid-1950s, it was becoming intuitively obvious to some of the Army's leaders that line units and partisans simply could not handle certain tasks. They often cited long-range reconnaissance as an example of a mission requiring a special formation. In the event of a war in Europe, the Army planned to hit targets in the enemy's intermediate rear with artillery and air strikes, using tactical nuclear weapons if necessary. To avoid indiscriminate fire, which would devastate the central European cities and countryside, field commanders needed to pinpoint enemy facilities and troop concentrations. Aerial reconnaissance, using cameras, radar, and infrared devices, would help, but could not substitute for an observer on the ground. A mission of this depth into the enemy rear was probably unsuitable for line units, and one could not be sure of the reliability, or even the presence, of partisans. The solution appeared to be specially trained teams of selected men with direct radio links to higher headquarters.

During the mid- to late 1950s, the U.S. Seventh Army in Europe joined other NATO contingents in experiments with long-range reconnaissance patrols (LRRP). As part of Exercise WAR HAWK in December 1956, VII Corps experimented with teams that infiltrated "enemy" lines by remaining in place, under cover, while the main force withdrew. The concept worked well enough that, by the autumn of 1957, the South European Task Force was organizing an airborne reconnaissance platoon, and V Corps was selecting and training personnel for LRRPs. In February 1958, V Corps's patrols practiced targeting for tactical nuclear strikes in Exercise SABRE HAWK, and the next year, V and VII Corps experimented with LRRPs in two separate field maneuvers in Germany. These exercises showed the considerable work that remained to be accomplished in such areas as communications and the use of helicopters. Nevertheless, the concept had progressed to the point that Seventh Army, in 1961, issued a doctrinal statement on the selection, training, organization, and employment of LRRPs.[4]

The LRRP concept soon gained widespread support in an Army that was reevaluating its force structure to conform with the Kennedy administration's strategy of flexible response. In May 1961, Continental Army Command, the agency responsible for Army doctrine, issued Directive 525-4, which defined for the entire Army the concept of small teams that were specially trained to reconnoiter for lengthy periods behind enemy lines and coordinate air and artillery strikes on lucrative targets. Directive 525-4 set the stage for a field manual on LRRP operations in 1962 and an organizational table for LRRP companies in 1964. The table provided for a LRRP company of three platoons, each with eight patrols of five men, and with Ranger-qualified personnel in the key positions. Written with tactical nuclear warfare and the European theater in mind, the table and manual envisioned the LRRP mission as "long-range reconnaissance, surveillance, and target acquisition" for a corps or field army.[5] Interestingly, the manual also stated that a LRRP could carry out certain demolitions "in conjunction with intelligence requirements" and locate and destroy "special intelligence" targets. Thus, on the eve of large-scale involvement in Vietnam, the Army acknowledged the need for a special unit to carry out some types of raids.[6]

For raids far behind enemy lines, the Army expected to rely largely on partisans trained by Special Forces. This organization traced its roots to the concept of special teams approved by Taylor in the summer of 1951. Modeled after the OSS's Operational Groups, these teams were designed to organize, supply, instruct, and lead partisans in attacks on Soviet communications and installations if the Red Army took advantage of American involvement in Korea to invade Western Europe. Despite opposition from the CIA and the Air Force, which had intended to keep the field of partisan warfare to themselves, the Army activated the 10th Special Forces Group in June 1952. If Special Forces advocates had earlier lumped Special Forces and Rangers together, they now made a clear distinction between the two concepts, implying that raids and patrols would waste the unique advisory skills of Special Forces. Col. Aaron Bank, the first chief of the 10th Group, argued that his troopers had "no connection with ranger-type organizations since their mission and operations are far more complex, time consuming, require much deeper penetration, and initially are often of a strategic character."[7]

In truth, the Special Forces mission did require a different type of individual than the Rangers. Although the Special Forces mission demanded a rugged volunteer in the Ranger mold, it also called for a soldier with the maturity, language skills, and cultural sensitivity to work with guerrillas for long periods with little guidance from higher levels. The organization predictably drew a number of unusual personalities, including nonconformists, adventurers, and others who were attracted by its unconventional nature. Particularly in its early years, it contained several displaced East Europeans who had joined the Army under a special dispensation of Congress, and it later added a number of

Cubans and other Latin American émigrés. Because of its unorthodox nature, the organization encountered problems in attracting Regular officers, who feared the impact that service with Special Forces would have on their careers, and, consequently, it drew most of its officers from the Reserves and enlisted ranks. Through the grapevine, Special Forces obtained several highly capable noncommissioned officers. Attracted by the independence of Special Forces, they volunteered despite the protests of superiors who feared the loss of their best men.[8]

If Special Forces personnel struck orthodox soldiers as mavericks, the organizational structure must have seemed radically unconventional. The basic unit, the A Team, fluctuated from 6 to 15 men before settling at a strength of 2 officers and 10 noncommissioned officers. The officers and 2 enlisted men provided skills in command, intelligence, and operations. Of the 8 remaining enlisted men, 2 each specialized in weapons, demolitions, communications, and medicine. With each individual cross-trained in another specialty, the A Team represented a flexible organization that could sustain losses and subdivide where necessary. In theory, it could support a 1,500-man guerrilla unit. Designed as a nucleus for a larger force, A Teams possessed obvious structural deficiencies for Ranger operations of any scale.

Likewise, training for Special Forces, while similar to Ranger training in its ruggedness, differed in its greater length and broader range of subjects. It took at least eight months to prepare an individual for service with Special Forces. After qualifying as parachutists, recruits received rigorous instruction in their specialties and some cross-training in the skills of their teammates. Demolitions experts, for example, constructed explosives and learned the critical points of dams, factories, and other potential targets, while communications personnel learned to use a small radio to transmit messages in Morse Code over a 1,500-mile range. Medics received six months of intensive training at Brooke Army Hospital in San Antonio and treated Special Forces personnel in the field. After individual training and more general instruction in guerrilla warfare, teams worked together, training in the field and studying the languages and customs of the geographic area where they would deploy in wartime. Even former Rangers and paratroopers were impressed with the complexity of the training.[9]

For all the differences between Special Forces and Rangers, the two concepts did seem strikingly similar to the uninitiated. Although Special Forces personnel were supposed to be primarily teachers, they were soon caught up in the Ranger mystique of the rugged individual. In large part, this image stemmed from Special Forces training, in which such Ranger-type subjects as conditioning, survival, and demolitions overshadowed other aspects of the mission. Indeed, Eddleman, as Army operations chief, complained in 1953 that the 10th Special Forces Group had received adequate training for commando–Ranger tasks, but not for the organization of guerrillas. The number of former Rangers in Special Forces and the tendency toward Ranger-style machismo strengthened the linking of the two concepts in many minds. For orthodox officers, the real concept of Special Forces was so radical and difficult to grasp that they focused on familiar traits, notably the Ranger-type ethos of the tough guy.[10]

The general lack of understanding of their mission made the 1950s a difficult decade for Special Forces. While they had managed to expand to 2,800 men in three groups by the end of the decade, they remained a relatively small clique with great esprit and camaraderie but isolated from the mainstream of the Army and public. Only occasionally did a correspondent venture to Fort Bragg, North Carolina, to see this collection of survivalists who ate snakes and jumped out of airplanes at night. Generals found the unusual training of Special Forces intriguing but had little idea how to employ them. The actual mission seemed esoteric, especially for commanders who were worried about tight budgets and manpower limits. Concerned about front-line strength in the event of a Soviet attack, army and corps leaders in Europe could hardly be receptive to Special Forces estimates of the time needed to organize guerrillas. At worst, Special Forces struck conventional officers as freewheeling buccaneers who disrupted otherwise orderly maneuvers with "raids" on headquarters and communications.[11]

To improve their respectability, and chances of survival as an organization, Special Forces could not object to, and in some cases welcomed, a series of new missions, including some Ranger-type tasks. With their cultural and language skills, they were a logical choice to train foreign troops, including conventional units and even some Ranger-type formations. By the late 1950s, the Army was adding deep-penetration operations by entirely American units to their list of missions. The Army's leaders were beginning to recognize that partisans, who generally lacked the equipment, training, and reliability of regular forces, were ill-suited for especially difficult and sensitive tasks. As the Army's experts in special warfare and apparent heirs to the commando tradition, Special Forces received the task of infiltration by land, sea, or air into enemy areas to attack key targets, rescue prisoners, and collect intelligence—a Ranger mission.

With the advent of the Kennedy administration, Special Forces received yet another mission: counterinsurgency. The Army's leaders might argue that any good soldier could fight guerrillas, but they knew that the president expected more from them than confident phrases. After the lean Eisenhower years, the Army could not afford to ignore counterinsurgency in any case, particularly since the other services were racing to organize special units and otherwise develop their resources in the field. To build its own capabilities, the Army naturally turned to Special Forces, which possessed the necessary background in foreign cultures and, as experts in unconventional warfare, would presumably know how best to combat guerrillas. In a field that would demand considerable improvisation on the part of the unprepared Army, Special Forces projected a mystique of individual "can-doism." Finally, they had been anointed for the role by the chief executive himself. Kennedy, a romantic idealist who believed that small elite groups could work wonders, had visited Fort Bragg, and, at the instigation of the commander of the Special Warfare Center, had authorized Special Forces to don the green beret, which they had worn for years in defiance of Army regulations prohibiting distinctive headgear.[12]

As Kennedy's chosen few, the Green Berets rocketed into the national limelight. They fit well with the sense of adventure and missionary drive of his "New Frontier." As the knights of his Round Table, they would lead the fight against the menace of Communist "wars of national liberation," using their brains and brawn to spread the gospel of Americanism to the contested nations of the Third World. The media soon adopted the theme, presenting the Green Berets, on the one hand, as brave, rugged outdoorsmen who could parachute, rappel down cliffs, and live off the land, and, on the other hand, as generous nation builders, eager to help the less fortunate. Comparisons to Daniel Boone, Kit Carson, and the Minute Men reassured Americans that the old virtues still lived. Cartoons, a Green Beret doll, and a novel by Robin Moore found appreciative audiences, and "The Ballad of the Green Berets," composed by a Special Forces medic named Barry Sadler, sold almost half a million copies in early 1966. In 1968, John Wayne's film *The Green Berets*, which portrayed Special Forces as tough humanitarians helping a beleaguered South Vietnam maintain its freedom, proved a big hit at the box office, if not with the critics. Special Forces eagerly encouraged the publicity, establishing an area at Fort Bragg where Green Berets showed off survival skills to applauding crowds while low-flying aircraft, dragging hooks, snatched other exhibitionists from the ground.[13]

Whatever the public popularity of Green Berets, the spectacle of them basking in acclaim aggravated an already deep antielitism in the Army. Orthodox officers sneered at what they dubbed "Jacqueline Kennedy's Own Rifles" and dismissed them as snake-eating publicity seekers. Even those who earlier had perceived a place for Special Forces in the Army were often startled by the publicity and repelled by publicity pictures of Green Berets skinning rabbits alive to impress their audience. Nor were chiefs of staff pleased with the attention received by Special Forces. Decker opposed the institution of the beret, and Harold Johnson, while publicly denying any grudge toward Special Forces, privately described them as nonconformists and fugitives from responsibility.[14]

Despite widespread antagonism within the Army toward the Green Berets, Special Forces grew rapidly, indeed, too rapidly for the good of the organization. Between 1961 and 1966, Special Forces expanded from 1,800 men in three understrength groups to 10,500 men in seven groups, not including the seven groups in the Army Reserve and four in the National Guard. While publicity helped swell the number of volunteers, it proved too much to expect Special Forces to increase sixfold in five years and maintain the same high standards. The number of first-time enlistees and young second lieutenants in this force of supposedly experienced soldiers increased dramatically, and the

**Movie actor John Wayne visits a Special Forces camp in Vietnam
(Dr. Homer House)**

Special Warfare Center, under pressure to turn out eight times as many students as before, saw its attrition rate drop from 90 percent in 1962 to 30 percent in 1964. To help the center find tough, mature recruits, Continental Army Command in early 1962 even considered the transfer of the Ranger program to Fort Bragg, but nothing came of the proposal.[15]

By that point, the distinction between Special Forces and Rangers had become practically nonexistent for many in the Army and society. Although the Army distinguished between the two concepts in some of its official literature and the views of some of its more thoughtful officers, it contributed to the confusion by transferring the official Ranger history and unit honors to Special Forces and by publicly referring to the Green Berets as heirs to the tradition of Rogers, the Rangers of World War II, and Merrill's Marauders. Many Army officers still viewed Special Forces as commandos and lumped all operations in the enemy's rear under the overall heading of "guerrilla activities." If the Army could not see the difference, one could hardly expect the public to do so. Certainly, the image of the Green Berets as tough, aggressive troopers in the mold of John Wayne drew more attention in the media than their nation-building role. On Capitol Hill, Senator Richard Russell of Georgia, the powerful chairman of the Senate Armed Services Committee, wanted to substitute the title "Rangers" for "Special Forces." The Army dodged that proposal, but the influx of rugged characters with few teaching skills into Special Forces during the mid-1960s testified to the common blurring of the two concepts.[16]

Among those who saw the difference between the two concepts, especially in the special warfare community, there still existed considerable support for a Ranger formation. Some advocates thought in terms of small units organized, equipped, and trained to fight guerrillas on their own terms. An even larger number envisioned a light unit that could conduct raids and reconnaissance and serve as a ready force. They did differ on the proper depth of Ranger missions. Hugh McWhinnie, a Green Beret who had fought with the Italian partisans in World War II, wanted a formation under the highest command levels for raids against the political and economic sources of the enemy's power. Dandridge Malone and Lewis Millett, the latter a former Medal of Honor winner who had helped establish the 101st Airborne's Recondo School, conceived of Rangers as operating in a "twilight zone" between the areas covered by shallow patrols and deeper regions allotted to partisans. All agreed that the Army's plan to rely on line units and partisans for Ranger tasks had proved inadequate. Another Green Beret, Thomas C. Wyatt, contended that Ranger training for individuals had not noticeably improved the ability of standard units to perform Ranger tasks, and an infantry captain, J. W. Nicholson, pointed out that the presence during the Cuban Missile Crisis of a Ranger unit, capable of quick strikes against missile sites, would have presented Kennedy with another option short of a major war.

Such arguments made little headway. When Col. Roger M. Pezzelle of the Special Warfare Center suggested that each Special Forces group include a Ranger company to carry out raids and prepare experienced personnel for service with the rest of the group, he received a cool response. His proposal eventually died in committee. When Ranger veterans pushed for Ranger battalions for commando and counterguerrilla operations during the Berlin Crisis in 1961,

Undersecretary of the Army Stephen Ailes responded that "due to the limited nature of the current mobilization, the modest strength increases, and the need to retain ranger-trained personnel in other combat units, it is not feasible to reactivate the Ranger Battalions at this time." The 1962 edition of the Army's manual on counterguerrilla operations made no provision for a special Ranger-type unit for such activities, save for a brief reference to LRRPs, and even that reference was absent from the 1963 version. Having agreed to expand Special Forces and grant the Ranger history to the Green Berets, the Army was in no mood to form a new Ranger unit.[17]

Although the Army had rejected the concept of Ranger formations, it had returned a long way toward the idea of special units for Ranger-type tasks. Given the Soviet nuclear arsenal and the growing threat of revolutionary wars in the Third World, it was becoming clear by the end of the 1950s that the United States must abandon massive retaliation and prepare for a broader array of contingencies, including situations in which other countries had found special units to be helpful. While the Army supported the new strategy of flexible response, in part to ensure a larger role in military policy, it continued to resist the notion of special units for special tasks. The obvious inadequacy of line units and partisans for certain Ranger missions, however, caused military leaders reluctantly to turn to special units. They approved the concept of LRRPs to support the Army's primary overseas task of the defense of Western Europe and allocated other Ranger tasks to Special Forces, free-spirited nonconformists who were different from Rangers but had enough similarities to confuse the uninformed. Once the press discovered the Green Berets, the ensuing publicity blitz, linking Special Forces with legendary Ranger heroes and qualities, not only further confused the two concepts but also contributed to an overblown image which inflated public expectations and aggravated antielite jealousies. Thus, by the time it deployed to Vietnam, the Army had recognized to some degree the need for special units, but it still showed little regard or grasp for special missions.

NOTES

1. Eddleman interview; Johnson interview, pp. 4–5; U.S. Army, *Ranger Training and Ranger Operations*, p. 333; Hauser, "Peacetime Army," p. 213; Douglas Kinnard, *The War Managers* (Hanover, N.H.: University Press of New England, 1977), pp. 10–11; USAMHI, "Senior Officers Debriefing Program: Palmer," p. 146; profiles in *Generals of the Army* and senior officers debriefing reports at USAMHI; Westmoreland, *Soldier Reports*; Col. Roger M. Pezzelle USA (Ret.), telephone interview with author, Fairfax, Va., 1 February 1989.

2. Cohen, *Commandos and Politicians*, pp. 23–25, 32, 41–47, 62–68; Tony Geraghty, *Inside the Special Air Service* (Nashville, Tenn.: Battery Press, 1980), pp. 15, 20–30, 47–49, 53–55, 83, 109.

3. Kimball, "We Need Intelligence," pp. 43–50; John W. Medusky, "Should We Have a Scout Platoon?" *Infantry School Quarterly* 45 (July 1955): 53–55; Bickford E. Sawyer, "Raid from the Sky," *Infantry School Quarterly* 42 (October 1953): 35–41.

4. Andrew J. DeGraff, "LRRP and Nuclear Target Acquisition," *Military Review* 40 (November 1960): 15–21; Joseph H. Devins, "Long Range Patrolling," *Infantry* 50 (October–November 1960): 34–38; Gordon L. Rottman, *U.S. Army Rangers and LRRP Units, 1942–1987* (London: Osprey, 1987), pp. 25–28; U.S. Army, Seventh Army, "Long Range Reconnaissance Patrols: Education and Training," unpublished manuscript, Vaihingen, Germany, 8 September 1961, p. 2, in USAMHI; Pezzelle interview. "Long-range patrol" (LRP) and "long-range reconnaissance patrol" (LRRP) have been used almost interchangeably. Here, LRRP will be used for both tactical and strategic long range patrols.

5. U.S. Army, Department of the Army, "Table of Organization and Equipment No. 7–157E: Infantry Long Range Patrol Company," 28 September 1964, Organizational History Branch, CMH.

6. Quotes from U.S. Army, Department of the Army, *Long Range Patrols: Division, Corps, Army*, FM 31–18 (Washington, D.C.: Department of the Army, June 1962), p. 3; see also pp. 5–7, 19–20, 25; Michael L. Lanning, *Inside the LRRP's: Rangers in Vietnam* (New York: Ivy Books, 1988), pp. 44–46; U.S. Army, "TOE No. 7–157E: Infantry Long Range Patrol Company," Organizational History Branch, CMH.

7. Quoted in Paddock, *Special Warfare*, p. 119; see also pp. 126–129; Simpson, *Green Berets*, pp. 16–20, 35; Bank, *From OSS to Green Berets*, pp. 156–171; "Organization, Strength, and Mission of the 10th Special Forces Group," U.S. Army, Office of the Chief of Staff, Decimal File, 1953 322 Joint Task Force & Miscellaneous Units Regt. . . . Corps Battalion, RG 319, MMHB, National Archives; Roger M. Pezzelle, "Special Forces," *Infantry* 49 (April 1959): 13–15; Edson D. Raff, "Fighting behind Enemy Lines," *Army Information Digest* 11 (April 1956): 16.

8. Simpson, *Green Berets*, pp. 20–26; Pezzelle interview; Col. Charles Norton USA (Ret.), interview by author, McLean, Va., 16 October 1985; Bank, *From OSS to Green Berets*, pp. 168–169, 176–177; Melvin R. Blair, "Toughest Unit in the Army," *Saturday Evening Post*, 12 May 1956, p. 89; Charles A. Dodson, "Special Forces," *Army* 11 (June 1961): 46; Shelby L. Stanton, *Green Berets at War: U.S. Army Special Forces in Southeast Asia, 1956–1975* (Novato, Calif: Presidio Press, 1985), p. 3; Norman and Spore, "Big Push, p. 36.

9. Simpson, *Green Berets*, pp. 36–40; Bank, *From OSS to Green Berets*, pp. 160–162, 173–176; Raff, "Behind Enemy Lines," pp. 16–17; Pezzelle, "Special Forces," p. 17; Stanton, *Green Berets at War*, pp. 3–4; Pezzelle interview.

10. The womanizing and roughhousing, such as the raids on North Carolina jails to free imprisoned comrades and the forced entries into German wine cellars, seem to have been regarded by Bank as the nature of a free-spirited unit, even if it did clash with the mature image that Special Forces was trying to project. See Aaron Bank, "The Birth of the Green Berets," *Gung Ho*, December 1983, pp. 54–56. See also Bank, *From OSS to Green Berets*, p. 175; Blair, "Toughest Unit," p. 93; Eddleman to Collins, 3 September 1953, and Eddleman to Collins, 15 October 1953, in U.S. Army, Office of the Chief of Staff, Decimal File, 1953, Joint Task Force and Miscellaneous Units, RG 319, MMHB, National Archives.

11. Simpson, *Green Berets*, pp. 48–50; Raff, "Behind Enemy Lines," p. 15; Stanton, *Green Berets at War*, pp. 2–4; R. W. Van de Velde, "The Neglected Deterrent," *Military Review* 38 (August 1958): 3–4; Blair, "Toughest Unit," pp. 41, 90, 93; Anthony Leviero, "Army Trains 'Liberation' Force to Fight behind Enemy Lines," *New York Times*, 30 August 1955, p. 1; Jack Raymond, "Elite Units Long a Source of Friction in U.S. Army," *New York Times*, 3 October 1964, p. 3; Bank, *From OSS to Green Berets*, pp. 165, 193–195; Bank, "Birth of the Green Berets," p. 55; Pezzelle interview; Joseph C. Lutz, "Special Forces: To Help Others Help Themselves," *Army* 33 (October 1983): 247.

12. Simpson, *Green Berets*, pp. 32–33, 50, 65–67; Stanton, *Green Berets at War*, pp. 7–9; Cable, *Conflict of Myths*, pp. 141, 145, 175–176; Anthony Harrigan, "A New Dimension in Special Operations," *Military Review* 41 (September 1961): 4–9; Pezzelle interview; Weigley, *History of the United States Army*, pp. 543–544; Yarborough interview, sess. 2, p. 25; Bowman, "Counterinsurgency Warfare," pp. 122–124; Frank A. McGregor, "Crusaders in Uniform: The Army Special Forces," *Infantry* 54 (March–April 1964): 10; Francis J. Kelly, *U.S. Army Special Forces, 1961–1971*, Vietnam Studies (Washington, D.C.: OCMH, 1973), p. 9.

13. Simpson, *Green Berets*, pp. 68–69, 95–96; Siegel, *Troubled Journey*, pp. 122–123, 131–132, 150; Hodgson, *America*, pp. 6–7, 493; C. L. Sulzberger, "Foreign Affairs: President Kennedy's Own Guerrillas," *New York Times*, 19 April 1961, p. 38; Dodson, "Special Forces," p. 44; W. D. McGlasson, "Special Forces: The New Elite," *National Guardsman* 18 (June 1964): 5; Jack Raymond, "Fighting Is Secondary to Army Special Forces," *New York Times*, 23 December 1964, p. 11; Neal J. Ahern, "What It Is That's So Special about Special Forces," *Army Reservist* 9 (November 1963): 5–6; "For 'Special Warfare,'" *New York Times Magazine*, 16 April 1961, sec. 6, pp. 20–21; Carroll B. Colby, *Special Forces: The U.S. Army's Experts in Unconventional Warfare* (New York: Coward McCann, 1964), pp. 3, 23–24; Moskos, *American Enlisted Man*, pp. 23–25; Robin Moore, *The Green Berets* (New York: Crown Publishers, 1965); Louis Calta, "Wounded Veteran Writes Song on Vietnam War," *New York Times*, 1 February 1966, p. 27; Suid, *Guts and Glory*, pp. 102–107, 222–235.

14. Simpson, *Green Berets*, pp. 96, 173–175; Johnson interview no. 12, tape 12, pp. 8–9; USAMHI, "Senior Officers Debriefing Program: Woolnough," Tab D, pp. 17–18; USAMHI, "Senior Officers Oral History Program: LTG Arthur S. Collins, Jr., interviewed by Col. Chandler Robbins III," Project 82-4 (Carlisle, Pa., 1982), pp. 229–230; USAMHI, "Senior Officers Debriefing Program: Hamlett," V:61; Joe Wagner, "Army Special Forces: Stepchild or Child Prodigy?" *Armed Forces Management* 12 (May 1966): 54–56.

15. Edward M. Flanagan, "Hit and Run—The Role of Special Forces," *National Guardsman* 15 (December 1961): 24; Simpson, *Green Berets*, pp. 67–69; Yarborough interview, sess. 2, p. 32; Norman and Spore, "Big Push," pp. 28–32; Hanson W. Baldwin, "Army Will Train Latin Guerrillas," *New York Times*, 5 April 1961, p. 1; "Army to Add 1,650 to Guerrilla Force," *New York Times*, 28 September 1962, p. 4; "Excerpts from President's Address to Coast Guard," *New York Times*, 4 June 1964, p. 27; Weigley, *History of the United States Army*, p. 544; Pezzelle interview; Stanton, *Green Berets at War*, p. 169; John B. Spore, "The U.S. Army in Vietnam," *Army* 16 (June 1966): 69.

16. Wagner, "Army Special Forces," p. 55; McGlasson, "Special Forces," p. 3; Yarborough interview, sess. 2, pp. 16, 21, and sess. 3, side 1, pp. 20–21; Simpson, *Green Berets*, p. 221, McGregor, "Crusaders," p. 11; Flanagan, "Hit and Run," p. 25; John R. Galvin, "Special Forces at the Crossroads," *Army* 23 (December 1973): 22–23; David J. Baratto, "Special Forces in the 1980's: A Strategic Reorientation," *Military Review* 63 (March 1983): 9; U.S. Army, Department of the Army, *Dictionary of United States Army Terms* (Washington: Department of the Army, 1962), p. 40; William H. Kinard, "This is Special Warfare—U.S. Army Style," *Army Information Digest* 15 (June 1960): 3–4, 10; Garrett interview; Norton interview; Paddock, *Special Warfare*, pp. 23–24, 165; Melvin L. Winkler, "The Army's Special Forces," *Army Digest* 21 (October 1966): 27; "Chairman Russell Wants Better Name for Special Forces; Doesn't Like 'Guerrilla'; Favors 'Ranger'," *Army, Navy, Air Force Journal* 98 (20 May 1961): 3.

17. Ailes quoted in Ailes to Altieri, undated, in Lisko Papers, USAMHI; see also James J. Altieri to President Kennedy, 25 August 1961, Lisko Papers, USAMHI; Pezzelle interview; Cable, *Conflict of Myths*, p. 142; Wyatt, "Butcher and Bolt," pp. 37–45; McCrorey, "Ranger Armor," p. 26; Hugh McWhinnie, "The Case for a Strategic Assault Force," *Infantry* 50 (June–July 1960): 22–25; Lewis L. Millett and Dandridge Malone, "Journey into the Twilight Zone: Bring Back the Proud Rangers," *Army* 14 (September 1963): 27–31.

11

Improvisation in Vietnam

President Johnson's decision in July 1965 to deploy 50,000 troops to South Vietnam concluded over 10 years of American efforts to prevent, short of massive military intervention, the unification of Vietnam under a Communist regime. American support for South Vietnam followed logically from the policy of containment, on which such a consensus existed that successive administrations never questioned the national interest in aiding the South. Obsessed with the threat of Communist expansion in Asia after the so-called loss of China, the United States funded the vain French attempt to restore colonial rule over Indochina and, after the Geneva Accords of 1954 divided the country, provided ever-increasing economic and military aid to South Vietnam. From the beginning, the new republic faced such overwhelming problems, including ethnic and religious divisions, a weak economy, political corruption, and subversion by North Vietnam, as to cast doubt on its viability as a nation. Despite the flow of American equipment, advisors, and a few ground troops, and despite the initiation of a bombing campaign against the North, South Vietnam appeared on the brink of collapse in the summer of 1965. Unwilling to accept the consequences of withdrawal or continued deterioration, Johnson committed the United States to a long, debilitating conflict which was to divide Americans and frustrate the efforts of their military forces.[1]

An Army that viewed itself, with good reason, as the most powerful, technologically advanced ground force in the world received a rude awakening in South Vietnam. As American troops arrived in the country, they found the terrain ill-suited for the type of warfare for which their weapons, training, and doctrine had prepared them. The humid jungles of the highlands and the tropical rain forests along the coast, with their heavy vegetation, broken terrain, and lack of roads or trails, provided concealment and hindered the maneuvering of larger units. The Viet Cong and North Vietnamese took full advantage of this terrain

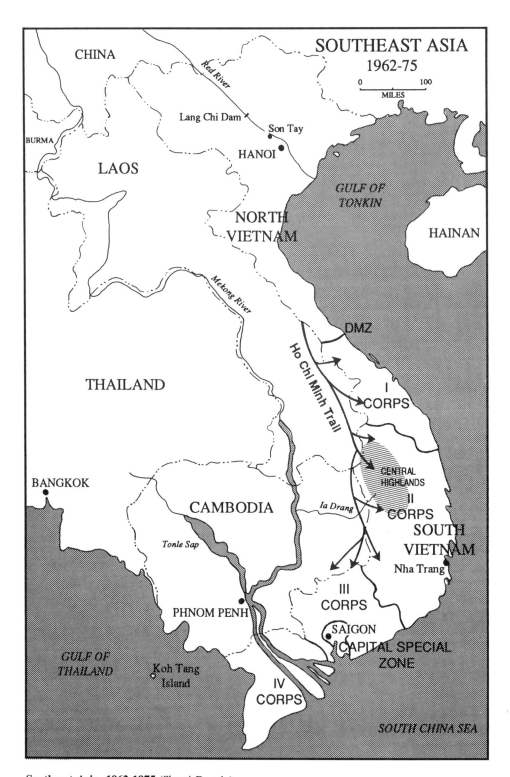

Southeast Asia, 1962-1975 (Sherri Dowdy)

in their tactics. More inured to the environment than their American counter-parts, the Communists proved to be tough, elusive foes. On occasion, they would mass their units and employ conventional tactics, particularly along South Vietnam's borders. Early in the war, American troops found it risky to operate in less than battalion strength in such areas. Suffering heavy casualties in clashes of large units, the Communists turned to small-unit tactics, inflicting losses in carefully planned ambushes and raids and then dispersing before the Americans could apply their superior firepower. Such a war placed a premium on patrol skills, aggressiveness, and discipline, as well as demanding small-unit leaders with courage, intelligence, and drive. In short, it presented a formidable challenge for the U.S. Army.[2]

Unfortunately for the Army, finding and fixing a crafty foe often proved incompatible with its reliance on mechanized mobility and firepower. Until late in the conflict, American commanders fought a big-unit war, seeking to inflict such heavy losses on the enemy's main forces that he would sue for peace. In the field, this translated into the use of mortars, artillery, helicopters, and aircraft to establish such a preponderance of fire as to wipe out everything in its path. The main task lay in finding the elusive Communists, and, toward that end, the Army employed a wide range of technology and techniques. Intelligence officers questioned informants and prisoners with the aid of Vietnamese interrogators and analyzed data from sensors and "people sniffers," helicopter-mounted devices that could detect microscopic particles emitted by humans. Units from company to brigade size swept suspected enemy areas, cordoned and searched villages, saturated alternate squares of terrain with patrols, and raced over the jungle in helicopters, ready to "pile on" suspected enemy concentra-tions. Such methods met with only indifferent success. The Communists generally were adept at avoiding the large, noisy American columns fumbling through the jungle, and, on the rare occasions when the Americans did make contact, the enemy could often slip away before American firepower became effective. If the Army wanted to find the enemy, it needed to use small patrols of squad or platoon size, precisely the kind taught by the Ranger school.[3]

Did Ranger training of small-unit leaders adequately prepare the Army for this type of warfare? Given the numerous factors affecting the performance of squads and platoons in Vietnam, a definitive answer to this question is probably impossible, but some observations can be made. Although many American field commanders praised the toughness, initiative, training, and morale of their infantry, others, particularly at the battalion and company levels, were not so favorably impressed. They noted that American soldiers seldom left trails and landing zones to venture into the bush, find the enemy, and pin him down, partly due to their training and partly because some carried as much as 50 or 60 pounds of equipment. Patrols all too often lost their way in the admittedly trackless jungle, seemed oblivious to the danger of mines and booby traps, and showed little concern for the security of their communications. Nor did they conduct proper ambushes, a subject that received little notice in unit training. Observers complained of the failure to place sentinels at the ambush site, the inability to remain silent, premature ambushes, and the tendency of trigger-happy soldiers to spray the fire of their automatic weapons over the heads of their opponents. Nevertheless, critics blamed a lack of training time, rather than faults in the instruction itself or the Army's methods, for these defects. As one lieutenant colonel stated, "The principles of patrolling and ambushing as taught in the Ranger course are tried and tested, and if unit commanders would apply those techniques, their ambushes would be successful."[4]

More alarming than poor techniques, failures of small-unit leadership presented a problem that went to the heart of Ranger training. The decentralized nature of operations in Vietnam, where company commanders often could not supervise the maneuvers of their squads and platoons, placed an enormous responsibility on the shoulders of junior officers, a burden that was compounded by the shortage of experienced sergeants. Green lieutenants, recently graduated from the Infantry Officer Basic Course or Officers Candidate School, were criticized by senior commanders for a lack of knowledge to detect faults in their units and willingness to correct those deficiencies. Too often, they turned to supporting firepower, rather than maneuver with available weapons, to meet tactical situations. These problems did not always, or even primarily, result from a lack of aggressiveness. Indeed, junior leaders frequently displayed too much boldness, imitating John Wayne in exposing themselves or recklessly leading frontal attacks on forts.[5]

American conduct of small patrols paled in comparison with those of other national forces in Vietnam, particularly the Australians. In contrast to the Americans, the Australians had focused on jungle warfare in their training and doctrine, and, while appreciative of technology, they recognized the preeminent role of the foot soldier in jungle tactics. At their Jungle Warfare Training Center, platoons practiced patrols and ambushes, relying on intelligence, mobility, stealth, and skillful tactics rather than firepower. A recruit normally devoted about 70 to 80 percent of his training to jungle warfare. Consequently, when the Australian brigade, with its high proportion of picked professionals, deployed to Vietnam, it quickly established a reputation for excellence in small-unit tactics. It should be said that the Australians seldom had to deal with large North Vietnamese units in their operating area, and at least part of their proficiency can be traced to their policy of rotating units rather than individuals on completion of their tour of duty in Vietnam. Nonetheless, their skill earned praise from the American commander, General Westmoreland, and other American officers.[6]

Although few American units could match the Australians at jungle warfare, some did adapt their training and tactics to the enemy, terrain, and missions that they faced in Vietnam. Brig. Gen. Willard Pearson, a brigade commander in the 101st Airborne Division, streamlined his intelligence organization to provide more timely information, arranged for the clandestine insertion of troops into operating areas, and stressed small night patrols, noise discipline, and deception plans to mislead the enemy. One of his subordinates, Lt. Col. Henry Emerson, turned his battalion into a "counterguerrilla spearhead," whose squads lived on rice for five days at a time and moved into the jungle at night to set ambushes along routes known to be used by the Communists. Other divisions attempted to improve their performance of small-unit operations through marksmanship training, programs for noncommissioned officers, and unit schools, notably the 25th Infantry Division's "ambush academy" and, in the United States, the 82d Airborne Division's "raider school," which was modeled on the Ranger course. With time, more American units turned to squad patrols, night missions, and ambushes to find, fix, and destroy the enemy.[7]

Most American commanders did not like the idea of using squads and platoons for independent operations. Especially in the war's early years, they claimed that the presence of large enemy units made such ventures too risky. The enemy, they warned, would soon find small patrols in his area, and if discovered, such patrols would be hard to rescue. Maj. Gen. Jonathan O. Seaman of the 1st Infantry Division said that it would have been "utter suicide" to allow his platoons to work independently, and Maj. Gen. W. R. Peers of the 4th Infantry Division later stated that he refused to let his companies operate over a kilometer, 1,000 meters, or an hour's distance apart, whichever was smallest.[8] Underlying many such comments was skepticism of the Army's ability to conduct small patrols in a Vietnam-type environment. One major went so far as to say:

> "As an Army, we are broadly representative of the general population—technically inclined, conditioned to a high standard of living, and, of greater significance, Western, largely white, and English speaking. Only with great difficulty can many of our soldiers who are drawn from that population be given more than superficial training of the type needed to make them effective."[9]

Did American soldiers really stumble through patrols because they were soft, technologically dependent Westerners? After all, the Australians, who earned so much praise for patrol techniques, were also English-speaking Caucasians. The argument that the affluent American standard of living had emasculated American soldiers did strike a responsive chord among senior officers who noted the cushy conditions in which many troops lived. In some areas of South Vietnam, engineers had constructed lavish base camps, complete with barracks, hospitals, airstrips, roads, and stores, where American infantry, after a day in the jungle, could return to eat hot food, purchase Cokes, ice cream, and radios, and even watch television. While a tribute to Army logisticians, such camps hardly created the proper atmosphere for the "lean, mean" force needed to go into the jungle and root out the enemy. Still, it must be said that not all, or even most, American units lived in such opulent conditions while in the field.[10]

More than inherent national traits or comfortable bases, Army personnel policies contributed to patrol deficiencies. On the American side, the war was fought, for the most part, by troops motivated only by a vague sense that Communism must be stopped before it reached the United States. To maintain morale, the Army limited service in Vietnam to a single year, a policy that created constant turnover within units, leading to disastrous consequences for unit cohesiveness and troop performance. To ensure their return to the "World," as they termed the United States, soldiers became extremely cautious in the last two months of their tour, just as they were developing expertise. Although officers also served one-year tours, they normally spent six months with American troops in the field, leaving the scene just as they began to develop insights into the country and the enemy. To complicate matters, graduates of the Ranger course represented only a small minority of the total number of officers. Thus, many, if not most, of the captains and lieutenants who led patrols were not Ranger-qualified.[11]

Thus, institutional obstacles to efficient patrolling proved too much for Ranger training to surmount. For all the talk of flexible response, the Army, in training, doctrine, organization, and mind-set, was oriented more toward tank infantry battles on the European plains than squad patrols in the jungles of Southeast Asia when it intervened in South Vietnam in 1965. To expect the Ranger course and improvised unit schools to overcome this orientation and, in a matter of weeks, make expert patrollers and woodsmen out of inexperienced lieutenants, was to demand more than these programs could deliver. With time, Army doctrine adjusted somewhat to the lessons of Vietnam, as patrol manuals placed more emphasis on careful preparation, noise discipline, local conditions, and ambushes.[12] As the Army adjusted its training and doctrine to meet the demands of Vietnam in the late 1960s, and as the expansion of the Ranger program provided more graduates to lead patrols, patrol performance improved, but by then, the Army was running out of time in its efforts to win the war before domestic opposition forced a withdrawal.

The prewar Army had recognized that some "Ranger" tasks lay so far beyond the capability of line troops that they had best be left to Special Forces, but it had not anticipated the number or variety of such missions in Vietnam. With its avowed emphasis on helping others to help themselves, the American effort in Vietnam seemed especially well suited for Special Forces. Well before the escalation of the summer of 1965, the Green Berets had been performing special missions in Southeast Asia and instructing units of the South Vietnamese Army (ARVN), including the nominally elite, but often unruly, force of shock troops known as the ARVN Rangers. Special Forces's main task throughout the war in Vietnam was to advise South Vietnamese Special Forces in the operation of the Civilian Irregular Defense Group (CIDG) program, which sought to maintain government control over ethnic minorities in remote regions of the country through the establishment of self-defending communities. The CIDG effort centered on the Montagnards, 700,000 primitive tribesmen in South Vietnam's Central Highlands. Beginning in November 1961, Special Forces teams deployed to the highlands, where they lived among the people, treated the sick, carried out civic action projects, built fortified camps, and trained small forces which patrolled surrounding areas. With time, the program expanded to include 100 camps from the Demilitarized Zone (DMZ) to the Gulf of Thailand.[13]

Special Forces devoted most of their time to counterinsurgency projects such as CIDG, but they also carried out special missions outside South Vietnam's borders. Although American-backed agents had been conducting sabotage and psychological warfare in North Vietnam since 1961, the program came of age with the formation of the Studies and Observation Group (SOG) in 1964 to advise and support South Vietnamese clandestine operations in surrounding countries. Its activities were monitored by the commander in chief of the Pacific theater and Military Assistance Command, Vietnam (MACV), the American joint headquarters in Saigon, but it received its orders directly from the Joint Chiefs of Staff in Washington, a complex arrangement that reflected the sensitive political nature of SOG's missions. As a joint unconventional warfare task force, SOG included personnel from all the services. Its 2,500 Americans and 7,000 Vietnamese were formed into operational commands, which were known as study groups in order to maintain their cover on organizational charts. Most of the Green Berets served in the Training, Ground, and Airborne Study Groups. They trained South Vietnamese personnel and served with them on Spike teams, which performed reconnaissance, and Search, Location, Annihilation, and Monitors (SLAM) companies, which engaged enemy forces located by Spike teams, rescued allied prisoners, and carried out ambushes and raids.

SOG's missions varied depending on the demands of higher levels and the nature of the operating area. In North Vietnam, SOG concentrated on the rescue of downed airmen, maritime raids along the coast, and psychological warfare, especially propaganda broadcasts. After SOG warned North Vietnamese fishermen against smuggling weapons and munitions into the South, radio intelligence reported that enemy troops complained of a drop in their supplies. SOG also attempted to interdict the flow of supplies along the Ho Chi Minh Trail in Laos, sending teams to watch traffic, call in air strikes, snatch prisoners, lay mines, and carry out ambushes. In Cambodia, SOG confined itself almost entirely to reconnaissance of enemy supply depots and sanctuaries in the border areas. There, as in the other two countries, SOG worked under restrictions limiting the depth of cross-border operations and the participation of Americans in those forays. The disclosure that Americans were conducting military operations in countries that were technically at peace with the United States would have created an uproar that the U.S. government did not want to face.

Even today, much information on SOG remains classified, but enough has surfaced to indicate that the program achieved only limited success at best. Although both Westmoreland and his successor, Gen. Creighton W. Abrams, praised SOG's efforts, the disappointing results and heavy losses of such SOG projects as LEAPING LENA, the early long-range reconnaissance effort in Laos, and the infiltration of Vietnamese teams and agents into the North hinted at serious problems. Part of the difficulty lay in precisely the reliance on indigenous troops that had made the Special Forces concept so attractive for special operations deep in the enemy's rear. All too often, South Vietnamese personnel proved ill-trained, inexperienced, and, in some cases, of dubious loyalty for such difficult, sensitive missions. After the exodus of dissidents from the North in the 1950s, a base of popular support for special operations no longer existed, and the Johnson administration's haste to begin operations left SOG with little time to develop one. Finally, SOG never had a clear objective for its activities. SOG did represent one of the earliest American efforts in a situation short of general war to bring under one joint agency all special operations, from Ranger reconnaissance and raids to such non-Ranger tasks as subversion and assassinations. Under the circumstances, fumbling improvisation was perhaps inevitable.[14]

If SOG projects often miscarried due to hasty improvisation, the war's most famous Ranger-type mission, the raid on the North Vietnamese prison camp at Son Tay, failed to rescue any prisoners largely because of the time required to mount the operation. In May 1970, Air Force intelligence located the camp and notified Brig. Gen. Donald D. Blackburn, the Joint Chiefs of Staff's advisor for special operations. After the joint chiefs approved a feasibility study in July, they formed a task force of representatives from the Pentagon and intelligence agencies to plan a rescue mission. As commander, Blackburn selected Air Force Brig. Gen. Leroy J. Manor, and, as the deputy in charge of the ground force, he chose an old friend, gruff, 52-year-old Col. Arthur D. "Bull" Simons, who had led Company B of the 6th Ranger Battalion in the capture of the lighthouse on Suluan Island in World War II. At Fort Bragg, Simons interviewed over 250 volunteers, mostly Green Berets. He selected 97, who went to Eglin Air Force Base for conditioning and training in weapons, night operations, survival, demolitions, communications, and joint rehearsals with Air Force counterparts selected by Manor. At a time of national anxiety over the plight of American prisoners of war, the plan for the raid received a warm reception at the White House, but developments in the Paris peace talks forced a postponement. Finally, on November 18, 1970, President Richard M. Nixon directed that the raid proceed.

By mid-November, the prisoners had long since left the camp. In July, the North Vietnamese had moved their captives due to flooding in the area. Although an agent notified Washington of the move, Blackburn recommended that the operation proceed, perhaps because he did not totally believe the report, and, in any case, he wanted to show that an all-American raid deep into North

Press briefing following the Son Tay raid. Left to right, Secretary of Defense Melvin R. Laird; Col. Arthur D. "Bull" Simons; Admiral Thomas H. Moorer, Chairman of the Joint Chiefs of Staff; and Brig. Gen. Leroy J. Manor. Note the 6th Ranger Battalion patch on Colonel Simons's shoulder. (Department of Defense and *Armed Forces Journal International*)

Vietnam was feasible. On the night of November 21, while Navy planes conducted a diversion along the coast, the raiders flew from Thailand through enemy radar cover to Son Tay. After a specially armed helicopter knocked out the towers on the walls, a 14-man assault team crash-landed inside the compound and rushed to the cell blocks. Simons's 22-man team was supposed to land outside, blow a hole in the wall, and destroy the garrison, but instead it landed at another camp, 400 yards to the south, where it wiped out a force which might have reinforced the prison. In the absence of Simons's team, the 20-man security group, which had been assigned to cover the approaches against reinforcement, broke into the compound and joined the assault team. By the time Simons arrived, the security group had confirmed that the camp was empty, and the colonel ordered a withdrawal. In a half hour, his force had surprised and eliminated the garrison, carried out a swift search, and conducted a smooth departure without losing a man.[15]

Despite the nearly flawless execution of the mission, the Nixon administration showed little receptivity to proposals for similar operations. Blackburn had hoped that the raid's success, demonstrating the vulnerability of North Vietnam, would lead his superiors to authorize a series of raids into the enemy's heartland. He particularly wanted to send a party of Green Berets to blow up the Lang Chi hydroelectric dam, a massive, Soviet-built complex on the Red River. American political leaders, however, were in no mood for further adventures into the North. The growth of the antiwar movement in the United States clearly illustrated the desire of many, if not most, Americans to wind down the war. While members of Congress expressed concern over the plight of the prisoners, several criticized the raid and accompanying bombings as a provocation that would only expand the conflict. From Nixon's point of view, the raid had already accomplished a purpose in demonstrating his administration's concern over the prisoners. He did not want to invest scarce political capital on further risky missions into the North.[16]

One can only wonder what Nixon would have decided if the Son Tay raid had achieved its objective. Although the task force had performed splendidly, it had not brought home a single prisoner. In the immediate aftermath, the intelligence community received most of the blame, but the evidence indicates that those agencies, on the whole, did well enough. The real culprit seems to have been the amount of time—six months—required to mount the operation. The Joint Chiefs of Staff had to create a series of ad hoc groups to determine the feasibility of the raid, plan the operation, and evaluate the plan. In the absence of an existing unit, the chiefs had to scrape together and train an ad hoc force of Green Berets and pilots for the mission. Once everything was in place, political leaders had to make the final decision to go ahead with the raid. An existing commando organization would have greatly expedited the process, but the services once again were forced to improvise a Ranger-type force. Considering the mission's complexity, it is a tribute to American technological skill, the dedication of the men in the force, the professionalism of Manor and Simons, and plain luck that it went as well as it did.[17]

Among so-called "recovery missions," operations to rescue prisoners or recover valuable objects, the Son Tay raid was unusual. Most of these Ranger-type missions took place inside South Vietnam and were carried out by native troops trained and advised by Special Forces. Under the supervision of the Joint Personnel Recovery Center, a separate office within MACV, Green Beret-advised teams conducted 91 rescue missions, 45 in response to reports of American prisoners. Of the 91 missions, 20 achieved success, rescuing 318 South Vietnamese soldiers and 60 civilians, but no American prisoners survived a rescue attempt. Some raids failed through lack of good intelligence, others due to a loss of surprise, and others, as in the case of Son Tay, because a delay in launching the mission allowed the Communists to move their captives. While Special Forces had developed considerable expertise in the escape and evasion of enemy search parties by individuals, it had not devoted much time or thought to techniques of larger-scale recovery operations. Nevertheless, in the absence of Ranger units, they and their protégés were the logical choices for the task.[18]

For recovery operations, as well as raids and other special missions within the borders of South Vietnam, Special Forces relied on mobile strike forces of mercenaries. These private armies, known as "Mike" Forces, grew out of the desire of the Green Berets for troops that could respond more rapidly than the apathetic South Vietnamese line units to threats to CIDG camps. In June 1965, General Westmoreland approved the formation of 550-man light battalions, one for each of the four corps tactical zones. These units, each commanded by an A Team, were manned by ethnic minorities, including Nungs, Rhades, and Montagnards, who were attracted by the higher pay and better working conditions. Initially, the Mikes served as compound guards and reaction forces that relieved threatened CIDG camps. By 1966, they were also conducting long-range reconnaissance and special missions into remote areas. As with so many other special units, they were frequently misused by officers who did not grasp their limitations, and they relied heavily on expensive helicopters for mobility. Nevertheless, they proved so useful that Westmoreland expanded the force to 18 battalions in 1966.

Smaller but otherwise similar to the Mike battalions, Mobile Guerrilla Forces operated for long periods in remote, enemy-held areas. At about the same time as Westmoreland's expansion of the Mike Forces, 5th Special Forces Group, 1st Special Forces—the headquarters for Special Forces in Vietnam—formed light companies, each containing 150 Vietnamese under an A Team. In a sense, the mobile guerrilla concept reflected the Special Forces philosophy of training natives for raids and reconnaissance, but it more closely approximated that of the *Chindits* and Marauders of World War II in its concept of a regular force that infiltrated deep into enemy territory and wreaked havoc for weeks before returning to friendly lines. After a scout platoon reconnoitered the target area, the Mobile Guerrilla Force would infiltrate into the region, usually by foot. For 30 to 60 days, at least in theory, it would harass enemy communications, call in air strikes, plant mines and booby traps, and collect information, while American aircraft provided air support and dropped food and ammunition in empty napalm containers. After two years of these operations, in 1968, the Mobile Guerrilla Forces merged with the Mike Forces and became a reaction force for CIDGs.

As reaction forces, independent of the cumbersome South Vietnamese command structure, Mike and Mobile Guerrilla Forces possessed some value, but for raids and reconnaissance deep into enemy territory, they displayed grave deficiencies. The very phrase "mobile guerrilla forces" misrepresented the nature of these units, since they did not come from the operational area and lacked the self-sufficiency to remain for long. These defects proved all the more serious since, by 1967, most of the old Viet Cong sanctuaries along the border had become staging areas for North Vietnamese regiments. Mobile guerrilla companies lacked the training, mobility, and elusiveness to work in that environment. Quickly detected, they could not evade the enemy and had to call for rescue under pressure. Although the Mobile Strike Forces enjoyed more success in light infantry missions, they suffered from a lack of aerial transportation as well as desertions and heavy losses, often through their misuse in prolonged combat by commanders who did not grasp their limitations.[19]

While the mobile strike forces and mobile guerrilla forces performed some long-range patrols, the bulk of the deep-reconnaissance missions assigned by MACV were handled by Special Forces's Greek-letter projects. American intelligence was finding that aircraft and sophisticated electronic gadgets could not substitute for a well-trained pair of human eyes on the ground. To reconnoiter remote areas, they turned to Special Forces–trained teams, of which the most notable served under Project DELTA. Formed in October 1964 by 5th Special Forces Group from the remnants of LEAPING LENA, DELTA assembled within one agency resources for both reconnaissance and exploitation. It possessed a "Strike Recondo Platoon" of 16 teams, each with three Green Berets and three troopers from South Vietnamese Special Forces, and a "Roadrunner Platoon" of 8 teams, each with four Vietnamese soldiers, who adopted the dress and equipment of the enemy. To react to reports from these teams, it could call on a battalion of ARVN Rangers. As a joint American Vietnamese project, DELTA received missions and supervision from both MACV and the South Vietnamese Joint General Staff.

In its missions, DELTA developed techniques that were later copied by other long-range patrols in Vietnam. DELTA teams usually infiltrated into their operational areas at twilight. To deceive the enemy, helicopters carrying a team made a number of fake descents before actually landing and inserting the group. Once on the ground, the Americans and South Vietnamese usually moved a short distance from the landing zone and waited until daylight to avoid a costly stumble into an enemy position in the dark. DELTA teams sometimes reconnoitered specific targets, but more often, they conducted a general survey of an area. As part of their mission, they frequently placed mines along infiltration routes, seized prisoners, called in air strikes and assessed the damage, and rescued downed aircrews. After five days, the maximum that a unit could last in the field with little sleep and resupply, the team was evacuated by helicopter in a procedure similar to the insertion. Secrecy was essential. If the team was detected, the enemy could either escape or annihilate the small group before ARVN Rangers could arrive.

Like other units performing Ranger-type missions in Vietnam, DELTA suffered from its status as an improvised, multinational unit under a Byzantine chain of command. To commit the Rangers, DELTA had to submit a request through several command levels to a Vietnamese general in Nha Trang. The unit's availability often depended on the whims of the South Vietnamese regime and jurisdictional disputes between officials at the district, sector, province, and national levels. A shortage of critical resources, especially airlift, compounded the problem. DELTA's six helicopters, which were provided by the South Vietnamese Air Force, did not meet the project's requirements, and the Green Berets had to turn to nearby units for support. At one point, the 1st Cavalry Division complained that DELTA was too expensive in aerial support for the quality of intelligence provided. To be sure, some grumbling can be traced to the reaction of orthodox officers to unconventional units and to personality conflicts between cavalry officers and Major Beckwith, DELTA's chief in 1965, but the criticism did point to a real problem in DELTA's organization.[20]

Nevertheless, DELTA's performance earned enough praise from high-ranking officers to encourage a proliferation of similar projects. Since DELTA concentrated its activities in the jungles of the north and in the Mekong Delta south of Saigon, the 5th Special Forces Group, in August 1966, formed Project OMEGA to carry out long-range patrols in the Central Highlands and Project SIGMA to cover the region just north of Saigon. After a year, these two projects turned over their assets to SOG, but SIGMA was soon replaced by Project RAPID FIRE, which conducted reconnaissance and ambushes along the border north of Saigon. Independently, Project GAMMA was collecting intelligence on North Vietnamese infiltration from Cambodia. In contrast to DELTA, the new projects used Mike companies as reaction forces and reported solely to I and II Field Forces, the American corps headquarters in central South Vietnam. Ethnic minorities, rather than Vietnamese Special Forces, provided the indigenous manpower: Sedangs and Montagnards in the case of OMEGA, and Cambodians and ethnic Chinese in the case of SIGMA, RAPID FIRE, and GAMMA. Like DELTA, however, these projects still relied on other units for helicopters and other support.[21]

In sum, Special Forces–led natives hardly represented a panacea for Ranger-type missions deep into enemy territory. On the one hand, their creation did expand the forces available to the allied effort while also involving more Vietnamese and ethnic minorities in a war that, in the final analysis, they must adopt as their own if South Vietnam was to maintain its independence. Relying on native personnel, SOG, the Mikes, Mobile Guerrilla Forces, and Greek-letter projects conducted special operations in enemy areas without risk to large numbers of Americans. On the other hand, the use of ethnic minorities and Vietnamese for Ranger missions created a new set of problems. The Army in general, and Special Forces in particular, were just beginning to examine the use of paramilitary units in a counterinsurgency situation when they became embroiled in Vietnam. As ad hoc organizations, these units lacked the training, equipment, esprit, stamina, and reliability of the picked troops of a Ranger unit. Their major advantage over such troops—their assumed familiarity and ability to blend into the operational area—often proved inapplicable in Vietnam, where many worked in regions far from their homes and therefore lacked a base of popular support for their activities. It was becoming clear that the Army needed special units of American troops for certain tasks, such as the Son Tay raid, and that Special Forces, as a cadre of trainers, was not the organization for such missions.[22]

Despite their problems, Special Forces–led reconnaissance teams achieved enough of a reputation that Westmoreland naturally turned to the Green Berets to run the MACV Recondo School. This program instructed selected allied personnel in the techniques of long-range patrols in the jungle. Instituted by the 5th Special Forces Group on a trial basis in January 1966, it received enough favorable reviews to merit the establishment in September of a more permanent, three-week course under the supervision of DELTA. During the first week, the 30 to 60 students in a class endured physical conditioning and training in methods of long-range reconnaissance, including communications, map and compass, procedures for insertion, and first aid. They then devoted the second week to practicing those techniques, calling in air strikes and carrying out escape and evasion, rappelling, and performing extraction by helicopter. During the third week, the classes carried out actual missions. The course proved a challenge for most students, almost half of whom did not finish it. Whether its three-week program would provide enough training to produce skilled jungle patrollers remained to be seen.[23]

Most graduates of the MACV Recondo School joined the new long-range reconnaissance patrols (LRRPs) that American units were forming to find the enemy so that the big units could destroy him with firepower. The elusiveness of the North Vietnamese and Viet Cong in the jungle, poor patrol methods, and the deficiencies of other sources of information caused American field commanders to turn to the concept that had received so much attention in the late 1950s. As one lieutenant colonel stated: "We can use some sophisticated detection devices, but we must rely mainly on the eyes and ears of the foot soldier. . . . Properly trained and led, small reconnaissance patrols could roam the country in depth and provide a wealth of information." By 1967, every division in Vietnam had a LRRP company, and by 1969 each of the separate brigades and field force commands boasted LRRPs. Also in 1969 the Army recognized the LRRP claim to the Ranger heritage by granting to LRRP companies the designation "Ranger."[24]

LRRPs may have borne the Ranger designation, but their organization, with its emphasis on reconnaissance and communications, differed greatly from that of the Rangers of World War II and Korea. A LRRP team generally contained anywhere from five to eight men, but six seems to have been the optimal number. Three to eight teams formed a LRRP platoon, and two to four platoons constituted a LRRP company. Although field force commands and independent brigades had LRRP units, most LRRP companies operated under the control of divisions. In some cases, the intelligence or operations officer on the division staff supervised the LRRP company and assigned missions in response to requests from subordinate units. Others allocated a LRRP platoon to each of their component brigades or attached their LRRPs to an air cavalry squadron, an arrangement calculated to meet the perennial need of LRRPs for helicopters and mobile, responsive reaction forces. Wherever LRRPs served, they relied on an assortment of gadgets that would have amazed Rangers of past wars, such as light radios with a range of 8 to 12 kilometers, strobes to signal aircraft, night vision devices, sensors, concussion grenades for prisoner snatches, harnesses for extraction by helicopters, and freeze-dried, concentrated "Lerp" rations.[25]

While the technology might have changed, the individuals who joined the LRRPs shared much with the Rangers of World War II and Korea. Young, cocky, and individualistic, they brawled with conventional troops and adopted nicknames like "Mad Dog," "Termite," "Mountain Man," and "Body Bag." They were attracted to the LRRPs by the challenge and status of an elite unit, the LRRP policy of time off between missions, the promise of adventure, and the greater room for individuality. The LRRPs drew these men from a variety of sources. Sometimes, commanders converted other units, such as reconnaissance or antitank platoons, into LRRPs. More often, they relied on volunteers. Since, as in past wars, subordinate commanders did not relish the idea of losing their best men and occasionally provided misfits, recruiters frequently turned to the replacement depots. Some LRRPs contained native troops, such as Montagnards, Nungs, and even a few former Viet Cong cadres. Although many of the officers were Ranger graduates, few of the enlisted men had attended Ranger School. A shortage of experienced team leaders proved to be one of the LRRPs' biggest problems, particularly given the constant turnover of personnel due to the rotation policy. Although most LRRPs improvised training courses for fillers, the replacement situation remained a major problem.[26]

Lack of training and experience proved a chronic problem for LRRPs. The Army's 1968 edition of the LRRP manual estimated that a LRRP required eight months of training to reach full proficiency. Those in Vietnam lacked the time and facilities to even approach that standard. Only a few LRRP members could attend the MACV Recondo School or train with the Australians and other foreign units that were experienced in jungle warfare. To train most of the volunteers, each field force, division, and brigade developed its own program. Relying largely on the Ranger manual, these courses stressed conditioning, weapons training, navigation, marksmanship, first aid, communications, and the methods of infiltration, terrain analysis, and ambushes. After instruction in patrol fundamentals, teams carried out missions in areas of limited enemy activity. Unfortunately, most programs lasted only 2 weeks, and some as little as 7 to 10 days. Compared to the grueling, 15-week training program of the SAS, this abbreviated, improvised schedule left much to be desired.[27]

The absence of a clearly defined mission also hampered LRRP operations. In theory, the main purpose of the LRRPs was to find the enemy so that the standard battalions could engage him. To carry out this task efficiently, LRRPs needed a clear directive that they focus on that function and not embroil themselves in combat. Unfortunately, prewar doctrine had included certain combat roles in the list of LRRP missions, and the emphasis in Vietnam would vary with the period of the war, the nature of the enemy, terrain and season, and the predilections of commanders who supervised the LRRPs. Early in the war, when the North Vietnamese often operated at division or regimental strength, LRRPs focused more on reconnaissance and the collection of intelligence, patrols of suspected enemy base areas, surveillance of infiltration routes, prisoner snatches, and occasionally spotting for air strikes. As enemy concentrations decreased in size and the number of contacts dropped, commanders increasingly authorized LRRPs to engage in combat when they found an enemy formation. LRRPs set ambushes, harassed enemy supply routes, and even served as reaction forces. Such tasks detracted from their primary mission of reconnaissance.[28]

The mission of a LRRP team from the 196th Light Infantry Brigade on July 14-16, 1967, furnishes an example of the way in which many LRRPs operated. During the week prior to the mission, the 196th had recorded two enemy sightings in the region southwest of the hamlet of Thanh My Trung. At noon on July 13, the 196th's intelligence officer directed the brigade's LRRP detachment to send a team to reconnoiter the area. After a day of preparation, including preliminary aerial reconnaissance of the target area, the team was inserted into a clearing by helicopters on the late afternoon of July 14. Running into the nearby woodline, the six team members proceeded through the thick underbrush in single file, looking for a good observation point. Following a night's stay in a canopied clearing, the team leader climbed a tree for a view of the surrounding area, but, while he was thus engaged, the other team members spotted a Viet Cong walking past the campsite. No one could be sure whether he had seen the patrol, but the possibility of compromise caused the detachment leader to direct the team by radio to leave the area. As they settled into their campsite the following night, members of the patrol thought they heard voices

Three members of a team from the LRRP detachment of the 196th Light Infantry Brigade race to board their helicopter for extraction.
(U.S. Army photograph)

and saw flashlights. Calling in artillery, they saw three Viet Cong flee from the shells. Their presence clearly compromised, the six patrollers proceeded to a landing zone the next morning for extraction, even as they heard firing in their rear from their overnight campsite.[29]

Of all the Army's activities in Vietnam, few have received more praise than the LRRPs. Even some of the most vocal critics of the Army's performance in Vietnam, such as Robert Asprey, have had favorable words for the patrols. Several generals approved of the concept, and some expressed great enthusiasm. General Peers of the 4th Infantry Division later stated, "In 1967, before we had any form of surveillance unit such as the people sniffer and the air cav with the scout unit, every major battle that the 4th Infantry Division got itself into was initiated by the action of a Long-Range Patrol; every single one of them." He credited LRRP reports for touching off the battle of Dak To, in which his division claimed 1,400 enemy dead. Maj. Gen. John H. Hay of the 1st Infantry Division called the LRRPs "one of the most significant innovations of the war."

Other generals—including Westmoreland, Lt. Gen. Stanley Larsen of II Field Force, Lt. Gen. Michael S. Davison of II Field Force, Lt. Gen. Frank T. Mildren of U.S. Army, Vietnam, Brig. Gen. E. R. Ochs of the 173d Airborne Brigade, Maj. Gen. Samuel W. Koster of the 23d Infantry Division, Maj. Gen. Harris W. Hollis of the 25th Infantry Division, Maj. Gen. Elvy B. Roberts of the 1st Infantry Division, and Brig. Gen. Jonathan R. Burton of the 3d Brigade, 1st Cavalry Division—also commended the LRRPs. One need not look hard for reasons for their popularity. They produced numerous contacts and very favorable "body counts," claiming 48 enemy dead for each of their own in one instance.[30]

On closer examination, however, the LRRPs do not present such a favorable picture. To be sure, many complaints came from antielitists who resented the special privileges of the LRRPs or from commanders who did not understand the concept. Others, though, pointed out some real problems, many of which resulted from hasty selection, organization, and training. LRRPs often proved easy to detect, due to noisy helicopter insertions and the desire of both the teams and their superiors for a fight despite the supposed emphasis on clandestine reconnaissance, and also because of carelessness on the part of the LRRPs. Even the 4th Infantry Division, which developed perhaps the best LRRP training program, complained of excessive movement, talking, and smoking by its teams in the field. When they sighted an enemy, teams found it difficult to remain still, observe, and provide valuable information on patterns of enemy movement. All too often, they blazed away with automatic weapons and then called headquarters for extraction, a dangerous procedure with an aroused enemy in pursuit. Many commanders resented the need to keep a reaction force and scarce helicopters ready for such missions, especially when reports from LRRPs gave little idea of the size of the enemy force. In sum, LRRPs achieved much in Vietnam, but not as much as a more established force, with adequate doctrine, thorough training, and superiors educated in its proper use, might have accomplished.[31]

As far as LRRP proponents in the Pentagon could see, LRRPs, by late 1968, had already accomplished enough to justify their presence in the postwar Army, and, to bolster their case, the advocates pushed for the redesignation of LRRPs as Ranger companies. Already, debate had begun within Army headquarters over the relative importance of Europe and the rest of the world in post-Vietnam Army strategy. Those who argued that the Army must be ready to intervene in future conflicts in the Third World viewed LRRPs as the type of unit necessary for counterguerrilla operations. One of them, Maj. Gen. Willard Pearson, who had been such an innovative brigade commander with the 101st Airborne in Vietnam, was now serving as the Army's director of individual training. In August 1968, he proposed to the assistant chief of staff for force development, Lt. Gen. Arthur S. Collins, Jr., redesignation of company-sized LRRP units as Ranger companies. "The term LRRP," Pearson bluntly stated, "is sterile, unappealing, and fails to motivate soldiers." On the other hand, the Ranger designation would give a "shot in the arm" to LRRP esprit. Having presented the issue in terms of morale, Pearson went on to state that LRRPs, by their performance in Vietnam, had justified their continuance in the postwar Army.[32]

By the time of Pearson's memorandum, "Ranger" had become a term of legendary connotations but no precise meaning. Although the 1962 edition of the Ranger manual had defined Ranger operations as "overt operations by highly trained units to any depth into enemy held areas for the purpose of reconnaissance, raids, and general disruption of enemy operations," use of the term had expanded to such a degree that it had almost ceased to have any meaning. Part of the problem lay in the definition of an enemy-held area in a war without front lines or any clear idea of the enemy's location. In this context, "Ranger" operations could mean anything from ordinary patrols to so-called "Eagle Flights," reconnaissances in force by American or ARVN platoons in helicopters. Commanders contributed to the confusion by their promiscuous use of the term to boost morale, drawing on its connotations of elite infantrymen and the skilled woodsmen of early America. In its publicity, the Army often compared the Vietnam War to the Indian Wars and claimed that it would use the skills of Rogers and other frontier scouts to defeat the Communists as they had defeated the Indians.[33]

Given the numerous connotations evoked by the term "Ranger," it is not surprising that Pearson's views ran into dissent on the Army Staff. Maj. Gen. Joseph A. McChristian, the Army's intelligence chief, drew a distinction between LRRPs, as collectors of intelligence, and Rangers as raiders. He feared that the redesignation of LRRP companies as Rangers would obscure their primary mission and asked that the Army choose another name more in line with that mission. To complicate matters, the LRRPs could not claim the Ranger lineage, since the Army, believing that it would never again activate Ranger units, had already designated 1st Special Forces as the regimental bearer of the Ranger unit history and honors from World War II and Korea. As an alternate parent unit, the keepers of the Army's organizational history considered the 75th Infantry, which traced its lineage to Merrill's Marauders of World War II fame. The Marauders were a different type of unit from the LRRPs, but they did have a unique character, a distinguished history, and, not least, an active veterans' organization.

In the end, the Army decided to give the Ranger title to the LRRPs and adopt the 75th Infantry as parent regiment for the new Ranger companies. On December 2, 1968, Westmoreland approved Collins's recommendation of the redesignation, which went into effect in February 1969. Announcements of the move emphasized that Rogers's Rangers had represented the "chief scouting arm of the British" and that the Army was merely returning to this earlier definition of the term "Ranger." Actually, the change in terms made little difference in the activities of the companies. While it did give the LRRPs a feeling of shared identity with Rangers of the past and thus improved morale, the lack of a true regimental headquarters meant that the LRRPs operated as independently as before.[34]

In the course of the war, the Army considered the formation of several of the more traditional Ranger units for service in Vietnam, but nothing came of the proposals. Vietnam had raised doubts about the ability of the standard division to perform in many different environments, despite the emphasis on flexibility in its design. As early as 1965, officers were discussing the conversion of armored and mechanized formations into light units and proposing special battalions with manportable equipment for lengthy operations in the jungle. Under the circumstances, it was probably inevitable that someone would propose a Ranger battalion, and, in the spring of 1967, the Infantry Center did so. According to Beckwith, who had moved to the Ranger School, Westmoreland liked the idea but decided that LRRPs would serve the purpose just as well. Gen. Fred C. Weyand, chief of II Field Force in the Tet offensive, later expressed regret that the Army had not activated a Ranger battalion. Experience had shown, he remarked, that "the higher the ratio of U.S. to indigenous personnel, the more effective the reconnaissance performed—a surprise to those who assume a U.S. infantryman cannot equal native personnel for performing reconnaissance."[35]

Weyand's comments provided a fine requiem for the concept of Ranger tasks conducted by standard infantry and native patrols. The Army had entered Vietnam confident that its infantry, led by officers schooled in the traditions of Rogers's Rangers and other Indian fighters, could handle counterguerrilla operations with a little help from native scouts and raiders. In practice, however, this concept had proved inadequate. Ethnic mercenaries and Vietnamese often proved ineffective due to lack of training and resources for the difficult missions assigned to them. Line units ran into so many difficulties that many officers despaired of the ability of their technologically-dependent legions to carry out basic, small-unit patrols in any environment similar to that of Vietnam. Unit leaders improvised special patrol teams which found a number of enemy troops but also ran into problems that a more professional force might have avoided. Still, the Army's experience did show the potential of special operations. Although the Son Tay raid had not achieved its objective, it did show the ability of a Ranger-type force, transported by helicopter, to infiltrate to the heart of the enemy's power and return safely. Son Tay, SOG operations, and other special activities encouraged military men to consider the possibilities and political benefits of joint special operations at the theater level. The question remained how the post-Vietnam Army would apply those lessons.

NOTES

1. George C. Herring, Jr., *America's Longest War: The United States and Vietnam, 1950–1975* (New York: Wiley, 1979), pp. vii–x, 8–11, 17, 40, 46, 50, 75, 107–108, 131–133, 140–144; Millett and Maslowski, *Common Defense*, pp. 545–549.

2. Robert B. Asprey, *War in the Shadows: The Guerrilla in History*, 2 vols. (Garden City, N.Y.: Doubleday, 1975), II:1113–1114; Gerald L. Tippin, "Reflections of a Battalion S-3," p. 63, Lawrence L. Mowery, "Vietnam Report," p. 296, and Albert N. Garland, "Reflections," p. 316, in Infantry Magazine, ed., *A Distant Challenge: The U.S. Infantryman in Vietnam, 1967–1972*, 2d ed. (New York: Jove Books, 1985); Jac Weller, *Fire and Movement: Bargain Basement Warfare in the Far East* (New York: Thomas Y. Crowell, 1967), pp. 73, 76, 90–93, 127–130; Doughty, *Evolution*, pp. 29–34, 38; David H. Hackworth, "Target Acquisition: Vietnam Style," *Military Review* 48 (April 1968): 73–75; John B. Spore, "The U.S. Army in Vietnam," *Army* 16 (May 1966): 83, (June 1966): 69; Anthony Harrigan, "Ground Warfare in Vietnam," *Military Review* 47 (April 1967): 63, 65; William L. Hauser, "Fire and Maneuver in the Delta," *Infantry* 60 (September–October 1970): 12–15; Frank L. Brown, "Combat Patrols," *Infantry* 58 (January–February 1968): 52; Carlisle L. Petty, "Don't Forget Nothing! Lessons Learned—Vietnam," *Army Digest* 21 (August 1966): 36; Millett and Maslowski, *Common Defense*, p. 554; Westmoreland, *Soldier Reports*, pp. 149–150.

3. Herring, *Longest War*, pp. 145–147; Westmoreland, *Soldier Reports*, pp. 142–147, 152–154; Weigley, *History of the United States Army*, pp. 545, 561–565; Asprey, *War in the Shadows*, II:1137, 1140, 1152, 1155, 1280; Charles B. MacDonald and Charles V. P. von Luttichau, "The U.S. Army in Vietnam," in Maurice Matloff, ed., *American Military History*, 2d ed., Army Historical Series (Washington, D.C.: OCMH, 1973), pp. 629, 634; Harrigan, "Ground Warfare," pp. 62–63, 67; Millett and Maslowski, *Common Defense*, pp. 558, 563; reports in HRC 314.82 Debriefing of Senior Officers, Historical Records Branch, CMH; Doughty, *Evolution*, pp. 29–38; Garland, "Reflections," p. 318; Mowery, "Vietnam Report," pp. 297–298; John R. Galvin, "Three Innovations: Prime Tactical Lessons of the Vietnam War," *Army* 22 (March 1972): 18–19; Hauser, "Fire and Maneuver," pp. 12–15; Weller, *Fire and Movement*, pp. 13, 18, 116, 128–131, 212–213; USAMHI, "Senior Officers Debriefing Program: Peers," III:16; Joseph A. McChristian, *The Role of Military Intelligence, 1965–1967*, Vietnam Studies (Washington, D.C.: OCMH, 1974), p. 156; David H. Hackworth, "Guerrilla Battalion—U.S. Style," *Infantry* 61 (January–February 1971): 27; John H. Hay, *Tactical and Material Innovations*, Vietnam Studies (Washington, D.C.: OCMH, 1974), p. 80.

4. Quote from Tippin, "Reflections," p. 67; see also pp. 67–73; Mowery, "Vietnam Report," pp. 297–298; Joseph W. Moore, "Impressions on a Third Tour," pp. 261–263, and Malcolm A. Danner and Billy J. Biberstein, "A View from the Enemy's Side: Thoughts of a Captured NVA Lieutenant," pp. 175, 179, in Infantry Magazine, ed., *A Distant Challenge: The U.S. Infantryman in Vietnam, 1967–1972*, 2d ed. (New York: Jove Books, 1985); Maj. Gen. George I. Forsythe, Lt. Gen. Frank T. Mildren, Maj. Gen. Elvy B. Roberts, and Lt. Gen. Julian J. Ewell in HRC 314.82 Debriefing of Senior Officers, Historical Records Branch, CMH; George C. Herring, Jr., "The 1st Cavalry and the Ia Drang Valley, 18 October–24 November 1965," in Charles E. Heller and William A. Stofft, eds., *America's First Battles, 1775–1965* (Lawrence: University Press of Kansas, 1986), p. 326; John Lance, "Commentaries on Jungle Warfare," *Infantry* 55

(January–February 1965): 54–56; Weller, *Fire and Movement*, pp. 124–125, 218; Thomas N. Greer, "Ambushing," in Albert N. Garland, ed., *Combat Notes from Vietnam*, 2 vols. (Fort Benning, Ga.: Infantry Magazine, 1968), I:75–78; Doughty, *Evolution*, p. 38; Allan W. Sandstrum, "Three Companies at Dak To," in John Albright, John A. Cash, and Allan W. Sandstrum, ed., *Seven Firefights in Vietnam* (Washington, D.C.: OCMH, 1970); Weigley, *History of the United States Army*, p. 564.

    5. Lance, "Jungle Warfare," p. 56; Mowery, "Vietnam Report," pp. 296, 299; Tippin, "Reflections," pp. 73–74; Weller, *Fire and Movement*, p. 93; HRC 314.82 Debriefing of Senior Officers: LTG Melvin Zais, CG, XXIV Corps, 26 June 69–18 June 70, p. 33, Historical Records Branch, CMH; Suid, *Guts and Glory*, p. 106; USAMHI, "Senior Officers Oral History Program: Collins," pp. 334–335.

    6. Weller, *Fire and Movement*, pp. 191–193, 198–206; Westmoreland, *Soldier Reports*, p. 258; McChristian, *Military Intelligence*, p. 105; comments of Shelby L. Stanton and George MacGarrigle, Histories Division, CMH on chapter draft.

    7. Weller, *Fire and Movement*, pp. 133–135; Hackworth, "Target Acquisition," pp. 73–79; Hackworth, "Guerrilla Battalion," pp. 22–28; David H. Hackworth, "Your Mission: Outguerrilla the Guerrilla," *Army Digest* 23 (July 1968): 60–62; Doughty, *Evolution*, p. 39; Tippin, "Reflections," pp. 69, 74; Mowery, "Vietnam Report," pp. 297, 299; Moore, "Impressions," p. 261; Frank J. Phelan, "Doi Ma Creek," p. 9, Joseph M. McDonnell, "The Rats of the Regulars," p. 101, and Robert F. Radcliffe, "Platoon," p. 22, in Infantry Magazine, ed., *A Distant Challenge: The U.S. Infantryman in Vietnam, 1967–1972*, 2d ed. (New York: Jove Books, 1985); Greer, "Ambushing," I:77; John A. Cash, "Ambush at Phuoc An," in John Albright, John A. Cash, and Allan W. Sandstrom, eds., *Seven Firefights in Vietnam* (Washington, D.C.: OCMH, 1970), pp. 59–60; HRC 314.82 Debriefing of Senior Officers: Col. W. F. Williams, 3d Brigade, 9th Inf., 1970, p. 9, and HRC 314.82 Debriefing of Senior Officers: Brig. Gen. E. R. Ochs, CG, 173d Airborne Brigade, 10 Aug 70–15 Jan 71, p. 3, in Historical Records Branch, CMH; Harrigan, "Ground Warfare," p. 62; Kenneth R. Minear, "Raiders for Freedom," *Army Digest* 21 (November 1966): 33; Weigley, *History of the United States Army*, p. 544.

    8. Quote from Jonathan O. Seaman, "Elements of Command," Seminar at Army War College, 4 February 1970, in "Senior Officers Debriefing Program: Seaman"; USAMHI, "Senior Officers Debriefing Program: Peers," III:16, 42–43.

    9. Quote from Zeb B. Bradford, "U.S. Tactics in Vietnam," *Military Review* 52 (February 1972): 74; see also Doughty, *Evolution*, pp. 31, 37, 39; Tippin, "Reflections," p. 64; Asprey, *War in the Shadows*, II:1292; Roger A. Beaumont and William P. Snyder, "Combat Effectiveness," in Sam C. Sarkesian, ed., *Combat Effectiveness: Cohesion, Stress and the Volunteer Military* (Beverly Hills, Calif: Sage Publications, 1980), pp. 49–50; HRC 314.82 Senior Officer Debriefing Report, Lt. Gen. A. S. Collins Jr., 7 Jan. 71, pp. 13–15, Historical Records Branch, CMH. It should be said that the North Vietnamese and Viet Cong occasionally did wipe out isolated patrols.

    10. Tippin, "Reflections," p. 64; USAMHI, "Senior Officers Debriefing Program: Peers," III:16, 42–43; Beaumont and Snyder, "Combat Effectiveness," pp. 49–50; HRC 314.82 Senior Officer Debriefing Report: Collins, pp. 13–15; USAMHI, "Senior Officers Debriefing Program: Palmer," pp. 204, 209; USAMHI, "Senior Officers Oral History Program: Kerwin," pp. 405–406; USAMHI, "Senior Officers Debriefing Program: Conversations between Lieutenant General Harry Lemley and Lieutenant Colonel Gerald F. Feeney," (Carlisle, Pa., 1974), V:23; Spore, "U.S. Army in Vietnam," *Army* 16 (May

1966): 83; Bradford, "Tactics," pp. 63–76; Weller, *Fire and Movement*, pp. 16, 118–119, 132; Moskos, *American Enlisted Man*, pp. 137, 153–154; Westmoreland, *Soldier Reports*, p. 154; comments of MacGarrigle, Col. Robert Sholly USA, and Lt. Col. Gary Bounds USA (Ret.) on the draft manuscript.

11. Moskos, *American Enlisted Man*, pp. 142–143, 151; Guenter Lewy, "The American Experience in Vietnam," in Sam C. Sarkesian, ed., *Combat Effectiveness* (Beverly Hills, Calif.: Sage Publications, 1980), pp. 102–104; USAMHI, "Senior Officers Oral History Program: Kerwin," p. 358; Garland, "Reflections," pp. 318–319; Paul Savage and Richard A. Gabriel, "Cohesion and Disintegration in the American Army: An Alternative Perspective," in Peter Karsten, ed., *The Military in America* (New York: Free Press, 1980), pp. 399–421; Adam Yarmolinsky, "The War and the American Military," in Anthony Lake, ed., *The Legacy of Vietnam* (New York: Council on Foreign Relations, 1976), p. 219; Weigley, *History of the United States Army*, p. 565; comments by Stanton and MacGarrigle on draft manuscript.

12. See U.S. Army, Department of the Army, *Combat Training of the Individual Soldier and Patrolling*, FM 21-75 (Washington, D.C.: Department of the Army, 1967); Cable, *Conflict of Myths*, pp. 113–115.

13. Kelly, *U.S. Army Special Forces*, pp. 7, 10–15, 33–34; Simpson, *Green Berets*, pp. 97–115, 202; Stanton, *Green Berets at War*, p. 91; Ronald H. Spector, *Advice and Support: The Early Years, 1941–1960*, U.S. Army in Vietnam (Washington, D.C.: CMH, 1983), pp. 349–355; Jeffrey J. Clarke, *Advice and Support: The Final Years, 1965–1973*, U.S. Army in Vietnam (Washington, D.C.: CMH, 1988), pp. 34–36, 70–72; James L. Collins, *The Development and Training of the South Vietnamese Army, 1950–1972*, Vietnam Studies (Washington, D.C.: OCMH, 1975), pp. 17–20, 33–38, 91; USAMHI, "Senior Officers Debriefing Program: Decker," IV:23.

14. Shelby L. Stanton, *Vietnam Order of Battle* (Washington, D.C.: U.S. News Books, 1981), pp. 251–252; Stanton, *Green Berets at War*, pp. 205–211; Simpson, *Green Berets*, pp. 143–149, 153; Westmoreland, *Soldier Reports*, pp. 106–109; Cable, *Conflict of Myths*, pp. 206, 211, 214, 220–221; Clarke, *Advice and Support: Final Years*, pp. 72–73; Benjamin F. Schemmer, *The Raid* (New York: Harper and Row, 1976), pp. 42, 46–51; USAMHI, "Senior Officers Debriefing Program: Peers," III:30, 72; Norton interview; Yarborough interview, II:29; Roger M. Pezzelle, "Military Capabilities and Special Operations in the 1980's," in Frank R. Barnett, B. Hugh Tovar, and Richard H. Shultz, eds., *Special Operations in U.S. Strategy* (Washington, D.C.: National Defense University Press, 1984), p. 141; "Perspectives on Military Special Operations at the Operational and Strategic Levels—MACSOG [Military Assistance Command, Studies and Observation Group], 1966–1968: Oral History Interview of MACSOG Commander: Major General John Kirk Singlaub USA Retired," interviewed by LTC John C. Woolfshlager, USAMHI.

15. Schemmer, *The Raid*, is the basic work on Son Tay. See also Earl H. Tilford, *Search and Rescue in Southeast Asia, 1961–1975* (Washington, D.C.: Office of Air Force History, 1980), pp. 104–112; Richard A. Gabriel, *Military Incompetence: Why the American Military Doesn't Win* (New York: Hill and Wang, 1985), pp. 42–49; Robert K. Ruhl, "Raid at Son Tay," *Airman* 19 (August 1975): 24–31.

16. Schemmer, *The Raid*, pp. 51–52, 259–260; U.S. Congress, Senate, Committee on Foreign Relations, *Bombing Operations and the POW Rescue Mission in North Vietnam*, 91st Cong., 2d sess., 1970, p. 7; Tad Szulc, "Fulbright Committee Asks

Explanation for Air Raids," *New York Times*, 24 November 1970, p. 1; Max Frankel, "Nixon and the Rescue Mission," *New York Times*, 24 November 1970, p. 14.

17. Schemmer, *The Raid*, pp. 211–212, 220, 229–230; Edward N. Luttwak, [comments on Pezzelle, "Military Capabilities and Special Operations in the 1980's"], in Frank R. Barnett, B. Hugh Tovar, and Richard H. Shultz, eds., *Special Operations in U.S. Strategy* (Washington, D.C.: National Defense University, 1984), pp. 155–156; Peter A. Kelly, "Raids and National Command: Mutually Exclusive!" *Military Review* 60 (April 1980): 20–25; Gabriel, *Military Incompetence*, pp. 19, 40; "Senior Officers Debriefing Program: Palmer," p. 146; Joshua Shani, "Airborne Raids: A Potent Weapon in Countering Transnational Terrorism," *Air University Review* 35 (March–April 1984): 46–49.

18. Schemmer, *The Raid*, pp. 237–238; Simpson, *Green Berets*, pp. 137–141; Kelly, *U.S. Army Special Forces*, p. 148; Stanton comments on manuscript.

19. Stanton, *Green Berets at War*, pp. 232–252; Clarke, *Advice and Support: The Final Years*, pp. 72, 203–206; Simpson, *Green Berets*, pp. 123–125, 133–135, 154–155; Stanton, *Vietnam Order of Battle*, pp. 244–245; Kelly, *U.S. Army Special Forces*, pp. 134–137, 141; HRC 314.82 Debriefing of Senior Officers: Colonel Harold R. Aaron, 5th Special Forces Group (ABN), 4 June 1968–29 May 1969, pp. 1–3; and HRC 314.82 Debriefing of Senior Officers: Colonel Jonathan F. Ladd, CO, 5th SFG, 4 June 67–4 June 68, pp. 1–2, 8–10, 98–99, in Historical Records Branch, CMH; Nicholas Sellers and Railey W. Macey III, "Special Forces Operations in the Delta," in Infantry Magazine, ed., *A Distant Challenge: The U.S. Infantryman in Vietnam, 1967–1972*, 2d ed. (New York: Jove Books, 1985), pp. 147–155; U.S. Army, Army Concept Team in Vietnam, "Final Report: Employment of a Special Forces Group (U)," JRATA Project No. (1B-154.0), 20 April 1966, pp. vii, 51, in Access and Release Branch, Adjutant General's Office, Alexandria, Va.

20. John D. Howard, "Recon," I:65, and James R. Davis, "Reconnaissance," I:69, in Albert N. Garland, ed., *Combat Notes from Vietnam*, 2 vols. (Fort Benning, Ga.: Infantry Magazine, 1968); Joel E. Sugdinis, "Intelligence," p. 17, and Robert G. Pasour, "Patrolling," p. 41, in Albert N. Garland, ed., *Infantry in Vietnam* (Fort Benning, Ga.: Infantry Magazine, 1967); Hay, *Innovations*, p. 123; Stanton, *Green Berets*, pp. 194–204, 212, 292; Clarke, *Advice and Support: Final Years*, pp. 72, 204–207; U.S. Army, "Employment of a Special Forces Group," pp. 22, 51; Beckwith and Knox, *Delta Force*, pp. 55–57, 62–71, 74–77; Debriefing of Senior Officers: Ladd, p. 10; HRC 314.82 Debriefing of Senior Officers: Major General John J. Tolson, Vietnam, p. 5, Historical Records Branch, CMH; "History of the 5th SF Grp ABN 1st SF, 1 October to 31 December 1964," pp. 26–29, 40–41, in U.S. Army, Adjutant General, Records of the 5th Special Forces Group, Accession No. 73A-3330, Box 14, RG 338, WNRC. Kelly provides a table of organization for DELTA on page 138 of *U.S. Army Special Forces*, but this table was not adopted in its entirety.

21. Stanton, *Green Berets at War*, pp. 187–188, 203–205, 208, 235; Clarke, *Advice and Support: Final Years*, pp. 204–205; Stanton, *Vietnam Order of Battle*, pp. 243–245; Kelly, *U.S. Army Special Forces*, p. 139; HRC 314.82 Debriefing of Senior Officers: Ladd, pp. 2–3, 99–100, Annex A, pp. 1–3; Memorandum for Record, MACV Commanders Conference, 24 September 1967, William C. Westmoreland Papers, Histories Division, CMH.

22. USAMHI, "Senior Officers Debriefing Program: Palmer," p. 146; Lt. Col. Joseph P. Argenterie USA, interview with author, Pentagon, Va., 18 April 1985; Simpson, *Green Berets*, p. 142; Asprey, *War in the Shadows*, II:1152; U.S. Army, Department of the Army, *Special Forces Operations*, FM 31-21 (Washington, D.C.: Department of the Army, 1965), pp. 181, 189-192.

23. Johnny Durden and Fred Sherrill, "Ranger Operations," *U.S. Army Aviation Digest* 16 (October 1970): 2-6; Stanton, *Green Berets at War*, p. 195; Kelly, *U.S. Army Special Forces*, p. 121; Operational Report, Lessons Learned (ORLL), of 5th Special Forces Group (ABN) for the Period Ending 30 April 1970, p. 30, in ORLLs, 5th SF Grp, 1970, Records of the 5th Special Forces Group, Accession No. 71A-4237, Box 1/15, RG 338, WNRC; HRC 314.82 Debriefing of Senior Officers: Ladd, pp. 77, 127-131; William Beecher, "A GI School Has 'Shoot Back' Targets," *New York Times*, 4 September 1966, p. 2; Lanning, *Inside the LRRP's*, pp. 59, 102; James R. Arnold, *Rangers*, Illustrated History of the Vietnam War (New York: Bantam Books, 1988), pp. 32-33; McChristian, *Military Intelligence*, p. 105.

24. Quote from Asprey, *War in the Shadows*, II:1152; see also Lanning, *Inside the LRRP's*, pp. 52-63; Harrigan, "Ground Warfare," p. 62; Gordon L. Rottman and Tim Moriarty, "Long Range Reconnaissance Patrol Companies," part I: "Vietnam," p. 2, in "75th Infantry," Organizational History Branch, CMH; Arnold, *Rangers*, p. 32; James E. Voyles, "Vietnam Rangers (LRRP)," *Gung Ho*, October 1984, p. 67; Stanton, *Vietnam Order of Battle*, pp. 53, 155, 161. See also the forthcoming Shelby L. Stanton, *Rangers at War* (New York: Crown Books, 1992).

25. 1st Lt. Robert J. Brown, CO, LRRP, 199th Infantry Brigade Separate (Light) to Commanding General, 199th Infantry Brigade, 7 October 1967, U.S. Army, 199th Infantry Brigade, Command Reports, 1967-1970, Accession No. 338-82-1502/1/1, RG 338, WNRC; Operational Report, Lessons Learned (ORLL) for Quarterly Period Ending 31 October 1967, 4th Infantry Division, 26 December 1967, U.S. Army, 4th Infantry Division, Formerly Classified Operations Report and Lessons Learned Oct. 1966-Dec. 1967, Accession No. 338-82-584/1-5/5, Box 5, RG 338, WNRC; "1st Air Cavalry Division Long Range Patrols," pp. 1-3, 7-8, ORLL, 1st Cavalry Division, Period Ending 31 October 1968, and Twenty-fifth Infantry, Company H (Ranger) Team 45, "Combat After Action Interview Report, Ranger Team 45 Contact, 3-4 Nov. 69," 20 February 1969, U.S. Army, Adjutant General, Records of the 1st Air Cavalry Division, Accession No. 73A-3330, Box 1/67, RG 338, WNRC; 1st Air Cavalry Division, ORLL, 1 August-31 October 1967, U.S. Army, 1st Air Cavalry Division, HHC, 228-07 Command Reports, Oct. 1965-Jan. 1968, Lessons Learned, Accession No. 338-82-1473, Box 2, RG 338, WNRC; Thomas J. Shaughnessy, "Rotors for the Rangers," *Army* 22 (May 1972): 38-42; Lanning, *Inside the LRRP's*, pp. 58, 111-113, 120-132, 145-148, 222-224; MACV Commanders Conference, encl. 9; USAMHI, "Senior Officers Debriefing Program: Peers," III:38; HRC 314.82 Debriefing of Senior Officers: Major General Donn R. Pepke, 4th Infantry Div., Republic of Vietnam, 30 Nov 68-10 Nov 69, Historical Records Branch, CMH; HRC 314.82 Debriefing of Senior Officers: Major General Harris W. Hollis, CG, 25th Infantry Division, U.S. Army, 15 September 1969-2 April 1970, pp. 15, 33, 39, Historical Records Branch, CMH; Hay, *Innovations*, p. 123; Stanton, *Vietnam Order of Battle*, p. 53.

26. Lanning, *Inside the LRRP's*, pp. 79-100, 143-144, 172; Arnold, *Rangers*, pp. 18, 40-41; MACV Commanders Conference, encl. 9; Gordon L. Rottman, *Army Rangers*, p. 31; Howard, "Recon," I:65-68; Tom P. Cable, "Long Range Patrol," *Army Digest* 23 (December 1968): 12; "1st Air Cavalry Division, Long Range Patrols"; Entry Dates, 25 September to 26 October 1967, U.S. Army, 4th Infantry Division, Company E, 20th Infantry, Daily Journals, 1967, Accession No. 338-82-638/1/1, Box 2, RG 338, WNRC; 1st Lt. Charles M. White, Executive Officer, LRRP, 199th Infantry Brigade to Commanding General, 199th Infantry Brigade, 10 October 1967, U.S. Army, 199th Infantry Brigade (Light), Company M, 75th Infantry, 2-12 Command Reports, 1967-1970, Accession No. 338-82-1502/1/1, RG 338, WNRC; 1st Lt. Arthur Tomascheck, Operations Officer, Company F, 75th Infantry, to Commanding General, 25th Infantry Division, 2 November 1969, U.S. Army, 25th Infantry Division, Company F, 50th Infantry, Formerly Classified After Action Reports, 1968, Accession No. 338-81-445/1-2, Box 1, RG 338, WNRC; ORLL of Company E, (Ranger) 75th Infantry for 1 May-31 July 1970, U.S. Army, 9th Infantry Division, Company E, 75th Infantry, Organizational History, Accession No. 338-81-1030/1/1, Box 1, RG 338, WNRC; Brown to Commanding General, 199th Inf. Brigade, 7 October 1967; ORLL, Company F, 75th Infantry (Ranger) Period Ending 31 Jan 70, U.S. Army, 25th Infantry Division, 75th Infantry (Ranger), Formerly Classified Status and After Action Reports, 1969-70, Accession No. 338-81-441/1-4, Box 4, RG 338, WNRC.

27. Maj. Gen. Willard Pearson, Director of Individual Training, DCSPER, to Maj. Gen. John R. Deane, Director of Doctrine and Systems, OACSFOR, 19 August 1968, in "75th Infantry," Organizational History Branch, CMH; Norton interview; Howard, "Recon," I:66; "1st Air Cavalry Division, Long Range Patrols," pp. 8-9; Brown to Commanding General, 199th Infantry Brigade, 7 October 1967; White to Commanding General, 199th Infantry Brigade, 10 October 1967; ORLL of Company E (Ranger) 75th Infantry, for 1 May-31 July 1970; ORLL of Company E (Ranger), 75th Infantry, Organizational History, Accession No. 338-81-1030/1/1, RG 338, WNRC; ORLL for Quarterly Period Ending 30 April 1967, p. 12, U.S. Army, 4th Infantry Division, Formerly Classified Operations Report and Lessons Learned, Oct. 1966-Dec. 1967, Accession No. 338-82-584/1-5/5, Box 12, RG 338, WNRC; Lanning, *Inside the LRRP's*, pp. 99-101, 107-109; Richard D. James, "Delta Team Is in Contact," *Infantry* 60 (November-December 1970): 13-14; HRC 314.82 Debriefing of Senior Officers: Pepke, p. 40; MACV Commanders Conference, encl. 9; HRC 314.82 Debriefing of Senior Officers: BG Jonathan R. Burton, Commanding General, 3d Brigade (Separate) 1st Cavalry Division (Airmobile) Period 10 April 71-13 Dec. 71, p. 7, Historical Records Branch, CMH; Cable, "Long Range Patrol," pp. 11-12; Col. Richard J. Keating USA, interview with author, Springfield, Va., 6 April 1986; Gen. William E. Depuy USA (Ret.), interview with author, Alexandria, Va., 30 September 1985, and personal communication to author, 10 June 1986; Beckwith and Knox, *Delta Force*, pp. 11-12, 18-19.

28. U.S. Army, *Long Range Patrols*, pp. 2-3; Rottman and Moriarty, "Long Range Reconnaissance Patrol Companies," p. 2; Tomascheck to Commanding General, 25th Infantry Division, 2 Nov 69; White to Commanding General, 199th Infantry Brigade, 10 Oct 67; ORLL of Company E (Ranger), 75th Infantry, for 1 May-31 July 1970; ORLLs of 4th Infantry Division; 1st Lt. Mills M. Byce, Operations Officer, Company F, 75th Infantry, to Commanding General, 25th Infantry Division, 30 November 1968, U.S.

Army, 25th Infantry Division, Company F, 50th Infantry, Formerly Classified After Action Reports, 1968, Accession No. 338-81-445/1-2, Box 1, RG 338, WNRC; Lanning, *Inside the LRRP's*, pp. 134-135, 142; James, "Delta Team," p. 12; Arnold, *Rangers*, pp. 34, 99; Richard G. Stilwell, "An Evolution in Tactics: The Vietnam Experience," *Army* 20 (February 1970): 22; HRC 314.82 Debriefing of Senior Officers: Ochs, pp. 3, 7-9; HRC 314.82 Debriefing of Senior Officers: Pepke, p. 4; HRC 314.82 Debriefing of Senior Officers: Burton, p. 5; HRC 314.82 Debriefing of Senior Officers: Hollis, pp. 33, 39; HRC 314.82 Debriefing of Senior Officers: Ewell, pp. 5-6; HRC 314.82 Debriefing of Senior Officers: Williams, p. 8; HRC 314.82 Debriefing of Senior Officers: MG John Hennessey, CG, 101st Airborne Division, Vietnam, May 1970-Jan 1971, p. 4, HRC 314.82 Debriefing of Senior Officers: Major General Edward Bautz, Jr., 25th Infantry Division, Vietnam, March 69-Dec. 70, pp. 5-7, and HRC 314.82 Debriefing of Senior Officers: Lt. Gen. Charles A. Corcoran, 23 May 68-23 Feb 70, p. 5, in Historical Records Branch, CMH; MACV Commanders Conference, encl. 9; Keating interview; Howard, "Recon," I:68; Hay, *Innovations*, p. 124; Robert C. Carroll, "Six Men Alone," *Infantry* 65 (January-February 1975): 41-43.

29. "VNI 50, 196th Light Infantry Brigade Contact of 14-16 July 1967," Historical Records Branch, CMH.

30. Peers quoted in Hay, *Innovations*, p. 124; Hay, *Innovations*, p. 126; see also Asprey, *War in the Shadows*, II:1290; USAMHI, "Senior Officers Debriefing Program: Peers," III:38, 52, 58; Lanning, *Inside the LRRP's*, pp. 77, 137, 161-170; ORLLs for 4th Infantry Division; 25th Infantry Division, ORLL for Quarterly Period Ending 31 July 1966, p. 13, in U.S. Army, 25th Infantry Division, Records of the 25th Infantry Division, AD-391 727 15/7, Access and Release Branch, Adjutant General's Office, Alexandria, Va.; Westmoreland, *Soldier Reports*, p. 280; Rottman and Moriarty, "Long Range Reconnaissance Patrol Companies," p. 2; Stanton, *Vietnam Order of Battle*, pp. 53, 155, 161; MACV Commanders Conference, encl. 9; HRC 314.82 Debriefing of Senior Officers: Burton, p. 6; HRC 314.82 Debriefing of Senior Officers: Ochs, p. 9; HRC 314.82 Debriefing of Senior Officers: Roberts, p. 9; HRC 314.82 Debriefing of Senior Officers: Hollis, p. 39; HRC 314.82 Debriefing of Senior Officers: Corcoran, p. 5; HRC 314.82 Debriefing of Senior Officers: Mildren, p. 34; HRC 314.82 Debriefing of Senior Officers: Major General S. W. Koster, Vietnam, p. 7, Historical Records Branch, CMH.

31. Lanning, *Inside the LRRP's*, pp. 171-175; Arnold, *Rangers*, pp. 99-101, 116-119; James W. England, *Long Range Patrol Operations: Reconnaissance, Combat, and Special Operations* (Boulder, Colo.: Paladin Press, 1987), pp. vi, 2-6; James, "Delta Team," p. 14; McChristian, *Military Intelligence*, p. 105; Depuy interview with author; Command Report, Operation FRANCIS MARION, 6 April-11 October 1967, U.S. Army, 4th Infantry Division, Formerly Classified Operations Reports and Lessons Learned, Oct. 1966-Dec. 1967, Accession No. 338-82-584/1-5/5, RG 338, WNRC; ORLL, Company F, 75th Infantry (Ranger), Period Ending 30 April 1970; ORLL for Period Ending 31 October 1968, 1st Cavalry Division, p. 12; MACV Commander's Conference, encl. 9.

32. Pearson quoted in Pearson to Deane, 19 August 1968; see also Lanning, *Inside the LRRP's*, p. 75; England, *Long Range Patrol Operations*, p. 5.

33. U.S. Army, [Foreword], in *Ranger Training and Ranger Operations*, January 1962; Shaun M. Darragh, "Rangers and Special Forces: Two Edges of the Same Dagger," *Army* 27 (December 1977): 14–19; Galvin, "Three Innovations," p. 18; John B. Spore, "The U.S. Army in Vietnam," *Army* 16 (May 1966): 82; Weller, *Fire and Movement*, p. 223; Hackworth, "Guerrilla Battalion," p. 28; Hackworth, "Mission," p. 61; "The Rangers Have a Long History," p. E6; A. Porter and S. Sweet, "Rangers Four," *Infantry* 56 (January–February, 1966): 60–61.

34. Quote from B. J. Sutton, "Merrill's Marauders," *Infantry* 59 (November–December 1969): 15; see also Maj. Gen. J. A. McChristian, Assistant Chief of Staff for Intelligence, to Assistant Chief of Staff for Force Development, 29 October 1968, and other correspondence in "75th Infantry," Organizational History Branch, CMH; Stanton, *Vietnam Order of Battle*, p. 154; Lanning, *Inside the LRRP's*, pp. 74–75; England, *Long Range Patrol Operations*, p. 6.

35. Weyand quoted in HRC 314.82 Debriefing of Senior Officers: LTG Fred C. Weyand, p. 8, Historical Records Branch, CMH; see also Beckwith and Knox, *Delta Force*, p. 87; Hanson W. Baldwin, "The All Purpose Army," *New York Times*, 15 August 1966, p. 4; Lance, "Jungle Warfare," pp. 52–53; Weller, *Fire and Movement*, p. 223; Weigley, *History of the United States Army*, p. 566.

12

"A Foot Infantry Battalion . . . Finest In The World"

The Vietnam War not only shattered the postwar anti-Communist consensus in the United States, it contributed to a crisis of confidence on the part of many Americans in their institutions. As the war dragged on without resolution, it sharpened divisions in a society that had already been polarized by the civil rights struggle, environmental and consumer movements, and other, seemingly intractable, economic and social issues. An increasingly vocal minority, based largely in colleges and universities, called for unconditional withdrawal from Vietnam, arguing that Americans were trying to impose their values on people who did not understand or desire them. Other Americans, including most of the middle class, dismissed student protesters as frivolous kids at best and "Red" agents at worst, and firmly believed that if the United States only applied its military power without limits, it would emerge victorious. These divisions, along with chronic inflation and unemployment, the political scandals of the Nixon administration, and the final collapse of South Vietnam in 1975 shook the belief of many Americans in their inherent goodness, their ability to solve problems, and the worth and universality of their values. Social critics deplored the materialistic, bureaucratized world they saw around them, and many individuals, feeling alienated from traditional standards, experimented with everything from illegal drugs and sexual mores to colorful clothing and men's hair salons. To be sure, most Americans did not abandon the old values and ideals, but they did view the world, and the role of the United States in it, with a considerably greater degree of cynicism.[1]

These new attitudes had their effect on American foreign policy in the 1970s. Disillusioned with 20 years of foreign adventures, Americans reacted against crisis diplomacy and further interventions abroad. Their leaders, in turn, were less certain of the role of military force in support of foreign policy. Some, such as Secretary of State Henry A. Kissinger, perceived an inevitable decline in American power and ability to protect its interests around the world. Under Nixon and Kissinger, American foreign policy entered a period of retrenchment, maintaining its commitments to NATO, Japan, and South Korea, but stipulating that client states elsewhere would have to provide the bulk of the manpower for their own defense. Retrenchment reached its apogee in the early years of President Jimmy Carter's administration, which advocated East-West détente, regional accommodation, restraint in the use of military force, and cuts in defense spending.[2]

For the Army, the 1970s brought hard times in ways other than lower defense budgets. For the first time since World War II, the military found its competence questioned, with critics savaging the officer corps as career-minded glory hunters and movies fostering the image of inept officers, drug-crazed soldiers, and mentally unbalanced veterans. However, the war had cost the Army much more than prestige. Because of President Johnson's refusal to raise taxes and mobilize the reserves, the Army had fought the war by juggling existing resources, with dire repercussions for unit readiness outside Southeast Asia. The absence of a decision in Vietnam, the massacre of Vietnamese civilians at My Lai and other scandals, and the collapse of support at home for the war created a moral crisis of which drug use, race riots, desertions, and murders of superior officers were only symptoms. Then came the postwar period, budget cuts, and the advent of an All-Volunteer Army which was hard-pressed to find qualified recruits. Within the Army, the experience of Vietnam was causing much soul searching on roles, tactics, and force structure. Although several younger officers foresaw more brushfire conflicts in an increasingly volatile, interdependent world, many of their superiors wanted to forget Vietnam and return to the Army's traditional focus on Europe, the one place, they argued, where defeat would have disastrous consequences for American interests. Thus, the Army of the period devoted much effort to modernizing heavy weapons, and to education and training in which the Arab-Israeli War of 1973, not the Vietnam War, was the model.[3]

The tilt toward Europe in forces and tactics had its effect on LRRPs. Many of the officers who believed that the Army must prepare for brushfire wars in the Third World saw LRRPs as essential to that role and tried to give them a more influential voice in Army policy-making circles by urging the designation of the director of the Ranger Department at Fort Benning as nominal commander of the 75th Infantry. Even with the backing of General Haines, commander of CONARC and a longtime Ranger partisan, the proposal was defeated by those in Army headquarters who argued that it would confer on the Ranger director only a vague, superficial status. Rejection of the proposal showed the direction in which LRRPs were heading. As brigades and divisions returned from Vietnam in the early 1970s, they inactivated their LRRPs, leaving the Army with only two active companies and a handful of National Guard LRRPs by October 1972. Commanders facing budget cuts and manpower ceilings were more likely to inactivate LRRPs than line units, particularly given their faith in sensors and other gadgets and the identification of LRRPs with a war that many soldiers wanted to forget. Where human observation was necessary, the Army believed Green Berets could do the job.[4]

Long-range reconnaissance was only one of a broad array of missions for which Special Forces were now responsible. Whenever the Army had encountered an unusual combat mission over the previous 10 years, it had tended to assign that task to the Green Berets, as the Army's experts in "special warfare." By 1970, their list of missions had grown to cover organization, training, and leadership of guerrillas, rescue, sabotage, civic action, counterinsurgency, instruction of foreign military and paramilitary forces, and such Ranger-type missions as raids, reconnaissance, surveillance, and target acquisition far behind enemy lines. Such a broad range of missions spread Special Forces thin. Many Green Berets complained that they should focus on the training of guerrillas and counterinsurgency but instead were receiving tasks, such as raids, reconnaissance, and ambushes, that wasted their unique abilities as cross-cultural trainers.[5]

Unfortunately for Special Forces, the war in Vietnam had dispelled much of the aura that had surrounded them in the heady days of Kennedy's New Frontier. Stories of Green Berets engaging in drunken brawls in bars and even shunning risky missions clashed with the chivalric image projected by the news media. The Rheault case, in which the commander of 5th Special Forces Group and seven of his men were charged with the murder of a Vietnamese contact, left a bad taste in many quarters. Literary works assailed Special Forces, and protests and biting reviews greeted the opening of John Wayne's hit film, *The Green Berets*.[6] Within the postwar Army, the image of Special Forces was almost as bad as among antiwar liberals. Even after MACV, in 1964, retrieved the 5th Special Forces Group from its semi-independent status under the CIA, it still seemed to many line officers to be an almost autonomous organization, with its own chain of command, funding, and supply system. The common feeling that the "green beanies" were out of control appeared confirmed by their use of such unauthorized items as tigerskin capes and elephant-hide boots, their reputation for drinking and brawling in Saigon bars, and the Rheault case. Finally, the attention that the Green Berets received created resentment among those who felt they were facing the same or greater risks without the headlines. Special Forces still enjoyed some defenders in high places, notably Westmoreland, but once those defenders retired, the Green Berets would be vulnerable to lingering antielitism.[7]

Despite its expanding responsibilities, therefore, Special Forces was hit hard by postwar cutbacks. By the end of 1974, the Army had inactivated four Special Forces groups, and the 7th Special Forces Group escaped a similar fate in 1979 only after an intensive lobbying effort. Most Vietnam veterans either retired or transferred to more conventional units. The three remaining, understrength groups lacked essential radio operators and medics. By the mid-1970s, the Army's resources for special operations seemed little better than they had been two decades before.[8]

Nonetheless, in this period of reorientation toward big-unit warfare, antielitism, and force cutbacks, the Army formed two new Ranger battalions. In part, this action can be explained by the fact that, for all the antipathy toward Special Forces and LRRPs, the Army seems to have departed Vietnam with more respect for the notion of specialization. As manpower levels dropped, the Army was looking for ways to make the best use of existing resources, and force planners were showing some receptivity to the idea of small, highly trained forces using the most advanced weapons to perform tasks formerly carried out by mass units. In a study for the Pentagon, the Advanced Research Projects Agency pointed out that developments in sensors, communications, night viewing devices, aerial fire support, and helicopters had provided such forces with the intelligence-gathering capability, firepower, and mobility to carry out tasks that had been unthinkable in past wars. Such studies created a more favorable environment for Ranger-type units than would initially appear to be the case.[9]

The actual impetus for revival of the Ranger battalions, as in World War II and the Korean War, came from the top of the Army hierarchy. On the surface, Gen. Creighton W. Abrams seemed an unlikely candidate for the role. Born to a railroad repairman in Agawam, Massachusetts, he had graduated from West Point in 1936. As a tank battalion commander during World War II, he spearheaded the drive by Patton's Third Army to relieve besieged Bastogne during the Battle of the Bulge. After the war, he had commanded the 3d Armored Division in Europe, directed Federal troops sent to police race riots in Mississippi and Alabama, and served as vice chief of staff before his tenure as commander of MACV. In 1972, he had succeeded Westmoreland as chief of staff. In many ways the opposite of his predecessor, Abrams was a gruff, no-nonsense leader who liked cigars and classical music. However, his reticence masked a powerful mind and an ability to get to the heart of a problem. No enthusiast of the Green Berets, he had felt so betrayed by the Rheault case that he had not attended the final Special Forces parade at Nha Trang. During his tenure as chief of staff, the Army saw an increase in heavy, conventional divisions and deep cuts in Special Forces.[10]

However, even as Abrams expanded the Army's conventional forces, he perceived a need for a rapidly deployable force able to respond to emergencies around the world. In the Middle East, the increasing dependence of the West on foreign oil, the volatility of the region, and the specter of another embargo raised the possibility that the United States might need to keep a force ready to seize the oil fields on a moment's notice. When Palestinian guerrillas hijacked four planes to Jordan in September 1970, the Army had been so unprepared to respond that commanders in Europe had considered dismounting some mechanized infantry units. The murder of Israeli athletes at the Munich Olympics

Gen. Creighton W. Abrams (U.S. Army photograph)

in 1972 and the worldwide alert of American forces during the Yom Kippur War in 1973 further drove home the value of a ready force. Abrams concluded that the 82d Airborne Division, despite its status as the nation's strategic reserve, lacked the ability to act quickly enough in a fast-developing crisis, and that Special Forces, as a cadre, did not have the organization to respond in strength to emergencies. Another kind of force was needed.

For this force, Abrams envisioned an elite formation, but not a special unit. Except for its light character, the force would use a fairly conventional organization and weapons to perform a mission that did not, nominally, lie outside the capacity of a well-trained standard unit. Its distinguishing feature lay in its ability to perform that task better than a line unit. At a time when the readiness of the Army to defend American interests was at a low ebb, Abrams wanted a force that he knew could deploy and fight at a moment's notice, without taking the time to organize and select the best troops for the mission. In short, under pressure, the Army was retreating from its old stance that one unit was as good as another, even for relatively conventional tasks.[11]

Some underlying motives might also have influenced Abrams's decision to revive the Ranger battalions. At a time when the U.S. Army was enduring severe criticism, the Rangers would show that the Army still contained some fighters, thus improving its image with the public and foreign military forces. As an Army loyalist, Abrams resented the favorable publicity surrounding the Marines and wanted to show that the Army could also produce crack light infantry. He realized that if the Army did not claim the mission of a force ready to respond to emergencies, the Marines, with their fleet-based units, probably would. Finally, although an elite unit, Rangers actually seemed conventional and accountable compared to the Green Berets, for whom Abrams harbored little affection. By taking some missions from Special Forces, the Rangers would make palatable deeper cuts in Special Forces.[12]

Within three months of the Yom Kippur War, Abrams acted to form the Rangers. On December 20, 1973, Army headquarters notified Gen. William E. Depuy of Training and Doctrine Command and Gen. Walter T. Kerwin of Forces Command of its intention to form one Ranger battalion immediately and two more by the end of the next fiscal year. Each of these light units would contain about 600 Ranger- and airborne-qualified soldiers, which the Army would draw from either its two LRRP companies, a Special Forces battalion, or normal recruiting procedures. The new battalions would serve as a force for rapid movement to any location in the world requiring an American military presence, as a model for joint training and exercises with foreign troops, and as trainers of foreign troops and irregulars. As a secondary task, the directive vaguely mentioned deep-penetration missions and long-range independent operations on foot in support of conventional forces in wartime. Clearly, Abrams was creating the Rangers for rapid reaction, not for raids or other established Ranger functions. Furthermore, he was proposing that they perform tasks that encroached on traditional Special Forces missions.[13]

Depuy moved quickly to clarify the concept. Hard-nosed and energetic, the TRADOC commander had impressed first Westmoreland and later Abrams with his brilliance and grasp of a number of topics. He could boast some experience with special operations through his service with the CIA in the late 1950s, his exposure to British ideas while attending the Imperial Defence College, and his tenure as operations officer at MACV and as the advisor to the Joint Chiefs for counterinsurgency and special activities. He now acted to delineate Ranger functions more clearly and to distinguish them from those of Special Forces. After conferring with Abrams, he provided his staff with substantially different guidance, reaffirming that training of foreign troops was a Special Forces mission and directing that Rangers focus on commando activities, such as raids. A Ranger battalion, Depuy stated, could receive missions to rescue American embassies and hijacked airliners, but he did not perceive these to be their main purpose. While acknowledging Abrams's desire for a rapidly deployable force, Depuy presented a much clearer view of the special tasks that a Ranger unit could perform.[14]

Abrams confirmed the change of concept at a meeting on January 21 in his office in the Pentagon. Before representatives from TRADOC, FORSCOM, and the Army Staff, he laid out his intention that the Rangers prepare for missions such as the raid on Son Tay and for "seizing something we wanted quickly," and that Special Forces continue to train and support native forces. He emphasized his desire that a Ranger battalion be "a foot infantry battalion . . . [the] finest in the world," a unit that could infiltrate by parachute, aircraft, foot, or boat to carry out platoon, company, or battalion-sized tasks.[15] They must not contain any hoodlums, and he warned that if they degenerated to that point, the Army would disband them. To ensure that this would not happen, the Army would impose no deadlines on the process of forming the battalions. After some debate over the location of the first battalion, Abrams decided that it would assemble and train its cadre at Fort Benning, with that post's range of instructional facilities, and then move to Fort Stewart, Georgia, which also had extensive training installations, housing, and an airfield capable of handling transports.[16]

Using Abrams's guidance, TRADOC drew up a summary doctrine for the Rangers. As a doctrinal statement, the paper represented a good start, but it left much to the intuitive sense of field commanders on proper Ranger missions and the role of the Rangers in strategy. The mission statement itself was vague, declaring only that a Ranger battalion "is normally employed against targets and under conditions which require the unique capabilities of the unit." The document did list a number of possible Ranger missions, including commando raids against missile sites and command posts, attacks on key communications centers and bridges, rescue of hostages and prisoners, and deployment as an advance force to show American resolve. It also pointed out the Rangers' lack of staying power for sustained combat and their need, in lieu of heavy weapons, to rely on stealth, surprise, audacity, and individual skills in attacks on fixed positions. Still, one does not sense a real grasp of, or certainly any commitment to, Ranger operations as part of a larger picture.[17]

TRADOC was also preparing an organizational table which, like earlier Ranger tables, envisioned a unit substantially smaller and lighter than its line counterpart. A Ranger battalion would consist of a headquarters contingent of 51 personnel and three "Ranger" companies, each with 7 officers and 172 enlisted men. In all, the battalion would contain 35 commissioned officers, 1 warrant officer and 552 enlisted men. Extremely light, it would carry no weapons heavier than 60-mm mortars, some machine guns, and a few 90-mm recoilless rifles as antitank weapons. A line infantry battalion, in contrast, could call on 4.2-inch and 81-mm mortars and more machine guns. The new Rangers lacked the equipment to communicate over long distances, a striking contrast to the LRRPs, and their transport was limited to a pair of jeeps. Their small supply echelon could support the unit for only five days at a time. Otherwise, the battalion would have to rely on others for administrative and logistical support.[18]

The problem of administrative and logistical support raised the sensitive issue of the proper headquarters to command the Rangers. Some officers envisioned the Rangers as part of the 82d Airborne Division, while others advocated their attachment to a corps or the formation of a Ranger brigade headquarters. In the end, FORSCOM rejected the idea of a central Ranger headquarters or other command levels between it and the battalions, and assumed direct peacetime control of the Rangers. According to the summary doctrinal statement, the Rangers in wartime would serve either directly under the president and Joint Chiefs of Staff or at the theater level until they were committed to a particular mission, at which point they would come under the headquarters responsible for the mission. In practice, many in the Army thought that the Rangers would serve under a corps, although some, especially in Special Forces, believed they should operate at a higher level, perhaps as part of a Joint Unconventional Warfare Task Force under theater control. Underlying the debate lay the ongoing uncertainty surrounding the Ranger mission.[19]

Along with missions, organization, and command and control, the Army needed to determine qualifications and a source for recruits. Abrams had made clear that the Army must take its time to ensure that the battalions contained elite, disciplined troopers, preferably Ranger and airborne-qualified. He did not want a rush job. However, Army headquarters wanted to activate the first battalion, even at reduced strength, by late January 1974. To enable the battalion to reach full strength by August 30 and a state of readiness by late December, the Army authorized the use of experienced troopers from Special Forces and the two remaining LRRP companies. The second battalion, which would have more time, would draw its cadre from units in the continental United States, and its remaining volunteers from new recruits who chose the Rangers through the

Army's "Unit of Choice" enlistment program. In the end, the Army dropped its stipulation that all personnel be graduates of the Ranger course. As TRADOC pointed out, 86 percent of a battalion would need to be Ranger-qualified for the unit to maintain a high readiness rating, a nearly impossible standard to meet. Therefore, the Army required only those above the rank of sergeant to be Ranger graduates. Other enlisted men would go to Ranger school after an initial period with their platoons.[20]

As recruiters canvassed the Army for volunteers, they found a mixed reception to the news of the Ranger revival. "Ranger-types" and those who thought that the Army should do more to prepare for crises in the Third World naturally applauded the action, but a curious combination of existing elites and old-guard antielitists, among whom the roughneck image of Rangers persisted, expressed irritation. Many saw little need for a ready force, given the presence of the 82d Airborne, the 1st Infantry Division, and Special Forces. Despite official denials, several Green Berets noted the cuts in their own units and saw an attempt to replace them with a relatively conventional force less stigmatized by Vietnam and more oriented toward Europe. On the other hand, some Special Forces officers were relieved that the Army had formed units which would take over some of their tasks, enabling the Green Berets to focus on their traditional mission of guerrilla war. Within the Army as a whole, of which the battalions were only a small part, the action does not seem to have created much of a stir. Most soldiers were probably more than willing to go along with the reasoning of the chief of staff.[21]

Whatever the attitudes of colleagues, the chance to lead a Ranger unit held enormous appeal for such ambitious, young infantry officers as Lt. Col. Kenneth C. Leuer and Lt. Col. A. J. "Bo" Baker. At Fort Benning, Leuer, a battalion leader with the 101st Airborne Division in Vietnam, joined 128 cadre to activate the 1st Battalion (Ranger), 75th Infantry on January 31, 1974. After some initial training at Fort Benning while filling the ranks, the 1st moved to Fort Stewart in July for individual and unit training. While the 1st prepared for action, Baker, a veteran of Project DELTA, was activating the 2d Battalion (Ranger), 75th Infantry at Fort Lewis, Washington, on October 1. Baker first screened Army personnel records for infantry leaders with combat experience, and then he and his sergeant major toured bases in the continental United States to interview prospective cadre. Because of the high priority that Abrams had placed on the project, they obtained most of the men whom they wanted, including Bob Howard, the most decorated soldier of the Vietnam War. After some instruction of cadre in early 1975, the 2d began full individual and unit training in March. The Army had planned to form a third battalion in January 1975, but it soon postponed the action, probably because of budget cuts.[22]

As in past years, the battalions proved a magnet for aggressive youngsters looking for excitement. At first, they contained many Vietnam veterans, but the proportion of these inevitably decreased over time. To replace them, the Army relied heavily on enlistees who volunteered specifically for the Rangers under the "Unit of Choice" program. Recruiting notices advertised the Rangers as the "go anywhere" soldiers, able to survive under the most difficult conditions, and stressed the challenge and self-discovery involved. By 1977, 65 to 75 percent of the battalions' ranks had enlisted in the Army specifically to join the Rangers. They included numerous bored teenagers, fed up with the routine of civilian life and attracted by the prospect of a hard, bare existence as part of the best unit in the Army. As of 1984, recruits had to possess a high school diploma, volunteer for the Rangers, achieve high scores on the Army's physical fitness and general aptitude tests, and pass a records exam, interview, and security check. Once in the Rangers, they could transfer at any time, and commanders retained the right to get rid of those who did not measure up to standards. Given these factors, morale, as expressed in low sick rates and high rates of reenlistment, remained at high levels.[23]

Part of the reason for the high morale lay in the training, which, in addition to being rigorous, emphasized esprit, realism, and the importance of individual and small-unit skills. Even before joining his unit, a prospective Ranger had to endure basic and advanced instruction, airborne training, and an indoctrination program of four weeks of instruction in weapons, navigation, and unit procedures. Once he joined the battalion, he received the usual heavy dose of physical conditioning, including 5-mile runs and 20-mile marches with full equipment. The battalion training schedules also stressed instruction in all infantry skills, especially marksmanship, hand-to-hand combat, and demolitions. Each individual practiced a specific technique or skill until he had performed it correctly, a process that the Army called "performance-oriented training." Some learned special skills, such as sniping, scuba diving, and free-fall parachuting. To prepare for missions in different environments, the Rangers trained in such diverse locations as Alaska for arctic warfare, the Panama Canal Zone for jungle tactics, California for instruction in amphibious techniques, and Fort Bliss, Texas, for desert operations. Frequently, they participated in joint exercises with other units.[24]

As Ranger battalions participated in joint training exercises, however, they found that field commanders had little idea of their proper employment. While the summary doctrinal statement for the Rangers provided some guidance, it proved too ambiguous for officers accustomed to clear, concise mission statements. Ranger doctrine obviously needed more development and integration into overall Army and joint doctrine, but at a time of great flux in tactics with the Army's adoption of the concept of maneuver warfare, the Army found it hard to define the Ranger role within a larger picture. Consequently, work on a Ranger doctrine seldom went much beyond a series of "operational capabilities" statements which commanders did not always read or, if they read them, did not always understand. However, in the summary statement, some semblance of a doctrine did exist, and a new generation of Ranger officers, more aware of the possibilities and perils of misuse, cited it to protest misuse. For example, when commanders used the 2d Battalion for deep reconnaissance, blocking positions, rear area security, and a ready reserve in a joint readiness exercise in 1976, the battalion commander complained that his Rangers were carrying out tasks more suitable for cavalry or light infantry.[25]

Underlying the confusion lay the fact that the American government and military in the mid-1970s were only beginning to come to grips with the concept of special operations. The shift to "flexible response" in the early 1960s, Vietnam, and an increasingly complex, turbulent world had created an environment in which special operations would be critical to the defense of American interests. However, the United States was not rising to the challenge. Part of the problem lay in the all-inclusive meaning of the phrase "special operations," which could be interpreted to signify anything from raids to military government to even such nominally conventional tasks as B-52 bombing missions and airmobile operations. To the extent Americans thought about many of these activities, such as raids and guerrilla warfare, they felt uncomfortable with them. They implied the use of military force in situations short of all-out war at a time when both military men and civilians were shying away from such involvements. Further, such activities as covert missions and psychological warfare struck both soldiers and civilians as "dirty" or "sneaky" and were viewed with distaste. Without a strategy for their use in support of American goals in peace and war, special operations forces languished and had to struggle to get funds for essential equipment, such as airlift.[26]

The lack of American thought on special operations was all too obvious in the *Mayaguez* affair. On May 12, 1975, the cargo ship USS *Mayaguez* was seized by Cambodian boarders, who apparently believed that the vessel was violating Cambodian territorial waters. After three days of fruitless diplomatic efforts to secure the ship's release, a hastily assembled task force of 228 Marines, supported by Navy vessels and Air Force planes, boarded the unoccupied *Mayaguez* and landed on neighboring Koh Tang Island, despite evidence that the Cambodians had removed the crew to the mainland. Simultaneous with the start of the operation, the Cambodians released the 40 crew members, but 18 Marines died in the assault. Perhaps with Son Tay in mind, policymakers had acted too quickly, where patience might well have assured better intelligence and planning and more resources for the operation. Intelligence failed to keep track of the crew's location, the essential element in planning, and also grossly misjudged resistance on Koh Tang, estimating it at 20 mostly elderly people rather than the 150 to 300 troops actually there. To perform the operation, the Pentagon relied on an ad hoc force which lacked the firepower and helicopters to properly support a landing and was handicapped by the tendency of President Gerald R. Ford and his aides to speak directly with officers on the scene, bypassing the chain of command. In evaluating the operation, one must remember the frustration of American leaders and their grim desire to show resolve only days after the final evacuation from Vietnam, but the chaotic nature of the rescue sent, at best, a mixed signal.[27]

While Americans were just beginning to grapple with the intricacies of special operations, other nations were showing the potential of such activities. Since its growing pains in the 1950s, the British Special Air Service had developed its techniques of reconnaissance and counterinsurgency to become perhaps the most professional special unit in the world. In Oman and Northern Ireland, the SAS showcased its skills in counterguerrilla operations and clandestine surveillance, and in 1980, an SAS team won fame for its rescue of hostages in the Iranian embassy in London. Although not a military unit, West Germany's GSG-9, an elite police counterterrorist force, earned international attention in October 1977 for its successful assault on a hijacked Lufthansa jet in Mogadishu, Somalia. Israeli elites were also establishing an international reputation. The Israelis had encountered their own problems with elites, abolishing the old "Palmach" over concerns about discipline, but Israeli paratroopers had spearheaded some of Israel's greatest successes in its wars with the Arabs. At Entebbe, Uganda on July 4, 1976, an elite Israeli counterterrorist force used a carefully prepared and rehearsed plan, good intelligence, surprise, rapid movement, and a few well-aimed shots to carry out one of the most successful hostage rescue missions in recent times.[28]

The media attention surrounding the war on terrorism thrust the Rangers back into the spotlight after years of obscurity. Through participation in parades and road races, and directives forbidding troops to engage in barroom brawls, Ranger commanders took pains to project a positive image in their communities, but, conscious of the resentment toward elites in the Army and antimilitary sentiment in the country as a whole, the battalions generally kept a low profile. As the press looked around for the American counterpart to the Israeli commandos and GSG-9, however, the Pentagon directed them to the Rangers. Reports spotlighted the tough training of the Rangers and their ability to deploy anywhere in the world. Much of the coverage had a certain James Bond quality, as the media focused on such exotic gadgets as starlight scopes, night goggles, and stun grenades of the type used by GSG-9 at Mogadishu. Actually, the Rangers used weapons and equipment which were fairly standard for infantry. Some Rangers grumbled about sensationalism, but the war on terrorism did give the battalions a raison d'être.[29]

The Ranger monopoly in the field of counterterrorism did not last long. For some time, the notion of a unit organized along the lines of the SAS had been pushed by several proponents, notably Depuy and Beckwith, the former chief of Project DELTA. Seizing on counterterrorism as a means of selling their concept, they argued that existing forces such as the Rangers were too heavy in men and equipment for the job and that the Army needed a unit of older, more self-reliant professionals for such missions and other clandestine tasks requiring a force of company size or smaller. They won the support of the Army Staff's

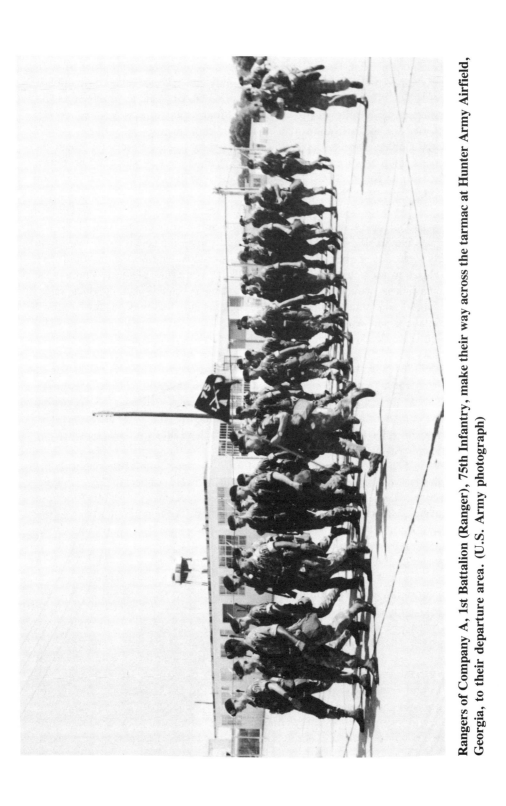

Rangers of Company A, 1st Battalion (Ranger), 75th Infantry, make their way across the tarmac at Hunter Army Airfield, Georgia, to their departure area. (U.S. Army photograph)

operations chief, Lt. Gen. Edward C. Meyer, who convinced the chief of staff, Gen. Bernard W. Rogers, to grant preliminary authority for such a formation in July 1977. When President Carter inquired about American resources for counterterrorism following the raid at Mogadishu, Rogers granted formal authority for the activation of a new unit, code named Delta Force, within Special Forces. Despite opposition from existing Special Forces units and the Rangers, both of whom felt that Delta was stealing their missions and best men, Beckwith, as commander of Delta, went ahead with efforts to recruit and train the SAS-type force.[30]

With the formation of Delta Force and expansion by other services of their special operations forces, duplication and confusion over missions was perhaps inevitable. Although Rangers claimed to be the country's primary light ready force, Marine battalion landing teams accompanying fleet units would often be closer to the action, as in the case of the *Mayaguez* incident. Under what circumstances would Rangers deploy? Rangers could also conduct raids, including amphibious forays in the commando tradition, against critical installations and personnel. However, the Special Forces mission statement still included attacks on strategic targets and the recovery of prisoners, and both elite, 14-man Navy Sea–Air–Land (SEAL) platoons and Marines could carry out amphibious raids. Finally, Delta Force, Special Forces, Rangers, and SEALs all claimed a role in the war against counterterrorism, and Special Forces had even formed a cadre, Project BLUE LIGHT, as an alternative to Delta Force within the existing Special Forces structure. It would require some time for the services to sort out roles for these forces and integrate them into a proper joint strategy for employment.[31]

The lack of an integrated joint force for special operations contributed to the failure of the Iranian rescue mission. On November 4, 1979, Iranian militants stormed the U.S. Embassy in Teheran and seized 60 American hostages. Although President Carter placed first priority on diplomacy to secure their release, he authorized planning for a rescue mission. Maj. Gen. John Vaught, a former Ranger, assembled and trained a joint task force, while his staff, built around an ad hoc joint committee of the Office of the Joint Chiefs of Staff, prepared a plan. By April, they had developed a scheme that seemed to overcome the enormous problems of terrain and logistics inherent in the task. When diplomatic efforts stalled, Carter, concerned that the Iranians might kill the hostages, directed the raid to proceed. On the night of April 24–25, six transport planes carried Delta and a small group of Rangers from the 75th Infantry to a remote location in the Iranian desert, where they would meet eight Navy helicopters to convey them to a staging point near Teheran. Only six helicopters made it through a desert sandstorm to the rendezvous, and one of these could not proceed due to a leaky hydraulic pump. Queried by his superiors, Beckwith recommended cancelation of the mission, and they agreed. While refueling before departure, one helicopter collided with a transport plane, causing an explosion which killed eight and injured five. Leaving the remaining helicopters intact, the force hurriedly boarded the transports and fled the site.[32]

For the Carter administration, the debacle at Desert One was a public relations disaster. Press and populace incredulously asked how the most technologically advanced nation in the world could have botched a critical military mission due to technical problems. Reporters focused on the quality of the helicopters and burrowed for information on "Charlie's Angels," as Delta Force became known. Reaction to the raid among the public followed the divisions that had developed in the country over the use of military force. Liberals were horrified that Carter would even consider such a move and expressed suspicion that the president, who was locked in a tough nomination battle with Senator Edward M. Kennedy, had directed the raid for political purposes. Conservatives criticized Carter as too indecisive and argued that the rescue plan from the beginning reflected an abort mentality and Vietnam-like reluctance to exert the necessary force to accomplish the task. The mission, some contended, should have employed 400 troops and 35 helicopters to end the crisis even if some hostages lost their lives in the process. As did most Americans, they wondered why the Israelis could conduct such an operation efficiently and the United States could not.[33]

In truth, the Entebbe raid had been a simple task compared to the mission into Iran, but the latter still reflected little credit on the American ability to perform such an operation. Once again, policymakers had improvised, rejecting existing contingency plans in favor of an ad hoc planning group and joint task force. The participation of each of the services, in particular the use of Marine helicopter pilots who were unseasoned in lengthy flights over difficult terrain, aroused suspicions that interservice rivalry, not efficiency, had determined the force's composition. From Carter to Vaught, the chain of command seemed clear, and Carter kept his promise not to interfere in the actual conduct of the operation. Below Vaught, however, command arrangements dissolved in confusion. An Air Force colonel technically commanded at Desert One, but he established no central command post nor did the helicopter pilots know his identity. In contrast to the *Mayaguez* affair, intelligence proved good, to the extent of pinpointing the location of the hostages in their rooms, but a complex rescue plan left little room for flexibility and almost no margin for error.[34] Finally, an obsession with secrecy precluded use of the contingency plan, limited the number of helicopters, prevented combined rehearsals, and generally hampered the planning and conduct of the mission from beginning to end.[35]

Six years after the revival of the Ranger battalions, confusion still characterized Ranger and other American special operations. This should not have been too surprising, for Abrams had created the Rangers less to carry out raids, reconnaissance, and other traditional Ranger missions than to provide crack troops that could compete with the Marines for the role of the nation's elite ready force. Only later did officers like Depuy develop the concept of Rangers as commandos, capable of numerous special operations in support of American interests. This proved to be a slow process in the atmosphere of the 1970s. Given détente, public sentiment against foreign adventures, and widespread doubts about the use of military force to support policy, both the Ford and Carter administrations focused more on domestic problems. Left to their inclinations, the services predictably focused on conventional warfare and consequently had to make up considerable ground with the rise of the threat of terrorism in the late 1970s. In a scene that was eerily reminiscent of the counterinsurgency fad of the early 1960s, services, agencies, and individuals competed for a piece of the action, resulting in conceptual confusion which contributed to the trauma of the Iranian rescue mission. However, by forming Rangers in 1974, the Army had shown a pragmatic realization of the need for elite units for certain contingencies, an advance over the old attitude that one unit was as good as any other. While the Army still faced a considerable task in defining roles and missions, it had nonetheless taken a very significant step.

NOTES

1. Ole R. Holsti and James N. Rosenau, *American Leadership in World Affairs: Vietnam and the Breakdown of Consensus* (London: Allen and Unwin, 1984), pp. xiii, 1, 16; Hodgson, *America*, pp. 136, 276–277, 392–395, 403–411, 493–494; Dickstein, *Gates of Eden*, pp. 213, 258, 267, 270–271; Leuchtenburg, *Troubled Feast*, pp. 174–184, 195, 234; Siegel, *Troubled Journey*, pp. 177–181, 195, 204–206, 224; Shils, "American Society," p. 44.

2. Herring, *Longest War*, p. 265; Donald B. Vought, "Preparing for the Wrong War?" *Military Review* 57 (May 1977): 19; Sam C. Sarkesian, *The New Battlefield: The United States and Unconventional Conflicts* (Westport, Conn.: Greenwood Press, 1986), pp. 24–25; Sam C. Sarkesian, "Special Operations Forces in the 1980's," in Stephen J. Cimbala, ed., *The Reagan Defense Program: An Interim Assessment* (Wilmington, Del.: Scholarly Resources, 1986), pp. 97–100; Millett and Maslowski, *Common Defense*, pp. 565–566, 569, 578, 582; William C. Westmoreland, *Report of the Chief of Staff of the United States Army, 1 July 1968 to 30 June 1972* (Washington, D.C.: Department of the Army, 1977), p. iv.

3. Hodgson, *America*, p. 354; Leuchtenburg, *Troubled Feast*, p. 184; Hauser, "Peacetime Army," pp. 214–215; Savage and Gabriel, "Cohesion and Disintegration," pp. 399–421; Suid, *Guts and Glory*, p. 3; Suid, "Film Industry," pp. ii–iii; Westmoreland, *Report of the Chief of Staff*, pp. 3–5, 8; Drew Middleton, "Military Worried at Reaction to Rising Costs, Argues 'Next War' Strategy," *New York Times*, 27 January 1973, p. 11; USAMHI, "Senior Officers Oral History Program: Collins," pp. 402–403; Millett and Maslowski, *Common Defense*, pp. 566–570, 579; Yarmolinsky, "American Military," pp. 221–222; Weigley, *History of the United States Army*, pp. 569, 573–584, 590–592; Sarkesian, "Special Operations Forces," p. 99; Doughty, *Evolution*, pp. 40–49; Vought, "Wrong War," pp. 22–23, 28–32.

4. Commanding Officer, CONARC, to HQ, Department of the Army, 15 December 1972; and Maj. Gen. Verne L. Bowers, Adjutant General, to Commanding Officer, CONARC, 22 February 1973, in "75th Infantry," Organizational History Branch, CMH; Rottman and Moriarity, "Long Range Reconnaissance Patrol Companies," p. 4; Henry G. Gole, "Bring Back the Long Range Reconnaissance Patrols," *Military Review* 61 (October 1981): 2–4; Barney Halloran, "Pros at the Survival Game," *Soldiers* 27 (July 1972): 21–23; Lanning, *Inside the LRRP's*, pp. 75, 176, 179, 184; Rottman, *Army Rangers*, p. 32; Pezzelle interview.

5. U.S. Army, Department of the Army, "Table of Organization and Equipment No. 31–105H: Special Forces Battalion, Airborne Special Forces Group," 10 June 1970; and U.S. Army, Department of the Army, "Table of Organization and Equipment No. 31–101H: Airborne Special Forces Group," 10 June 1970, in Organizational History Branch, CMH; U.S. Army, Department of the Army, *Special Forces Operations: U.S. Army Doctrine*, FM 31–21 (Washington, D.C.: Department of the Army, February 1969); Courtney M. Rittgers, "The Hard Corps Soldier," *Soldiers* 33 (January 1978): 11; John M. Collins, *Green Berets, SEAL's, and Spetsnaz: U.S. and Soviet Special Military Operations* (Washington, D.C.: Pergammon Brassey's, 1987), pp. 23–24.

6. Renata Adler of the *New York Times* denounced Wayne's movie as "a film so unspeakable, so stupid, so rotten and false in every detail that it . . . becomes an invitation to grieve, not for our soldiers or for Vietnam, . . . but for what has happened to the fantasy-making apparatus in this country;" see Renata Adler, "Screen: 'Green Berets' as Viewed by John Wayne," *New York Times*, 20 June 1968, p. 49. See also "150 Picket Opening of 'Green Berets'; Signs Score Wayne," *New York Times*, 20 June 1968, p. 49; Charles Mohr, "U.S. Special Forces: Real and On Film," *New York Times*, 20 June 1968, p. 49; A. H. Weiler, "John Wayne's 'Green Berets' a Box Office Triumph," *New York Times*, 3 January 1969, p. 20; Moskos, *American Enlisted Man*, pp. 23–24; "Green Beret Chief Held in Slaying of a Vietnamese," *New York Times*, 6 August 1969, p. 1; Drew Middleton, "Returning Green Berets Face Uncertain Future," *New York Times*, 12 March 1971, p. 16; Jane E. Brody, "Green Beret Losses Laid to Leadership Struggle," *New York Times*, 17 May 1968, p. 3; Terence Smith, "Questions in Green Beret Affair," *New York Times*, 15 August 1969, p. 10; Donald Duncan, *The New Legions* (New York: Random House, 1967).

7. Clarke, *Advice and Support: Final Years*, pp. 196–199, 203; David Halberstam, *One Very Hot Day* (Boston: Houghton Mifflin, 1968), pp. 63, 97–98; Stanton, *Green Berets at War*, pp. 186–187, 261, 268; Middleton, "Uncertain Future," p. 16; Raymond, "Elite Units Long a Source of Friction in U.S. Army," p. 3; Tom Buckley, "Green Berets Try to Shed Reputation as Derring Do Unit," *New York Times*, 23 January 1967, p. 1; Simpson, *Green Berets*, pp. 217–220, 223; Garrett interview; Norton interview; Galvin, "Special Forces," p. 21; David C. Schlacter and Fred J. Stubbs, "Special Operations Forces: Not Applicable?" *Military Review* 58 (February 1978): 18.

8. Rittgers, "Hard Corps Soldier," pp. 10–11; Collins, *Green Berets*, p. 24; Steve Huettel, "Special Forces: Army's First Unconventional Unit," *Fayetteville Observer*, 15 June 1982, p. 1.

9. Hauser, "Peacetime Army," p. 217; Middleton, "Military Worried at Reaction to Rising Costs, Argues Next War Strategy," p. 11; John M. Mattisse, "Independent Action Forces," *Marine Corps Gazette* 56 (October 1972): 13.

10. "Abrams, Creighton William Jr., (1914–1974)," in Robert McHenry, ed., *Webster's American Military Biographies* (Springfield, Mass.: Merriam, 1978), pp. 1–2; Barney Halloran, "Fightingest General," *Soldiers* 27 (August 1972): 6–9; Clarke, *Advice and Support: Final Years*, p. 361; USAMHI, "Senior Officers Oral History Program: Collins," p. 233; USAMHI, "Senior Officers Debriefing Program: Peers," III:81; Stanton, *Green Berets at War*, pp. 261, 268; Weigley, *History of the United States Army*, pp. 573, 585.

11. Keating interview; Argenterie interview; Creighton W. Abrams, "Chief of Staff Reports on the Posture of the Army," *Army Logistician* 6 (May–June 1974): 36; Vought, "Wrong War," p. 19; Zeb B. Bradford and Frederic J. Brown, *The United States Army in Transition* (Beverly Hills, Calif: Sage Publications, 1973), pp. 29, 83; Pezzelle interview; James Adams, *Secret Armies: Inside the American, Soviet, and European Special Forces* (New York: Atlantic Monthly Press, 1987), pp. 71–72, 78; Barry M. Blechman and Stephen S. Kaplan, *Force without War: U.S. Armed Forces as a Political Instrument* (Washington, D.C.: Brookings Institution, 1978), pp. 260–278; Cohen, *Commandos and Politicians*, p. 49; USAMHI, "Senior Officers Debriefing Program: Palmer," p. 146; Drew Middleton, "Army Shifts Forces in Attempt to Gain Flexibility in Crisis," *New York Times*, 3 May 1974, p. 40.

12. Middleton, "Army Shifts Forces," p. 40. On the Marine issue, see Depuy interview with author; regarding Abrams as an Army loyalist, see USAMHI, "Senior Officers Debriefing Program: Palmer," p. 480. See also Drew Middleton, "Army Molds Elite Ranger Unit for Deployment to Trouble Spots," *New York Times*, 25 October 1974, p. 41; Lt. Gen. Donald H. Cowles, DCSOPS, to Gen. William E. Depuy, TRADOC, Gen. Walter T. Kerwin, FORSCOM, undated, "1st Battalion, 75th Infantry," Organizational History Branch, CMH.

13. HQ, Department of the Army, to Commanding Officer, Training and Doctrine Command (TRADOC), 20 December 1973, and HQ, Department of the Army, to Commanding Officer, Forces Command (FORSCOM), 28 December 1973, in "1st Battalion, 75th Infantry," Organizational History Branch, CMH.

14. "William E. Depuy," HRC 201 Biographies, Historical Records Branch, CMH; USAMHI, "Senior Officers Debriefing Program: Palmer," p. 478; Memorandum for Record, 17 January 1974, "1st Battalion, 75th Infantry," Organizational History Branch, CMH; Kinnard, *War Managers*, pp. 40–41.

15. Memorandum for Record, 22 January 1974, "1st Battalion, 75th Infantry," Organizational History Branch, CMH.

16. Ibid.; Commanding Officer, FORSCOM, to HQ, Department of the Army, 16 January 1974, "1st Battalion, 75th Infantry," Organizational History Branch, CMH.

17. U.S. Army, Training and Doctrine Command (TRADOC), "Revised Ranger Battalion Summary Doctrinal Statement," 10 December 1974, p. 2, USAMHI.

18. U.S. Army, Department of the Army, "Table of Organization and Equipment No. 7-85H: Ranger Infantry Battalion," 30 May 1974, and U.S. Army, Department of the Army, "Table of Organization and Equipment No. 7-87H: Ranger Company, Ranger Infantry Battalion," 30 May 1974, Organizational History Branch, CMH; James M. Dubik, "Ranger Training," *Infantry* 67 (May–June 1977): 41; Robert M. Killebrew, "Has Light Infantry Really Had Its Day?" *Army* 29 (December 1979): 45; Tom Hamrick, "The Black Berets," *Army* 27 (May 1977): 31–32; U.S. Army, 2d Battalion (Ranger), 75th Infantry, "Unit Historical Report, 1976," pp. 8–10, Unit Histories Files, USAMHI;

Argenterie interview; Middleton, "Army Shifts Forces," p. 40.

19. Commanding Officer, FORSCOM, to HQ, Department of the Army, 16 January 1974; General Orders no. 127, HQ, FORSCOM, 25 January 1974, "1st Battalion, 75th Infantry," and General Orders no. 1365, HQ, FORSCOM, 16 September 1974, "2d Battalion, 75th Infantry, (Formerly Company H)," in Organizational History Branch, CMH; U.S. Army, "Revised Ranger Battalion Summary Doctrinal Statement," 10 December 1974; Darragh, "Rangers and Special Forces," p. 18; USAMHI, "Senior Officers Oral History Program: Warner," p. 161.

20. Commanding Officer, FORSCOM, to HQ, Department of the Army, 16 January 1974; HQ, Department of the Army, to Commanding Officer, FORSCOM, 25 January 1974; Commanding Officer, TRADOC, to Department of the Army, 22 February 1974; and Commanding Officer, FORSCOM, to Commanding Officer, TRADOC, 28 February 1974, in "1st Battalion, 75th Infantry," Organizational History Branch, CMH; U.S. Army, 2d Battalion (Ranger), 75th Infantry, "Annual Historical Supplement, Calendar Year 1974, 2d Battalion (Ranger), 75th Infantry," p. 5, Unit History Files, USAMHI; Walter F. McTernan, "Rangers and Recon Marines," *Infantry* 72 (May–June 1982): 21.

21. "The Rangers Are Back," *Army Reserve* 20 (July–August 1974): 8; USAMHI, "Senior Officers Debriefing Program: Palmer," pp. 146–147; Robert D. Heinl, Jr., "Berets: Another Vietnam War Casualty," *Army Times*, 12 June 1974, p. 13; Michael Getler, "Green Berets Yielding to Rangers," *Washington Post*, 30 April 1974, p. 14; Argenterie interview; Norton interview; Simpson, *Green Berets*, p. 142.

22. "Kenneth C. Leuer," HRC 201 Biographies, Historical Records Branch, CMH; General Orders no. 127, HQ, FORSCOM, 25 January 1974; "Ranger Unit Waits," *Army Times*, 5 March 1975, and Department of the Army to HQ, FORSCOM, 9 September 1974, in "3d Battalion, 75th Infantry (Formerly Company F)," Organizational History Branch, CMH; "Rangers Are Back," pp. 8–9; U.S. Army, 1st Battalion (Ranger), 75th Infantry, "Rangers Lead the Way: A Brief History" (Fort Stewart, Ga., 1976), p. 8; U.S. Army, 1st Battalion (Ranger), 75th Infantry, "Rangers Lead the Way: An Overview" (Hunter Army Airfield, Ga., 1983), p. 7; Argenterie interview; 2d Ranger Battalion, "Unit Historical Report, 1974," USAMHI; General Orders no. 1365, HQ, FORSCOM, 16 September 1974; U.S. Army, 2d Battalion (Ranger), 75th Infantry, "Rangers Lead the Way: A Brief History," (Fort Lewis, Wash., 1981), p. 10. To make available spaces in the Army's force levels for the Ranger battalions, the Army inactivated the last two LRRP companies in the active Army in late 1974. See Rottman, *Army Rangers*, p. 32.

23. Hamrick, "Black Berets," pp. 29–33; "The Challenge of Combat Arms," Army advertisement, 1987; advertisement in *Sports Illustrated*, 20 May 1985, pp. 84–85; Bruce W. Gaffner, "The 2nd Battalion," *Gung Ho*, October 1984, p. 29; Millard Barger and Benjamin F. Schemmer, "An Exclusive AFJ Interview with John O. Marsh Jr., Secretary of the Army," *Armed Forces Journal International* 122 (May 1985): 48; "It Takes Dedication To Be A Ranger," *Pentagram News*, 10 February 1977; U.S. Army, 1st Ranger Battalion, "Rangers Lead the Way: An Overview," 1983 ed., p. 25; Geoffrey Norman, "Black Berets to the Rescue," *Esquire*, 11 April 1978, p. 44; Art Harris, "The Wild Bunch, Heroes Once More: Return of the Rangers: 'Our Job Is to Kill,'" *Washington Post*, 4 November 1983, sec. 4, p. 1; Argenterie interview.

24. U.S. Army, 1st Ranger Battalion, "Rangers Lead the Way: An Overview," 1983 ed., pp. 24–25; 2d Ranger Battalion, "Unit Historical Report, 1976," USAMHI; U.S. Army, 2d Ranger Battalion, "Rangers Lead the Way: A Brief History," 1981 ed., pp.

10–13; McTernan, "Rangers," p. 21; Hamrick, "Black Berets," pp. 30–31; Zack Richards, "Rangers: Anytime, Anywhere," *Soldiers* 32 (February 1977): 22–23; Dubik, "Ranger Training," pp. 41–42; Gaffner, "2nd Battalion," pp. 27–30; William L. Walter, "Ranger Indoctrination Program/Ranger Orientation Program/Pre Ranger," *Gung Ho*, October 1984, p. 92; Harris, "Wild Bunch," sec. 4, p. 1; Argenterie interview; Rottman, *Army Rangers*, pp. 46–48; 1st Special Operations Command (Airborne), "Annual Historical Review, FY 1983–1986," Appendix H, pp. 14–22, Public Affairs Office, 1st Special Operations Command (Abn), Fort Bragg, N.C.

25. BRAVE SHIELD XIV AAR, pp. 1–2, 11–13, in 2d Ranger Battalion, "Unit Historical Report, 1976," USAMHI; Weigley, *History of the United States Army*, pp. 578–582.

26. Maurice Tugwell and David Charters, "Special Operations and the Threats to United States Interests in the 1980's," pp. 30–31, and Edward N. Luttwak's comments on the Pezzelle article, pp. 155, 164, in Frank R. Barnett, B. Hugh Tovar, and Richard H. Shultz, eds., *Special Operations in U.S. Strategy* (Washington, D.C.: National Defense University, 1984); Schlacter and Stubbs, "Special Operations Forces," pp. 15–17; Argenterie interview; Keating interview; Angelo Codevilla, "Special Operations," *Journal of Defense and Diplomacy* 3 (June 1985): 27; William H. Burgess III, "Strategic Targeting," *Armed Forces Journal International* 122 (March 1985): 66–67; Hamrick, "Black Berets," p. 28; Deborah G. Meyer and Benjamin F. Schemmer, "An Exclusive AFJ Interview with Noel C. Koch, Principal Deputy Assistant Secretary of Defense, International Security Affairs," *Armed Forces Journal International* 122 (March 1985): 50.

27. The rescue would have been a logical mission for the Rangers, but the 2d Battalion was too far from the scene and not yet ready, having just started unit training; see Argenterie interview. See also J. A. Messegee, Robert A. Peterson, Walter J. Wood, J. B. Hendricks, and J. Michael Rodgers, "'Mayday' for the *Mayaguez*," *U.S. Naval Institute Proceedings* 102 (November 1976): 93–111; J. M. Johnson, Jr., R. W. Austin, and D. A. Quinlan, "Individual Heroism Overcame Awkward Command Relationships, Confusion, and Bad Information Off the Cambodian Coast," *Marine Corps Gazette* 61 (October 1977): 24–34; Tilford, *Search and Rescue*, pp. 146–154; Donald E. Carlile, "The Mayaguez Incident: Crisis Management," *Military Review* 56 (October 1976): 3–14; Shani, "Airborne Raids," pp. 44–52; U.S. Congress, House Committee on International Relations, Subcommittee on International Political and Military Affairs, *Seizure of the Mayaguez*, 94th Cong., 1st sess., 1975, pt. 3, pp. 310–317; pt. 4, pp. 60–65, 71–76, 84–85, 91, 95, 115–126; Gabriel, *Military Incompetence*, pp. 61–83; Kelly, "Raids and National Command," pp. 22–25; Philip Shabecoff, "Questions on Ship Rescue Persist Despite Briefings," *New York Times*, 20 May 1975, p. 1; Drew Middleton, "Heavy Resistance Surprised the Marines," *New York Times*, 16 May 1975, p. 14.

28. Geraghty, *Inside the Special Air Service*, pp. 120–123, 136, 141, 167–172, 179–180; Cohen, *Commandos and Politicians*, p. 73; Adams, *Secret Armies*, pp. 78–81, 85–87, 179, 186–187, 190–192; Benjamin Netanyahu, "Operation Jonathan: The Rescue at Entebbe," *Military Review* 62 (July 1982): 2–23; Douglas Menarchik, "Strike Against Terror! The Entebbe Raid," *Air University Review* 31 (July–August 1980): 65–76; Shani, "Airborne Raids," pp. 43–50; David Eshel, *Elite Fighting Units* (New York: Arco, 1984), pp. 72, 76, 80. For information on other elites, see Eshel; also see William R. Farrell, "Military Involvement in Domestic Terror Incidents," *Naval War College Review* 34

(July–August 1981): 61.

29. 2d Ranger Battalion, "Unit Historical Report, 1976," p. 7, USAMHI; Hamrick, "Black Berets," pp. 32–33; U.S. Army, 2d Ranger Battalion, "Rangers Lead the Way: A Brief History," 1981 ed., p. 9; Menarchik, "Entebbe Raid," p. 66; Argenterie interview; Norman, "Black Berets," pp. 43–46; Meyer and Schemmer, "Interview: Koch," p. 50.

30. Beckwith and Knox, *Delta Force*, pp. 94–108, 120–129, 142, 163; personal correspondence, Depuy to author, 10 June 1986; Adams, *Secret Armies*, pp. 99–100; Farrell, "Military Involvement," p. 62; Robert A. Manning and Steven Emerson, "Special Forces: Can They Do the Job?" *U.S. News and World Report*, 3 November 1986, p. 38.

31. Collins, *Green Berets*, pp. 26–30; Adams, *Secret Armies*, pp. 100–101; Robert S. Dudney, "Return of America's Secret Warriors," *U.S. News and World Report*, 15 November 1982, p. 39; Baratto, "Special Forces," p. 5; Richard Halloran, "Green Berets Tackle a New Job," *New York Times*, 13 October 1976, p. 45; Schlacter and Stubbs, "Special Operations Forces," pp. 18–19; Darragh, "Rangers and Special Forces," p. 18.

32. The standard source on the Iranian rescue mission is Paul B. Ryan, *The Iranian Rescue Mission: Why It Failed* (Annapolis, Md.: U.S. Naval Institute Press, 1985). See also U.S. Joint Chiefs of Staff, Special Operations Review Group, "Iran Rescue Mission: Group Analyzes Reasons for Failure" (hereafter cited as Holloway Board, pt. 1) *Aviation Week and Space Technology*, 15 September 1980, pp. 68–70; Beckwith and Knox, *Delta Force*, pp. 187–195, 252–256, 268, 274–283; Robert L. Earl, "A Matter of Principle," *U.S. Naval Institute Proceedings* 109 (February 1983): 32–33; Benjamin F. Schemmer, "Presidential Courage and the April 1980 Iranian Rescue Mission," *Armed Forces Journal International* 118 (May 1981): 60; Gabriel, *Military Incompetence*, pp. 85–102.

33. Ryan, *Iranian Rescue Mission*, pp. 15, 96–98, 102–104, 126; see also Philip Taubman, "Months of Plans, Then Failure in the Desert," *New York Times*, 26 April 1980, p. 1, and other articles in *New York Times*, 26–28 April 1980; Richard Burt, "Many Questions, Few Answers in Iran Mission," *New York Times*, 11 May 1980, sec. 4, p. 3; Earl, "Matter of Principle," p. 30.

34. For more on the plan, see Ryan, *Iranian Rescue Mission*, pp. 1–2. It included the capture by a Ranger company of an airfield where the rescue party and freed hostages would transfer from helicopters to transport planes for the flight back to the United States; see George C. Wilson, "For Rangers in Egypt, Bunker 13 Proved a Harbinger of Future," *Washington Post*, 25 April 1982, p. 15.

35. Holloway Board, pt. 1, pp. 63–64, 69–70; U.S. Joint Chiefs of Staff, Special Operations Review Group, "Report Cites Mission's Lack of Review," *Aviation Week and Space Technology*, 22 September 1980, p. 140; U.S. Joint Chiefs of Staff, Special Operations Review Group, "Review Group's Conclusions Reported," *Aviation Week and Space Technology*, 29 September 1980, p. 89; Ryan, *Iranian Rescue Mission*, pp. 3, 18–20, 25, 39–40, 81, 116–117, 127; Shani, "Airborne Raids," pp. 46, 48, 51; Gabriel, *Military Incompetence*, pp. 87, 93–113; Beckwith and Knox, *Delta Force*, pp. 224–225, 258, 295; U.S. Congress, House Committee on Appropriations, Subcommittee on Department of Defense, *Department of Defense Appropriations for 1981, Pt. 4: Hostage Rescue Mission*, 96th Cong., 2d sess., 1980, pp. 608–610; Alexander Scott, "The Lessons of the Iranian Raid for American Military Policy," *Armed Forces Journal International* 117 (June 1980): 26–32; Earl, "Matter of Principle," pp. 32–36; Schemmer, "Presidential Courage," p. 61. Much controversy has surrounded the use of the Navy's HH-53

helicopter, which was designed for minesweeping and rescue missions at sea rather than flights over difficult terrain, but its range and cargo capacity, as well as the omnipresent concern for secrecy, assured its use over such alternatives as the Army's C-47 helicopter.

13

"Ronnie's Rangers"

The fiasco in Iran strengthened the conservative tide which, in November 1980, carried Ronald Reagan into the White House. The new president and his advisors saw the landslide victory as a mandate for their worldview and massive rearmament. Alarmed by the rise of Marxist regimes in Asia, Africa, and Central America, they perceived most, if not all, of the world's troubles as emanating from the Kremlin. The Soviets, they argued, were using psychological warfare, subversion, surrogates, and occasional outright intervention to foment unrest in the Third World and encourage the triumph of Marxist movements. Furthermore, while the United States had been cutting its defense budget since the Vietnam War, the Soviets had been increasing military expenditures and improving their ability to project power into distant areas. In response, the Reagan administration planned to strengthen ties with anti-Communist allies, expand the American military presence around the globe, and provide aid to resistance movements attempting to overthrow Communist regimes. To meet these new commitments, it wanted to increase defense spending by over $300 billion over five years. This enormous buildup would take place across the board but with a special emphasis on conventional forces, adding B-1 bombers, M-1 tanks, and enough vessels for a 600-ship Navy.[1]

As they pondered the Soviet threat to Western Europe and the Third World, American strategists were concerned about the menace posed by Soviet special units, or *Spetsnaz*. The Soviets, they noted, had employed special operations for years, most recently in Afghanistan where Soviet commandos had seized critical points and assassinated Afghan leaders in advance of the main invasion force. In the event of a Soviet offensive in Europe, planners anticipated preliminary attacks by airborne troops, naval infantry, and saboteurs against storage sites for nuclear missiles, communications facilities and key airfields, ports, and industries. NATO could also expect long-range patrols to locate targets for Soviet air strikes, and for hit squads to attempt to eliminate NATO's leaders. Echoing the *Brandenburgers* of World War II, many *Spetsnaz* would use NATO uniforms and equipment. Experts could not confirm the size of these forces but believed enough existed to present a major threat to NATO's rear.[2]

Once again, the threat posed by special units of a possible enemy prompted the United States to expand its own Special Operations Forces (SOF). However, the civilians and retired officers in the Reagan administration who provided the impetus for the buildup did so for pragmatic reasons which went beyond concern about the threat of *Spetsnaz* or even embarrassment over the debacle at Desert One. In their view, SOF represented a cheap, low-profile alternative to conventional forces for most prospective crises in the Third World. Given their estimate of the nature and dimensions of the threat, few were disturbed by the use of SOF and "dirty" tactics in situations short of all-out war. Accordingly, Secretary of Defense Caspar W. Weinberger, in his *Defense Guidance* for 1981, laid out a five-year plan for expansion of SOF. As with so many Reagan defense initiatives, the plan emphasized increased funds for men and equipment rather than real thought on doctrine and strategy.[3]

More than other service chiefs, the Army's leadership showed a readiness to support expansion of SOF. Secretary of the Army John O. Marsh, a distinguished-looking Virginia lawyer and former congressman, could boast more exposure to special operations than most of his colleagues. As counselor to President Ford, he had participated in the deliberations during the *Mayaguez* crisis, and he later served as chairman of the Presidential Intelligence Coordination Group, which reorganized the intelligence community. His chief of staff, Gen. Edward C. Meyer, had earned a reputation in the Army as a strong supporter of SOF. He had backed Colonel Beckwith's efforts to create Delta Force and, as chief of staff, had established the clandestine Intelligence Support Activity to provide the human intelligence so absent in earlier crises.[4]

With Marsh's strong backing, Meyer directed an extensive buildup of Army SOF. The Army announced plans to add another Special Forces group, restore existing groups to full strength, increase spending on communications equipment and training for special operations, and establish a separate career branch for special operations. The latter step was especially welcome to Special Forces officers, who had complained for years, to no avail, about slow promotions in branches that showed little appreciation of their abilities. In October 1982, the Army also formed 1st Special Operations Command as a headquarters under FORSCOM for Ranger, Special Forces, psychological warfare, and civil affairs units in the continental United States. Ostensibly, the Army created 1st SOCOM to improve its planning, research and development, and training in special operations, but Meyer also hoped that the new headquarters would be a step toward a true joint agency in the field. In this, he would be disappointed, for the other services would consent only to a weak Joint Special Operations Command, with authority to coordinate training and develop joint doctrine and equipment, but little else.[5]

As the debate over JSOC showed, considerable opposition to the SOF buildup remained, both within the military and society. It discomfited liberals, who feared the new SOF would draw the country into more Vietnams. It aroused still-strong antielite sentiment within the services, as, once again, line officers grumbled that elite forces would take the best men from their units. It even stirred misgivings among career servicemen with considerable experience in special operations, such as Colonel "Bull" Simons and Gen. Robert C. Kingston. Some believed that the Pentagon was spending enormous sums without sufficient thought on the subject, while others feared that too rapid a buildup would create a glut of amateurs and careerists in a complex field. Furthermore, many thought that the Pentagon by forming such agencies as JSOC and 1st SOCOM was only creating more layers of needless bureaucracy. The SOF buildup reminded them too much of the counterinsurgency fad of the early 1960s, a craze which had produced a rapid expansion of forces but little long-term improvement in American capabilities in the field.[6]

While the Rangers did not share in the initial expansion of SOF and ongoing discussions at the Infantry Center had not produced a Ranger doctrine, the battalions were making important refinements in the operational capabilities statements which passed for doctrine. By 1983, the list of missions provided in these statements had grown more focused. Raids and attacks on communications centers continued as possible tasks, but the statements also listed interdiction of enemy lines of supply as a legitimate mission and placed more emphasis on the Ranger role as an advance force to show American resolve. Not only did hostage rescue no longer appear on the list, but the statements stressed that long-range reconnaissance and rear security could not be considered proper Ranger missions. The authors were obviously worried about the problem of misuse, for they devoted a long section to the need to use such units wisely, keeping in mind the investment in training which each Ranger represented. Such conceptual debates escaped most of the Ranger rank and file. At Fort Stewart, Fort Lewis, and points around the world, they continued training, restless for action.[7]

They finally found action on the lush, green Caribbean island of Grenada. For some time, the Reagan administration had been warily watching Grenada's Marxist government buy Soviet arms and build an airport capable of handling Soviet "MiG" fighters and bombers. When a coup in mid-October 1983 plunged Grenada into anarchy, Reagan and his advisors decided to act, partly to restore order and ensure the safety of American medical students on the island, but mainly to rid the region of the regime. After planning an evacuation of the students, the Navy-dominated staff of Atlantic Command, from October 21 to 23, changed gears and prepared a plan for Marines and Army units to occupy the island, landing on opposite sides and then converging on the capital of St. George's. JSOC would play a major role, as Delta operatives would capture the Richmond Hill prison and SEALs would reconnoiter landing areas, seize the main radio station, and rescue the island's governor general. The two battalions of Rangers, transported by Air Force SOF, were originally supposed to seize the airfields at Point Salines, on the southwest tip of the island, and Pearls, to the northeast, in advance of the 82d Airborne Division and the Marines respectively, but a revised plan provided for both battalions to land at Salines. When Caribbean states requested American intervention, Reagan, on October 23, directed that the operation, code-named URGENT FURY, proceed.

Given overwhelming American military power, the issue was never in doubt, but American SOF again ran into trouble. Technical problems with aircraft and JSOC's attempts to crowd several reconnaissance missions into the early morning hours of October 25 forced many SOF to conduct their missions in daylight. While SEALs captured the radio station, Delta's morning attack on the prison failed with heavy losses, and the SEALs who rescued the governor general needed help from the Marines. Meanwhile, the Rangers, reduced to a contingent from each battalion due to lack of airlift, were making a daylight parachute jump from 500 feet to avoid antiaircraft fire at Salines. Amazingly, they landed with little loss and secured the airfield and surrounding heights. They contacted students at nearby True Blue campus, only to find that other students were at the Grand Anse campus near St. George's. The next day, the 2d Battalion, using Marine helicopters, conducted a well-coordinated operation to secure the students at Grand Anse. As Marines and paratroopers converged on St. George's, the 2d Battalion carried out a successful but costly attack on the Grenadian Army barracks at Calvigny on October 27. Although the assault met little opposition, two were killed and seven wounded in a helicopter crash. Sobered by the experience, the Rangers returned to Fort Stewart on October 28, leaving the 82d Airborne Division and Marines to mop up the remaining pockets of resistance. They returned to a nation which, except for some criticism from liberals and media, was rejoicing over a long-awaited military success.[8]

In private, military analysts were not so impressed with the American performance. Despite the longstanding American concern over Grenada, prior planning and intelligence had been inadequate. The invasion force had little idea of the strength or dispositions of their opponents, or the location of the students they were supposed to save. Rushed planning produced an ad hoc, interservice collection of units that had trouble working, or even communicating, with each other. JSOC's performance, in planning and execution, was a disappointment. Overambitious planning and repeated changes in missions and schedules threw parachuting Rangers and heliborne Delta troopers in front of an alerted enemy in broad daylight. Only extraordinary luck enabled the Rangers to complete their jump without heavy casualties. For all the confusion, the services did accomplish their missions with dispatch, but the nasty experience of SOF showed that they still had much to learn about the proper use of such forces.[9]

Few could find much fault with the Rangers themselves. They returned to Hunter Army Airfield, near Fort Stewart, and to Fort Lewis, cocky and full

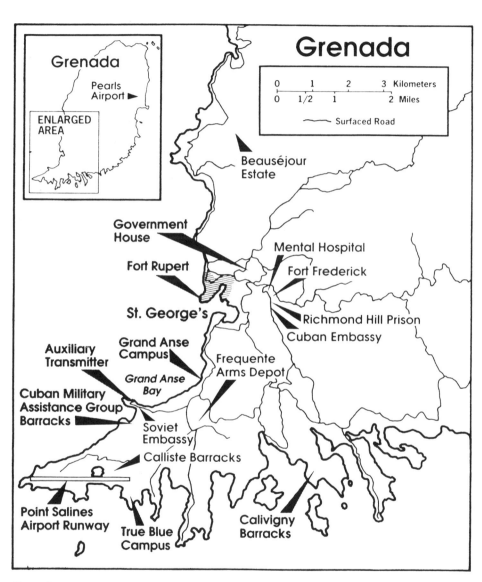

Grenada

Jim Kistler and *Parameters: U.S. Army War College Quarterly.*

Rangers advance from the airstrip at Point Salines in Grenada (U.S. Army Military History Institute)

of war stories for appreciative audiences. In a bar at Fort Stewart, "Ronnie's Rangers" drank whiskey, danced under an American flag, and fired shotgun blanks at the ceiling, while one patriot with a black beret, shaved head, and golden earring rasped into a microphone, "You guys kicked ___ in Grenada."[10] Reporters heard stories of a Ranger who accidentally parachuted into the sea near Salines and then walked ashore with his rifle and pack, and of a Ranger who used the blade of a hot-wired bulldozer as a shield in an attack on an enemy position. The unit bulletin board at Hunter Army Airfield soon filled with thank-you notes from proud Americans, and Vietnam veterans noted that civilians in bars were buying drinks for them for the first time in years. The Rangers had reason to be proud. They had planned well, deployed quickly, and fought with courage and dash. They received their share of medals issued for the invasion, including a Valorous Unit Award, and a 2d Battalion medic who won the Silver Star was introduced by President Reagan during his State of the Union address.[11]

The Ranger performance in Grenada helped prompt the Army to expand the Ranger force. Responding to Ranger complaints that the lack of an overall command structure hampered their operations in Grenada, the Army, in July 1984, formed a 130-man Ranger regimental headquarters. Under Col. Wayne E. Downing, a Vietnam veteran who had served with both the 1st and 2d Battalions, the new 75th Infantry headquarters would mainly supervise training, develop doctrine, and provide a liaison between higher levels and the battalions, which could now focus on training and combat. The Army also activated the long-awaited 3d Battalion (Ranger), 75th Infantry in October. The expansion was hailed by Rangers, some of whom talked of a possible 4th Battalion, but met with less enthusiasm in other quarters. Critics noted the cost in funds and loss of leaders among other units and questioned whether the Army needed another Ranger battalion. Many feared that, by forming a regimental headquarters, the Army was merely adding another bureaucratic layer between higher levels and the Rangers.[12]

The Ranger expansion was only part of the Reagan administration's continuing efforts to upgrade SOF. Shortly before the invasion of Grenada, Deputy Secretary of Defense Paul Thayer had directed the services to draw up master plans for expansion of their SOF and improvements in such areas as command organizations, training, equipment, and personnel policies. In response, the Navy laid plans to increase its SEAL force from 41 to 70 platoons by 1990, the Air Force announced its intention to purchase more SOF transports and helicopters, and the Marines sought to endow their amphibious units with a capacity for special operations. The Army was already proceeding with plans to form another Special Forces group, and, over the next three years, it added an aviation task force, psychological operations battalion, and support units to 1st SOCOM. It even revived LRRPs in the form of "Long-Range Surveillance Units" to conduct deep reconnaissance and observation for corps and divisions.[13]

In their efforts to upgrade SOF, advocates still ran into strong opposition within the Pentagon. The perennial fixation on a conventional war in Europe, a general lack of understanding of special operations, and antielitism within the services resulted in slow promotion of SOF officers and diversion to other areas of funds for SOF expansion. The joint command structure for SOF remained weak. In yet another attempt to coordinate special operations among the services, the Pentagon created a Joint Special Operations Agency in January 1984, but the organization possessed little power beyond an advisory role. In early 1985, the Department of Defense estimated that, after three years of buildup, SOF had achieved readiness levels of only 63 percent. Frustrated by the slow pace of SOF reform, Noel C. Koch, the Pentagon official who supervised SOF, complained to the media of obstruction, especially within the service bureaucracies, and pointed to many instances where SOF had been hampered in their work by a lack of equipment. When Weinberger's office arranged a compromise in a dispute over Air Force efforts to transfer responsibility for SOF helicopters to the Army, Koch, in May 1986, resigned, charging duplicity in the handling of the affair.[14]

At this point, Congress joined the fray. With the hijacking of a TWA jet to Lebanon, the murder of an American citizen aboard an abducted Italian cruise liner, and similar terrorist acts, counterterrorism had again become a major issue. SOF not only appealed to members of Congress as a response to terrorism but also as a smaller and, for the most part, cheaper alternative to conventional forces. The House Armed Services Committee had formed a special panel to oversee SOF improvements, and Congress had been generous with funds for SOF. Members had observed service obstructionism to the buildup with growing irritation, and some, despairing of the willingness of the armed forces to make needed reforms, talked of a new "sixth service" for SOF. In the end, Congress would not go that far, but it did, in October 1986, create a new joint Special Operations Command under an Assistant Secretary of Defense for Special Operations and Low Intensity Conflict. Congress trusted that the four-star rank of SOCCOM's head, and the presence of an upper-level office on the subject would ensure that special operations received a fair hearing in future bureaucratic and budgetary battles within the Pentagon.[15]

SOF needed all the help that they could get, for, in the last years of the decade, they were still plagued by chronic equipment shortages, shortfalls in trained manpower, and general lack of readiness. Contrary to the popular image, SOF generally used standard equipment, but they did require some special items, such as sophisticated communications, bubble-less SCUBA gear, and transport planes and helicopters which could infiltrate deep into enemy territory in the dark. All too often, the services diverted funds for this equipment to more conventional projects. They also tended to assign personnel to special operations for only a few years before rotating them to other duties, leaving little time to develop the cultural expertise needed in such areas as unconventional warfare and psychological operations. Observers noted the shortage of language-qualified personnel in Special Forces and questioned whether the Green Berets possessed the training to elude security troops in the enemy's rear areas in the event of a major war. Many also urged the Pentagon to deploy SOF closer to prospective trouble spots, where they would be in a better position to react in a crisis.[16]

Underlying readiness shortfalls was the continuing lack of a strategy for the use of SOF in support of American objectives. While still at the Pentagon, Noel Koch confessed that "the services, and we ourselves, to be perfectly honest, have little more than an intuitive sense of what these forces ought to be doing."[17] In part, the absence of a strategy reflected the lack of a clear definition of special operations as well as the discomfort of an open, democratic, Judeo-Christian society with such activities as psychological warfare and assassination, but it also resulted from divisions over policy. Debate continued, within and outside the government, over a definition of American interests and the question of when and where to employ military forces in support of those interests. Within the administration, Secretary of State George P. Shultz argued that military forces should play an active role in support of American foreign policy, while Secretary Weinberger wanted to rule out military force except in cases where the United States could employ its full resources, with popular backing, in pursuit of a strategy of "victory." In the absence of a consensus on such basic questions, no blueprint for SOF could exist. As one observer put it, the ability to swim unusual distances, parachute stealthily, live off the land, and shoot like John Wayne was of little use if the troops possessing these qualities were not serving a coherent strategy.[18]

Within and outside the military, SOF continued to arouse mixed emotions. Public attitudes toward SOF reflected those toward the military in general, with pro-military types viewing SOF as near superhuman figures and antimilitarists seeing them as lawless misanthropes, with few views falling between the extremes. Many Americans revelled in a certain commando chic roughly based on John Wayne's portrayal, but with a new slant introduced by Chuck Norris and Sylvester Stallone in the post-Vietnam era: the notion of a tough, resourceful hero forced to confront and overcome, on his own, a corrupt "Establishment." Others saw SOF as cold-blooded killers unfit for civilized society, a perception reinforced by press reports of embezzlement of funds by Delta Force troopers and profiles of maladjusted ex-Green Berets, trying to adjust to civilian life after carrying out assassinations in Southeast Asia. Within the services, much antielitism remained, but more officers were showing a willingness to live with elite units. The generation which had fought World War II was giving way to the Vietnam veterans, who could be expected to display a greater appreciation for the subtle nuances of the use of force in the 1980s. Consequently, discussions of elites focused not so much on whether they should exist but whether they should expand any further.[19]

As the 1980s came to a close, no Ranger doctrine as yet existed, but the 75th Ranger Regiment, the new designation of the 75th Infantry after 1986, seemed to be making progress in efforts to educate field commanders on the Ranger concept. In lieu of a formal doctrine, Ranger commanders continued to rely on operational capabilities statements, but these guides did little better than earlier circulars in clearly defining the Ranger mission. Consequently, observers held different ideas of that mission. Diplomats and grand strategists viewed the Rangers as valuable for a show of resolve, almost as a counter on a gameboard. More orthodox generals saw them as an elite unit to seize key targets in advance of a more conventional force. Those within the special operations community stressed the role of Ranger raids in the interdiction of communications and recovery of personnel and valuable equipment. Under these circumstances, education of field generals on the Ranger mission continued to be a challenge, but by the end of the decade, signs of progress could be detected. Early reports indicate that the employment of Rangers in Panama as part of Operation JUST CAUSE was handled with more competence than was the case in Grenada, but the Rangers did not participate in the war with Iraq, which fit the mold of a big-unit, mechanized conflict.[20]

At the least, the use of the Rangers in Panama represents a step in the right direction after a period in which the Reagan administration, for all its efforts to build up Rangers and other SOF and provide them with the bureaucratic clout to ensure their survival, devoted little real thought to their purpose, missions, and employment. Reagan and his advisors backed expansion of SOF, including Rangers, not so much because they understood the use of these units as because of the threat of Soviet SOF, particularly in the Third World, and the desire to respond in kind. Some officials, such as Secretary Marsh and General Meyer, had a better grasp of special operations but still backed expansion before doctrinal development in order to lock in the buildup against a backlash from the many officers who preferred to spend funds on more conventional forces. Consequently, the services still had not devoted much real thought to special operations and their integration into strategy by the time of the invasion of Grenada, and SOF performance in Grenada reflected that state of affairs. Despite encouraging steps since then, it still is too early to tell whether Reagan's buildup of Rangers and other SOF heralded the start of a true American capability in special operations or another passing fancy.

NOTES

1. Carter himself later said that the failure of the rescue mission marked a turning point in his bid for re-election; see Ryan, *Iranian Rescue Mission*, p. 101. See also Sarkesian, "Special Operations Forces," pp. 93–94, 101–103; C. N. Donnelly, "Operations in the Enemy Rear," *Infantry* 71 (March–April 1981): 24–25; Collins, *Green Berets*, pp. 4, 40–47; James K. Oliver and James A. Nathan, "The Reagan Defense Program," in Stephen J. Cimbala, ed., *The Reagan Defense Program* (Wilmington, Del.: Scholarly Resources, 1986), pp. 1–3, 13; Millett and Maslowski, *Common Defense*, pp.

583–584; Noel C. Koch, "Special Operations Forces: Tidying Up the Lines," *Armed Forces Journal International* 126 (October 1988): 104; Cimbala, *Reagan Defense Program*, pp. xvii, xx; "Introduction," pp. 1–15, "Keynote Address by the Honorable John O. Marsh Jr., Secretary of the Army," pp. 19–20, and Gen. Richard G. Stilwell's comments, pp. 44–46, in Frank R. Barnett, B. Hugh Tovar, and Richard H. Shultz, eds., *Special Operations in U.S. Strategy* (Washington, D.C.: National Defense University, 1984).

2. Collins, *Green Berets*, pp. 52, 62, 71; Donnelly, "Operations I," pp. 24–28, and C. N. Donnelly, "Operations in the Enemy Rear II," *Infantry* 71 (May–June 1981): 29–35; Viktor Suvorov, "*Spetsnaz*: The Soviet Union's Special Forces," *Military Review* 64 (March 1984): 30–46; John J. Dziak, "The Soviet Approach to Special Operations," in Frank R. Barnett, B. Hugh Tovar, and Richard H. Shultz, eds., *Special Operations in U.S. Strategy* (Washington, D.C.: National Defense University, 1984), pp. 95–113; Adams, *Secret Armies*, pp. 135–136.

3. Richard Halloran, "Military Is Quietly Rebuilding Its Special Operations Forces," *New York Times*, 19 July 1982, p. 1; Kenneth J. Alnwick, "Perspectives on Air Power at the Low End of the Conflict Spectrum," *Air University Review* 35 (March–April 1984): 17; Michael E. Haas, "Special Forces for Special Problems," *U.S. Naval Institute Proceedings* 109 (July 1983): 110–111; Neil C. Livingstone, "Fighting Terrorism and 'Dirty Little Wars,'" *Air University Review* 35 (March–April 1984): 6, 9, 13; Collins, *Green Berets*, pp. 73–75; Noel C. Koch, "Special Operations Forces," *Defense '83* (July 1983): 9–13; Lutz, "Special Forces," p. 248; interview between Steve Huettel of the *Fayetteville Observer* and Secretary of the Army John Marsh, undated, Public Affairs Office, 1st Special Operations Command, Fort Bragg, N.C.; "Introduction," pp. 1–15, Marsh's address, p. 18, and Stilwell's remarks, p. 45, in Barnett, Tovar, and Shultz, eds., *Special Operations in U.S. Strategy*.

4. "John O. Marsh," HRC 201 Biographies, Historical Records Branch, CMH; Marsh address, p. 22; Barger and Schemmer, "Interview: Marsh," p. 44; Adams, *Secret Armies*, pp. 211–212.

5. The Army did not actually establish a separate career branch until 1987, and when it did, the new branch was just for Special Forces; see General Order no. 135, HQ, Department of the Army, 19 June 1987, Organizational History Branch, CMH. See also "Green Berets To Be Expanded," *Army* 33 (May 1983): 30–32; Deborah G. Meyer, "Army OK's Special Operations Field, New Special Forces Group," *Armed Forces Journal International* 120 (July 1983): 8; "Army Rebuilding Counterinsurgency Forces," *Fayetteville Times*, 23 August 1982, p. 1; Dudney, "America's 'Secret' Warriors," pp. 37–38; Richard Halloran, "Army Plans New Command to Curb Leftist Insurgencies," *New York Times*, 17 September 1982, sec. 2, p. 6; Sarkesian, "Special Operations Forces in the 1980s," p. 104; 1st SOCOM, "Annual Historical Review, FY 1983–1986," pp. 45–48, 65, 1st Special Operations Command, Fort Bragg, N.C.; Rittgers, "Hard Corps Soldier," p. 11; Collins, *Green Berets*, pp. 23–26; "Press Release: U.S. Army 1st Special Operations Command (Airborne)," 1st SOCOM, Fort Bragg, NC; interview between *Fayetteville Times* and Marsh, undated, 1st SOCOM, Fort Bragg, N.C.; Office of the Assistant Secretary of Defense for Public Affairs, "Responses for Use Upon Query," [re: activ of 1st Special Operations Command,] Public Affairs Office, 1st Special Operations Command, Fort Bragg, N.C.; Lutz, "Special Forces," p. 251; Ryan, *Iranian Rescue Mission*, p. 145; Adams, *Secret Armies*, p. 209.

6. Meyer and Schemmer, "Interview: Koch," pp. 40, 52; Noel C. Koch and J. Michael Kelly, "Two Cases against A Sixth Service for Special Ops," *Armed Forces Journal International* 123 (October 1985): 102–109; Adams, *Secret Armies*, pp. 211, 218; Dudney, "America's Secret Warriors," p. 13; Sarkesian, *New Battlefield*, p. 158.

7. U.S. Army, 1st Ranger Battalion, "Rangers Lead the Way: An Overview," 1983 ed., pp. 12–15; Schlacter and Stubbs, "Special Operations Forces," p. 25.

8. Mark Adkin, *URGENT FURY: The Battle for Grenada* (Lexington, Mass: D. C. Heath, 1989) is probably the most thorough unclassified source. See also Jonathan M. House, "The U.S. Army in Joint Operations," draft manuscript, pp. 177, 194, 207–208, Military Studies Branch, CMH; Daniel R. Bolger, "Special Operations and the Grenada Campaign," *Parameters: USAWC Quarterly* 18 (December 1988): 49–61; Adams, *Secret Armies*, pp. 225–252; Timothy Ashby, "Grenada: Soviet Stepping Stone," *U.S. Naval Institute Proceedings* 109 (December 1983): 30–35; Langhorne A. Motley, "The Decision to Assist Grenada," Current Policy no. 541, U.S. Department of State, 24 January 1984; Anthony Payne, Paul Sutton, and Tony Thorndike, *Grenada: Revolution and Invasion* (New York: St. Martin's Press, 1984), pp. 148–159; B. Drummond Ayres, Jr., "Grenada Invasion: A Series of Surprises," *New York Times*, 14 November 1983, p. 1; Jim Shults, "Rangers in Grenada," *Gung Ho*, October 1984, pp. 75–78; Jay Finegan, "Army Rangers Tell Tale of U.S. Invasion," *Air Force Times*, 14 November 1983, p. 1; Gabriel, *Military Incompetence*, pp. 149–157, 162–171; Stephen Harding, *Air War Grenada* (Missoula, Mont: Pictorial Histories Publishing Company, 1984); Edward N. Luttwak, *The Pentagon and the Art of War* (New York: Simon and Schuster, 1984), p. 57; Eshel, *Elite Fighting Units*, pp. 131–140.

9. Adkin, *URGENT FURY*, pp. 128, 134, 334, 336; U.S. Senate, Armed Services Committee, *Organization, Structure, and Decisionmaking Procedures of the Department of Defense, Part 8*, 98th Cong., 1st sess., 1983, pp. 287–291, 329–330; Gabriel, *Military Incompetence*, pp. 150, 153, 173–179; Luttwak, *Pentagon and the Art of War*, pp. 53–57, 237–238, 268; Bill Keller, "Reports Cite Lack of Coordination during Invasion of Grenada," *New York Times*, 4 December 1984, p. 14; Bolger, "Special Operations," p. 56; Daniel P. Bolger, "Operation Urgent Fury and Its Critics," *Military Review* 66 (July 1986): 58–69; Sarkesian, "Special Operations Forces in the 1980s," p. 110; Rick Maze, "Report Faults Military Performance in Grenada," *Air Force Times*, 23 April 1984, p. 49; John H. Cushman, Jr., "Pentagon Study Faults Planning in Grenada," *New York Times*, 12 July 1986, p. 1; Drew Middleton, "Operation on Grenada: How Forces Performed," *New York Times*, 28 October 1983, p. 12; Adams, *Secret Armies*, pp. 231–232, 237, 241, 252; Manning and Emerson, "Special Forces," p. 42; Ayres, "Grenada Invasion," p. 1; Rick Maze, "Intelligence 'Limited' Before Grenada Action," *Air Force Times*, 21 November 1983, p. 4.

10. Harris, "The Wild Bunch," sec. 4, p. 1.

11. Ibid.; B. Drummond Ayres, Jr., "Rangers Back from Grenada Reveling in Praise as Heroes," *New York Times*, 11 November 1983, p. 1; Shults, "Rangers in Grenada," p. 77; Don Hirst, "Ranger Medic to Receive Silver Star for Heroism During Grenada Action," *Army Times*, 13 February 1984, in "2d Battalion, 75th Infantry," Organizational History Branch, CMH; David Bailey, "'As Intense as Vietnam:' Rangers Recount Invasion," *Florida Times-Union*, 3 November 1983, pp. A1, A4; Argenterie interview; U.S. Senate, Armed Services Committee, *Department of Defense Authorization for Appropriations for FY 1985, Part 2*, 98th Cong., 2d sess., 1984, pp. 507, 523, 537;

Barger and Schemmer, "Interview: Marsh," p. 48; Luttwak, *Pentagon and the Art of War*, pp. 55, 268; Eshel, *Elite Fighting Units*, p. 140; comments by Romana Danysh, Organizational History Branch, CMH, on the manuscript.

12. U.S. Army, 75th Infantry (Ranger) Regiment, "Annual Historical Review, 1984," Historical Records Branch, CMH; U.S. Army, HQ, 1st Special Operations Command (Airborne), "75th Ranger Regiment Statement of Operational Capabilities," 14 September 1984, U.S. Army, HQ, 75th Infantry (Ranger) Regiment, Fort Benning, Ga.; Millard Barger and Deborah G. Meyer, "An Exclusive AFJ Interview with MG John W. Foss, USA, Chief of Infantry," *Armed Forces Journal International* 123 (October 1985) 88; Barger and Schemmer, "Interview: Marsh," pp. 46, 48; Meyer and Schemmer, "Interview: Koch," p. 40; Gary L. Bounds and Scott R. McMichael, "Counting Costs of Elite Forces," *Army* 35 (November 1985): 25, 32; 1st SOCOM, "Annual Historical Review, FY 1983–1986," p. C-1, 1st SOCOM, Fort Bragg, N.C.; Sarkesian, *New Battlefield*, p. 156.

13. Adams, *Secret Armies*, p. 220; "Military Chiefs Resist Improving Special Forces, Official Says," *New York Times*, 27 May 1984, p. 41; 1st SOCOM, "Annual Historical Review, FY 1983–1986," pp. 28, 32–35, 1st SOCOM, Fort Bragg, N.C.; Clinton H. Schemmer, "House Panel Formed to Oversee Special Ops Forces," *Armed Forces Journal International* 122 (October 1984): 15; *Department of Defense Authorization for Appropriations for FY 1985, Part 2*, p. 591; Benjamin F. Schemmer, "Commandant Directs Marines to Sharpen Their Inherent Special Ops Capability," *Armed Forces Journal International* 123 (October 1985): 24–25; Rottman, *Army Rangers*, pp. 45–46; Sarkesian, *New Battlefield*, p. 156; Collins, *Green Berets*, pp. 26, 28; U.S. Army, Department of the Army, "Table of Organization and Equipment 7-157L: Airborne Infantry Long Range Surveillance Company," 1 April 1985, Organizational History Branch, CMH.

14. Koch, "Special Operations Forces," pp. 8–13; Meyer and Schemmer, "Interview: Koch," pp. 36–40; Sarkesian, *New Battlefield*, pp. 134–135, 159–160, 184–185; Adams, *Secret Armies*, pp. 263–269, 272, 281–284; Collins, *Green Berets*, pp. xiii, 3, 5, 13, 56–58, 68; "Military Chiefs Resist," p. 41; Bill Keller, "Conflict in Pentagon Seen as Hurting Elite Units' Buildup," *New York Times*, 6 January 1986, p. 1; Manning and Emerson, "Special Forces," p. 39; Ryan, *Iranian Rescue Mission*, p. 124; Sarkesian, "Special Operations Forces," pp. 96, 103; Koch, "Special Operations Forces: Tidying Up the Lines," pp. 105, 108, 110; Farrell, "Military Involvement," p. 60.

15. Koch, "Special Operations Forces," pp. 8–13; Meyer and Schemmer, "Interview: Koch," pp. 36–40; Schemmer, "House Panel Formed," pp. 15–18; Dan Daniel, "U.S. Special Operations: The Case for a Sixth Service," *Armed Forces Journal International* 123 (August 1985): 70–75; Koch and Kelly, "Two Cases Against a Sixth Service," pp. 102–109; Sarkesian, *New Battlefield*, pp. 134–135, 159–160, 184–185; Adams, *Secret Armies*, pp. 263–272, 281–284; Collins, *Green Berets*, pp. xiii, 3, 5, 13, 56–58, 68; "Military Chiefs Resist Improving Special Forces," p. 41; Keller, "Conflict in Pentagon," p. 1; Manning and Emerson, "Special Forces," p. 39; Ryan, *Iranian Rescue Mission*, p. 124; Sarkesian, "Special Operations Forces," pp. 96, 103; Koch, "Special Operations Forces: Tidying Up the Lines," pp. 105, 108, 110; Farrell, "Military Involvement," p. 60; Michael Ganley, "Congress Creates New Unified Command for SOF and New Civilian SOF Chief," *Armed Forces Journal International* 124 (November 1986): 20–22.

16. Collins, *Green Berets*, pp. 30–31, 63, 66, 69, 82, 89, 95–96; Adams, *Secret Armies*, pp. 323–334; Livingstone, "Fighting Terrorism," p. 14; Manning and Emerson, "Special Forces," pp. 39–42; Koch, "Special Operations Forces: Tidying Up the Lines," pp. 108, 110.

17. Meyer and Schemmer, "Interview: Koch," p. 40.

18. Codevilla, "Special Operations," p. 27; see also Ibid., pp. 40, 42; Collins, *Green Berets*, pp. 1, 3, 16, 42–43, 71; Sarkesian, *New Battlefield*, pp. 159–160, 200, 299; Sarkesian, "Special Operations Forces," p. 104; Tugwell and Charters, "Special Operations," pp. 27–43; Pezzelle, "Military Capabilities and Special Operations in the 1980s," p. 149; Vincent Davis, "The Reagan Defense Program: Decision Making, Decision Makers, and Some of the Results," in Stephen J. Cimbala, ed., *The Reagan Defense Program* (Wilmington, Del.: Scholarly Resources, 1986), pp. 36, 50.

19. Suid, "Film Industry," pp. 182, 224; Richard Halloran, "Army's Special Forces Try to Rebuild Image by Linking Brains and Brawn," *New York Times*, 21 August 1982, p. 8; Philip Taubman, "Former Green Berets Found to Sell Military Skills to Foreign Regimes," *New York Times*, 9 December 1981, p. 1; Philip Taubman, "The Secret World of a Green Beret," *New York Times Magazine*, 4 July 1982, sec. 6, p. 18; "Army Inquiry Embarrasses Intelligence Units," *New York Times*, 1 December 1985, p. 23; Adams, *Secret Armies*, pp. 215–217, 287; Bounds and McMichael, "Counting Costs," pp. 24–32; Davis, "Reagan Defense Program," p. 51.

20. General Orders no. 7, "75th Ranger Regiment," HQ, Dept. of the Army, 14 February 1986, Organizational History Branch, CMH; U.S. Army, "75th Ranger Regiment Statement of Operational Capabilities"; Barger and Meyer, "Interview: Foss," p. 82; Glenn M. Harned, "Special Operations and the Airland Battle," *Military Review* 65 (September 1985): 73, 76, 80–81; Argenterie interview; 1st SOCOM, "Annual Historical Review, FY 1983–1986," p. 6, 1st SOCOM, Fort Bragg, N.C.; Collins, *Green Berets*, pp. 24–25; Bounds and McMichael, "Counting Costs," p. 26; "Ranger Missions," *Gung Ho*, October 1984, p. 79; Sarkesian, "Special Operations Forces," p. 112; Dennis Steele, "Operation Just Cause," *Army* 40 (February 1990): 40; David Hughes, "Night Airdrop in Panama Surprises Noriega's Forces," *Aviation Week and Space Technology*, 1 January 1990, pp. 30–31; "Operation Just Cause: Critique and Reply," *Parameters: USAWC Quarterly* 20 (March 1990): 100–102.

Conclusion

Problems of war and peace used to be much less complex for the United States. During the nineteenth century, Americans relied on the oceans, the European balance of power, and weak neighbors for security, enabling them to maintain a minimal military establishment. When the United States finally did intervene in two world wars, its war effort assumed the nature of a crusade, employing huge armies of conscripts with almost unanimous popular support against aggressors perceived as threats to Western civilization. Mass warfare had been the focus of American military thinking ever since the Civil War. While the Army fought the nineteenth-century counterpart of brushfire wars in its clashes with the Indians, it could usually muddle through such conflicts with little loss of national prestige or harm to the national interest. Except for such disasters as Custer's Last Stand, the Army's failures received little attention and generally proved only temporary setbacks on the road to eventual victory.

This state of affairs was changing by 1945. As the leader of the so-called Free World in the emerging struggle to contain Communism, the United States was assuming new responsibilities and facing new challenges, including such complex forms of conflict as revolutionary warfare and terrorism. These conflicts could erupt at a moment's notice or drag on for years, often presented an ambiguous threat, and contained complicated political, economic, and social elements. They therefore did not lend themselves to national crusades and the mobilization of conscript armies. For the first time in its history, the United States needed a large professional standing army, with all the connotations of empire and world policeman which such an army evoked.

This force would necessarily include Rangers and other specialists for special tasks. The Army could, and for a long time did, cling to the illusion that well-trained standard units, with a little extra instruction in some cases, could perform most Ranger missions. With time, the fallacy of this stance became obvious. A line unit could not possibly train for all the special missions which it might receive and, at the same time, maintain its readiness for its primary task. It also took time for a line unit to reorganize for a special mission and train its personnel for the job. The transition promised to be especially difficult for American infantrymen, accustomed as they were to tactics emphasizing combined arms and firepower. A unit of specialists offered a much greater prospect for success, a key factor in operations whose fate would have major implications for the interests and prestige of the United States.

Nevertheless, the Army formed Ranger units only grudgingly. This reluctance can be traced to several factors, including the reputation of Rangers as disciplinary headaches. To be sure, many, if not most, Rangers were highly motivated individuals who joined out of a desire to be part of one of the Army's best outfits. Ranger formations, however, did tend to draw a type of recruit who saw war as an adventure, a form of release, and expressed impatience with the routine of peacetime. In action, the aggressiveness, self-reliance, and skill of Rangers exemplified the best qualities of the American soldier, but the independence and pugnacity which made them useful in Ranger operations often translated into disrespect for authority and irritation with procedure, characteristics which made the Rangers more of a challenge in the barracks than in combat. Discipline in such a unit was possible but demanded strong, even charismatic leaders, like Darby and Frederick. Still, the concern over discipline was not totally without foundation. The experience of the ARVN Rangers and French paratroopers, and even the recent scandal involving Delta Force, show the problems posed by elites who get out of control.[1]

The issue of discipline was only one of the reasons for the Army's often jaundiced attitude toward the Rangers. Within Army intellectual and social circles ran a strong current of egalitarianism which rejected the notion of a special and, thus, privileged group. Reflecting the society from which they came, conventional officers saw themselves as professionals who performed an unpleasant but necessary service, and they expressed disdain for mavericks who seemed to delight in violence. They viewed Ranger operations as underhanded, overpublicized, lacking in tangible benefits, and a distraction from the main task of destroying the enemy's main forces. Furthermore, they pointed to the real problems created by the formation of Ranger units. Fears that the Rangers would drain the conventional army of small-unit leaders proved to be exaggerated, but the difficulty in finding suitable volunteers as the Ranger force expanded indicates that the argument did possess some validity. Lacking their own support apparatus and needing highly qualified replacements, Ranger units could be an administrative nuisance. Any decision to form or expand a Ranger force involved costs as well as benefits.

For all the problems attendant to Rangers and the antagonism which they aroused, the recurring need for Ranger units caused their periodic revival, although it generally took a crisis and support from the highest levels to overcome opposition. Repeatedly, when the Army found itself unready for a

particular strategic or tactical challenge, it turned to Ranger formations to right
the balance. Whether in World War II, when a green U.S. Army faced the
prospect of a clash with a battle-hardened foe, or in Korea and Vietnam, when
American troops struggled to cope with unfamiliar enemy tactics and terrain, or
in the 1970s, when an Army traumatized by Vietnam tried to meet its commitments in a turbulent world, the experience or real possibility of defeat or
embarrassment made the Army more receptive to change. Even then, the backing
of an influential patron often proved necessary. In some cases, such leaders as
MacArthur and Kennedy supported Ranger-type units because of an appreciation
for the moral factor and the ability of small, elite forces to achieve results out
of all proportion to their size. More frequently, such figures as Marshall,
Collins, and Abrams backed Ranger units out of pragmatism and a readiness to
try new ideas.

      Whatever the impetus for the creation of Ranger units, it did not reflect
an enduring commitment to Ranger operations as part of an overall strategy. In
some cases, as in Korea and Vietnam, the Army formed Ranger units to try out
new tactics and techniques. Thus, the Rangers in Korea represented an
experimental response to the Army's problems with infiltration, raids, and
guerrilla tactics by the North Koreans. In other cases, the Army created a
provisional Ranger-type unit to carry out a single mission. The 1st Special
Service Force, GALAHAD, and Bull Simons's task force at Son Tay all fit this
description. Still other Ranger units came into existence to meet longer-term, but
still temporary, needs. The 1st Ranger Battalion in World War II was supposed
to provide combat experience for American troops through raids, and later
Ranger battalions were to spearhead amphibious landings. The Rangers of the
early 1970s differed from earlier versions in that they existed less to carry out
specific tasks than to perform missions not inherently special but important
enough to demand an especially capable force. In that respect, they were a sign
that the Army was recognizing the value of an elite force to handle small-scale
contingencies, although a designated airborne battalion probably could have
performed that task just as well.

      The history of Ranger-type units, once formed, has tended to fall into
a general pattern. Initial success and support from field commanders impressed
with their abilities usually results in expansion of the Rangers. In this expansion,
the Rangers frequently experience problems in maintaining the high standards of
a smaller force, as in the case of Darby's Rangers before Cisterna. Furthermore,
the original, temporary purpose for the units often passes, leaving them without
a mission. However, once in existence, Ranger units, like most institutions,
usually prove difficult to disband. More frequently, field commanders employ
the otherwise inactive Rangers for missions ill-suited to their training and
organization, as in the case of GALAHAD at Myitkyina and the Rangers in
Korea. When the Rangers do receive a special mission, a decline in standards,
coupled with overconfidence of both Rangers and their superiors as a result of

earlier feats, can lead to disaster, as was the case with Cisterna.

Disasters like Cisterna and the Iranian rescue mission show some of the factors contributing to failed Ranger missions, just as Sened and Cabanatuan illustrate elements underlying successful Ranger operations. Certain conditions, such as rugged terrain and a fluid, lightly manned enemy front, facilitate infiltration. Obviously, it aids the task if any accompanying conventional operations are proceeding well and the enemy has lost cohesion. Experience shows that the different components of the attacking force need to be well trained and accustomed to working together. Strong, resourceful leadership and a clear chain of command are essential. To accomplish its task, a Ranger mission must have good intelligence, based in part on a thorough reconnaissance of the target area and a simple, yet flexible, plan. Successful execution, in turn, depends largely on skill in such light infantry tactics as the use of terrain and existing cover, rapid movement, surprise, and shock at the point of attack. Finally, it helps to have on the scene superiors who appreciate Ranger operations and understand the proper use of Ranger units.[2]

Unfortunately, few high-ranking officers have possessed any comprehension of the role of the Rangers. Proper employment of the Rangers demands sensitivity to their special nature as a light force containing highly motivated and specially trained personnel but lacking the staying power and fire support for either static defense or conventional offensive operations. Many commanders did not recognize these limitations and employed the Rangers like any other infantry unit. Others sensed the difference but misused Rangers anyway, partly due to a need for troops and partly because Ranger inactivity might cause morale problems among the high-spirited Rangers and resentment among line units in combat. Given the orientation toward big-unit warfare, the lack of a clear concept of Rangers in the Army, and the generally temporary status of Ranger units during those rare periods when they did exist, the puzzlement of senior officers over a proper role for the Rangers is not surprising. A doctrine laying out Ranger capabilities and limitations and their place in strategy would have furnished a basis for education in higher-level schools, but the Army seldom furnished any such guide, in part because Ranger missions can be notoriously difficult to define. If the capture of critical points constitutes a Ranger mission, how does one define a critical point? Still, some kind of guidance was necessary for field commanders, who all too often viewed the Rangers as tough guys, rather than specialists.

The subject of toughness, specifically concern about the toughness of American soldiers, recurs frequently in the Ranger story. Such anxieties hardly constitute a new or unique theme within Western democracies. One can trace them back, at least, to the Social Darwinism at the turn of the century, when a British staff officer expressed concern that Western civilization eroded the military virtues, leaving the West vulnerable to the rugged representatives of more primitive societies.[3] Similar fears that affluence was emasculating

American society could be heard among American military officers during World War II, the Korean War, and the Vietnam War. Whether these concerns were true misses the point, for many officers believed them to be true. They saw Ranger training and operations as a corrective, preparing American boys for the fight against battle-hardened Germans, Japanese, and Communists. While such preparation was undoubtedly preferable to none at all, one can seriously question whether a few raids or a mere eight weeks of Ranger training would go far enough to create skilled leaders of small, line combat units. Yet, if Ranger training did nothing else, it did create a certain esprit and contributed to the image of Rangers as "tough guys."

The image of tough guys predominated even more in society, which, in its reactions to Rangers, split along traditional divisions in American attitudes toward warfare and the military. In *Soldiers and Civilians*, Marcus Cunliffe distinguished three American outlooks toward the military: the Quaker, which sees warfare as tragic and wasteful and feels ill at ease with martial values; the Rifleman, which believes in the toughness, self-reliance, and natural fighting ability of the American soldier; and the Chevalier, which views warfare and the military as romantic and heroic.[4] Cunliffe was focusing on nineteenth century America, but one may see vestiges of those attitudes toward the military in general and the Rangers in particular 100 years later. A sizable segment of society combined elements of the Rifleman and Chevalier in its idolization of Rangers as rugged, resourceful supermen, heirs to the place held by such legendary frontiersmen as Daniel Boone, Kit Carson, and Robert Rogers. The image of the romantic hero, fostered by radio, television, books, and newspapers held an especially strong appeal in an impersonal age of mass marketing, mass media, and technology. Not everyone had such a favorable view of the Rangers. As antimilitary sentiment revived in the late 1960s, one detected among liberals and much of the press elements of the Quaker view in their perception of Rangers as societal misfits or hoodlums.

Thus, because of antimilitarism and romanticization among the public, as well as antielitism and orientation toward a mass war among professional soldiers, society and the Army never developed a clear idea of Ranger operations or the Ranger concept during the period from World War II to Grenada. "Ranger" meant different things to different people at different times. It could signify specialists for special missions, such as raids and reconnaissance. It also could mean elite troops for particularly difficult, hazardous infantry missions. Finally, it could stand for tough, skilled individual infantrymen. The numerous legends attached to the term further blurred its meaning, evoking as they did the image of the rugged frontier hero who could do anything, a view unfortunately held by too many modern field commanders toward their Ranger units. Under these circumstances, it is not surprising that the Army has encountered problems in its use of the Rangers, and that the bitter lessons learned as a result are too often forgotten until the next war.

NOTES

1. See Cohen, *Commandos and Politicians*, for a broader discussion of the problems of elite units in democracies.

2. King's *Rangers* has a fine section on the factors underlying successful Ranger operations. See also McMichael, *Light Infantry*, p. 236.

3. Lloyd, *History of Infantry*, pp. vi–vii.

4. Cunliffe, *Soldiers and Civilians*, pp. 413–418.

Bibliographical Essay

REFERENCE WORKS

As a basic guide to finding aids, the author turned to the brief but comprehensive "Finding Aid Finder: A Bibliography of Tools for Research and Writing in United States History and Related Fields," prepared for in-house use by Dr. I. B. Holley, Jr., of Duke University. For government documents, see *Monthly Catalog of U.S. Government Publications*, its *Cumulative Subject Index, 1900–1971*, the *Cumulative Index of Congressional Committee Hearings*, and the *Index to U.S. Government Periodicals*; also see Roberta A. Scull, *A Bibliography of U.S. Government Bibliographies, 1968–1976*, 2 vols. (Ann Arbor, Mich.: Pierian Press, 1975–1979). The subject catalogues of the Library of Congress, the library of the U.S. Military Academy at West Point, and Perkins Library at Duke University also provided numerous titles for investigation.

Of the more specialized bibliographies, the most valuable were Robin Higham, *A Guide to the Sources of United States Military History* (Hamden, Conn.: Archon Books, 1975–1981); John E. Jessup and Robert W. Coakley, *A Guide to the Study and Use of Military History*, 2d ed. (Washington, D.C.: Office of the Chief of Military History, 1982); Myron J. Smith, *The Secret Wars: A Guide to Sources in English* (Santa Barbara, Calif.: ABC–Clio, 1980–1981); HRC 461 Bib—Rangers in the Historical Records Branch of the U.S. Army Center of Military History; and *Air University Library Index to Military Periodicals, 1949–* , an invaluable source for professional journals. For unit histories, see Charles E. Dornbusch, *Histories of American Army Units, World Wars I and II and Korean Conflict with Some Earlier Histories* (Washington, D.C.: Department of the Army, 1956); Office of the Chief of Military History, *Unit Histories of World War II* (Washington, D.C.: OCMH, 1950); and USAMHI, *United States Army Unit Histories*, Special Bibliography no. 4

(Carlisle Barracks, Pa.: USAMHI, 1971). Many of the collections at the National Archives, notably the classified decimal files of the Adjutant General's Office, the observer reports of Army Ground Forces, and the records of Allied Force Headquarters in the Mediterranean, have their own indexes. See also *Catalog and Index to Historical Manuscripts, 1940–1966*, a very useful guide to the collection of unpublished manuscripts at the Center of Military History. Since the author completed his research, an additional bibliography of note has appeared: Roger A. Beaumont, *Special Operations and Elite Units, 1939–1988: A Research Guide* (Westport, Conn.: Greenwood Press, 1988).

Bibliographies were not the only finding aids which the author utilized. In a conceptual study, dictionaries are essential; see especially James T. Adams, ed., *Dictionary of American History*, 7 vols., rev. ed. (New York: Scribner's, 1976); John R. Elting, Dan Cragg, and Ernest L. Deal, *A Dictionary of Soldier Talk* (New York: Scribner's, 1984); Edward S. Farrow, *A Dictionary of Military Terms* (New York: Crowell, 1918); Max B. Garber, *A Modern Military Dictionary* (Washington, D.C.: Max B. Garber, 1936); Eric Partridge, *Origins: A Short Etymological Dictionary of Modern English* (New York: Macmillan, 1963); the 1944, 1950, 1953, 1958, and 1961 editions of the *Dictionary of United States Army Terms*; and the 1953, 1955, 1957, 1959, 1963, 1964, 1968, and 1974 editions of the *Dictionary of Military and Associated Terms* produced by the Joint Chiefs of Staff. For biographical information, see Dumas Malone, ed., *Dictionary of American Biography*, 22 vols. (New York: Scribner's, 1933); T. M. Dunleavy, ed., *Generals of the Army* (Washington, D.C.: Dunleavy Publishing, 1953–1956); and Robert McHenry, ed., *Webster's American Military Biographies* (Springfield, Mass.: Merriam, 1978). John K. Mahon and Romana Danysh, *Infantry, Part I: Regular Army*, Army Lineage Series (Washington, D.C.: OCMH, 1972) provided helpful data on Ranger unit lineages.

ARCHIVES

Most upper-level military records are stored at the Modern Military Headquarters Branch of the National Archives in Washington, D.C. Material on the Rangers of World War II is scattered throughout these papers. Some items can be found in the Adjutant General's decimal file and classified decimal file in RG 407, while other important documents are stored in the decimal files of the War Department's Operations Division in RG 165. See also the intelligence reports numerical file of Army Ground Forces in RG 337; the material on Second Army's Ranger School in the project decimal file of Second Army's Adjutant General, RG 337, Boxes 1156–1161; the Top Secret Decimal File of 12th Army Group's Adjutant General, Box 32, in RG 331; and the ABC Decimal File of the Army Staff's Plans and Operations Division in RG 319; as well as the decimal file of SHAEF's G-1 section and the subject, decimal, and numeric files of SHAEF's G-3 section in RG 331. Upper-level records for the Rangers of the Korean War are much more concentrated; see especially Box 380 of the Army G-3's decimal file for March 1950–1951 in RG 319. Also important for the period are Boxes 92 and 94 of the Operations Division's general decimal file for 1950–1951 in RG 319. Thus far, declassification of the Army's post–Korean War records has not proceeded much past the mid-1950s, except for some Vietnam War records. Some records on the Ranger concept in the 1950s can be found in the decimal file of the Adjutant General of Army Field Forces, 1951–1952, in RG 337; the inspection reports of the Combat Arms Advisory Group for 1951–1954 in RG 337; Boxes 12 and 15 of the Chief of Special Warfare's Top Secret Decimal Files, 1951–1954 in RG 331; and the Army G-3's general decimal file for 1954 and the Chief of Staff's decimal file for 1953-1954, both in RG 319.

Records of Army units and headquarters in the field are deposited at the Washington National Records Center in Suitland, Maryland. In the World War II Operations Reports of RG 407, researchers can find the reports and other records of all six Ranger battalions in World War II, the 1st Special Service Force, and the few surviving records of Merrill's Marauders. Within the microfilmed documents of Allied Force Headquarters in RG 331, one can find some documents pertaining to the role of commandos in Allied operations in the Mediterranean. The records of the Chief of Staff and G-3 of Sixth Army in RG 338 contain some valuable items, particularly regarding the training of the 6th Ranger Battalion, and the administrative file of the Historical Division of the European Theater of Operations in RG 332 has a brief report on the Rangers in Box 55. Material on the Ranger companies in Korea is much more scattered. One must go to the command reports and journals of the corps and divisions of Eighth Army and the command reports of the Japan Logistics Command and nonorganic units in RG 407; post–World War II unit histories in Boxes 567443 and 568445 of RG 338; and Boxes P486–487, P559, P570, P572, P596, and P732 of the Eighth Army records in RG 338. See also Boxes 3, 7, 748–749, 752, and 840–843 of the records of the Eighth Army G-3 in RG 338. Box 874 of the Army Intelligence section's decimal file for 1941–1948 in RG 319 provides some information on the Ranger concept between World War II and Korea. The Army has been declassifying records pertaining to Vietnam, and records of divisions, the 5th Special Forces Group, and other units, notably the 75th Infantry, in RG 338 are now open to researchers. Access numbers can be obtained from the Access and Release Branch of the Adjutant General's Office, Alexandria, Virginia.

The U.S. Army Center of Military History has a number of records worthy of examination by researchers of Ranger history. Of special interest, especially for researchers of the Korean War Rangers, are the collection of unpublished manuscripts prepared by the center's historians, notably Martin Blumenson, "Action on Hill 628, 8th Ranger Infantry Company (Airborne)," and

"Hwachon Dam"; Eighth U.S. Army Korea, "Special Problems in the Korean Conflict," and "Task Force Byorum"; Office of the Chief of Army Field Forces, "Annual History, 1 January–31 December 1950"; and Edward C. Williamson, "Chip Yong-ni: Defense of the South Sector of 23rd Regimental Combat Team Perimeter by Company G, 13–15 February 1951." Arranged by unit, the files of the Organizational History Branch contain invaluable documents on recent Ranger history, as well as the 1984 annual report of the 75th Infantry (Ranger) Regiment. The heart of the center's historical collections lies in its archives. See especially HRC 314.7 Ranger Battalion; HRC 314.82 Debriefing of Senior Officers, which contains reports from several officers in Vietnam; HRC Geog L. Italy 370.2–Anzio, including press releases on the Rangers of World War II; HRC Geog V. Korea 350.5, which has clippings on Collins's attitudes toward the Rangers at the start of the Korean War; and 370.64 Guerrilla Warfare, U.S. Army. The archives and library also have the reports of the Williams and Haines boards, including comments on the Ranger School, field manuals and regulations, and tables of organization and equipment. In preparation, but available for this book, was Jonathan M. House, "The U.S. Army in Joint Operations," a product of CMH's Military Studies Branch.

Another major source for documents relating to Ranger history, particularly personal papers, is the U.S. Army Military History Institute at Carlisle Barracks, Pennsylvania. Of papers in the institute's archives, the most productive were the collections of James J. Altieri, Theodore J. Conway, Chester B. Hansen, Korean War interviews, Louis F. Lisko, John P. Lucas, Merrill's Marauders, John W. O'Daniel, the Ranger Collection, Matthew B. Ridgway, World War II Miscellaneous, and William P. Yarborough. Supplementing these papers, the institute has conducted interviews with leading figures in the recent history of the U.S. Army. Interviews that were especially enlightening on the Ranger concept were those with Paul D. Adams; Arthur S. Collins, Jr.; George H. Decker; Paul L. Freeman; Barksdale Hamlett; Harold K. Johnson; Walter T. Kerwin, Jr.; Harry Lemley; Frank Pace, Jr.; Bruce Palmer, Jr.; William R. Peers; Jonathan O. Seaman; Volney F. Warner; James K. Woolnough; and William P. Yarborough. The library possesses unit histories and old tables of organization and equipment, as well as the transcript of a lecture on Rangers given by Col. William O. Darby at the Army and Navy Staff College on 27 October 1944; an Army Field Forces letter, dated 22 October 1951, establishing the Ranger course; a copy of the tentative manual prepared by the Ranger Training Center in 1950; unit historical reports for the 2d Battalion (Ranger), 75th Infantry, in 1974 and 1976 and the summary doctrinal statement for the Rangers, dated 15 November 1974; and a Seventh Army paper on long range patrols, dated 8 September 1961.

These four repositories furnished the bulk of the primary documentation on the Rangers, but other archival collections helped fill in the story. The George C. Marshall Papers and the Lucian K. Truscott, Jr. Papers at the George C.

Marshall Research Library in Lexington, Virginia, provided essential information on the origins of the World War II Rangers. The library of the U.S. Army Infantry School in Fort Benning, Georgia, furnished some invaluable documents on the origins of the Ranger School. The library of the John F. Kennedy Special Warfare Center at Fort Bragg, North Carolina, has a microfilm set of key documents on the Rangers of World War II. This collection was compiled by Harry Perlmutter, a former sergeant with Darby's 1st Ranger Battalion; another set is available at the library of the U.S. Military Academy at West Point. In addition to its finding aids for records of units in Vietnam, the Access and Release Branch of the Army Adjutant General's Office maintains microfiche copies of many unit records. At the Library of Congress, the author was able to view films relevent to the Ranger concept, including *Darby's Rangers* (Warner Brothers, 1958), *The Devil's Brigade* (David Wolper, 1968), *The Green Berets* (Warner Brothers, 1968), and *Northwest Passage* (Metro Goldwyn Mayer, 1940).

INTERVIEWS AND CORRESPONDENCE

Several individuals who were intimately involved in the Ranger story gave freely of their time and knowledge, not only by granting often lengthy interviews but also by painstakingly checking interview notes for accuracy. Without their generosity, a major part of the story would have been lost. Those interviewed included Lt. Col. Joseph P. Argenterie USA, Pentagon, Virginia, 18 April 1985; Col. Robert W. Black USA (Ret.), Carlisle, Pennsylvania, 22 March 1984; Gen. Theodore J. Conway USA (Ret.), Durham, North Carolina, 2 May 1984; Col. Herman W. Dammer USA (Ret.), McLean, Virginia, 23 August 1984; Gen. William E. Depuy USA (Ret.), Alexandria, Virginia, 30 September 1985; Brig. Gen. John W. Dobson USA (Ret.), Hilton Head, South Carolina, 16 November 1984; Gen. Clyde D. Eddleman USA (Ret.), Arlington, Virginia, 13 September 1988; Col. Robert W. Garrett USA (Ret.), Potomac, Maryland, 8 October 1985; Col. James F. Greene, Jr., USA (Ret.), Carlisle, Pennsylvania, 8 March 1984; Col. Richard J. Keating USA, Springfield, Virginia, 6 April 1986; Col. Charles Norton USA (Ret.), McLean, Virginia, 16 October 1985; Col. Roger M. Pezzelle USA (Ret.), Fairfax, Virginia, 1 February 1989; Harry Perlmutter, Fort Bragg, North Carolina, 25 April 1984; members of the Ranger Battalions Association, Carlisle, Pennsylvania, 4 May 1984; and Maj. Gen. John K. Singlaub USA (Ret.), Alexandria, Virginia, 1 February 1989.

Agencies of the Department of the Army, when contacted, were forthcoming with informational material on the current Rangers. The public affairs office of the Department of the Army provided "Rangers Lead the Way: A Brief History," regarding the background and activities of the 1st Battalion

(Ranger), 75th Infantry, as of 1976. The public affairs office of the 1st Special Operations Command (Airborne) at Fort Bragg, North Carolina, presented the author with a copy of their annual historical review for 1983–1986 as well as papers relating to the announcement to the press of the creation of 1st SOCOM; "Rangers Lead the Way: An Overview," the 1983 edition of the informational booklet on the 1st Battalion; and "Rangers Lead the Way: A Brief History," the 1981 edition of the corresponding pamphlet for the 2d Battalion. In addition, the 75th Ranger Regiment provided the author with its "Statement of Operational Capabilities," dated 14 September 1984.

PUBLISHED PRIMARY SOURCES

Congressional documents provided some helpful material on the recent history of the Ranger concept, particularly with regard to overall policy and some specific operations. Regarding particular operations, see Senate Committee on Foreign Relations, *Bombing Operations and the POW Rescue Mission, North Vietnam*, 91st Cong., 2d sess., 1970; House Committee on Foreign Relations, Subcommittee on International Political and Military Affairs, *Seizure of the Mayaguez*, 94th Cong., 1st sess., 1975; House Committee on Appropriations, Subcommittee on the Department of Defense, *Department of Defense Appropriations for 1981, Pt. 4: Hostage Rescue Mission*, 96th Cong., 2d sess., 1980; and Senate Committee on Armed Services, *Organization, Structure and Decision-making Procedures of the Department of Defense, Part 8*, 98th Cong., 1st sess., 1983, on Grenada.

In addition to the information provided by public affairs offices, the Department of the Army and its predecessor, the War Department, have published a number of works relating to the Ranger concept over the years. Among field manuals, note especially *FM 21–50: Ranger Training*, August 1957; *FM 21–50: Ranger Training and Ranger Operations*, January 1962; *FM 21–75: Infantry Scouting, Patrolling, and Sniping*, February 1944; *FM 21–75: Combat Training of the Individual Soldier and Patrolling*, January 1962; *FM 21–75: Combat Training of the Individual Soldier and Patrolling*, 1967; *FM 31–18: Long Range Patrols: Division, Corps, and Army*, June 1962; and *FM 31–21: Special Forces Operations*, 1965 and February 1969. See also *ROTC Manual 145–60: Small Unit Tactics, including Communications*, 1954; *Ranger* (Fort Benning, Ga.: Infantry School, 1959); and a training circular, *TC 31–20–1: The Role of U.S. Army Special Forces: Airborne: Tips for Leaders*, 1976. For background on the commandos, U.S. War Department, Military Intelligence Service, *British Commandos*, Special Series no. 1 (Washington, D.C.: U.S. War Department, August 1942), proved especially helpful, and U.S. War Department, *Infantry in Battle*, 2d ed. (Washington, D.C.: Infantry Journal Press, 1939) revealed much on pre-World War II infantry doctrine.

All of the unit histories examined cover Ranger-type units in World War
II. James J. Altieri, *Darby's Rangers* (Durham, N.C.: Seaman Printery, 1945)
covers Darby's three battalions, and Henry S. Glassman, *"Lead the Way
Rangers!"* A History of the 5th Ranger Battalion (Markt Grafing, Germany:
Buchdruckerei Hausser, 1945) performs the same function for the 5th Ranger
Battalion. Rudder's 2d Ranger Battalion receives attention in a series of company
histories, including Morris Prince, "Company A, 2nd Ranger Battalion: Overseas
and Then—Over the Top!," in the 2d Ranger Battalion's records at Suitland,
Maryland; Edwin M. Sorvisto, *2nd Ranger Battalion: Roughing It with Charlie*
(Williamstown, N.J.: Antietam National Museum, n.d.); and Alfred E. Baer, Jr.,
D for Dog: The Story of a Ranger Company (Memphis, Tenn., 1946). See also
Joseph H. Ewing, *29 Let's Go! A History of the 29th Infantry Division in World
War II* (Washington, D.C.: Infantry Journal Press, 1948) for the 29th Ranger
Battalion. For the 1st Special Service Force, see Robert D. Burhans, *The First
Special Service Force: A War History of the North Americans, 1942–1944*
(Washington, D.C.: Infantry Journal Press, 1947). For Merrill's Marauders and
its successor, the Mars Task Force, see U.S. War Department, Military
Intelligence Division, *Merrill's Marauders, February–May 1944*, American
Forces in Action series (Washington, D.C.: War Department, 1945) and John
H. Randolph, *Marsmen in Burma* (Houston, Tex.: Gulf Publishing, 1946).

Most memoirs that were examined also focused on the period of World
War II. For the memoirs of an early "Ranger," see John S. Mosby, *Mosby's
War Reminiscences*, rev. ed. (New York: Pageant Books, 1958). Some revealing
information on the origins of the Ranger concept in World War II can be found
in the reminiscences of British commandos, including John Durnford-Slater,
Commando (London: Kimber, 1953); Simon Christopher Joseph Fraser Lord
Lovat, *March Past: A Memoir* (New York: Holmes and Meier, 1978); Murdoch
C. McDougall, *Swiftly They Struck: The Story of No. 4 Commando*, 2d ed.
(London: Arms and Armour, 1986); and Peter Young, *Commando* (New York:
Ballantine, 1969). Memoirs and journals produced by ex-Rangers and veterans
of Ranger-type units include Robert H. Adleman and George Walton, *The
Devil's Brigade* (Philadelphia: Chilton Books, 1966); James J. Altieri, *The
Spearheaders* (Indianapolis, Ind.: Bobbs–Merrill, 1960); John F. Hummer, *An
Infantryman's Journal* (Manassas, Va.: Ranger Associates, 1981); Charles N.
Hunter, *GALAHAD* (San Antonio, Tex.: Naylor, 1963); William L. Newnan,
Escape in Italy: The Narrative of Lt. William L. Newnan, U.S. Rangers (Ann
Arbor, Mich.: University of Michigan Press, 1945); and Charlton Ogburn, Jr.,
The Marauders, 2d ed. (New York: Harper and Bros., 1959). William O. Darby
and William H. Baumer, *Darby's Rangers: We Led the Way* (San Rafael, Calif.:
Presidio Press, 1980) was based on interviews with Colonel Darby. Memoirs of
higher-ranking officers provided relatively little information specifically on the
Rangers, but they were quite revealing on the overall outlook of higher-level
commanders; see especially Edmund F. Ball, *Staff Officer with the Fifth Army*

(New York: Exposition Press, 1958); Omar N. Bradley, *A Soldier's Story* (New York: Holt, 1951) and Bradley's pseudo-autobiography with Clay Blair, *A General's Life* (New York: Simon and Schuster, 1983); Mark W. Clark, *Calculated Risk* (New York: Harper, 1950); J. Lawton Collins, *Lightning Joe: An Autobiography* (Baton Rouge: Louisiana State University Press, 1979); Lucian K. Truscott, Jr., *Command Missions: A Personal Story* (New York: E. P. Dutton, 1954); and Albert C. Wedemeyer, *Wedemeyer Reports!* (New York: Holt, 1958). Important memoirs for the period since World War II include Aaron Bank, *From OSS to Green Berets: The Birth of Special Forces* (Novato, Calif.: Presidio Press, 1986); Charlie A. Beckwith and Donald Knox, *Delta Force* (New York: Harcourt, Brace and Jovanovich, 1983); J. Lawton Collins, *War in Peacetime: The History and Lessons of Korea* (Boston: Houghton Mifflin, 1969); Anthony B. Herbert, *Soldier* (New York: Holt, Rinehart and Winston, 1973); Matthew B. Ridgway, *The Korean War* (Garden City, N.Y.: Doubleday, 1967) and *Soldier: The Memoirs of Matthew B. Ridgway* (New York: Harper, 1956); Maxwell D. Taylor, *Swords and Plowshares* (New York: Norton, 1972); and William C. Westmoreland, *A Soldier Reports* (Garden City, N.Y.: Doubleday, 1976).

Other published primary sources took a variety of forms. Most are discussions by professional officers and academics of contemporary defense issues, including commandos and Rangers; see Frank R. Barnett, B. Hugh Tovar, and Richard H. Shultz, eds., *Special Operations in U.S. Strategy* (Washington, D.C.: National Defense University Press, 1984); Zeb B. Bradford, Jr., and Frederic J. Brown, *The United States Army in Transition* (Beverly Hills, Calif.: Sage Publications, 1973); Stephen J. Cimbala, ed., *The Reagan Defense Program: An Interim Assessment* (Wilmington, Del.: Scholarly Resources, 1986); Morris Janowitz, *The Professional Soldier* (Glencoe, Ill.: Free Press, 1960); Roger Keyes, *Amphibious Warfare and Combined Operations* (Cambridge: Cambridge University Press, 1943); Edward N. Luttwak, *The Pentagon and the Art of War* (New York: Simon and Schuster, 1984); S. L. A. Marshall, *Men against Fire: The Problem of Battle Command in Future War* (Washington, D.C.: Combat Forces Press, 1947); Charles C. Moskos, *The American Enlisted Man: The Rank and File in Today's Military* (New York: Russell Sage, 1970); and Sam C. Sarkesian, *Combat Effectiveness: Cohesion, Stress and the Volunteer Military* (Beverly Hills, Calif.: Sage Publications, 1980), and his *The New Battlefield: The United States and Unconventional Conflicts* (Westport, Conn.: Greenwood Press, 1986). Some published collections of papers that have provided information include Martin Blumenson, *The Patton Papers*, 2 vols. (Boston: Houghton Mifflin, 1972–1974); Alfred D. Chandler Jr. and Stephen E. Ambrose, eds., *The Papers of Dwight David Eisenhower: The War Years*, 9 vols. (Baltimore, Md.: Johns Hopkins University Press, 1970); and U.S. Congress, *American State Papers, Class V: Military Affairs*, vol. 1 (Washington, D.C.: Gales and Seaton, 1832). Among the most productive sources were personal accounts of combat, including Ralph Ingersoll, *The Battle Is the Payoff*, Fighting Forces Series (Washington, D.C.: Infantry Journal Press, 1943) for World War II; S. L. A. Marshall, *Notes on Infantry Tactics in Korea* (Baltimore, Md.: Johns Hopkins University, Operations Research Office, 1951) on Korea; and Albert N. Garland, ed., *Combat Notes from Vietnam*, 2 vols. (Fort Benning, Ga.: Infantry Magazine, 1968) and *Infantry in Vietnam* (Fort Benning, Ga.: Infantry Magazine, 1967); Infantry Magazine, ed., *The U.S. Infantryman in Vietnam, 1967–1972*, 2d ed. (New York: Jove Books, 1985); Joseph A. McChristian, *The Role of Military Intelligence*, Vietnam Studies (Washington, D.C.: OCMH, 1974); and Jac Weller, *Fire and Movement: Bargain Basement Warfare in the Far East* (New York: Thomas Y. Crowell, 1967) on Vietnam. See also Carroll B. Colby, *Special Forces: The U.S. Army's Experts in Unconventional Warfare* (New York: Coward McCann, 1964); Arthur Goodfriend, *Scouting and Patrolling: The Soldier, the Enemy, the Ground* (Washington, D.C.: Infantry Journal, 1943); Langhorne A. Motley, "The Decision to Assist Grenada," Current Policy no. 541 (Washington, D.C.: Department of State, 1984); Lord Louis Mountbatten, *Report to the Combined Chiefs of Staff by the Supreme Allied Commander, Southeast Asia, 1943–1945* (London: HMSO, 1951); and William C. Westmoreland, *Report of the Chief of Staff of the United States Army, 1 July 1968 to 30 June 1972* (Washington, D.C.: Department of the Army, 1977).

ARTICLES

The author examined articles in the *New York Times*, as well as both popular and professional journals, only a few of which can be mentioned here. For the period prior to World War II, see especially John R. Elting, "Further Light on the Beginnings of Gorham's Rangers," *Military Collector and Historian* 12 (Fall 1960): 74–77; Carl E. Grant, "Partisan Warfare, Model 1861–1865," *Military Review* 38 (November 1958): 43–46; Larry Ivers, "Rangers in Florida—1818," *Infantry* 53 (September–October 1963): 37; John K. Mahon, "Anglo-American Methods of Indian Warfare, 1676–1794," *Mississippi Valley Historical Review* 45 (September 1958): 254–275; Maurice Matloff, "The American Approach to War, 1919–1945," in Michael Howard, ed., *The Theory and Practice of War* (London: Cassell, 1965), pp. 215–229; J. M. Scammell, "Light Infantry," *Infantry Journal* 44 (September–October 1937): 428–429; John W. Wright, "An American Corps D'Elite," *Infantry Journal* 28 (May 1926): 481–484; and Otis E. Young, "United States Mounted Ranger Battalion, 1832–1833," *Mississippi Valley Historical Review* 41 (December 1954): 453–470.

For the Ranger concept in World War II, see especially Robert P. Arnoldt, "The Dieppe Raid: A Failure That Led to Success," *Armor* 90

(July–August 1981): 12–19; Glen S. Barclay, "Butcher and Bolt: Admiral Roger Keyes and British Combined Operations, 1940–1941," *Naval War College Review* 35 (March–April 1982): 18–29; Martin Blumenson, "Darby," *Army* 32 (January 1982): 37–39; J. Hughes-Hallett, "The Mounting of Raids," *Military Review* 31 (May 1951): 85–93; Thomas M. Johnson, "The Army's Fightingest Outfit Comes Home," *Reader's Digest*, December 1944, pp. 51–54; R. E. Laycock, "Raids in World War II," *Military Review* 28 (March 1949): 93–97; Milton Lehman, "The Rangers Fought Ahead of Everybody," *Saturday Evening Post*, 15 June 1946, pp. 28–29; James B. Lyle, "Divide and Conquer: Capture of Butera Sicily by the First Ranger Battalion Illustrates Tactics of Village Fighting," *Infantry Journal* 56 (February 1945): 21–24; Scott R. McMichael, "Common Man, Uncommon Leadership: Colonel Charles N. Hunter With GALAHAD in Burma," *Parameters: USAWC Quarterly* 16 (Summer 1986): 45–57; Henry A. Mucci, "Rescue at Cabanatuan," *Infantry Journal* 56 (April 1945): 15–19; "The Rangers," *Life*, 31 July 1944, pp. 59–63; Charles W. Schreiner, "The Dieppe Raid: Its Origins, Aims, and Results," *Naval War College Review* 25 (May–June 1973): 83–97; George R. Shelton, "The Alamo Scouts," *Armor* 91 (September–October 1982): 29–30; James H. Stone, "The Marauders and the Microbes," *Infantry Journal* 64 (March 1949): 4–11; Bruce Thomas, "The Commando," *Harper's*, March 1942, pp. 438–440; "Truscott's Rangers," *Newsweek* 20 (31 August 1942): 21–22; Brian Loring Villa, "Mountbatten, the British Chiefs of Staff, and Approval of the Dieppe Raid," *Journal of Military History* 54 (April 1990): 201–226; Alexander M. Worth, Jr., "Supporting Weapons and High Ground: The Rangers at Salerno," *Infantry Journal* 56 (May 1945): 33–34; and Leilyn M. Young, "Rangers in a Night Operation," *Military Review* 24 (July 1944): 64–69.

Articles relating to the Rangers during the period leading up to and including the Korean War are not as numerous but are still plentiful. See "Army Ranger Companies," *Army, Navy, Air Force Journal* 88 (14 October 1950): 168; Martin Blumenson, "The Rangers at Hwachon Dam," *Army* 17 (December 1967): 36–40; Waller B. Booth, "The Pattern That Got Lost," *Army* 31 (April 1981): 62–67; "The Champs Have a New Competitor," *Combat Forces Journal* 1 (December 1950): 7; Shaun M. Darragh, "Hwanghae Do: The War of the Donkeys," *Army* 34 (November 1984): 66–75; D. B. Drysdale, "41 Commando," *Marine Corps Gazette* 37 (August 1953): 28–32; "The New Ranger Company," *Military Review* 31 (May 1951): 31–35; "Parachute Operation Which Neutralised Communist Defenses near Seoul," *Illustrated London News*, 7 April 1951, p. 531; Rod Paschall, "Special Operations in Korea," *Conflict* 7, no. 2 (1987): 155–178; "Ranger Companies," *Combat Forces Journal* 1 (December 1950): 34; "The Rangers," *National Guard* 5 (May 1951): 20; "The Rangers Lose," *Time*, 3 September 1951, p. 25; J. P. O. Twohig, "Are Commandos Really Necessary?" *Canadian Army Journal* 3 (December 1949): 19; John G. Van Houten, "The Rangers Are Back," *Army Information Digest* 6 (August

1951): 35–41; and R. C. Williams, "Amphibious Scouts and Raiders," *Military Affairs* 13 (Fall 1949): 155–157.

Given the shortage of unclassified documentation, much of this book's coverage of the period since the mid-1950s relies on articles. For the 1950s and 1960s, including the Vietnam War, see especially Melvin R. Blair, "Toughest Outfit in the Army," *Saturday Evening Post*, 12 May 1956, pp. 40–41; Richard J. Buck, "Rangers Are the New Look," *Combat Forces Journal* 5 (August 1954): 44; Tom P. Cable, "Long Range Patrol," *Army Digest* 23 (December 1968): 10–13; Captain Tactic, "U.S. Grant Wasn't a Trooper," *Combat Forces Journal* 5 (May 1955): 49–50; Robert C. Carroll, "Six Men Alone," *Infantry* 65 (January–February 1975): 41–43; Andrew J. DeGraff, "LRRP and Nuclear Target Acquisition," *Military Review* 40 (November 1960): 15–21; Joseph H. Devins, "Long Range Patrolling," *Infantry* 50 (October–November 1960): 34–38; Charles A. Dodson, "Special Forces," *Army* 11 (June 1961): 44–52; John Durden and Fred Sherrill, "Ranger Operations," *U.S. Army Aviation Digest* 16 (October 1970): 2–6; Robert C. Fox, "The New Ranger," *Infantry* 57 (November–December 1967): 47–50; Richard D. James, "Delta Team Is in Contact," *Infantry* 60 (November–December 1970): 12–15; Gerald W. Johnson, "Aquabush," *Infantry* 62 (January–February 1972): 50–53; James K. McCrory, "Ranger Armor," *Armor* 76 (January–February 1967): 24–31; Hugh McWhinnie, "The Case for a Strategic Assault Force," *Infantry* 50 (June–July 1960): 22–25; Armistead D. Mead, "Ranger Type Training for Infantry Units," *Infantry School Quarterly* 46 (April 1956): 33–36; Lewis L. Millett, "Recondo: Patrol of Opportunity," *Army* 10 (February 1960): 54–57; Lewis L. Millett and Dandridge Malone, "Journey into the Twilight Zone: Bring Back the Proud Rangers," *Army* 14 (September 1963): 27–31; Jim Mintner and Paul Price, "Rangers Ready!" *Army Information Digest* 8 (January 1953): 13–20; John G. Pappageorge, "Raid and Destroy!" *Infantry* 51 (July–August 1961): 2–5; Ronald L. Paramore, "Ranger," *Infantry* 61 (May–June 1971): 18–20; Roger M. Pezzelle, "Special Forces," *Infantry* 49 (April 1959): 13–19; Edson D. Raff, "Fighting behind Enemy Lines," *Army Information Digest* 11 (April 1956): 12–19; "Ranger Training," *Infantry* 51 (May–June 1961): 34–35; "Ranger Training Today," *Army Information Digest* 14 (January 1959): 55–58; "The Rangers Have a Long History," *Army Times,* 11 March 1964, p. E6; "Researcher Turns Ranger to Probe Military Skills," *Army Times*, 25 April 1959, p. 19; Robert K. Ruhl, "Raid at Son Tay," *Airman* 19 (August 1975): 24–31; Thomas J. Shaughnessy, "Rotors for the Rangers," *Army* 22 (May 1972): 38–42; A. Porter and S. Sweet, "Rangers Four," *Infantry* 56 (January–February 1966): 60–61, (March–April 1966): 12–13, (May–June 1966): 9–10, (July–August 1966): 10–11; Joseph Windsor, "Rugged and Ready," *Infantry School Quarterly* 42 (January 1953): 94–103; Thomas C. Wyatt, "Butcher and Bolt," *Army* 10 (May 1960): 37–45.

The increasing interest in SOF since the Vietnam War has been demonstrated by the plethora of articles that have appeared on the subject since that time. See Kenneth J. Alnwick, "Perspectives on Air Power at the Low End of the Conflict Spectrum," *Air University Review* 35 (March–April 1984): 17–28; David J. Baratto, "Special Forces in the 1980's: A Strategic Reorientation," *Military Review* 63 (March 1983): 2–14; Daniel R. Bolger, "Operation URGENT FURY and Its Critics," *Military Review* 66 (July 1986): 58–69, and "Special Operations and the Grenada Campaign," *Parameters: USAWC Quarterly* 18 (December 1988): 49–61; Gary L. Bounds and Scott R. McMichael, "Counting Costs of Elite Forces," *Army* 35 (November 1985): 24–32; William H. Burgess III, "Strategic Targeting," *Armed Forces Journal International* 122 (March 1985): 66–75; Donald E. Carlile, "The Mayaguez Incident: Crisis Management," *Military Review* 56 (October 1976): 3–14; Angelo Codevilla, "Special Operations," *Journal of Defense and Diplomacy* 3 (June 1985): 18–27; Ernest W. Cooler, "The Ranger Course," *Infantry* 70 (September–October 1980): 30–36; Steve Crawford, "Desert Combat Added to Ranger School Classload," *Army* 34 (November 1984): 26–28; Shaun M. Darragh, "Rangers and Special Forces: Two Edges of the Same Dagger," *Army* 27 (December 1977): 14–19; James M. Dubik, "Ranger Training," *Infantry* 67 (May–June 1977): 40–42; Robert L. Earl, "A Matter of Principle," *U.S. Naval Institute Proceedings* 109 (February 1983): 29–36; John R. Galvin, "Special Forces at the Crossroads," *Army* 23 (December 1973): 21–24; Michael Ganley, "Congress Creates New Unified Command for SOF and New Civilian SOF Chief," *Armed Forces Journal International* 124 (November 1986): 20–22; Warren D. Garlock and Michael L. Lanning, "Ranger Training: A Part of the Army's Future?" *Infantry* 62 (November–December 1972): 28–30; Henry G. Gole, "Bring Back the Long Range Reconnaissance Patrols," *Military Review* 61 (October 1981): 2–10; Barney Halloran, "Pros at the Survival Game," *Soldiers* 27 (July 1972): 21–23; Tom Hamrick, "The Black Berets," *Army* 27 (May 1977): 28–33; Glenn M. Harned, "Special Operations and the Airland Battle," *Military Review* 65 (September 1985): 72–83; William J. Holton, "The TAC Role in Special Operations," *Air University Review* 28 (November–December 1976): 54–68; J. M. Johnson Jr., R. W. Austin, and D. A. Quinlan, "Individual Heroism Overcame Awkward Command Relationships, Confusion, and Bad Information Off the Cambodian Coast," *Marine Corps Gazette* 61 (October 1977): 24–34; Peter A. Kelly, "Raids and National Command: Mutually Exclusive!" *Military Review* 60 (April 1980): 19–26; Noel C. Koch, "Special Operations Forces," *Defense '83* (July 1983): 8–13, and "Special Operations Forces: Tidying Up the Lines," *Armed Forces Journal International* 126 (October 1988): 104–112; J. A. Messegee, Robert A. Peterson, Walter J. Wood, J. B. Hendricks, and J. Michael Rodgers, "'Mayday' for the Mayaguez," *U.S. Naval Institute Proceedings* 102 (November 1976): 93–111; Deborah G. Meyer, "Army OK's New Special Operations Field, New Special Forces Group," *Armed Forces Journal International* 120 (July 1983): 8; Deborah G. Meyer and Benjamin F. Schemmer, "An Exclusive AFJ Interview with Noel C. Koch," *Armed Forces Journal International* 122 (March 1985):

36–52; Geoffrey Norman, "Black Berets to the Rescue," *Esquire*, 11 April 1978, pp. 43–46; William D. Phillips, "Ranger Desert Phase," *Infantry* 74 (March–April 1984): 10–12; "The Rangers Are Back," *Army Reserve* 20 (July–August 1974): 8–9; Zack Richards, "Rangers: Anytime, Anywhere," *Soldiers* 32 (February 1977): 20–23; Benjamin F. Schemmer, "Commandant Directs Marines to Sharpen Their Inherent Special Ops Capability," *Armed Forces Journal International* 123 (October 1985): 24–25; David C. Schlacter and Fred C. Stubbs, "Special Operations Forces: Not Applicable?" *Military Review* 58 (February 1978): 15–26; Viktor Suvarov, "*Spetsnaz*: The Soviet Union's Special Forces," *Military Review* 64 (March 1984): 30–46; U.S. Joint Chiefs of Staff, Special Operations Review Group, "Iran Rescue Mission: Group Analyzes Reasons for Failure," *Aviation Week and Space Technology*, 15 September 1980, pp. 61–71, 22 September 1980, pp. 140–144, 29 September 1980, pp. 84–91.

SECONDARY SOURCES

Several general sources provided essential contextual material for this study. Roger A. Beaumont, *Military Elites* (Indianapolis, Ind.: Bobbs–Merrill, 1974) and Eliot A. Cohen, *Commandos and Politicians: Elite Military Units in Modern Democracies*, Harvard Studies in International Affairs, no. 40 (Cambridge, Mass.: Harvard University Press, 1978) were invaluable starting points for a work on special units. Among studies of American military history, see especially Maurice Matloff, ed., *American Military History*, 2d ed., Army Historical Series (Washington, D.C.: OCMH, 1973); Allan R. Millett and Peter Maslowski, *For the Common Defense: A Military History of the United States of America* (New York: Free Press, 1984); Russell F. Weigley, *The American Way of War: A History of United States Military Strategy and Policy* (New York: Macmillan, 1973); and Russell F. Weigley, *History of the United States Army*, 2d ed. (Bloomington: Indiana University Press, 1984). Regarding American society during this period, see Charles C. Alexander, *Holding the Line: The Eisenhower Era, 1952–1961* (Bloomington: Indiana University Press, 1975); John M. Blum, *V Was for Victory: Politics and American Culture during World War II* (New York: Harcourt, Brace and Jovanovich, 1976); Morris Dickstein, *Gates of Eden: American Culture in the Sixties* (New York: Basic Books, 1977); Geoffrey Hodgson, *America in Our Time* (Garden City, N.Y.: Doubleday, 1976); Ole R. Holsti and James N. Rosenau, *American Leadership in World Affairs: Vietnam and the Breakdown of Consensus* (London: Allen and Unwin, 1984); William E. Leuchtenburg, *A Troubled Feast: American Society Since 1945*, rev. ed. (Boston: Little Brown, 1979); Keith L. Nelson, ed., *The Impact of War on American Life: The Twentieth Century Experience* (New York: Holt, Rhinehart and Winston, 1971); J. Ronald Oakley, *God's Country: America in the Fifties* (New York: Dembner Books, 1986); Richard Polenberg, *War and Society:*

The United States, 1941–1945 (Philadelphia: J. B. Lippincott, 1972); and Frederick F. Siegel, *Troubled Journey: From Pearl Harbor to Ronald Reagan* (New York: Hill and Wang, 1984). Works on military education gave clues to the intellectual climate in the American officer corps; see Harry P. Ball, *Of Responsible Command: A History of the Army War College* (Carlisle Barracks, Pa.: Alumni Association of USAWC, 1983) and George S. Pappas, *Prudens Futuri: The U.S. Army War College* (Carlisle Barracks, Pa.: Alumni Association of USAWC, 1967).

Despite the aura of legend surrounding the early Rangers, some scholarly works have managed to treat the subject more or less dispassionately. See John R. Cuneo, *Robert Rogers of the Rangers* (New York: Oxford University Press, 1959) on Rogers; North Callahan, *Daniel Morgan: Ranger of the Revolution* (New York: Holt, Rhinehart and Winston, 1961) and Don Higginbotham, *Daniel Morgan: Ranger of the Revolution* (Chapel Hill: University of North Carolina Press, 1961) on Morgan; Walter P. Webb, *The Texas Rangers*, 2d ed. (Boston: Houghton Mifflin, 1965) on the Texas Rangers; and V. C. Jones, *Ranger Mosby* (Chapel Hill: University of North Carolina Press, 1944) on Mosby. For the context in which these men operated, see Correlli Barnett, *Britain and Her Army, 1509–1970: A Military, Political, and Social Survey* (New York: William Morrow, 1970); John Childs, *Armies and Warfare in Europe, 1648–1789* (New York: Holmes and Meier, 1982); Marcus Cunliffe, *Soldiers and Civilians: The Martial Spirit in America, 1775–1865* (Boston: Little Brown, 1968); Robin Higham and Carol Brandt, eds., *The United States Army in Peacetime: Essays in Honor of the Bicentennial* (Manhattan, Kans.: Military Affairs, 1975); Don Higginbotham, *The War of American Independence: Military Attitudes, Policies, and Practices* (New York: Macmillan, 1971); Samuel P. Huntington, *The Soldier and the State: The Theory and Politics of Civil-Military Relations* (Cambridge, Mass.: Harvard University Press, 1957); Douglas E. Leach, *Arms for Empire: A Military History of the British Colonies in North America* (New York: Macmillan, 1973); E. M. Lloyd, *A Review of the History of Infantry*, 2d ed. (Westport, Conn.: Greenwood Press, 1976); John K. Mahon, *The War of 1812* (Gainesville: University of Florida Press, 1972); and Robert M. Utley, *Frontier Regulars: The United States Army and the Indian, 1866–1890* (New York: Macmillan, 1973). Francis Parkman, *The Battle for North America*, 2d ed. (Norwalk, Conn.: Easton Press, 1987) and Kenneth Roberts, *Northwest Passage*, 4th ed. (New York: Ballantine, 1964) are critical to an understanding of the development of the Ranger legend.

A number of studies relating to the Rangers of World War II have appeared over the years. The best analysis is Michael J. King, *Rangers: Selected Combat Operations in World War II*, Leavenworth Papers no. 11 (Fort Leavenworth, Kans.: Command and General Staff College, 1985). See also Jerome J. Haggerty, "A History of the Ranger Battalions in World War II" (Ph.D. dissertation, Fordham University, 1982). More specific studies include

Forrest B. Johnson, *Hour of Redemption: The Ranger Raid on Cabanatuan* (New York: Manor Books, 1978); Michael J. King's excellent *William Orlando Darby: A Military Biography* (Hamden, Conn.: Archon Books, 1981); Ronald L. Lane, *Rudder's Rangers* (Manassas, Va.: Ranger Associates, 1979); and Scott R. McMichael's article on the 1st Special Service Force in his *A Historical Perspective on Light Infantry*, Research Survey no. 6 (Fort Leavenworth, Kans.: Combat Studies Institute, 1987). The World War II Rangers received much of their inspiration from the British commandos; see John W. Gordon, *The Other Desert War: British Special Forces in North Africa, 1940-1943* (Westport, Conn.: Greenwood Press, 1987); James D. Ladd, *Commandos and Rangers of World War II* (New York: St. Martin's, 1978); and Hilary St. George Saunders, *Combined Operations: The Official Story of the Commandos* (New York: Macmillan, 1943). Regarding the *Chindits*, see Shelford Bidwell, *The Chindit War: Stilwell, Wingate, and the Campaign in Burma, 1944* (New York: Macmillan, 1979) and Christopher Sykes, *Orde Wingate* (Cleveland, Ohio: World, 1959). The U.S. Marine Corps Historical Branch's multivolume *History of U.S. Marine Corps Operations in World War II*, as well as Jeter A. Isely and Philip A. Crowl, *The U.S. Marines and Amphibious War: Its Theory and Practice in the Pacific* (Princeton, N.J.: Princeton University Press, 1951) cover the exploits of the Marine Raiders. The best book on the Dieppe raid, Brian L. Villa, *Unauthorized Action: Mountbatten and the Dieppe Raid* (New York: Oxford University Press, 1989) appeared too late to be of use in this narrative. For context and some operational details, *The U.S. Army in World War II*, the Army's official history of that conflict, proved invaluable; see also Marshall Becker, *The Amphibious Training Center*, Study no. 22 (Washington, D.C.: Army Ground Forces, 1946), and Bell I. Wiley and William P. Govan, *History of the Second Army*, Study no. 16 (Washington, D.C.: Army Ground Forces, 1946), for data on training camps involved in the Ranger story. For Army doctrine, organization, and preparedness, see Martin Blumenson's article, "Kasserine Pass," in Charles E. Heller and William A. Stofft, eds., *America's First Battles, 1775-1965* (Lawrence: University Press of Kansas, 1986). On the American soldier, see Samuel A. Stouffer, *The American Soldier*, 3 vols. (Princeton, N.J.: Princeton University Press, 1949) and Martin Van Creveld's *Fighting Power: German and U.S. Army Performance, 1939-1945* (Westport, Conn.: Greenwood Press, 1982). Some biographies of leading military figures involved in the Ranger story include Martin Blumenson, *Mark Clark: The Last of the Great World War II Commanders* (New York: Congdon and Weed, 1984); D. Clayton James, *The Years of MacArthur*, 3 vols. (Boston: Houghton Mifflin, 1970-1985); William M. Leary, ed., *We Shall Return! MacArthur's Commanders and the Defeat of Japan* (Lexington: Univ. Press of Kentucky, 1988); Forrest C. Pogue, *George C. Marshall*, 4 vols. (New York: Viking Press, 1963-1987).

The best available study on the Rangers in Korea is Robert W. Black, *Rangers in Korea* (New York: Ballantine, 1989). Alfred H. Paddock, Jr., *U.S.*

Army Special Warfare: Its Origins: Psychological and Unconventional Warfare, 1941–1952 (Washington, D.C.: National Defense University Press, 1982) shows the interrelationship between the Ranger concept and the birth of Special Forces. Robert A. Doughty, *The Evolution of U.S. Army Tactical Doctrine, 1946–1976* Leavenworth Papers no. 1 (Fort Leavenworth, Kans.: Combat Studies Institute, 1979), and Roy Flint's "Task Force Smith and the 24th Division: Delay and Withdrawal, 5–19 July 1950," in Charles E. Heller and William A. Stofft, eds., *America's First Battles, 1775–1965* (Lawrence: University Press of Kansas, 1986), cover Army organization and doctrine during the period. See Morris J. MacGregor, Jr., *Integration of the Armed Forces, 1940–1965*, Defense Studies Series (Washington, D.C.: OCMH, 1981) for background on blacks in the military. More general histories of the war in Korea include T. R. Fehrenbach, *This Kind of War: A Study in Unpreparedness* (New York: Macmillan, 1963); and S. L. A. Marshall, *The River and the Gauntlet* (New York: Morrow, 1953).

The Ranger concept in the 1950s and the Vietnam period is only beginning to receive serious attention from scholars. Rick Atkinson, *The Long Gray Line* (Boston: Houghton Mifflin, 1989) discusses Ranger training as part of the story of the West Point Class of 1966. Thus far, the best books available on long-range reconnaissance patrols are popular accounts, including James R. Arnold, *Rangers*, Illustrated History of the Vietnam War (New York: Bantam Books, 1988); Michael L. Lanning, *Inside the LRRP's: Rangers in Vietnam* (New York: Ivy Books, 1988); and Gordon L. Rottman, *U.S. Army Rangers and LRRP Units, 1942–1987*, Osprey Elite Series (London: Osprey, 1987). Soon to appear is Shelby L. Stanton, *Rangers at War* (New York: Crown Books, 1992). A scholarly overall history of Special Forces remains to be written, but more specialized studies include Francis J. Kelly, *U.S. Army Special Forces, 1961–1971*, Vietnam Studies (Washington, D.C.: OCMH, 1973); Charles M. Simpson III, *Inside the Green Berets: The First Thirty Years* (Novato, Calif.: Presidio Press, 1983); Shelby L. Stanton, *Green Berets at War: U.S. Army Special Forces in Southeast Asia, 1956–1975* (Novato, Calif.: Presidio Press, 1986); and Shelby L. Stanton, *Vietnam Order of Battle* (Washington, D.C.: U.S. News Books, 1981). Benjamin F. Schemmer, *The Raid* (New York: Harper and Row, 1976) provides an in-depth study of the Son Tay raid. Of other elite units in the world, the British Special Air Service was perhaps the most renowned; their tale is told in Tony Geraghty, *Inside the Special Air Service* (Nashville, Tenn.: Battery Press, 1980). Larry E. Cable, *Conflict of Myths: The Development of American Counterinsurgency Doctrine and the Vietnam War* (New York: New York University Press, 1986) and Stephen L. Bowman, "The Evolution of United States Army Doctrine for Counterinsurgency Warfare from World War II to the Commitment of Combat Units in Vietnam" (Ph.D. dissertation, Duke University, 1985) cover the counterinsurgency craze. General studies on the Vietnam War include Robert B. Asprey, *War in the Shadows: The Guerrilla in History*, 2 vols. (Garden City, N.Y.: Doubleday, 1975); Jeffrey J. Clarke,

Advice and Support: The Final Years, 1965–1973, U.S. Army in Vietnam (Washington, D.C.: CMH, 1988); John H. Hay, Jr., *Tactical and Material Innovations*, Vietnam Studies (Washington, D.C.: OCMH, 1974); George C. Herring, Jr., *America's Longest War* (New York: Wiley, 1979); Neil Sheehan, *A Bright Shining Lie: John Paul Vann and America in Vietnam* (New York: Random House, 1988); Ronald H. Spector, *Advice and Support: The Early Years, 1941–1960*, U.S. Army in Vietnam (Washington, D.C.: CMH, 1983); and Earl H. Tilford, *Search and Rescue in Southeast Asia, 1961–1975* (Washington, D.C.: Office of Air Force History, 1980). For analyses of the war movies that influenced public perceptions of the Rangers, see Lawrence H. Suid, "The Film Industry and the Vietnam War" (Ph.D. dissertation, Case Western University, 1980), and Lawrence H. Suid, *Guts and Glory: Great American War Movies* (Reading, Mass.: Addison–Wesley, 1978).

 Secondary sources on the Ranger concept since 1974 have had to work without several primary sources, resulting in an incomplete picture. Of available studies, the most complete is John M. Collins, *Green Berets, SEAL's, and Spetsnaz: U.S. and Soviet Special Military Operations* (Washington, D.C.: Pergammon-Brassey's, 1987); also helpful are James Adams, *Secret Armies: Inside the American, Soviet, and European Special Forces* (New York: Atlantic Monthly Press, 1987) and David Eshel, *Elite Fighting Units* (New York: Arco, 1984). For specific operations, see Mark Adkin, *URGENT FURY: The Battle for Grenada* (Lexington, Mass.: D. C. Heath, 1989); Richard A. Gabriel, *Military Incompetence: Why the American Military Doesn't Win* (New York: Hill and Wang, 1985); Stephen Harding, *Air War Grenada* (Missoula, Mont.: Pictorial Histories Publishing Company, 1984); and Paul B. Ryan, *The Iranian Rescue Mission: Why It Failed* (Annapolis, Md.: U.S. Naval Institute Press, 1985).

Index

A Team, 158, 177
Abrams, Creighton W., 174,
199, 201, 202, 233; attitude
toward special units, 198, 200;
background, 198
Acheson, Dean, 103
Achnacarry Castle, Scotland, 19,
36
Adams, James Y., 109, 120
Adler, Renate, 211 n.6
Advanced Research Projects
Agency, 198
Afghanistan, 217
Aguinaldo, Emilio, 9 n.12
Ailes, Stephen, 163
Alamo, siege of, 58
Alamo Scouts, 82, 86, 88, 100,
106
Allen, Terry M., 24, 26, 45
All-Volunteer Army, 196
Altieri, James J., 26
American Civil War, 5, 6, 112,
231
American Revolution, 3, 4, 145
amphibious operations, 13, 14,
17, 24, 30 n.2, 36, 96
Anderson, Dorsey B., 118

anti-Communism, 139, 146, 195,
217
anti-elitism, 231–35; during
1950s and 1960s, 155, 159,
160, 163, 184; during Korean
War, 120, 126, 128, 129,
131–33; in early America, 4;
in the World War II-era, 15,
37, 45, 49, 63, 75; postwar,
97, 98; post-Vietnam, 197,
198, 203, 219, 224, 225
anti-militarism, 146, 148, 196,
235
Anzio, Italy, Battle of, 57, 61
Apaches, 14
Aparri, Philippines, 90
Arab-Israeli War of 1973, 196,
200
arditi, 6
Argyle, Scotland, 19
Armies, British, Eighth, 28
Armies, U.S.: First, 68, 69, 71,
72, 75, 107; Second, 23, 47,
109, 140; Third, 72, 140, 198;
Fifth, 41, 42, 44, 58, 61, 125;
Sixth, 44, 81, 82, 84–86, 88,
90, 91 n.2, 95, 129; Seventh,

companies: Church's, 2;
Gorham's, 2; Morgan's, 4;
Mosby's, 5; Rogers's, 1–4,
7, 19, 185, 186
Companies, U.S.: 1st Ranger
Infantry (Abn.), 118, 119, 124;
2d Ranger Infantry (Abn.),
110, 118, 124; 3d Ranger
Infantry (Abn.), 118, 119, **127**;
4th Ranger Infantry (Abn.),
118, 124; 8th Ranger Infantry
(Abn.), 119; 8213th Army
Unit, 106; A, 1st Battalion
(Ranger), 75th Infantry, **207**;
B, 6th Ranger Battalion, 174;
Eighth Army Ranger, 106,
112; Marauder, 108; Ranger
volunteer, 5
Containment, 97, 167. *See also*
Cold War; United States,
foreign policy
Conway, Theodore J., 17
Corps, North Korean, I, 118
Corps, U.S.: I, 118, 126; II,
28, 35; III, 74; V, 156;
VI, 57, 61; VII, 156; VIII,
71; IX, 118, 123; XX, 72; I
Field Force, 179; II Field
Force, 179, 184, 186
Corregidor Island, Philippines,
siege of, 11, 81, 83, 88
Cota, Norman D., 69
Counterguerrilla operations, 5,
105, 147, 148, 155, 156, 159,
163, 169–172, 184, 186, 206.
See also counterinsurgency;
Ranger, counterguerrilla
operations
Counterinsurgency, 147, 155,
156, 159, 172, 197, 201, 206,
219. *See also* counterguerrilla
operations; Ranger,
counterguerrilla operations

Counterterrorism, 206, 208, 210,
224
Crockett, Davy, 146
Cuban Missile Crisis, 162
Cunliffe, Marcus, 235
Custer's Last Stand, 58, 231

Dahlonega, Georgia, 140
Dahlquist, John E., 140
Dammer, Herman W., 24, 26, 40
Darby, William O., **43**, 74, 84,
96, 125, 145; background, 17;
Cisterna, 58, 60, 75 n.2;
death, 61; and formation of 1st
Ranger Battalion, 18, 32 n.15;
leadership qualities, 17,
58 n.23, 232; in North Africa,
24, 26, 28, 29; Sicily and Italy,
36–43, 53 nn.14, 16, 57
Darby's Rangers, 145
Davison, Michael S., 184
Decker, George H., 147, 160
Defense Guidance for 1981, 218
Delta Force, 206, 208, 209,
218–20, 232
Deogarh, India, 49
Deolali, India, 49
Department of the Army. *See*
U.S. Army Staff
Department of Defense, 103,
108, 147, 174, 184, 198, 201,
205, 206, 219, 224, 225
Depuy, William E., 200, 201,
206, 210; background 201
Dernaia Pass, Tunisia, 28
Détente, 196, 210
Devers, Jacob L., 60, 62, 98,
131
The Devil's Brigade, 145
Dieppe, France, 19, 20, 29, 36,
40; casualties, 20; lessons,
20, 96; reasons for the raid,
19

About the Author

DAVID W. HOGAN, JR. is a historian in the Contingency Operations and Low Intensity Conflict Branch at the U.S. Army Center of Military History. He received his B.A. from Dartmouth College in 1980 and his Ph.D. from Duke University in 1986. After teaching at Elon College, he joined the Center in 1987. He is the author of *U.S. Army Special Operations in World War II* and numerous book reviews.